Debating Democracy's Discontent

Essays on American Politics, Law, and Public Philosophy

EDITED BY

Anita L. Allen and Milton C. Regan, Jr.

Oxford University Press

1998

[redacted]

Oxford University Press, Great Clarendon Street, Oxford OX2 6DP

Oxford New York
Athens Auckland Bangkok Bogotá Buenos Aires Calcutta
Cape Town Chennai Dar es Salaam Delhi Florence Hong Kong Istanbul
Karachi Kuala Lumpur Madrid Melbourne Mexico City Mumbai
Nairobi Paris São Paulo Singapore Taipei Tokyo Toronto Warsaw

and associated companies in
Berlin Ibadan

Oxford is a registered trade mark of Oxford University Press

Published in the United States
by Oxford University Press Inc., New York

First published 1998

British Library Cataloguing in Publication Data
Data available

Library of Congress Cataloging in Publication Data
Data available

ISBN 0–19–829484–0
ISBN 0–19–829496–4 (pbk.)

1 3 5 7 9 10 8 6 4 2

Typeset by Hope Services (Abingdon) Ltd.
Printed in Great Britain
on acid-free paper by
Biddles Ltd., Guildford and King's Lynn

[redacted]

To Paul, Adam, and Ophelia Castellitto.

*To my father, Milton C. Regan, and the memory of my mother,
Lucie Richardson Regan.*

ACKNOWLEDGEMENTS

We would like to thank the contributing authors for participating in our ambitious project. Many of the essays in this book originated as papers delivered at the American Political Science Association meetings in 1995 and 1996, or as symposium papers. On April 21–22 1997, Georgetown University's Law Center, Department of Government, and Department of Philosophy hosted the McDonough Symposium: "Debating Democracy's Discontent: America in Search of a Public Philosophy." Professor Michael Sandel and most of the other contributors to this volume appeared at that memorable event. We would like to thank Law Center Dean Judith Areen for encouraging us to bring the McDonough Symposium to Georgetown University. We would also like to thank the Bernard P. McDonough Foundation, the McDonough Family, and the Marmac Corporation for generous support.

Anita L. Allen
Milton C. Regan, Jr.

CONTENTS

IV. Living with Difference

V. Law, Morals, and Private Lives

VI. Self-Government and Democratic Discontent

VII. A Reply to His Critics

NOTES ON CONTRIBUTORS

Anita LaFrance Allen is Professor of Law at the University of Pennsylvania. She recently was Professor and Associate Dean for Research and Scholarship at Georgetown University Law Center. She holds a law degree from the Harvard Law School, and a Ph.D. in Philosophy from the University of Michigan. She has been a Visiting Professor at the Harvard Law School and in the Philosophy Department at the University of Pennsylvania. Professor Allen is the author of many essays on ethics, privacy, race policy, literature, and legal philosophy. She is also author of *Uneasy Access: Privacy for Women in a Free Society* and co-author of *Privacy: Cases and Materials*.

Christopher Beem is the Director of the Council on Civil Society, a project of the Institute for American Values and the University of Chicago Divinity School.

Ronald S. Beiner is Professor of Political Science at the University of Toronto. He holds a BA in political science and philosophy from McGill University and a D. Phil. from Oxford. Prior to joining the faculty at Toronto Professor Beiner was a lecturer at the University of Southampton, and has been a Visiting Professor at the Hebrew University of Jerusalem. He is the author of many articles and *What's the Matter With Liberalism?*, which was awarded the Canadian Political Science Association's Macpherson Prize for best book published in political theory, and *Political Judgment*.

William E. Connolly is Professor of Political Science at Johns Hopkins University. His most recent books are *The Ethos of Pluralism* and *The Immodesty of Secularism* (forthcoming).

Jean Bethke Elshtain is Laura Spelman Rockefeller Professor of Social and Political Ethics in the Divinity School at the University of Chicago. She also sits on the University's Committee on International Relations and teaches in the Department of Political Science. Professor Elshtain holds a Ph.D. from Brandeis University. Her books include *Public Man, Private Woman: Women in Social Thought*; *The Family in Political Thought*; *Meditations on Modern Political Thought*; *Women and War*; *Democracy on Trial*, and *Augustine and the Limits of Politics*.

Amitai Etzioni is the first University Professor of the George Washington University. Prior to this appointment he was Professor of Sociology at Columbia University for twenty years. He has served as a Senior Adviser in the White House during the Carter administration, Thomas Henry Carroll Ford Foundation Professor at the Harvard Business School, and President of the American Sociological Association. Professor Etzioni founded the Center for

Policy Research, and still serves as its director. He is the editor of *The Responsive Community: Rights and Responsibilities*, and founder and director of the Communitarian Network. His many books include: *Modern Organizations; Political Unification; The Active Society; Social Problems; An Immodest Agenda; The Moral Dimension: Toward a New Economics; The Spirit of the Community: Rights Responsibilities and the Communitarian Agenda*. Professor Etzioni's most recent book is *The New Golden Rule: Community and Morality*.

James E. Fleming is Associate Professor of Law at Fordham University. He holds an undergraduate degree from the University of Missouri, a law degree from Harvard, and an MA and Ph.D. from Princeton. Professor Fleming teaches Constitutional Law and Theory, Jurisprudence, and Remedies. He is a co-author of *American Constitutional Interpretation*, and many articles.

Bruce Frohnen is currently a legislative assistant to US Senator Spencer Abraham and a lecturer at Catholic University. He holds a BA from California State University, MA's from both the University of California (Davis) and Cornell University, a Ph.D. from Cornell, and a JD from the Emory Law School. His publications include the books, *The New Communitarians and the Crisis of Modern Liberalism* and *Virtue and the Promise of Conservatism: The Legacy of Burke and Tocqueville*.

William A. Galston is Professor in the School of Public Affairs at the University of Maryland and Director of the University's Institute for Philosophy and Public Policy. He is a former Deputy Assistant to President Clinton for Domestic Policy and is currently a senior adviser to the Democratic Leadership Council and the Progressive Policy Institute. He is the author of six books and numerous articles in the areas of political philosophy, public policy, and American politics. His books include *Justice and the Human Good; Liberal Purposes: Goods, Virtues, and Diversity in the Liberal State*; and *Virtue*.

Will Kymlicka is Research Director of the Canadian Center for Philosophy and Public Policy at the University of Ottawa and also a Visiting Professor of Philosophy at Carleton University. He holds a BA from Queen's University and a D.Phil. from Oxford. He has held research fellowships at Princeton, Queen's, Toronto, Ottawa, and the European University Institute. Professor Kymlicka is the author of three books: *Liberalism, Community, and Culture; Contemporary Political Philosophy*; and *Multicultural Citizenship*, which was awarded the Macpherson Prize in political theory by the Canadian Political Science Association. Professor Kymlicka has also published numerous articles and has edited three books.

Linda C. McClain is Associate Professor of Law at Hofstra School of Law. She holds an undergraduate degree from Oberlin College, and an MA from the University of Chicago. She received her JD from Georgetown and holds an LL M from New York University. She has been a Visiting Professor at the University of Virginia Law School. Professor McClain teaches Property, Jurisprudence, and seminars on Feminist Legal Theory, and Law and the

Welfare State. Prior to joining the faculty at Hofstra she was an associate with the New York firm of Cravath, Swaine, and Moore.

Clifford Orwin is Professor of Political Science at the University of Toronto. He holds an AB in Modern History from Cornell University and an MA and Ph.D. from Harvard. He has published numerous articles and is the author of *The Humanity of Thucydides* (Princeton, 1997) and co-editor of *The Legacy of Rousseau* (Chicago, 1997).

Thomas L. Pangle has been a Professor in the Department of Political Science at the University of Toronto since 1979. He is a graduate of Cornell University and earned his Ph.D. at the University of Chicago in 1972. He has taught at Yale, Dartmouth, the University of Chicago, and the Ecole des Hautes Etudes en Sciences Sociales, Paris. He is a recipient of the Guggenheim Fellowship and a three-time recipient of fellowships from the National Endowment for the Humanities. His books and co-authored books include, *Montesquieu's Philosophy of Liberalism; The Spirit of Modern Republicanism; The Ennobling of Democracy: The Challenge of the Post-Modern Age; The Learning of Liberty: The Educational Ideas of the American Founders*; and the forthcoming *Justice Among Nations: What Political Philosophy Teaches About the Moral Basis of International Relations*. His most recent edited work is *Political Philosophy and the Human Soul: Essays in Memory of Allan Bloom*.

Philip Pettit is with the Research School of Social Sciences at the Australian National University. He has been Visiting Professor of Philosophy at Columbia University, in New York.

Milton C. Regan, Jr. is Professor of Law at Georgetown University Law Center. He holds a BA from the University of Houston, an MA from the University of California at Los Angeles, and a JD from Georgetown. Professor Regan was law clerk to Supreme Court Justice William Brennan and to Justice Ruth Bader Ginsburg when she sat on the Federal Court of Appeals. He is a former Adjunct Professor of Urban Affairs at the University of Maryland. Professor Regan practiced law with the New York firm of Davis, Polk & Wardwell before becoming a legal academic. As a lawyer he specialized in defense of professionals, white-collar criminal defense, and *pro bono* representation of tenant associations. He is the author of the recent book, *Family Law and the Pursuit of Intimacy*. Professor Regan's forthcoming second book, *Alone Together: Law and the Meanings of Marriage*, will be published by Oxford University Press.

Nancy Lipton Rosenblum is Henry Merritt Wriston Professor at Brown University. She holds a BA from Radcliffe College and a Ph.D. in political science from Harvard, where she was then an Associate Professor in the Department of Government. Professor Rosenblum is the author of many articles and books including *Another Liberalism: Romanticism and the Reconstruction of Liberal Thought* and *Bentham's Theory of the Modern State*, and is the editor of *Thoreau: Political Writings*, Cambridge Texts in the History of Political Thought, and *Liberalism and the Moral Life*.

Richard Rorty is University Professor of the Humanities at the University of Virginia. He holds a Ph.D. from Yale. He taught at Yale, Wellesley College, and Princeton prior to joining Virginia's faculty. Professor Rorty is the author of *Philosophy and the Mirror of Nature*. His recent books are *Objectivity, Relativism and Truth* and *Essays on Heidegger and Others*.

Michael J. Sandel is Professor of Government at Harvard University. He holds an undergraduate degree from Brandeis University and a D.Phil. from Oxford. Professor Sandel teaches courses in contemporary political philosophy and the history of political thought. He also teaches on law and political theory at Harvard Law School, and chairs the University's Advisory Committee on Free Speech. He has been honored with fellowships from the Ford Foundation, the American Council of Learned Scholars, and the National Endowment for the Humanities. Professor Sandel has lectured widely in the USA and abroad. His books include: *Democracy's Discontent: America in Search of a Public Philosophy*; *Liberalism and Its Critics*; and *Liberalism and the Limits of Justice*. He has also published articles in the *New Republic*, the *Atlantic Monthly*, the *New York Review of Books*, and the *New York Times Book Review*.

Richard Sennett is University Professor of the Humanities at New York University. He holds a BA with special honors from the University of Chicago and a Ph.D. from Harvard. He has held several distinguished fellowships and is currently a fellow of the American Academy of Arts and Sciences and the Royal Society of Literature. He has been a Visiting Professor at many noted schools, including the University of London, the Collège de France, and the Harvard Graduate School of Design. Professor Sennett founded the New York Institute for the Humanities, serving as its first Director. He is currently the Chair of the Council on Civil Society. Professor Sennett is the author of *Families Against the City*; *The Uses of Disorder*; *The Fall of Public Man*; *Authority*; and *The Conscience of the Eye*; as well as co-author of *19th Century Cities* and *The Hidden Injuries of Class*. He also edited a collection of writings in urban studies, *Classical Essays on the Culture of Cities*. Professor Sennett's most recent book is *Flesh and Stone: the Body and the City in Western Civilization*.

Mary Lyndon Shanley is Margaret Stiles Halleck Professor of Political Science at Vassar College. She specializes in the history of political philosophy; feminist theory; and women, politics, and the law. Professor Shanley graduated from Wellesley College, and received both her MA and Ph.D. from Harvard University. She is the author of *Feminism, Marriage and the Law in Victorian England* and the co-editor of *Feminist Interpretations and Political Theory* and *Contentious Concepts: Feminist Essays in Political Theory*.

Andrew W. Siegel is Greenwall Fellow in Bioethics and Health Policy at Johns Hopkins and Georgetown Universities. He has served as a Legislative Fellow for Senator Edward M. Kennedy on the Labor and Human Resources Committee and as Staff Attorney for the NIH-DOE Task Force on Genetic Testing. He holds an undergraduate degree from the University of Oregon, and a JD and Ph.D.

in Philosophy from the University of Wisconsin-Madison. Dr. Siegel has taught Philosophy at Georgetown and Johns Hopkins, and Law at Georgetown and the University of Wisconsin. Professor Siegel's published articles include "On Narcissism and Veiled Innocence: Prolegomena to a Critique of Law" in the *International Journal of Law and Psychiatry*.

Charles Taylor is Professor of Philosophy at McGill University in Quebec, Canada. He has had a very distinguished international teaching career, having taught at Oxford University, Princeton University, the University of California at Berkeley, and the University of Frankfurt in Germany. His publications include four books: *Sources of the Self* (1979); *The Malaise of Modernity* (1991); *Multiculturalism and the Politics of Recognition* (1992); and *Philosophical Arguments* (1992).

Mark Tushnet is Carmack Waterhouse Professor of Law at the Georgetown University Law Center. Professor Tushnet holds a BA from Harvard and both an MA and JD from Yale. After receiving his JD, Professor Tushnet served as a clerk to US Supreme Court Justice Thurgood Marshall and then on the faculty of the University of Wisconsin Law School. He is the co-author of widely used casebooks on federal jurisdiction and constitutional law. His other recent writings include *The NAACP's Legal Strategy Against Segregated Education, 1925–1950* (winner of the Littleton Griswold Award of the American Historical Association); *Red, White and Blue: A Critical Analysis of Constitutional Law*; and *Making Civil Rights Law: Thurgood Marshall and the Supreme Court, 1936-1961*. He is a former secretary of the Conference on Critical Legal Studies, and a recent recipient of a Guggenheim Fellowship.

Jeremy Waldron is the Maurice and Hilda Friedman Professor at Columbia University Law School in New York. His books include *Theories of Rights* (1984), *The Right of Private Property* (1988), *Nonsense on Stilts* (1988), and *Liberal Rights: Collected Papers* (1993).

Michael Walzer is a permanent faculty member of the Institute for Advanced Study in Princeton, New Jersey. Prior to joining the Institute, Dr. Walzer taught at Princeton and Harvard Universities. He is a graduate of Brandeis University and holds a Ph.D. from Harvard. He also studied at Cambridge University as a Fulbright Fellow. Dr. Walzer is the editor of *Dissent* and a contributing editor of the *New Republic*. He is the author of numerous articles as well as fourteen books including *Just and Unjust Wars; Spheres of Justice; What It Means to Be an American; Civil Society and American Democracy; Thick and Thin: Moral Argument at Home and Abroad;* and *Pluralism, Justice, and Equality*.

Robin West is Professor of Law at the Georgetown University Law Center. She holds a JD from the University of Maryland, as well as a JSM from Stanford. Professor West has taught at the University of Maryland Law School and has been a Visiting Professor of Law at the University of Chicago Law School and Stanford Law School. Her extensive publications include three books, *Narrative, Authority, and the Law*; *Progressive Constitutionalism: Reconstructing the Fourteenth Amendment*; and *Caring for Justice*.

Joan C. Williams is Professor of Law at American University. She has an undergraduate degree from Yale, a master's degree in City Planning from MIT, and a law degree from Harvard. Professor Williams has taught as a Visiting Professor at both the Harvard and the University of Virginia Law Schools. She has published a number of articles on various topics including gender and family issues in the law, legal theory and jurisprudence, and property law. She is the author or co-author of two forthcoming books: *Reconstructing Gender* and *Land Ownership and Use.*

INTRODUCTION

The Quest for a Post-Liberal Public Philosophy

RONALD S. BEINER

MICHAEL SANDEL'S *Democracy's Discontent*[1] is by far the most ambitious recent attempt to make the civic republican tradition relevant to current dilemmas. It is entirely appropriate, then, that it has elicited the illuminating and intellectually rich chapters assembled in this volume, including responses to Sandel by many of the leading political and constitutional theorists of our time. Sandel's argument has two main strands. Part One of *Democracy's Discontent* offers a root-and-branch challenge to the grip exercised by procedural liberalism over American constitutionalism in recent decades.[2] Following a general characterization, by Sandel, of the meaning of contemporary liberalism, the main topics of chapter 3 are freedom of religion, free speech, and the regulation of pornography; the main topics of chapter 4 are abortion, homosexuality, and no-fault divorce laws. As one would expect, Sandel's claims in this area are vigorously contested by legal scholars committed to the basic tenets of liberal jurisprudence. Part Two of Sandel's book lays out a history of civic republican politics in America and its progressive eclipse from Thomas Jefferson to Ronald Reagan. Here, too, Sandel's provocative claims are scrutinized and challenged by thinkers who are more skeptical of the attractions of civic republicanism. The result is a full-blown philosophical dialogue on issues of the greatest theoretical and political moment.

I

In 1982, Sandel published *Liberalism and the Limits of Justice*, a penetrating theoretical challenge to Rawlsian liberalism. This major work soon came to be associated with an important current within contemporary theory that was subsumed, not necessarily by its proponents, under the label "communitarianism." This had the happy effect of organizing theoretical discussion along what appeared to be clear lines of debate; it had the unhappy effect of lumping together theorists with overlapping but still importantly distinguishable intellectual and moral concerns. More to the point, making "community" in the abstract the point of contention between liberals and their critics often caused considerable confusion about the real basis of the theoretical challenge, by Sandel and others, to the 1970s–1980s-style version of the political philosophy of liberalism, as I will now try to go on to explain.[3]

There are real perils in using "community" as the banner under which to rally critics of procedural liberalism. There are, of course, all kinds of communities: big and small, national and local, liberal and illiberal. It is not terribly helpful to be told that community is a good, and that a philosophy that diminishes the importance of community is deficient, until we have more information about the kinds of communities that we are supposed to be defending.[4] Just as a quick antidote to abstract theorizing about the attractions of community as such, consider a few instantiations of community in its concrete diversity: an Amish village, a suburban bridge club, a local chapter of the "Nation of Islam," a skinhead youth gang, a college fraternity, a clandestine organization of Irish-Americans constituted for the purpose of fund-raising for the Irish Republican Army. Each of these in some respect confers a sense of belonging that allows its members to transcend their bare individuality. Is it therefore true that they all offer commensurable experiences of something—"community"—that, for the very reason that it involves a mode of belonging, is morally superior to individuality? The problem of community was put on the theoretical agenda by critics of liberal individualism such as Sandel, Charles Taylor, Michael Walzer, Robert Bellah, and Christopher Lasch, and they did so by addressing questions both to liberalism as a social philosophy and to the kind of society we think of as a liberal society. They asked whether liberalism as a basically individualistic creed could do justice to the richly textured narrative histories and socially constituted practices by which individuals in any society come to acquire meaningful selves. And they asked, quite properly, whether liberal societies, which basically define and understand themselves within a framework of individualistic categories, can offer the rich experiences of coinvolvement and communal solidarity that make for a meaningful human life. The chief point that these critics of liberalism were trying to make is that if we are restricted in our thinking about social and political life to an exclusively individualist moral language (for example, the moral language employed in the work of John Rawls, Ronald Dworkin, Bruce Ackerman, to say nothing of Robert Nozick), then we find ourselves confined within an unacceptably narrow horizon of moral and social experience. It is true that we need a richer and more encompassing moral-political vocabulary than the one we get from procedural liberalism, but this surely does not entail the notion that any and all experiences of "community" elevate us to a higher plane of moral experience.

Sandel is well aware of these perils of appealing to community in the abstract. In an important review essay on Rawls's *Political Liberalism* published in the *Harvard Law Review* in 1994, Sandel goes out of his way to insist that it was not at all the intention of so-called communitarians like himself to sanctify community as such as the ultimate standard of right; rather, the intention was to highlight issues of substantive good, present or absent in liberal societies, that were shunned on principle by proponents of neutralist liberalism like Rawls and Dworkin and their followers.[5] The real issue in the debate with Rawls and his followers, as Sandel rightly says, is whether a liberal theory of justice can be vindicated while avoiding appeal to one among a set of rival and controversial conceptions of the good.[6] Again, what is unfortunate about the term "communitarian" is that it suggests that the ultimate standard of theoretical judgment is community as an indiscriminate good. While it is true that some of the writings of so-called communitarians gave some encouragement to this notion,[7] none of these theorists were prepared to hold fast to the banner of community expressed as a full-blown principle of ultimate philosophical judgment, and all of them more or less renounced the communitarian label as a helpful or illuminating description of their thought.[8]

If the appeal to community is meaningless in advance of a clear specification of the community being celebrated, which community does Sandel mean to champion: is it the immediate locality, friends and neighbors one knows personally, or some much larger nationwide community of citizens, the vast majority of whom are in any literal sense strangers? Is it one's family, in the literal sense, or a metaphorical "family" of citizens stretching from coast to coast? In his works prior to *Democracy's Discontent*, Sandel has always been reluctant to specify which of these communities should be privileged, and in his new book, that reluctance to opt for one kind of community or the other is still very much present.[9] In order to dramatize the issue, let us contrast Sandel with one of his putative allies in the assault upon procedural liberalism, namely Alasdair MacIntyre. There is no such ambivalence in MacIntyre: he opts decisively for the local—"schools, farms, other workplaces, clinics, parishes"[10]—as the privileged locus of communal goods. MacIntyre writes:

> when practice-based forms of Aristotelian community are generated in the modern world, they are always, and could not but be, small-scale and local. . . . modern nation-states which masquerade as embodiments of community are always to be resisted. The modern nation-state, in whatever guise, is a dangerous and unmanageable institution, presenting itself on the one hand as a bureaucratic supplier of goods and services, which is always about to but never actually does, give its clients value for money, and on the other hand as a repository of sacred values, which from time to time invites one to lay down one's life on its behalf . . . it is like being asked to die for the telephone company. [So] the liberal critique of those nation-states which pretend to embody the values of community has little to say to those Aristotelians, such as myself, for whom the nation-state is not and cannot be the locus of community.[11]

Sandel is obviously not a pure communitarian localist like MacIntyre, for his project, a revival of civic republicanism, must in some quite large measure involve community in a pan-national sense. Moreover, Sandel, notwithstanding his criticisms of distributive justice as the dominant liberal preoccupation, is a strong supporter of the welfare state, which he would prefer to "beef up" or make more robustly egalitarian rather than diminish. In this sense, Sandel's difference with welfare liberals like Rawls and Dworkin concerns only the *grounds* of one's egalitarian commitment (or perhaps the rhetoric in which one would like to see it enveloped), not its substance. For MacIntyre, the modern state, far from being redeemed by its redistributive function or its provisions for social welfare, is a monstrosity of liberal-bureaucratic impersonality, Nietzsche's "coldest of all cold monsters." For Sandel, on the other hand, the issue is not whether to accept or reject the welfare state, but whether to mobilize support for it in a language of distributive justice and the entitlements of rights-bearing individuals (which Sandel sees as having proven ineffective) or in a language of civic solidarity and the pursuit of a common good (which he sees as more promising).[12]

Admittedly, there are some significant tensions in Sandel's argument. Sandel, like Charles Taylor, is keen to present himself as a "Tocquevillean decentralist" (this is Taylor's self-description), but, as Clifford Orwin remarks in his critique of Sandel, it is hard to see how one can argue for state decentralization and at the same time expect public authority to be equal to the task of resisting corporate power and combating social inequality.[13] More generally, as Michael Walzer points out in his chapter in this book, Sandel never really comes to terms with the *tension* between local communities on the one side and national community on the other.[14] Clearly, what Sandel is hoping for is that experiences of local allegiance and experiences of nation-wide civic allegiance will work together, reinforcing each other, as they did in nineteenth-century America as depicted by Tocqueville.[15] But as Walzer again persuasively argues, contemporary America, with all its ethnic and racial heterogeneity, is vastly different from the social conditions that characterized Tocqueville's America.[16] As various commentators in this volume highlight in different ways, there is no way of guaranteeing that different kinds of community will not make contradictory rather than complementary claims upon their members.[17] My point here is not that one ought to rule out the possibility of a harmony between allegiance to local communities and allegiance to a larger civic community; the point is that there is no guarantee that in appealing to community one is appealing to a singular good, and no guarantee even that any particular community embodies a good at all. As Orwin rightly puts it: "Community . . . cannot serve as a moral principle; rather our moral principles must furnish the basis of our community." In fact, it is quite clear that one of Sandel's deliberate intentions in writing *Democracy's Discontent* is to move discreetly away from the language of community—presumably in order to avoid the confusions introduced by treating community as an ultimate philosophical standard.[18] In *The New Golden Rule*, Amitai Etzioni has remarked that the term "communitarian" is not to be found in the index of Sandel's book;[19] this is obviously no accident. But switching from the language of community to a language of civicism and republican virtue does not necessarily by itself banish the tensions that were previously expressed in the appeal to different kinds of communal embeddedness.

II

The theoretical armature upon which *Democracy's Discontent* is built is a remarkably simple one. The entire work revolves around a sharply drawn contrast (much *too* sharply drawn, critics contend) between two rival conceptions of political association, corresponding to two rival conceptions of political freedom. The first conception, liberal proceduralist, is centrally defined by a vision of moral agency, of rational individuals as autonomous choosers of their own ends; with this goes an understanding of politics that leaves maximal space for the exercise of moral autonomy, and that tries to maximize possibilities of practical consensus in a radically pluralist society by steering away as much as possible from the political endorsement of morally and philosophically controversial notions of the good.[20] The rival conception, civic-republican, is preoccupied with problems of character formation and the fostering of virtues conducive to deliberative self-rule. Because civic republicanism involves a much more ambitious idea of politics than what we associate with liberal politics, it also requires, so to speak, a much more ambitious cultural infrastructure, supplied by citizens with deep identities rather than shallow identities. Again, this way of characterizing the moral alternatives will be strongly contested by Sandel's liberal critics. In any case, on the basis of this theoretical contrast, Sandel develops basically two ambitious historical narratives: first, an account of a global shift, over the course of the middle decades of this century, of jurisprudential norms (with respect to family life, religious affiliations, sexual identity, patriotism, and so on) in the direction of the liberal conception of moral autonomy; then, on a larger canvas, an account of the transformation of the social and economic structures of American life, played out in political debates stretching across the whole history of the republic. Here too, the story is one of an inexorable waning of the civic-republican vision, culminating in a near-total eclipse, in recent decades, of civic republican aspirations, in favor of an idea of politics that privileges the individual's autonomous choice of ends. Sandel tries hard to hold out hope that the candle of the civic republican ideal continues to flicker, but when one runs through the various episodes of his story, one is left, irresistibly, with a considerably grimmer picture of the fate of republican ideals.

In one important sense, at least, *Democracy's Discontent* is more faithful to the communitarian ideal than *Liberalism and the Limits of Justice* was. Sandel's first book pursued the argument about the strengths and weaknesses of liberalism at the level of general (that is, universalist) principles, whereas *Democracy's Discontent* analyzes the liberal legacy in one particular society. It is, as Michael Walzer says, an exercise in "immanent social criticism"—in

Walzer's view, "social criticism as it ought to be written."[21] But whereas the earlier book had assured us that, whatever certain philosophers may presuppose, selves have deep attachments and are rooted in constitutive communities because that is what a coherent theory of the self requires, we learn from Sandel's more recent book that the living of a certain kind of history can do much to loosen our attachments and uproot us from our constitutive communities. What are the major episodes in Sandel's history of liberal America? The central story in chapter 5 is the eclipse of Jefferson's vision of the virtue and independence of yeoman farmers and the move towards large-scale manufacturing within the political economy of the early republic. The central story in chapter 6 is the eclipse of "the artisanal republican tradition"[22] and the failed struggle of the Knights of Labor against the wage system. The central story of chapter 7 is the contest between the decentralist vision of Louis Brandeis and Woodrow Wilson and the nationalizing impulse of Theodore Roosevelt and Herbert Croly during the Progressive era. Chapter 8 continues chapter 7's story of the displacement of the "political economy of citizenship" by the "political economy of growth and distributive justice"[23] as this unfolded in the Keynesian regime of Franklin Delano Roosevelt. In the final two chapters, we get a few glimmers of the vanquished republican tradition (notably, in the civil rights movement of Martin Luther King, Jr.), but Sandel leaves no doubt that the last few decades have seen the more or less total triumph of the procedural republic, with almost every aspect of economic, legal, and cultural life helping to consolidate it. According to Sandel, throughout this whole series of continuous debate across American history, right up until the most recent decades, *both* sides in each debate appealed to civic considerations (what organization of economic and political life will form better citizens?), but the clear implication of his narrative is that the outcome of these debates has pushed the civic impulse right outside the bounds of contemporary American political life.

In every one of these stories, the bad guys win and the goods guys lose. My impression is that Sandel wants more than anything to write a hopeful book; but the tale he tells is a woeful one. The book is the story of how people in modern America progressively lose the sense that they have meaningful control over their own affairs. The world of *Democracy's Discontent* is a bit like the antiworld of Tocqueville's America—that is, a world where the basic institutions that structure the lives of citizens do not lay a foundation for meaningful self-government, but render that very thing impossible or nearly so. Does Sandel offer solutions? One gets the sense in reading the book that he does very much *want to*.[24] If "public philosophy" got us into this mess, then public philosophy can somehow show us the way out of it. Overall, the narrative of the book, the rather discouraging story it tells about the social and economic process whereby American life has been relentlessly "modernified," seems to me a lot more persuasive than the book's implicit promise that political theory can offer a source of civic edification. This is not to say that modern citizenship is necessarily doomed. People can find modest ways (and very occasionally, quite spectacular ways) of regenerating the civic resources of their lives. As Sandel rightly reminds us, this was—in its essential meaning—the achievement of the civil rights movement in America.[25] And it is also the aspiration that now animates the valiant efforts of Ernesto Cortes, Jr. and others in the IAF (Industrial Areas Foundation)—again, precisely a movement of civic regeneration.[26] Sandel sees signs of hope in a few other places—the heartening response to the final moments of Bobby Kennedy's career; new initiatives in urban theory; antiWal-Mart campaigns—but, let's face it, these intimations of a renewed civicism offer a slender basis upon which to challenge (politically rather intellectually) the overwhelmingly dominant public philosophy described in Sandel's book.

Is Sandel's story just one big lament? Is the whole thing just the construction of an antiliberal mythology that has little relevance to the economic and political realities that we face today? Even if one entirely accepts the historiographical accuracy of Sandel's history of America, the civic-republican dream is, surely, irrecoverable. Each of the battles in the Sandelian cosmic war between liberalism and republicanism was decisively won by the liberal side, and the losers in these battles (Jeffersonian yeomen, civic-minded artisans, Knights of Labor, corner-store pharmacists) have no sociological or political basis for resuming the fight. So if one takes Sandel's narrative at face value, one is tempted to concede the point to one of his critics who writes:

> Are you a communitarian who is sick and tired of hearing that you see the past through rose-tinted glasses? Is it irksome for you to waste so much time denying claims that communitarians sigh nostalgically for a past that never existed? Then stay away from *Democracy's Discontent*, in which Michael Sandel unwittingly vindicates the charges levelled by communitarianism's critics.[27]

But here one must fill in more of the theoretical background in order to have a more subtle appreciation of what Sandel is up to.

A decisive moment in the articulation of contemporary liberalism occurred when Ronald Dworkin wrote that liberal equality demands that "political decisions must be, so far as is possible, independent of any particular conception of the good life, or of what gives value to life. Since the citizens of a society differ in their conceptions, the government does not treat them as equals if it prefers one conception to another."[28] From Sandel's point of view, this articulation of neo-Kantian liberalism has dramatic moral and political consequences that actually shape in crucial ways the contemporary political landscape. Although Sandel never comes right out and says so explicitly, I think he believes that the political discrediting of American liberalism in the 1980s must be interpreted in conjunction with this philosophical endorsement, by Dworkin and others, of "official neutrality amongst theories of what is valuable in life."[29] Rightly or wrongly, liberalism came to be seen as indifferent to moral concerns and cultural anxieties that were, not unreasonably, widespread among American citizens following the turbulent decades of the 1960s and 1970s. Reaganite conservatism succeeded in thoroughly discrediting American liberalism by portraying it as the ideology of a morally indifferent and nonjudgmental culture (think of John Travolta's brilliant parody, near the beginning of *Pulp Fiction*, of the anything-goes philosophy of liberal Amsterdam!—a society where the legal order exists in order to encourage maximum self-indulgence). This association between liberalism and nonjudgmentalism destroyed the political credibility of the Democratic Party for a whole generation, until Bill Clinton put it back on the political map by returning to moral themes that earlier Democrats had failed to address. As Sandel rightly points out: "A politics that brackets morality and religion too completely soon generates its own disenchantment. Where political discourse lacks moral resonance, the yearning for a public life of larger meaning finds undesirable expression. Groups like the Moral Majority seek to clothe the naked public square with narrow, intolerant moralisms. Fundamentalists rush in where liberals fear to tread."[30] Sandel puts the point even more directly in a column in the *New Republic*: "Democrats . . . resisted the politics of virtue, not by disputing conservatives' particular moral judgments but by rejecting the idea that moral judgments have a place in the public realm . . . the Democrats' rejection of the politics of virtue carried a high price, for it left conservatives with a monopoly on moral discourse in politics."[31] So a great deal is at stake, politically, in Sandel's quarrel with neutralist liberalism: nothing less than the political redemption of egalitarian politics in America. If egalitarians and center-leftists come to present themselves in terms closer to Sandel's vocabulary of civic virtue and more remote from the procedural-neutralist vocabulary of his liberal adversaries, this will have real political advantages in re-equipping the American left.[32] *This*, it seems clear, is the real point of Sandel's grand narrative of republican virtues and deep identities.

Sandel tends to postulate Dworkinian liberalism as the telos of American life, and therefore he projects Dworkin and Rawls back into key episodes in American political history, reading these historical turning points as anticipations of the telos: the Rawlsian-Dworkinian procedural liberalism of the 1970s. Sandel makes such ambitious use of this interpretive grid that it begins to sound like a full-blown "philosophy of history," or what postmodernists call a "metanarrative." One should not be surprised if all of this makes Sandel easier prey for critics in the historical profession. Yet his historical claims are rather peripheral to his primary theoretical project, as I understand it; the real project is to reorient the terms by which the contemporary American left defines itself. Even if the civic-republican vision as a global political possibility is not recoverable (and everything in Sandel's own narrative suggests it is not), it will do liberals and social democrats a lot of good to engage with Sandel's antiliberal narrative (a narrative of virtues, character building, and civic agency rather than a narrative of rights, autonomy, and self-chosen identity). Indeed, some of these good effects have already been apparent in the new (post-neo-Kantian) generation of liberal theory in the last decade or so. The sketching of the relevant political context should help us to understand the central preoccupation of Sandel's work, namely, the need to open up more space for moral deliberation and civic character-building as a way of refuting the long-unchallenged presumption that only the New Right in America upholds moral standards and takes seriously the moral commitments (of faith, patriotism, devotion to family and neighborhood) that are central to the identity of most Americans.[33]

III

Democracy's Discontent has already elicited lively critical responses—very well represented in the chapters that follow—and there is no doubt that Sandel's book will continue to generate fruitful controversies. Liberals, of course, will complain that Sandel attributes to them theoretical vices that they actually avoid, or the avoidance of which is consistent with the liberal tradition at its best.[34] (See, for instance, the chapters by Richard Rorty, William Galston, and Will Kymlicka, which offer powerful restatements of the central liberal idea, as each of them conceives it.) Liberal theorists will also complain that Sandel highlights the virtues of the civic republican tradition and downplays its vices in a way that obscures why liberal politics came to be seen as more attractive than the politics of republican virtue. (See, especially, Nancy Rosenblum's chapter.) Feminists will charge that Sandel romanticizes the traditional family, and that he gives insufficient attention to the patriarchalism of a male-dominated history that is even more deeply inscribed in the civic republican tradition than it is in the liberalism criticized by Sandel. (See, for instance, the interesting dialogue between Mary Lyndon Shanley and Robin West.[35]) Aristocratic conservatives will argue that Sandel fails to go far enough in his philosophical interrogation of liberalism, and will accuse him of failing to acknowledge to what extent the cultural pathologies he rightly traces in contemporary society are intimately related to modern egalitarianism. (See, for instance, the fine chapters by Thomas Pangle and Clifford Orwin.) Historians of American political thought will challenge the historical accuracy of the liberal/republican dichotomy upon which Sandel structures his narrative.[36] Analysts of public policy and American law will question his interpretations of the American legal tradition as well as the feasibility and coherence of his prescriptions. (See, for instance, Shanley on family law; Andrew Siegel on the abortion issue; James E. Fleming and Linda C. McClain on constitutional issues concerning privacy or autonomy; discussions, by West and by Fleming and McClain, of the moral analysis of homosexuality offered by Sandel; Joan Chalmers Williams on Sandel's treatment of religion; Mark Tushnet on Sandel's championing of American federalism; and Milton Regan on how the modern corporation fits into Sandel's civic republican narrative.) Finally, even those broadly sympathetic to Sandel's project may find themselves wishing for less reliance upon historical narrative, which merely whets their appetite for a more direct political-philosophical grounding of Sandel's substantive political vision. Again, fine statements of each of these kinds of challenges are made available within the covers of this volume.

This is a formidable array of critical responses; some of these challenges arose in response to Sandel's first book, and it would have been unreasonable to expect that the narrative presented in his second book would satisfy or silence all of these various critics. I do not have the space in this introduction to address each of these sets of critics or to evaluate the justice or injustice of their critical challenges.[37] Sandel himself will be pursuing many of these lines of dialogue in his conclusion to this volume, and one wishes him well in tackling such challenging and spirited responses to his work. Whether one is persuaded by Sandel or persuaded by his critics, one cannot help concluding that only a radical interpretation of our moral and political condition could spawn debates of this scope and depth.

Rather than trying to engage in these multifaceted debates, either on Sandel's side or on that of his critics, I want to limit myself to highlighting one key aspect of Sandel's theoretical approach, and to discuss briefly why I think its centrality to his thought poses an important problem for those, like myself, who are sympathetic to his project. If there is one notion that, more than any other, defines the Sandelian enterprise, it is the one announced in the subtitle of his book: public philosophy. As William Galston explains in his contribution to this volume, the notion is not exactly free of ambiguity. Notably, we need to ask: What is the relationship between the Rawlsian political philosophy challenged in chapter 1 of the book, and the "public philosophy" disclosed in the central chapters of Sandel's narrative? It may help to distinguish two possible ways of thinking about public philosophy: (1) an implicit but nonetheless cohering set of conceptions associated with the reigning social, economic, and political practices of a society (this is more or less the way William Galston presents the idea of public philosophy in his chapter in this volume); (2) an explicit articulation of theoretical principles that has some significant causal role in the evolution of such practices. I am not sure whether Sandel would be eager to embrace a fully ambitious version of this second rendering of the public philosophy idea (indeed, I am pretty sure he would prefer to disavow it), but the way in which he talks about the battle of public philosophies, and the fact that it figures so centrally in his historical narrative, suggests that Sandel's conception of public philosophy is closer to the second of these two accounts than he sometimes professes. Sandel would deny, I think, that he attributes any particularly strong causal agency to "official" philosophical articulations of the public philosophy. Still, his narrative reads *as if* the key actors in American history had already read Rawls's philosophy of procedural liberalism, and were guided by it in shaping the American polity in a Rawlsian direction.

There are elements of *both* of the two conceptions I've distinguished in Sandel's explicit account of public philosophy in his preface to the book. He writes:

> philosophy inhabits the world from the start; our practices and institutions are embodiments of theory. We could hardly describe our political life, much less engage in it, without recourse to a language laden with theory—of rights and obligations, citizenship and freedom, democracy and law. Political institutions are not simply instruments that implement ideas independently conceived; they are themselves embodiments of ideas. . . . My aim is to identify the public philosophy implicit in our practices and institutions and to show how tensions in the philosophy show up in the practice. If theory never keeps its distance but inhabits the world from the start, we may find a clue to our condition in the theory that we live. Attending to the theory implicit in our public life may help us diagnose our political condition.[38]

This important passage does not quite resolve the ambiguities that trouble me. If Sandel really means to put the principal stress in this account on the quasi-philosophy "implicit in our practices and institutions," then in principle it would be possible for one to tell exactly the same story about the American public philosophy even if philosophers like John Rawls and Ronald Dworkin had never written their books or were entirely unknown to a larger lay citizenry outside the academy. On the other hand, when Sandel talks about "theory embodied in practice" and "philosophy inhabiting the world," he unmistakably implies that academic political philosophy makes a big difference to the shape of practices and institutions crystallized in a particular public philosophy. Reading *Democracy's Discontent*, it is difficult not to get the impression that Sandel thinks that the American polity would not be in the sorry shape it is in if it were not the case that John Rawls is America's leading contemporary public philosopher. The fact that his account of public philosophy in chapter 1 focuses on Rawls and Rorty[39] reinforces the sense one has that contests within philosophy in the ordinary sense guide his subsequent chronicle of the unfolding of the American *Geist*.

Therefore, while it's not Sandel's intention to inflate the causal efficacy of ideas having their source in the realm of philosophy, the way in which he tells his story (as prestructured by one all-important quarrel between philosophers) smacks of idealism.[40] Consider once again all the liberal-republican battles that Sandel narrates, and whose loss by the republican side he laments: an agrarian versus commercial political economy; a political economy of free labor versus a political economy of wage labor; industrial democracy versus big government; the political economy of citizenship versus the Keynesian preoccupation with growth and consumerism. In each of these cases, it seems to me that one can tell a story that has much less to do with competing public philosophies and much more to do with the all-too-tangible evolution of economic and sociological realities. There is in each case a more-or-less materialist explanation for why the winners won and the losers lost, and the attempt to tell the story at the level of self-interpretations that could have been otherwise (and are therefore in principle reversible) tends to put an overly idealist gloss on social and economic history. This problem is particularly well illustrated in a striking passage in the book where Sandel writes: "The problems in the theory of procedural liberalism show up *in the practice it inspires*. Over the past half-century, American politics has come to embody the version of liberalism that renounces the formative ambition and insists government should be neutral toward competing conceptions of the good life."[41] One feels compelled to ask: How can a theory articulated in *1971* "inspire" a half-century of political practice?[42]

It strikes me that Sandel faces a problem whichever way he goes with his concept of public philosophy. If he really wants to make the deficiencies of Rawlsian and Dworkinian political philosophy central to the story that he wants to tell about American history, then he is lumbered with a rather implausible view of the causal efficacy of ideas *vis-à-vis* social reality—which is something he clearly wants to avoid. On the other hand, Sandel could—and should—stick with the notion that a public philosophy is implicit in social practices (economic practices, norms of constitutional law, the character of political relationships), waiting to be teased out by an activity of social interpretation, or self-interpretation (precisely what defines Sandel's enterprise). But if one thinks this through, then it turns out that the promise of a Sandelian public philosophy is less than it appears to be at first glance. For it then follows that the consciously or philosophically articulated version of the public philosophy (for instance, Rawls's political philosophy) is more the *expression of* than the *source of* what is embodied in social practices (i.e. the philosophy doesn't "inspire" but merely crystallizes what's already implicit in the practices). This has rather deflating consequences for the enterprise of a renewed contest of public philosophies. Even if one persuades philosophers of the deficiencies of the reigning public philosophy, what reason is there to believe that the practices themselves will change? And if the practices don't change, then neither does the public philosophy! If one rejects an idealist account of the causal efficacy of philosophical theories (as Sandel says he does), then there is not much reason to hope that the mere articulation of new philosophical ideals will change the existing public philosophy. Writing a book like *Democracy's Discontent* surely will not by itself transform apathetic, disconnected, politically alienated quasi-citizens of contemporary America into Sparta-like paragons of republican virtue, nor will it turn hyper-individualistic consumers into wholehearted citizens preoccupied with the common good.[43] This of course certainly does not mean that telling the kind of civic narrative that Sandel offers is a pointless endeavor. If we lower our expectations to more modest proportions, Sandel's book does precisely what any good work of social criticism ought to do: it helps those who find themselves unsatisfied or unfulfilled by existing social arrangements articulate or clarify to themselves some of the sources of their dissatisfaction. *Democracy's Discontent*, rightly understood, does not magically transport us into a new public philosophy; rather, it provides us with theoretical insights and historical terms of comparison by which we can submit to critical analysis and judgment the public philosophy we now have and will continue to have for the foreseeable future.

Those who expect from social theorists like Sandel the redesign of an entire social order are asking too much. What we need most urgently from political theory are the philosophical resources to be fearlessly self-critical as a society. For this purpose, we need alternative vocabularies that pose a radical challenge to the reigning vocabulary of our society—intellectual equipment for thinking outside the boundaries of our present condition. *This* is what Sandel and other critics of liberal theory and liberal practice try to furnish: certainly not some miraculous cure for the "dysphoria" of citizens in our "joyless polity,"[44] but at least a set of theoretical categories that will help us articulate what it means for a society to be deprived of public happiness.

I

Reviving Civic Virtue

1

The Retrieval of Civic Virtue: A Critical Appreciation of Sandel's *Democracy's Discontent*

THOMAS L. PANGLE

MICHAEL SANDEL'S *Democracy's Discontent* is a powerful academic expression of, and reflection upon, the moral malaise that is ever more profoundly and precipitously seizing hold of American democracy. Sandel has responded to our "predicament," or "the anxiety of the age," as he calls it, by elaborating in the first place a severe—even gloomy—indictment of America's reigning "liberal public philosophy." By "public philosophy" Sandel means "the theory we live": "for all we may resist such ultimate questions as the meaning of justice and the nature of the good life, what we cannot escape is that we live some answer to these questions—we live some *theory*—all the time."[1] What is more, in today's America, and more generally in contemporary liberal democracy, the implicit theory that gives the "answer" to these "ultimate questions" is a (or the) chief force shaping and distorting our lives. To the question: "Why is American politics ill equipped to allay the discontent that now engulfs it?" Sandel insists that "the answer lies beyond the political arguments of our day, in the public philosophy that animates them."

Our Reigning Public Philosophy

What then is the defining heart of this public philosophy that shapes us? According to Sandel, at the center of our public philosophy is a celebration of the liberation of the individual from all ties of solidarity or obligation that are not autonomously chosen. This moral outlook, which finds its best known systematic expression in the philosophy of John Rawls, locates self-worth not in a person's aims but instead in a person's exercise of his or her right to choose among aims. Rights, or legitimate liberties, take priority over the good; choice over fulfillment or dedication.

Politically, the dominant public philosophy expresses itself in what Sandel, following Judith Shklar, calls "the procedural republic." In this civic vision, government, law, and public policy are understood as lacking any legitimate authority to foster virtue or to repress vice, to shape personal ends or notions of happiness, to define the ultimate worth or dignity of any human beings. Government is required to be neutral as regards all such concerns; political life ought to focus exclusively on protecting, enabling, and expanding opportunities and capacities for personal choice among ends, among attachments, among obligations, and among objects of reverence. Law and public policy are forbidden to pass moral judgments on citizens' religious faith or piety, on their character or their mores, on their industriousness or their laziness, on their sense or their lack of civic spirit and responsibility. What public life ought to honor or promote is only whatever sorts of behavior and outlook, whatever kinds of institutions and practices, liberate individuals, as choosing beings, from all unchosen constraints—be those constraints grounded in custom, or tradition, or purported revelation, or family, or patriotism, or ethnic and national identity.

The Indictment of Our Reigning Public Philosophy

Now why precisely, according to Sandel, is this public philosophy gravely flawed? Sandel presents his case in part formally, and in part by weaving it into a narrative account of constitutional and political history. It seems to me that there are at least seven major rubrics of Sandel's indictment that can be distilled from his book taken as a whole.

First, our liberal public philosophy is incapable of fostering, or justifying the attempt to foster, those specific civic virtues or character traits that are necessary for the vigorously deliberative self-government that is *either* a chief constituent of human flourishing *or*, arguably, an important prerequisite of even that voluntarist freedom that liberalism celebrates.[2]

Second, the notion of the self as "unencumbered" by unchosen ties is so narrow and impoverished, and so self-centered, that this notion ignores the rich, manifold moral bonds that constitute and give dignity to our imbedded spiritual existences as members of human and transhuman wholes—family, nation, religious call and commandment, tradition, the environment or the natural whole. Our public philosophy lacks a vocabulary in which we might articulate these dimensions of our existence, and all the attendant hopes and longings.[3]

Third, the political vision of the procedural republic frustrates our natural need to express or to enact this rich matrix of attachment, of obligation, and of aspiration in our *public* life, as citizens whose civic activity bespeaks our entire being.[4]

This inarticulateness conduces, in the fourth place, to a tolerance that is a mere toleration, a "thin pluralism" of coexisting but mutually hostile or indifferent multicultural posturings, rather than the "higher pluralism of persons and communities who appreciate and affirm the distinctive goods their lives express."[5]

In the fifth place, the more we accept this conception of ourselves as unencumbered, the more isolated or atomized we become, as individuals in modern society: this conception of the self contributes to the sense of powerlessness that increasingly engulfs modern mass society—a sense of loss of control that is not only intrinsically demoralizing, but that contributes to civic apathy, cynicism, and heartless individualism.[6]

In the sixth place, this public philosophy helps to create a spiritual vacuum—the "naked public square"—that is all-too-easily filled by petty moralisms on the one hand and intolerant extremisms on the other. The neutralism of liberal public philosophy toward all higher claims and ends leaves liberalism with no strong philosophic answer to, or defense against, intensely felt religious or ideological views that seek to elevate public life by *imposing* a unified and unifying spiritual agenda. Nay, this neutralism, by its banality and trivialization of life, unwittingly invites and fosters such movements.[7]

Finally, the liberal public philosophy is self-contradictory or incoherent inasmuch as it corrodes or fails to sustain even the *minimal* bonds of fraternity, and the *modest* sense of personal responsibility and willingness to sacrifice, that are required to maintain the basic procedures of the procedural republic, especially when that procedural republic has assumed its most modern form as the liberal welfare state.[8]

Resuscitating Civic Republicanism

But Sandel's book is far from being just a critique or a diagnosis of our spiritual ills: the book is above all what C. B. Macpherson called "an essay in retrieval." In the opening chapter, and in the second and longest part, Sandel elaborates a richly illuminating, and sometimes inspiring, synoptic historical narrative showing how relatively recent is the attainment of cultural hegemony by procedural liberalism, with its "voluntarist" conception of the self. This triumph comes only at the end of a long and depressing process whereby a competing and mitigating "civic republican" strand of American public philosophy was gradually eclipsed. This alternative public philosophy was powerfully present at the founding, and waged a mighty if losing struggle throughout the nineteenth century and well into the twentieth—meeting its "demise" only in the late New Deal. It is to the regeneration of this older and sounder republican moralism that Sandel looks, with fond but qualified hope.[9] As Sandel says, arguing against Justice Stevens's defense in *Thornburgh* v. *American College of Obstetricians* (1986) of the Court's fundamental civic premises in *Roe* v. *Wade*:

the liberal conception of the person on which Stevens' view relies is not characteristic of our political and constitutional tradition as such. The image of the person as a freely choosing, unencumbered self has only recently come to inform our constitutional practice. Whatever its appeal, it does not underlie the American political tradition as a whole, much less "the public culture of a democratic society" as such [quoting Stevens].[10]

The alternative, civic republican public philosophy is rooted in Aristotle—but also in Machiavelli, whose "more modest version" Sandel seems to favor.[11] The classical republican tradition puts self-government at the heart of the definition of democratic or republican freedom and dignity. This older perspective stresses the civic virtues deliberative self-government requires in the citizenry, and makes the formation of character—that is, the fostering of the capacities for active citizenship—a chief and direct aim of legislation and public policy. In the narrative that takes up the bulk of the second part of the book, Sandel tells a moving and melancholy story—not so much nostalgia as lament—that relates how dramatically the public philosophy of the last fifty years has drifted away from these originally strong republican concerns.

Thus the labor movement in its youth, and throughout most of the late nineteenth century, challenged capitalism on *civic* grounds, arguing for limits on working hours, and changes in working conditions, that would enable workers to perform "public duties."[12] But at the end of the century there emerged the new, more effective union movement that made prosperity and fair distribution of wealth its overriding aims.

Thus, again, the striking contrast Sandel draws between the Progressive era's reform agenda and spirit, and the agenda and spirit that came to predominate in the New Deal:

The economic arguments of our day bear little resemblance to the issues that divided Theodore Roosevelt and Woodrow Wilson, Herbert Croly and Louis D. Brandeis. They were concerned with the structure of the economy and debated how to preserve democratic government in the face of concentrated economic power. We are concerned with the overall level of economic output and debate how to promote economic growth while assuring broad access to the fruits of prosperity. . . . Beginning in the late New Deal and culminating in the early 1960s, the political economy of growth and distributive justice displaced the political economy of citizenship.[13]

Thus, yet again, the profound difference between the aims of Brandeis, in his concern with the overweening power of big business, and the narrower aims of Ralph Nadar or Mark Green: the latter are chiefly concerned with the good of the citizen as *consumer*; Brandeis and his colleagues were concerned with the citizen as *producer*, as worker and owner, as possessor of some real economic independence, and as politically empowered.[14]

The same contrast, essentially, distinguishes Brandeis and the great New Deal antimonopolist Thurman Arnold:

> Unlike antimonopolists in the tradition of Brandeis, Arnold sought not to decentralize the economy for the sake of self-government but to regulate the economy for the sake of lower consumer prices. . . . For Brandeis, antitrust was an expression of the political economy of citizenship, concerned with preserving an economy of small, independent producers. For Arnold, antitrust had nothing to do with the producer ethic of the republican tradition; its purpose was to serve the welfare of consumers.[15]

The same shift throws into gear the Keynesian revolution in economics:

> From Jefferson to Brandeis, republicans worried more about conditions of production than about conditions of consumption because they viewed the world of work as the arena in which, for better or for worse, the character of citizens was formed. . . . Keynesians, by contrast, focused on consumption and wanted to increase "the propensity to consume." . . . The New Deal differed from earlier reform movements in precisely this respect; it sought better to satisfy Americans' wants and ends, not to elevate or improve them. "The New Deal is attempting to do nothing to *people*," Tugwell insisted, "and does not seek at all to alter their way of life, their wants and desires."[16]

But What is Virtue?

Now it is in the course of Sandel's historical narrative, some of whose highpoints I have limned, that we gain more concrete indications of just what the specific civic virtues or qualities of character are that Sandel seeks to regenerate. But we get these indications, not so much from Sandel's own words, as from the sources he quotes. Sandel himself stands back in some hesitation from those sources, and himself speaks more in generalities, not to say abstractions. And this brings me to my critical observations. To begin with, I wonder whether a more systematic, direct, specific, and argumentative presentation and analysis of the virtues, and thus of the human good, is not essential, if we are to have clarity as to what it is we are seeking to encourage, and therefore what direction it is in which we are to move, if we agree to follow Sandel's lead. For must we not apply to Sandel's own project the strictures he applies to Justice Stevens's appeal to the liberal and voluntarist public philosophy? Immediately after the words we quoted above, in which Sandel rejects Stevens's attempt to claim the liberal outlook as the only truly American or even authentically democratic outlook, Sandel goes on to observe of this liberal public philosophy that

> any role it may play in the justification of liberalism must therefore depend on moral argument, not cultural interpretation or appeals to tradition alone. If liberals want to bracket controversial moral questions in a way that assures individual choice (Stevens' way over White's), they must affirm after all a conception of the person in which the self is prior to its ends. They cannot avoid confronting the difficulties that this conception of the person entails.[17]

Must not Sandel, for his part, also go beyond cultural interpretation and appeals to tradition; must he not affirm a specific conception of the person, and, what is more, present a "moral argument," which includes an adequate "confronting" of "the difficulties that this conception of the person entails?" But does not such an argument require, as a minimal beginning, a clear and distinct account of precisely what character traits and what ways of life we will be aiming for, if we revivify the classical republican outlook?

One can certainly generate a list of specific virtues from the historical sources and authorities that Sandel cites in the course of his narrative. What are those specific virtues? What concrete picture do they begin to give us of the human types, of the ways of living and relating to one another, that we are going to be fostering if and to the extent that we truly retrieve the civic republican tradition, and do not use it merely as a vague source of critical and uplifting rhetoric?

In the foreground is a stress on the virtues of family and marital fidelity, conceived as "being sacred" and "noble" in "purpose"[18] (quoting the words of the Court in *Griswold* v. *Connecticut*)—as opposed to a contrary, liberal, or voluntarist outlook which asserts that "the marital couple is not an independent entity with a mind and heart of its own, but an association of two individuals each with a separate intellectual and emotional makeup"[19] (quoting the Court in *Eisenstadt* v. *Baird*). The civic republican spirit leads married persons "to describe their family life in terms of their duties as husbands, wives, and parents," as opposed to today's liberal public philosophy that leads people to describe family life "more as a relationship of persons behind the roles."[20] The civic republican outlook is, to say the least, at a sharp tension with "no-fault" divorce, for the "old law," inspired by civic republican principles, "implied a 'right' to remain married if one adhered to one's marriage contract," while the "new law elevates one's 'right' to divorce by permitting divorce at either party's request"; "under the old law the adulterous husband or wife typically had to pay for his or her infidelity with a disadvantageous property or alimony award," while "today, in contrast, there are no penalties for adultery and no rewards for fidelity."[21] "The new law fails to respect mothers and homemakers of traditional marriages"; "it penalizes women whose economic reliance on their husbands expressed the mutual dependence of traditional marital roles."[22]

Closely linked to family virtue are the economic virtues of the workplace and the market as well as of household management: honesty,[23] frugality,[24] industry,[25] craftsmanship,[26] simplicity of manners[27]; and, more generally, economic independence or even self-sufficiency, epitomized in the exemplars of the yeoman farmer, the small businessman, and the self-employed craftsman or artisan.[28] The most prominent vices attacked in the course of the narrative are also economic: luxury,[29] venality,[30] and avarice.[31] It is surprising, however, to observe how rarely the narrative refers to charity or generosity. In fact, if I am not mistaken, the virtue of charity is mentioned only once, as a private virtue promoted by Ronald Reagan[32]—though the much vaguer virtue of "social sympathy," or a "feeling for the wants" as well as a "sense of the rights" of others, does figure.[33] I noted no reference to generosity, nor for that matter to friendship—despite the invocation of Aristotle, in whose moral and political philosophy no virtue figures so large as the virtue of friendship.

Returning to the specific virtues that *are* evoked by Sandel's narrative, we find next in order of prominence the virtues of "self-control,"[34] including "discipline,"[35] "moderation,"[36] "temperance,"[37] and even "self-denial,"[38] as well as a capacity for shame.[39] Here it is striking to observe that we find, if I am not mistaken, no reference to control of anger or of indignation—despite, again, the repeated reference to classical republicanism. For the civic-educational reflections of classical republicanism (Ciceronian and Stoic no less than Platonic-Aristotelian) may be said to be deeply preoccupied with the problem of the moderating of indignation, and more generally the sublimating of that whole problematic part of the human soul that Plato calls "spiritedness" (*thumos*).

Sandel's narrative surely does echo the spirit of classical republicanism insofar as his quoted sources invoke, in close conjunction with virtues of self-control, the kindred virtues of obedience,[40] respect for authority,[41] orderliness,[42] "equality of station,"[43] and reverence for tradition.[44] And of course there is abundant reference to religious piety, and to obedience to God and His commandments.

But in counterpoint to this stress on equal obedience to law and lawful authority, including higher or transhuman law and authority, is the repeated invocation of manliness, manly pride, and courage[45]; the prominent place assigned to manliness is associated with the moral value of the "rigors of war."[46]

And with these last we finally reach unquestionably political or civic virtues—for, to a surprising degree, the virtues that are actually mentioned in the course of Sandel's narrative are as often as not personal, not to say private, rather than distinctly civic or political (a bridge of a sort is suggested by the invocation of the "community service" promoted by Ronald Reagan's Task Force on Private Sector Initiatives[47]). The political virtues praised, in addition to military courage and manly pride, are a "positive passion for the public good, the public interest, honour, power and glory, established in the minds of the people," as opposed to the vices of "avarice and ambition," and of "rage for profit and commerce" (quoting John Adams)[48]; the "love of fame," as "the ruling passion of the noblest minds," a motive "which would prompt a man to plan and undertake extensive and arduous enterprises for the public benefit" (quoting Hamilton),[49] "a vision of republican glory and greatness," of "grandeur and glory," (again quoting Hamilton)[50]; a patriotic sense of union and national identity.[51]

Last but not least, Sandel's favored sources of inspiration speak emphatically of the virtue of wisdom, by which they mean not only, and not even chiefly, farsighted practical judgment[52]: no, these sources—Jacksonian democrats, the Knights of Labor, Theodore Roosevelt—have in view the noble employment of genuine leisure in a life of the mind pursued for its own sake.[53] In other words, Sandel's sources (though apparently not Sandel himself, for the contrast between his characterization of the sources and what they actually say in the passages he quotes in this regard are striking) agree with Socrates that wisdom is not to be reduced to being simply a civic virtue. Given Sandel's struggle, near the end of the book, to find in the civic republican tradition some basis for cosmopolitanism, his failure to focus on the transcivic dimension of intellectual virtue is especially surprising: for it is in the intellectual virtues or the life of the mind that the classical tradition from Socrates to the Stoics locates the only sure foundation, at once solid and sublime, for a cosmopolitan virtue and cosmopolitan civic consciousness (see above all the famous "Dream of Scipio" with which Cicero closes his *Republic*).

When we step back and survey the results of our attempt to generate a list of the specific virtues that Sandel's narrative calls up, we cannot help but begin to wonder whether there are not major lacunae in the tabulation. What about justice? Or can we leave it at the assumption that "everybody knows" what justice is or demands? But it suffices to recall our current burning debate over so-called "affirmative action" (racial preferences) to recognize at once that there are in fact deep and intense disagreements over what justice means—in principle, and not merely in application. Can one turn seriously to the civic republican strand in our tradition of public philosophy without confronting the fact that classical republicanism has a conception of justice that severely challenges, in important respects, the current procedural-republican conception? In Sandel's book, justice is indeed mentioned, but almost exclusively in connection with the morally deficient liberal and procedural public philosophy. That impoverished public philosophy stresses distributive justice, understood as the egalitarian redistribution of material welfare.[54] Does not the civic or classical republican outlook understand distributive justice rather differently? Does the civic republican tradition not argue that while justice as fairness means equality in *some* sense, this "equality" must be further analyzed? According to the classic Aristotelian analysis in Book Five of the *Nicomachean Ethics*, strict or arithmetical equality characterizes only commutative justice, the justice that prevails in law courts and in the marketplace, where each plaintiff or negotiator is conceived as possessing equal claims. But distributive justice is a higher form of fairness; it is the fairness that prevails in the allocation of office and honor, as well as dishonor. Here justice consists not in a simple equality of persons, but in an equality of value between what is distributed to each person and that person's deserts or merits.[55]

This conception of distributive justice is indeed "aristocratic" (as opposed to plutocratic): for is not the civic republican democratic tradition inspirited with a powerful aristocratic component? Thomas Jefferson's famous and influential educational proposals were explicitly aimed at insuring "that those persons, whom nature hath endowed with genius and virtue, should be rendered by liberal education worthy to receive, and able to guard, the sacred deposit of the rights and liberties of their fellow citizens, and that they should be called to that charge without regard to wealth, birth, or other accidental condition or circumstance." For, Jefferson goes on to declare, these latter, "whom nature hath fitly formed and disposed to become useful instruments for the public," are more likely to come from the poor than from the rich or middle class.[56] Jefferson therefore proposed publicly funded scholarships for higher education: "by this means," he explains in *Notes on the State of Virginia*, "the best geniuses will be raked from the rubbish annually." It is these few of whom Jefferson later speaks, in a famous letter to John Adams, as "the natural aristocracy": "the natural aristocracy I consider as the most precious gift of nature, for the instruction, the trusts, and government of society. . . . May we not even say that that form of government is the best which provides the most effectually for a pure selection of these natural *aristoi* into the offices of government?"[57]

Sandel cannot help but acknowledge this aristocratic dimension in American civic republicans' arguments about the true nature of justice:[58]

> What troubled the revolutionary leaders most of all was the popular politics increasingly practiced in the state legislatures. They had assumed that under republican government, a "natural aristocracy" of merit and virtue would replace an artificial aristocracy of heredity and patronage . . . .
>
> Despite their revision of classical republican assumptions, the framers of the Constitution . . . continued to believe that the virtuous should govern . . . The framers rejected the notion that the people possessed sufficient virtue to govern directly. But they retained the hope that the national government they had designed would be led by enlightened statesmen like themselves, who would possess the virtue and wisdom that ordinary citizens and local representatives lacked. . . .
>
> The aim was to design a system that would, in Madison's words, "extract from the mass of society the purest and noblest characters which it contains"[59] . . . This aim distances Madison from modern-day interest-group pluralists who invoke his name.[60]

But so far as I can see, Sandel never really comes to terms with these arguments that insist on the need to temper democracy and equality. All that one finds are occasional fastidious expressions of discomfort at such unfashionable sentiments.[61] But how can Jeffersonian republicanism be appealed to, once this aristocratic cornerstone of authentic Jeffersonianism is hidden away in embarrassment? Is this not a bit like Callias holding a party to honor philosophy, and then asking Socrates, beforehand, please not to cause a scene by questioning anyone about justice? Is there not perhaps an inadequate, a truncated, meditation on virtue, and especially on justice, at work in the American tradition, even or precisely in its most "civic republican" strand? And does Sandel do much to repair that inadequacy?

Nor is it only as regards the preeminent virtue of justice that one must entertain doubts as to the adequacy of Sandel's richly thought-provoking book. It is illuminating to compare the virtues mentioned or discussed in Sandel's narrative with the virtues elaborated in classic philosophic treatments of the virtues, from Aristotle to Hume. By making such a comparison we begin to become more acutely aware of the grave questions that would have to be addressed in any thoroughgoing attempt to return to a politics of civic virtue—if we are, in Sandel's words, not to "avoid confronting the difficulties that this conception of the person entails."[62]

An Agenda for a Rigorous Investigation of Republican Virtue

To begin with, must one not establish, on the basis of argument and analysis, some priorities of intrinsic rank among the many virtues or candidates for virtue? Which of the virtues are more important or essential and which less? Which are central and which ancillary? For example, is manliness as crucial as it appears from the sources Sandel evokes, and if so, just which sort of manliness—and why? What is the argument for the crucial significance of distinctively manly qualities of character in a strong republic? Surely in our time this argument needs to be restated, and can by no means be taken for granted. And if, in response to our query, Sandel wishes to abandon the reverence for manliness so strongly testified to in his sources, then again we must demand from him his argument. Why is the academically fashionable denigration of manliness anything more than another manifestation of slavishly conventional clinging to the mutilated or bankrupt contemporary public philosophy? If we are to resuscitate civic republicanism, why, and how, are we to jettison the celebration of manliness that is so central to that older republican tradition?

To move to another kind of basic question: are all of the virtues that *appear* to be virtues actually capable of retaining that precious title once they are exposed to searching scrutiny? For example, is the passion for glory, the love of fame, as unambiguously a mark of nobility as John Adams and Alexander Hamilton, following Machiavelli, seem to have supposed?[63] Or is this passion, as Aristotle and Socrates contended, only the essential raw material for great excellence: a material that can also take on the form of great vice, and therefore a material which, in order to become true virtue, is in need of refinement and shaping through critical scrutiny and severe discipline? After all, is there no connection between what Sandel praises as "a vision of republican glory and greatness"[64] and the proclivity to imperialism? And what about the "passion for power," or "ambition"? As regards this spiritual drive, Sandel's narrative manifests a striking tergiversation. On one and the same page we are given a quotation from a great authority (John Adams) celebrating the "passion for power" as a leading civic virtue, and then, seven lines later, we are told by Professor Sandel that the Founders viewed power as a "corrupting force"—as is illustrated by quoting Adams again, in an attack on "ambition" as a great civic vice.[65] So which is it? Or is there not indicated here a genuine conundrum, calling for profound reflection?

Then in the third place, one must ask whether all of the civic virtues invoked by Sandel, even those that survive critical scrutiny, are compatible and harmonious one with another. Are there not severe unexplored tensions among some of the apparently highest of the virtues that Sandel's narrative evokes? For example, does even the noble or purified love of fame necessarily go easily with strong and solid attachment to the family, or with the prosaic satisfactions of independent craftsmanship? Does the passionate sense of honor, does proud manliness, does the drive for economic self-sufficiency, sit easily with authentic biblical piety—or is there not here a plethora of problems crying out for long meditation?

Lastly, one must ask how the virtues are to be ranked or prioritized in terms of their relative feasibility for us, given the conditions of our contemporary society. Is it not possible or even likely that we may have to make painful choices between, on the one hand, cultivating lesser, but more attainable virtues and, on the other hand, running greater risks with the entire project of ennoblement in order to prevent the extinction of the greatest and truest forms of human flourishing?

These are questions and tasks of prioritizing that, so far as I know, have never been avoided by any previous serious theorist of virtue. Aristotle's *Ethics* would be unthinkable without his elevation of pride and his denigration of humility, or without his conspicuous silence on piety as a moral virtue; the same theorist's *Politics* culminates in a critique of the Spartan cult of manliness and a rigorous argument for the superiority of the intellectual virtues; the Platonic dialogues mean nothing if they do not teach that the core of true virtue is knowledge or wisdom, the core of vice ignorance; Hobbes's moral and political philosophy is centered on the critique of Aristotelian pride and the argument for the sanctity of promises; the argument of Kant's *Groundwork* elevates the good will, or reverence for the pure form of legislation, over all other traditional moral and civic virtues, and most strikingly over wisdom; Nietzsche's superman is "Caesar with the soul of Christ." But what sort of human being and what code of the virtues is Sandel talking about? What is a "multiply-encumbered self," and on what basis does such a self make fundamental decisions about noble and base, right and wrong? These questions take on a real bite when we observe that Sandel concedes that there is a specific new "corruption to which multiply-encumbered citizens are prone": "the drift to formless, protean, storyless selves, unable to weave the various strands of their identity into a coherent whole."[66]

I confess that I do not see in this book a firm and well-argued basis, as opposed to an earnest wish, for avoiding this new and potentially devastating corruption of the human spirit. But if this terrible new corruption is a real danger inherent in his project; if it is true, as Sandel explicitly affirms, that the critique of, and the movement away from, the "unencumbered self" runs the real risk of producing psychologically rudderless creatures who circulate, glazed-eyed and herd-like, around a kind of lifelong spiritual shopping mall, then one may, and one must, legitimately ask whether an intransigent adherence to the idea of the unencumbered self might not give individuals a more sterling personal integrity, a greater strength of will and sense of responsibility, and a more vigorous capacity for treasuring and sustaining at least a modicum of self-government. One may and must ask whether in our age it may not be the intransigently unencumbered self, with its proud assertion of personal rights, and the attenuated virtues that derive from such proud independence that is not closer to the classical republican ideal.

But this points to an even broader and deeper kind of critical question that must be raised in the course of any sustained theoretical attempt to revive civic virtue. Are the civic virtues, is republican self-government or participation in deliberative politics, to be understood chiefly as an end, that is, as intrinsically good, because constitutive of human fulfillment? Or is civic virtue to be understood finally and chiefly as instrumental, as a *means* for protecting and securing subpolitical or transpolitical goods? Sandel does, indeed, raise this crucial question; but he never, as it seems to me, really grapples with it, or recognizes its weighty urgency. He instead reproduces a wavering or even a confusion that is found in the widely diverse sources he employs to evoke the meaning of civic virtue.

Sandel admits that the philosophic tradition of civic republicanism exhibits a deep division on this momentous issue:

> The strong version of the republican ideal, going back to Aristotle, sees civic virtue and political participation as *intrinsic* to liberty; given our nature as political beings, we are free only insofar as we exercise our capacity to deliberate about the common good, and participate in the public life of a free city or republic. More modest versions of the republican ideal see civic virtue and public service as *instrumental* to liberty; even the liberty to pursue our own ends depends on preserving the freedom of our political community, which depends in turn on the willingness to put the common good above our private interests.[67]

But this formulation of the "more modest" version is simply incoherent, or self-contradictory: for how can we put the common good "above" our private interests when that good, or public service to it, is merely instrumental to the pursuit of "our own ends"?! Sandel inadvertently reproduces here a glaring incoherence in the "more modest" version—which he ascribes to Machiavelli, as interpreted by Quentin Skinner, although in fact a careful reading of Machiavelli would show that Machiavelli is not guilty of the absurdity thus attributed to him. On the contrary: Machiavelli's outlook is ruthlessly coherent and consistent. Machiavelli is the source of that conception of virtue (*virtù*) that inspires the famous remark of Hamilton that Sandel repeatedly quotes: "the love of fame is the ruling passion of the noblest minds."[68] This remark implies that a clear-sighted person would never put the common good "above" his greatest personal good or pleasure found in fame. This remark implies, in the famous words of *Cato's Letters*, that

> when we call any man disinterested, we should intend no more by it, than that the turn of his mind is towards the publick, and that he has placed his own personal glory and

pleasure in serving it. To serve his country is his private pleasure, mankind is his mistress, and he does good to them by gratifying himself. Disinterestedness, in any other sense than this, there is none. . . . as selfishness is the strongest bias of men, every man ought to be upon his guard against another, that he become not the prey of another . . .

No wise man, therefore, will in any instance of moment trust to the mere integrity of another . . . [69]

This Hamiltonian or Machiavellian outlook is directly contradicted by George Washington—contrary to Sandel's assertion that Hamilton correctly describes the ruling passion of the Founders.[70] When called to lead the Virginia defenses in 1775, Washington wrote to a friend that "no man can gain any Honour by conducting our Forces at this time, but rather lose in his reputation": he therefore chose to forfeit, he wrote, "what at present constitutes the chief part of my happiness; i.e. the esteem and notice the country has been pleased to honour me with." Similarly, when called to serve as the nation's first President, Washington judged the office as hardly likely to enhance, as more likely to jeopardize, his already glorious repute; still, he wrote to Henry Lee, "if I know myself . . . regard for my own fame will not come in competition with an object of so much magnitude."[71] And is not the outlook expressed by Washington evidently the truer? For once we begin to understand public service or virtue as ultimately an instrument for the acquisition of personal fame, power, wealth, and empire—as Machiavelli argues we should, and the imperialistic Roman republicans did—have we not lost sight of what truly dignifies humanity, and ennobles politics? We may invoke here the testimony of Sandel himself (contradicting what he says later in his book): "a wholly instrumental defense of freedom and rights not only leaves rights vulnerable but fails to respect the inherent dignity of persons. The utilitarian calculus treats people as means to the happiness of others, not as ends in themselves, worthy of respect."[72]

The contradiction in which Sandel thus becomes entrammelled can only be resolved, I believe, by his following consistently his deepest and noblest insight, into the noninstrumental, intrinsic and ultimate, value of civic virtue. Such a move would require an ascent from the more "modest" (and, we now see, incoherent or self-contradictory) version to the Aristotelian version of civic republicanism.

Yet to return to Aristotle is not to find simple or easy answers. It is rather to become aware of what is truly perplexing about virtue. If Sandel were to reconsider Aristotle attentively, he would, I suggest, be forced to enlarge considerably his conception of virtue, and of what Aristotle—and the entire classical tradition stretching at least up to Jonathan Swift—means by "virtue." For that tradition, contrary to what Sandel says and suggests, does not conceive of republican liberty and participation in deliberative self-government as the fullest and most complete realization of human flourishing or excellence. Aristotle insists that civic virtue (*arete politike*) can be maintained as a key constituent of human fulfillment if and only if such virtue is seen as partial, as incomplete, as pointing beyond itself to a virtue that ultimately transcends politics: in the first place, to moral virtue (*arete ethike*), which Aristotle distinguishes from civic virtue,[73] and then, in the final analysis, to contemplative or theoretical virtue, culminating in the imitation of and the meditation on God and the cosmos as a whole, the cosmos within which the human things occupy only a subordinate place or status.[74] This keystone of authentic classical republicanism gives it an obvious kinship with the biblical tradition. But concern for a virtue linked to divinity, this crown of classical republicanism, has been amputated in Sandel's account or invocation—despite our catching glimpses of it shining out from the sources he quotes, such as Roger Williams, Abraham Lincoln, Theodore Roosevelt, Ronald Reagan, and Martin Luther King.

This animadversion brings me to my final critical reflection. The argument, and indeed the structure, of Sandel's book is complicated in a very puzzling way by the fact that he charges our liberal public philosophy with having neglected or diminished a whole range of spiritual goods and concerns that extend way beyond what can be included as aspects of or means to civic virtue, republican self-government, or deliberative citizenship. But a curious effort is made to shoehorn these spiritual goods into the category of civic virtue. In the Introduction and Conclusion, and throughout the longer Part Two of the book, Sandel speaks as if his main aim is the regeneration of the civic virtues needed for self-government. But in Part One, and periodically in Part Two, the spiritual goods Sandel focuses on—family; independence and fulfillment in productive work; respect for the environment; the life of the mind; and, above all, religion—can by no means be understood simply or even mainly as valuable or as valued for their contribution to self-government. Take, as a foremost example, the family: of course, we value family life in part because it serves as a school for good citizenship. But surely what we value by far the most in family life is intrinsic to the family—and not instrumental to citizenship. Or consider, similarly, our concern for freedom of speech. It is true, as Sandel argues following Meikeljohn, that freedom of speech receives a high justification as a prerequisite and constituent of open deliberative self-government. But surely we also value freedom of speech for its role in cultural, artistic, scientific, philosophic, and religious life—none of which we treasure chiefly because of their contribution to self-government (though they indeed make such a contribution). We cherish these dimensions of spiritual life above all because of their transpolitical and inherent value.

Sandel somehow recognizes this difficulty from time to time, as when he speaks of "the higher pluralism."[75] But the content and character of this "higher pluralism" remains foggy, and its relation to civic virtue obscure.

The problem is especially acute in Sandel's treatment of religion, which is praised in this book in almost exclusively instrumental terms. When talking of the importance of the Church in the lives and aspirations of African-Americans, for example, Sandel speaks as if their Christian faith were mainly important for its political role, for its usefulness in fostering civic spirit and civic action, primarily in the civil rights movement. But surely, from the point of view of the faithful adherents of Christianity, such a characterization is narrow to the point of verging on blasphemy. In this optic, religion is reduced to being a means for secular or mundane ends. Such a perspective fails to acknowledge the supreme value of the Church as the avenue to transpolitical and indeed transcendent goods. From such a vantage point we lose sight of the spirituality that responds to the call of suprarational revelation, and that obeys the Living and Eternal God's commandments—divine laws that demand far more than what can be comprehended as useful for earthly civic well-being.

This dimension of transcendence—so powerfully evident in religion, but unmistakably present also in love and in friendship, in the family conceived as sacred, in our reverence for the environing whole of nature, and in our longing for and openness to completion through contemplation—must be made a more thematic cynosure of our analysis of what has been neglected or diminished by the public philosophy that now reigns among our democratic elites. Otherwise, we will continue to lack, I fear, an adequate beginning point for our diagnosis of democracy's discontent.

2

Virtue *en Masse*

JEREMY WALDRON

IN this chapter, I consider how some of the arguments of Michael Sandel's book *Democracy's Discontent* fare when related explicitly to the conditions of modern social and political life. I shall argue, first, that Sandel's liberal opponents are more sensitive than he is to the sociological circumstances which ought to frame any attempt to use politics to inculcate ethical virtue. And I shall argue, secondly, that Sandel's discussion of specifically civic or political virtue is undermined by a failure to take seriously points made more than 150 years ago by Benjamin Constant about the scale of modern politics and the possibilities for agency that that generates.

I

The attractive thing about *Democracy's Discontent* is that it promises not just an abstract case for the civic republican vision of political community, but a vision essentially *for us*—as indeed the logic of Michael Sandel's argument requires—a vision embedded in a retelling of our history and related intimately and in detail to the all-too-concrete predicaments and panics of modern American society. It is a pity therefore that the author is content to state the position of his liberal or proceduralist opponents in terms which remain abstract and philosophical.

At the beginning, Sandel emphasizes the importance to the liberal vision of the principle of *neutrality*. In chapter 1, he mentions two arguments for liberal neutrality: (1) the Kantian celebration of the autonomous, choosing self, rejecting the heteronomy that state perfectionism necessarily involves; and (2) the utilitarian defense of neutrality, identified by Sandel with the work of J. S. Mill. Of the latter, Sandel's summary version is as follows:

> The state should not impose on its citizens a preferred way of life, even for their own good, because doing so will reduce the sum of happiness, at least in the long run.

Now that's a pretty sound-bite rendering of Mill. It is not complemented by any discussion of why or how Mill thought imposing a shared way of life would reduce the sum of happiness. Indeed, Sandel's critique of this position is simply the familiar critique of utilitarian morality—that it takes preferences for granted, etc. This is unfortunate because it ignores what is original, interesting, and historically concrete in Mill's argument. I would like to talk a little more about this, because it is relevant to a wider theme that I want to take up.

Sandel observes that "the idea that government should be neutral on the question of the good life is distinctive to modern political thought." Another way of putting that is to say that the liberal principle of neutrality can be understood as a response to certain features of modernity. In the early modern period, the case for toleration and state neutrality on matters of religion was the Lockian view that state imposition could not produce religious belief but only a mockery of religious belief. This—or rather the moral version of it (i.e. the moral version of a view originally about religion), which by the way I think is at the heart of Kant's position—is not something that Sandel considers. Its continuing centrality to the liberal case is evidenced by the fact that it is also the argument at the heart of Ronald Dworkin's position in *Life's Dominion*. But let that pass. What is important to see is that the modern liberal case for neutrality begins with this concern and amplifies it in relation to the historical conditions of modernity. For of course the reason Mill thought state imposition of moral principles would diminish human happiness was his apprehension about what such imposition would involve in the circumstances of mass society. It would involve, not coercion at the point of a sword, nor anyone being burned at the stake, but dull grey, fearful mass conformism, dictated by something like a moral version of the fashion industry, engendering and sustaining shallow mockeries of moral commitment in the repetitive, thoughtless, sound-bite form which is the only way in which ethical ideals can be transmitted under the auspices of political and social authority in a modern mass society. In other words, Mill's case in *On Liberty* is not just an abstract formulation of the principle of utility together with the harm principle; it is a sociologically sensitive piece of theorizing—every bit as concrete in its orientation as Sandel's own best work. Mill's writing is an attempt to consider what would become of our moral lives and our ethical ideals if "the engines of moral repression" were made more powerful than they already were in the mid-nineteenth century.

Remember Mill's account of the deadened way in which even pleasures (let alone ethical ideals) are pursued *en masse* in the society he saw around him:

> [E]veryone lives as under the eye of a hostile and dreaded censorship. Not only in what concerns others, but in what concerns only themselves, the individual or the family do not ask themselves—what do I prefer? Or, what would suit my character and disposition? Or, what would allow the best and highest in me to have fair play, and enable it to grow and thrive. They ask themselves, what is suitable to my position? What is usually done by persons of my station and pecuniary circumstances? . . . I do not mean they choose what is customary, in preference to what suits their own inclination. It does not occur to them to have any inclination, except for what is customary. Thus the mind

itself is bowed to the yoke: even in what people do for pleasure, conformity is the first thing thought of; they like in crowds. . . . (*On Liberty*, ch. 3, para. 6)

(By the way: it is a mockery—very close to the opposite of the truth—to think that the appropriate way to criticize this argument is to say—as Sandel does—that utilitarians like Mill take preference formation for granted!) Remember too Mill's sociological speculations in chapter 3 of *On Liberty*—"A people, it appears, may be progressive for a certain length of time and then stop"—and the "warning example" in the case of China of how a once progressive society became "stationary":

They [the Chinese] have succeeded beyond all hope in what English philanthropists are so industriously working at—in making a people all alike, all governing their thoughts and conduct by the same maxims and rules; and these are the fruits. The modern *regime* of public opinion is, in an unorganized form, what the Chinese educational and political systems are in an organized; and unless individuality should be able successfully to assert itself against his yoke, Europe, notwithstanding its noble antecedents and its professed Christianity, will tend to become another China. (*On Liberty*, ch. 3, para. 17)

Progress is the important thing for Mill, and the issue in the passage just quoted is the relation between progress and uniformity. It is progress that offers to improve human happiness (by which Mill meant not so much the mere satisfaction of preferences, but the sort of decrease in misery that things like better medical or better sanitation or better educational arrangements would involve—see the passage on "wretched social arrangements" in *Utilitarianism*). And the utilitarian case for neutrality—if that is what it is—is that the political, or worse, the social imposition of ethical ideas and ways of life will destroy the spirit of originality and individuality that animates progress of this and every sort.

I mention these familiar points (I hope they are familiar) because Mill's case is a case for neutrality which sounds a warning that ought to be of some concern to those like Sandel who take moral and ethical ideals seriously. Sandel sometimes seems to suggest that it is liberalism's fault that shallow and potentially oppressive groups like the Moral Majority seek to colonize the public sphere:

a politics that brackets morality and religion too soon generates its own disenchantment. Where political discourse lacks moral resonance, the yearning for the public life of larger meaning finds undesirable expression. Groups like the Moral Majority seek to clothe the public square with narrow, intolerant moralisms.[1]

But Mill's warning is that these may be exactly the sort of moralisms we can expect when the coercive forces of government and the mass opinion it both shapes and panders to are put at the service of "moral ideals."

It is, as I said, a pity that Sandel neglects this more sociological side of Mill's argument—not just because he fails therefore to do justice to the liberal case for neutrality, but also because the question of how traditional moral ideals fare in modern circumstances of mass society (and also global society) is in fact supposed to be a dominant theme in Sandel's book. For example, near the end of the book, in a passage on "voluntarist freedom," Sandel writes:

> The liberal self-image and the actual organization of modern social and economic life are sharply at odds. Even as we think and act as freely choosing, independent selves, we confront a world governed by impersonal structures of power that defy our understanding and control. The voluntarist conception of freedom leaves us ill-equipped to contend with this condition.[2]

Here Sandel is suggesting that the liberal ideals of freedom and autonomy are sociologically *not available* in modern circumstances. And what I am suggesting is that, also, in modern circumstances of mass society, the Aristotelian ideal of a polity devoted to the inculcation of genuine full-blooded virtue may not be sociologically available either.

II

This brings me to my second point about the relation between the critique of liberalism and the conditions of modernity. Surely it is incumbent on any defender of civic republicanism to ponder whether traditional ideals of civic participation can possibly make sense when we shift from the Athenian *polis* or Florentine city state to a continental nation of a quarter of a billion people.

One way of reading *Democracy's Discontent* is to see it as a late twentieth-century response—or perhaps as a late twentieth-century refusal to concede anything—to the famous comparison which Benjamin Constant essayed, at the beginning of the nineteenth century—between the liberty of the ancients and the liberty of the moderns. Constant is not mentioned by name in Sandel's book. But Sandel's case could be read as a refusal to accept Constant's view that:

> We [in modern society—even in 1819, when Constant was writing] can no longer enjoy the liberty of the ancients, which consisted in an active and constant participation in collective power. Our freedom must consist of peaceful enjoyment and private independence.

Sandel is sensitive to the issue of political scale. He raises the question of size a number of times. He uses a phrase from Brandeis—"the curse of bigness." He talks of "an economy too vast to admit republican hopes of mastery."[3] He talks of " 'the curse of bigness' railed against by republicans"[4] and he talks too of "the gap between the terms of political community and the scale of economic life."[5] But he does not yield to Constant's point. Indeed it is remarkable how much democratic ideals and participatory practice have flourished in the twentieth century, notwithstanding Constant's transvaluation of participatory values. The modern revival of republican thought is a tribute to the fact that the impulse to ancient liberty is somewhat stronger in the modern world (at least among legal scholars and political theory graduate students) than Constant believed. Apparently, it continues to answer to some fairly deep human needs.

Nevertheless it would be wrong to dismiss Constant's point altogether, for—as with Mill—we need to look at and evaluate not just the position that Constant takes, but his reasons for that position. For the reasons are not just something that Mill or Constant make up—considerations which we are free to reject as we reject their politics (if we do). Reasons purport to appeal to something that *is* the case and connect it with things the theorist thinks *we* think or should think are important. So we need to consider whether there is something in the reasoning that is important to us, even if we would rather reject the conclusion.

Let us look then at Constant's argument (not his conclusion, his *argument*) to see whether there is anything that a theorist like Sandel ought to ponder. Constant's reasoning was as follows:

> [T]he size of a country causes a corresponding decrease of the political importance allotted to each individual. The most obscure republican of Sparta or Rome had power. The same is not true of the simple citizen of Britain or the United States. His personal influence is an imperceptible part of the social will which impresses on the government its direction. . . . The share which in antiquity everyone held in national sovereignty was by no means an abstract presumption as it is in our own day. The will of each individual had real influence: the exercise of this will was a vivid and repeated pleasure. Consequently the ancients were ready to make many a sacrifice to preserve their political rights and their share in the administration of the state. Everybody, feeling with pride all that his suffrage was worth, found in this awareness of his personal importance a great compensation. This compensation no longer exists for us today. Lost in the multitude, the individual can almost never perceive the influence he exercises. Never does his will impress itself upon the whole; nothing confirms in his own eyes his own cooperation.[6]

There is no denying these points that Constant makes about the effects of size, even if—eventually—we want to reject Constant's conclusion. We cannot pretend that the United States has the population of *quattrocento* Florence, just because we would like to call ourselves civic republicans. We have to think hard about what to do with the undeniable facts that Constant draws our attention to. The points that Constant emphasizes are important and ought to be taken very seriously in a theory of virtue. (And modern civic republicanism is in part a theory of virtue—civic virtue.) Let me explain.

Virtue is a matter of how an individual is disposed to act, and a matter also of his self-control in action. What virtue amounts to and what is required of agents or citizens in the way of virtue should surely be sensitive to the nature of agency that is possible in the area of life with which we are concerned. It should also be sensitive, at least in part, to the phenomenology of agency in that area. Whether an agent (participating in a certain form of life) is able—or not—to "perceive the influence he exercises" will affect the sort of care he is required to take and the sort of awareness he is required to have of what is going on around him. Acting in a way that has a direct and visible effect is one thing; acting in circumstances where the effects, though momentous, accrue indirectly because of one's participation along with thousands or millions of others, is quite another thing. Both forms of action may be ethically significant, and both may require guidance and frameworking by a theory of virtue. But it would be surprising if the same theory of virtue—or even the same sort of theory of virtue—applied to the two modes of action. Virtue is about the control of action and the self-control of agents—initially it concerns the conscious control, eventually the habitual control. But either way, it will be affected by the circumstances in which the moral dimensions of a form of behavior make themselves apparent to the agent.

What I am saying is that if the scale of political organization is so different as to enable only civic agency of a quite different sort, then it is likely that our thinking about "the qualities of character necessary to the common good of self-government" will have to be different too. Just because we reject Constant's conclusion, it does not mean we are entitled to treat his reasons for that conclusion as though they had no impact in our own thinking. We cannot just *decide* that traditional civic virtue still makes sense, if the social conditions for its development and exercise patently no longer exist and if it is not in our power to restore those conditions.

Certaintly, if we are going to persevere with a republican commitment to active civic participation, notwithstanding the point that individual citizens can almost never perceive the influence they individually exercise, then we will have to develop conceptions of virtue that are appropriate to agency of that sort. For example, there is still a tendency among citizens to worry all the time about whether they can—individually—make a difference when they engage themselves in politics or social activity. It is a common phrase, among well-intentioned American college students, for example. And where the individual difference they make is indiscernible (because they are acting together with thousands or millions of others) they may say things like "I don't matter" or "My vote is wasted" or "It makes no difference what I do."

It seems to me that an education in civic virtue in (and for) the modern world ought to involve education out of that way of thinking, and in its place education in the logic and ethics of collective action. For that, I would urge upon citizens of the modern republic, not a rereading of Jefferson's apotheosis of the individual yeoman farmer, but perhaps the section in Derek Parfit's book *Reasons and Persons* entitled "Five Mistakes in Moral Mathematics."

In general, if conditions have changed, then we cannot infer what modern civic virtue is from what it has in the past been taken to be. In addition—and this is an important supplementary point that comes from Machiavelli and Max Weber—we cannot infer what political virtue is from what we would like it to be. It is possible that civic virtue for the modern world is unfamiliar and counterintuitive. It may even be the case that the virtues required for political engagement in mass society are not best taught in the face-to-face circumstances of family or small-town Main Street. From a Machiavellian perspective—and I mean the Machiavelli who thought seriously about politics not just about statecraft (i.e. I mean the Machiavelli who cautioned us against judging tumultuous politics as necessarily undesirable)—"Mr. Smith Goes to Washington" may be a cautionary tale about inappropriate forms of civic education. It may be the case that if we persevere with the sincere/heroic individualism of civic virtue as it is conceived by its most nostalgic proponents, we will be bringing up a generation of citizens quite unprepared for the messy and congested reality of political life, and for the moral possibilities it actually does offer.

One could go on in this vein—indicating ways of thinking, talking, and acting in politics that are often presented as civic virtue, but which perhaps ought to be rethought in the light of what Constant says about both the reality and the phenomenology of politics in the modern world. For example, we think it important and virtuous—human, bringing things down to earth, the importance of the concrete narrative, etc.—to draw lessons from individual stories. But we need to balance this in sensible civic thinking with some awareness of the scale on which we are proceeding. Two hundred and sixty million is a huge number of people, and there is some virtue in acknowledging that among such a number of people engaged in dense interaction, if anything can go wrong it will, and so there may be room for some care in inferring general lessons from particular anecdotes.

Styles of politics—whether they are apprehensions about freedom and progress or whether they are concerns about traditional virtues—are not to be chosen arbitrarily or willfully—not even by liberals. They ought to be the product of thought about the conditions of political life. My general point in this section, then, is the same as the point I made in the first section of the chapter. We should not be in the business of lambasting liberalism unless we are sure that there is nothing to learn from the aspects of modernity that liberals have taken seriously in their arguments. We may not want their conclusions. But we have to consider how our conclusions—or in this case, Michael Sandel's conclusions—fare in the light of their premises. In fact, however, those who call themselves civic republicans are—in my experience—often the least inclined to undertake this rethinking about whether there is anything distinctive about modern conditions that calls for a different conception of virtue or a different account of politics. And they are also the most inclined to disparage or slight such modes of sociologically sensitive rethinking when conducted by their opponents.

Let me reiterate. I am not arguing that Benjamin Constant's case makes civic republicanism obsolete, and that we should all (as Constant urges) become private-realm liberals. I am arguing that the premises of Constant's discussion do need to be taken seriously—by us and by Sandel. And if they are taken seriously, they may necessitate a rethinking of civic virtue—both of what it is and how, more structurally, it is related to the agency conditions of collective action.

3

Reworking Sandel's Republicanism

PHILIP PETTIT

IN *Democracy's Discontent*[1] Michael Sandel describes "America in search of a public philosophy," as the book's subtitle puts it. He documents the commitment to the procedural republic that he finds in the public life of the United States today and he sets up a contrast between this philosophy and the older American commitment to civic republicanism.

The aim of the book is to rekindle enthusiasm for republicanism and to dampen the contemporary ardor for liberalism: for liberalism, that is, in the broad sense in which liberals may be conservative as well as progressive.[2] The book attempts to achieve this end by taking us through developments in constitutional law and political economy where we can see liberal ideals taking over from republican ones and where we can gain a palpable sense of the loss involved in the retreat from republicanism.

I find Sandel's claims engaging—engaging, in particular, for the wealth of detail with which he documents them—and on the whole congenial. But in one crucial respect they leave me unhappy. They are worryingly indeterminate about the precise nature of America's lost republican ideals, about what those ideals would require of us as citizens, and about where they would lead governmental policy. Whenever the book focuses on such matters, it fades out before achieving a sharp level of resolution.

I raise this complaint in a spirit of construction, however, not despair. For it turns out that if Sandel will only go along with the characterization of republicanism which I have defended elsewhere[3]—and which, in broad outline, Quentin Skinner[4] pioneered—then he can escape such charges of indeterminacy and still uphold most of the themes that he parades. Let him allow us to rework his narrative a little, restructuring it around this account of republicanism, and he can tell a story that has a much greater claim on our attention. So at any rate I shall argue.

My chapter is in three sections. In the first, I summarize the salient points in Sandel's original narrative, identifying the indeterminacies that worry me. In the second I present the elements in my account of republicanism that are

Reprinted with permission from the *Journal of Philosophy*, 95 (1998), 73–96.

relevant to that narrative. And then in the third section I rework the narrative around those elements, showing how the worrying indeterminacies are thereby removed.

1. Sandel's Original Narrative

Neglecting his own order of exposition, I think we can identify five salient themes in Sandel's book. These are:

(1) American constitutional law has become rights-based in practice and therefore neutral in aspiration: it aspires to impose no particular values;
(2) this neutralism shows up also elsewhere: for example, in a preference-based pattern of economic policy-making; and
(3) in an interest-based way of conceptualizing and organizing politics.
(4) In making a concern for civic virtue irrelevant, such developments contrast with older, republican ways of thinking; and
(5) we would do well to adopt such ways of thinking in preference to contemporary liberalism.

First theme

The first theme, bearing on a rights-based interpretation of constitutional law, is the main topic of the first half of Sandel's book. He thinks of the rights-based approach as one that abstracts away from particular accounts of what is good and valuable and that tries to argue, independently of any particular conception of the good, that certain rights are sacrosanct. They have a claim on state and society that is prior to the claim of any alleged good.

Sandel argues that such a concern for rights was not particularly prominent in discussions around the time of the War of Independence and the constitutional convention. "Only in the final week of the convention, as the proposed constitution was being prepared for submission to Congress, did George Mason of Virginia rise to say he 'wished the plan had been prefaced with a Bill of Rights.' "[5] Of course it is true that the Anti-Federalists used the absence of a bill of rights as an argument against the Constitution. But this did not come of a commitment to a rights-based way of thinking, according to Sandel. "In opposing the Constitution, they sought to limit national power, and they found in the bill of rights the most popular, though not necessarily the most effective, way of doing so."[6] When James Madison proposed a bill of rights, then—the proposal, somewhat amended, was adopted in 1791—he did not do so out of a personal commitment to a rights-based approach. "This reversal reflected shrewd political strategy and astute political science."[7]

It was only in the aftermath of the Civil War, according to Sandel's story, that the rights-based approach began to come into its own. The Thirteenth, Fourteenth, and Fifteenth Amendments to the Constitution were designed to ensure the emancipation and equal status of slaves. But the second of those measures had a further, incidental effect. "The Fourteenth Amendment also imposed on the states certain restrictions that would transform the role of the Supreme Court in protecting individual rights. It established that no state may 'abridge the privileges or immunities of citizens of the United States' or 'deprive any person of life, liberty, or property, without due process of law' or deny to any person 'the equal protection of the laws.' "[8]

Sandel goes on to argue that this Amendment empowered the Supreme Court to protect individual rights from state infringement and that in doing so it led to the appearance, over a number of generations, of a distinctively rights-based approach. Thus when the famous *Lochner* v. *New York* (1905) judgment struck down a law prohibiting the employment of bakery employees for more than sixty hours per week, the Court used the words: "The general right to make a contract in relation to his business is part of the liberty of the individual protected by the Fourteenth Amendment."[9]

The Lochner approach was given up by the Court in the period of the New Deal. But the way of thinking that it encapsulated became ever more entrenched, according to Sandel's account. Perhaps there was no right of the kind alleged in the Lochner judgment; perhaps the will of the democratic majority should be given sway in such cases. But there were other rights that should be protected, and protected even against democratic majorities. And those rights enjoyed precisely the status of trumps that the Lochner Court had given to the right to make employment contracts.

Which rights had that trumping status? Well, the reason that the right to make employment contracts of any kind was not a protected right, according to critics of the Lochner Court like Oliver Wendell Holmes, was that its claim to be a right was predicated on the truth of a particular economic philosophy.[10] And so the rights that should be protected naturally came to be depicted as rights of such a fundamental kind that their acceptance did not presuppose any particular conception of the good life or the good society. This approach was established after the Second World War, when the Court came to represent the Constitution as a framework of rights that is neutral among different ends.

Sandel goes on to illustrate the neutralism—the no-value neutralism, as he views it—that he finds in judgments of the Court over the past few decades. He sees it in the tendency to think of religious liberty, for example, not as freedom of conscience in an area of agreed and special importance for human beings, but as the freedom to choose on matters of personal preference: on matters about the importance of which the Court has no opinion.[11] He sees it in development of the doctrine that the content of a given sort of speech is irrelevant to the question of whether the Court ought to protect the freedom of that kind of speech: there is no distinction that the Court is entitled to make between low-value and high-value expression.[12] And he sees it in the shift from a civic to a voluntarist way of defending privacy. Under the civic defense, privacy should be protected so far as it fosters social institutions—say, the institution of marriage—that are of agreed importance; under the voluntarist defense, privacy should be protected so far as it enables individuals to exercise their autonomy in a way that, however unimportant or even obnoxious it may seem to most of us, is consistent with a similar exercise of autonomy on the part of others.[13]

Second theme

I have given a lot of attention to the first theme in Sandel's book—that American constitutional law has become rights-based and neutralist—mainly because he himself devotes all of the first part of his book to it. His second theme, asserting the presence of a similar no-value neutralism in American economic thinking, emerges in the second part of the book. But it emerges only at the end of a detailed historical discussion of how thinking about political economy developed in the United States over the past two hundred years. And when it appears it does not receive the same sort of documentation that he gives to the first.

Sandel's historical discussion of the development of thinking about political economy is the most riveting part of the book. He documents a continuing concern, from the period of the Constitution down to the New Deal, with the effect of economic arrangements on the citizenry. The fear throughout this period is that such arrangements can subjugate workers and render them incapable of achieving the independence and civic virtue that republicanism has always looked for in citizens.

Should there be widespread manufacturing industry in America—this, as distinct from an economy of independent farmers—given the subject status of industrial workers? No, thought Jefferson in the early days of the republic: "Dependence begets subservience and venality, suffocates the germ of virtue, and prepares fit tools for the designs of ambition."[14] But didn't the Lowell industrial model of the Jacksonian era offer some hope? Not according to protectors in 1834 who objected to "that haughty, overbearing disposition, that purse-proud insolence" that they found in their employers.[15] The position of industrial workers, as it was seen by artisan republicans, was often no better than that of southern slaves: they were "wage slaves" rather then "chattel slaves" but the dependence they suffered was none the less real for that.[16]

Still, wasn't there a basis for consolation in the fact that industrial workers, as free laborers, could aspire to owning and working land of their own in an expanding America? There was, according to the proponents of the free-labor movement in the 1850s and 1860s. But alas the free soil rapidly ran out and by 1870, two-thirds of productively engaged Americans were wage-earners.[17] The Knights of Labour articulated a widely felt discontent about the standing of wage-earners but the failure of their own attempts to establish cooperatives meant that the discontent was unrelieved. As they saw it, workers could never become self-supporting and could not hope to enjoy the proper status of a citizen: "no man whose bread and that of his children are dependent on the will of any other man, or who has no interest in his work except to please an employer, fulfills these conditions; a farmer of his own land does fulfill them."[18]

The upshot, as Sandel tells his story, is that with no hope of a republican reconciliation with the nature and conditions of industrial employment, people generally moved over to a different conception of economic arrangements. They ceased to worry in the name of republican values about the effects of such arrangements. They consoled themselves with the thought—ultimately the value-neutral thought—that if workers voluntarily entered into employment relations then, however demeaning those relations might be, they presumably answered to the preferences of the workers. This neutralism in economic thinking reached its apogee in the rise of consumerism. The best economic arrangements are not those that satisfy some pre-given conception of the good, such as that which republicanism offers; according to the consumerist credo, they are the arrangements that best answer to the preferences that people reveal in their consumption choices, including their choice of job. "Instead of asking how to elevate or improve or restrain people's preferences, it asks how best—most fully, or fairly, or efficiently—to satisfy them."[19] The lesson is that "government should not form or revise, or for that matter even judge, the interests and ends its citizens espouse; rather, it should enable them to pursue these interests and ends, whatever they may be, consistent with a similar liberty for others."[20]

Third theme

So much for the no-value neutralism that Sandel finds in contemporary American thinking about constitutional law and the political economy. His third theme is very closely related, as I see it; indeed it is so closely related that it barely receives separate mention. Not only is America neutralist in its attitude to constitutional law and the political economy, according to this third theme, it is also neutralist in its attitude to politics. There is no longer an assumption, as there used to be in republican days,[21] that politics is about the deliberative identification and cooperative pursuit of certain common goods: the plural reference to "common goods" is appropriate, because people may not agree on any unitary account of the common good.[22] Rather politics is conceptualized as a process of competitive bargaining between different interest-groups, which involves no attempt to evaluate the propriety of any of the interests represented.

This theme is very prominent in the works of another self-described republican, Cass Sunstein,[23] and it is remarkable that Sandel makes no reference to the fact. But it is clear that he shares Sunstein's sense that interest-group politics represents a betrayal of American republican ideals, one that parallels the betrayal that he documents in a rights-based constitutional law and in a preference-based political economy. Thus he rightly castigates "modern-day interest-group pluralists" for invoking the name of Madison. "For Madison, the reason for admitting interests into the system was not to govern by them but to disempower them, to play them to a draw, so that disinterested statesmen might govern unhindered by them."[24]

Fourth theme

And so we come finally to the theme in regard to which I find fault with Sandel's book and believe that his narrative needs reworking. He counterpoints the neutralist tradition described in his first three themes with the republican approach that he takes—surely rightly—to have marked earlier stages, in particular the founding stage, of American public life. The main point of contrast is predictable. The public philosophy of today—"the assumptions about citizenship and freedom that inform our public life"[25]—eschews all values in favor of a no-value neutralism. The earlier public philosophy looked unashamedly for a certain sort of virtuous citizenry and insisted that social and political institutions should be designed so as to form people in that virtuous mold: it ascribed a committed, formative role to those institutions, not the role of a neutral referee.[26]

At this point we naturally wait on more. We want to be told exactly why the republican philosophy required a virtuous citizenry; exactly what sort of virtue it recommended; and exactly how the institutions of government were supposed to facilitate that civic virtue and advance republican ideals. We want to be told more, in other words, on three crucial issues: first, the nature of the republican ideals that mandate civic virtue; second, the nature of the virtue that they mandate; and third, the nature of the institutions and programs whereby that virtue is to be encouraged and those ideals promoted. Sandel does tell us something more about these things, though only in a series of short comments that are distributed throughout the book. But what he tells us falls well short of a satisfying account.

What, according to Sandel, are the central republican ideals? The ultimate ideal, we are told, is republican freedom or liberty as distinct from liberal freedom or liberty.[27] So what is this republican freedom? In most of his utterances, Sandel suggests that he follows the "strong version of the republican ideal,"[28] according to which being free essentially—he would say, "intrinsically"—involves "sharing in self-government."[29] "Republican political theory teaches that to be free is to share in governing a political community that controls its own fate."[30] He distinguishes this strong version from "more modest versions of the republican ideal," according to which the relation between self-government and freedom is instrumental rather than definitional. He appears to be well-disposed to such versions of the ideal so far as they agree with the strong version that, even if instrumental, the relationship between self-government and liberty is nonetheless "internal". Yet he does not explain what an internal connection involves.[31] I shall return to this theme later but for the moment I simply note that his own way of speaking clearly suggests that he thinks of liberty, in the "strong" republican manner, as being definitionally tied up with participation in government.

What sort of virtue, to move to the second issue, does liberty in this sense mandate? What does the republican "conception of the good society" as a self-governing republic require of its members?[32] The answer given, at its most explicit, is this: "republican theory does not take people's existing preferences, whatever they may be, and try to satisfy them. It seeks instead to cultivate in citizens the qualities of character necessary to the common good of self-government. Insofar as certain dispositions, attachments, and commitments are essential to the realization of self-government, republican politics regards moral character as a public, not a private, concern."[33] What qualities of character are to be cultivated? Those which are necessary for people to be able to deliberate fruitfully about the common good and to help shape the society's destiny. We are told that they include "a knowledge of public affairs and also a sense of belonging, a concern for the whole, a moral bond with the community."[34]

So much for the nature of the republican ideal, according to Sandel, and the nature of the civic virtue it requires. What, finally, of the institutions and programs whereby such virtue is to be facilitated and the republican ideal promoted? The institutions are not to be exclusive of the nonmainstream, the nonmale and the nonpropertied, in the manner of premodern republics.[35] And neither are they to be invasive and homogenizing, for Sandel's republican hero is Tocqueville, not Rousseau. "Unlike Rousseau's unitary vision, the republican politics Tocqueville describes is more clamorous than consensual. It does not despise differentiation. Instead of collapsing the space between persons, it fills this space with public institutions that gather people together in various capacities, that both separate and relate them. These institutions include the townships, schools, religions, and virtue-sustaining occupations that form the 'character of mind' and 'habits of the heart' a democratic republic requires."[36]

These remarks on the sorts of republican institutions for which he looks do not yet tell us where Sandel thinks that his ideal state will go on important matters of public policy. But he offers a number of comments, often in passing, that indicate the drift of his expectations. Thus he is in favor of greater equality. "The republican tradition teaches that severe inequality undermines freedom by corrupting the character of both rich and poor and destroying the commonality necessary to self-government."[37] And while he has sympathy for those communal conservatives who see a greater role for morals in public life,[38] he clearly thinks that bringing issues of morality into politics will not necessarily turn back the clock on a range of social issues. He suggests that what is wrong with the liberal tolerance of homosexuality, for example, is not that it runs counter to the moralistic views of many and is indeed a form of tolerance but that it does not directly challenge those moralistic views, as presumably a republican approach would do: "unless those views can be plausibly addressed, even a court ruling in their favor is unlikely to win for homosexuals more than a thin and fragile toleration."[39] More generally he argues that going republican does not mean giving up on individual rights, only providing them with a new foundation. "Rights can be defended on a number of grounds, including the grounds that respecting certain rights is a way of cultivating civic virtue or of encouraging among citizens certain worthy practices or beliefs or qualities of character."[40]

I am unhappy, as I said, with Sandel's comments on these three issues: the nature of the ideal that republicans espouse, the nature of the civic virtue it requires, and the nature of the public institutions and programs that it would support. Apart from leaving the connection between self-government and liberty underspecified—talk of an internal connection is just not good enough—he fails to explain how self-government is supposed to be implemented, especially in a society as complex and large as the United States today, and he fails to say anything about how self-government is going to be made proof against what Jefferson himself described as the tyranny of the majority. When he goes on to say that republican liberty and self-government require civic virtue in the citizenry, he remains studiously uncommitted on what the content of that virtue is supposed to be; we are referred, vaguely, to the qualities essential for participants in self-government. And this worrying indeterminacy about republican freedom and republican virtue carries over into a similar, breezy vagueness about the institutions and programs that such freedom and virtue are going to support or, when examples are given, about why they are going to support them. How can Sandel be sure, for example, that the virtuous citizens of his self-governing republic will really be tolerant of homosexuality? We are never told.

Fifth theme

The fifth and final theme that I mentioned in describing Sandel's book is that we should give up the liberalism that constitutes America's current public philosophy and endorse instead the republicanism that emerges in his narrative. I shall not say much about this claim except to note that it is advanced, not by showing the merits of republicanism, but rather by displaying the weakness of the liberal alternative. In his opening chapter he considers three defenses of contemporary liberalism: a utilitarian defense, a Kantian defense, and a defense on minimal, pragmatic grounds. He argues against utiliarianism that it does not respect differences between persons; against Kantianism that it does not enable us to vindicate particularistic, communal attachments; and against minimalism that pragmatic resolutions are often just not available: moral and religious convictions cannot always be put aside, as in the abortion debate, and putting them aside in other cases may erode "the moral and civic resources necessary to self-government."[41]

You can't beat something with nothing and what worries me about this way of arguing for republicanism is that it is essentially negative. Perhaps that is as it has to be, given the vagueness that I have alleged in Sandel's characterization of republicanism. But it would have been much more satisfying had we been given a less elusive account of the approach and a more positive argument in its favor.

2. Elements for a Reworking of the Narrative

In this section I am going to present three elements in my own account of republicanism and then show, in the section following, how Sandel's story can be reworked around those elements and how the problems raised for the story can be thereby removed or at least diminished. The first of my three elements bears on the definition of republican liberty, the second on the relationship between liberty in that sense and the institutions—including institutions of self-government—that support it, and the third on the relationship between those institutions and civic norms and virtues.

The Definition of republican liberty

When Sandel goes along with the view of republican liberty which holds that "to be free to share in governing a political community that controls its own fate,"[42] then he follows the neo-Athenian reading of republicanism popularized in recent times by Hannah Arendt; indeed he refers to Aristotle and Arendt as the sources of the view.[43] That reading associates republicanism with what Benjamin Constant, early in the last century, called the liberty of the ancients and it lets liberalism claim the liberty of the moderns: this is liberty in the sense of being let alone, liberty as noninterference.[44] Where liberalism would allow each person full control over his or her own domain of action, within limits dictated by the need for social coordination, republicanism on this account would allow each person partial control over the domain of everyone's action: the sort of control allegedly exercised by the citizens of classical Athens. Where liberal freedom consists in having nearly global control over a small domain, republican freedom would consist in having a small degree of control over a global domain: that of what everybody does.

Sandel allows that for Machiavelli, as Quentin Skinner has argued,[45] most people pursue freedom in a sense that does not give them a share in government. "A small part of them wishes to be free in order to rule; but all the others, who are countless, wish freedom in order to live in security."[46] And he happily concedes that James Madison was primarily concerned to guard against "elective despotism"[47]—hardly the concern of someone who thought of freedom as sharing in self-government—and that he and the other framers of the constitution pursued a "revision of classical republican assumptions,"[48] as Sandel thinks of those assumptions. But when he suggests that the doctrines of Machiavelli and Madison are just variations on his own neo-Athenian themes, then I think he is quite wrong. What we find in Machiavelli and Madison—and what we find in the long tradition of republicanism in the period in between[49]—is a distinct neo-Roman republicanism, Ciceronian rather than Aristotelian in inspiration. This is the account of republicanism, in particular of republican freedom, that I wish to introduce as the first element in a reworking of Sandel's story.

The republican tradition from Machiavelli to Madison saw the Roman constitution through the eyes of Polybius and saw the practice of Roman politics through the eyes of Livy, Plutarch, Sallust, Tacitus, and of course Cicero himself. These republicans pictured Athens, rightly or wrongly, in the critical terms suggested by Polybius: as a ship without a captain, buffeted by the storms of popular opinion. They traced the Athenian problem to excessive reliance on pure democracy and saw the Roman republic, by contrast, as a constitution in which government was built on a democratic foundation but was better devised to guard against problems of faction and demogoguery and tyranny. The principal devices they celebrated in Rome were the dispersion of democratic power across different assemblies, adherence to a more or less strict rule of law, election to public office, limitation on the tenure of public office, rotation of offices among the citizenry, and the like. These devices provided the checks and balances whereby a republic might hope to constitute a government that was at once popular and stable.[50]

The key idea in this neo-Roman tradition is republican freedom, for it is the freedom ideal that provides the argument, ultimately, for recourse to such institutions. Republican freedom, however, is distinct both from liberty as noninterference and from liberty as democratic participation.[51] It is a negative form of liberty, like the liberal ideal. But it requires something other than the absence of interference. It requires the absence of dependency upon the will of another and the absence of vulnerability to interference at the will of that other: it requires the absence of mastery or domination by any other. The antonym of freedom for the republican conception is not restraint as such but rather slavery and, more generally, any position of subjection. A person is free, and a person acts freely, just to the extent that they are not exposed, in the way a slave is exposed, to the arbitrary interference of another: to the sort of interference that only has to track the *arbitrium*—the will or judgment—of the interfering power.

Freedom as nondomination differs in two striking ways from freedom as noninterference. The conceptions will agree that someone who is subject both to domination and to interference is unfree and that someone who is subject to neither domination nor interference is free. Where they differ is in the judgments made about those who are dominated but not actually interfered with—say, the subjects of a kindly master—and about those who are not dominated but are interfered with: say, the citizens who are bound by a regime of law that, as they themselves see it, tracks their common interests and ideas and is the contrary of arbitrary interference.

The sort of republicanism associated with the English commonwealthman tradition, ultimately the sort of republicanism shared by the American founders, was forthright on both of these themes. The commonwealthmen insisted, first of all, that being subject to another in the manner of a slave made a person unfree, even if the other was not disposed to interfere. Algernon Sydney could write, for example, in the late 1600s that "he is a slave who serves the best and gentlest man in the world, as well as he who serves the worst."[52] And Richard Price could add in the century following: "Individuals in private life, while held under the power of masters, cannot be denominated free, however equitably and kindly they may be treated."[53]

The commonwealthmen also insisted, to move to the second point of contrast with liberalism, that so far as a rule of law was genuinely nonarbitrary—so far as it tracked the interests and ideas of citizens—to that extent it did not compromise their liberty. Not only did it protect people against a compromise of their liberty by others, it did not itself impose the sort of compromise that would have to be justified by such protection. John Locke, the hero of eighteenth-century American republicans, is a good example of this attitude. He argues for a "freedom from Absolute, Arbitrary Power" as the essential thing, and the thing that marks the contrast with slavery.[54] And that leads him to represent law as in no way a restriction on freedom: "that ill deserves the Name of Confinement which serves to hedge us in only from Bogs and Precipices . . . the end of Law is not to abolish or restrain, but to preserve and enlarge Freedom."[55] Richard Price again echoes this theme when he writes: "Just government . . . does not infringe liberty, but establishes it. It does not take away the rights of mankind but protect[s] and confirm[s] them."[56]

Liberty and republican institutions

So much for the first of the three elements I want to introduce. The second bears on the relationship between liberty in the sense of nondomination and those public institutions whereby such liberty is secured for the citizens of an ideal republic. The institutions that were taken to be required for the promotion of republican liberty are various, though they are almost all of a Roman provenance. They include institutions like a rule of law that governs everyone alike—even a monarch, if there is a monarchy; a dispersion of the powers given to those who make and run the law among many hands; a restriction on the tenure with which public office is held; a dispensation that allows for public discussion of important issues, for public deliberation over how to resolve them and for a degree of public participation in their resolution; an arrangement for the appointment of certain officers by a system of voting or lottery or a mixture of both; and so on. The second element I want to introduce bears on how such institutions, assuming that there is a uniquely appropriate set for any social situation, are going to relate to the freedom of the citizens that they are meant to support. Since the institutions were usually taken to include some measures of participatory government, this element bears in part on how participatory institutions are going to relate to the freedom of participating citizens.

Sandel is right that in the republican, even in the neo-Roman republican, way of thinking there is an intimate connection envisaged between the institutions that support freedom—between the constitution of the free society—and the freedom that they support. It is this connection, for example, that allows Montesquieu—in many ways, a covert republican—to speak now of freedom in the constitution, now of freedom in the citizen.[57] But the connection is not the definitional connection that relates freedom to participatory institutions when it is said, as Sandel says, that to be free is to share in the self-government of a community. And neither is it the causal connection that relates freedom as noninterference to certain protective institutions: the connection whereby the presence of those institutions comes to inhibit potential offenders and thereby to have the causal effect of enhancing the freedom as noninterference of others. The connection between freedom as nondomination and relevant institutions is constitutive, as I shall put it, and not definitional or causal.[58]

Consider the connection between the antibodies that make someone immune to a certain disease and that immunity itself. The connection is not definitional, since immunity to the disease can be defined and understood without reference to the antibodies. But neither is the connection causal, for it is not as if the immunity is something distinct from the antibodies; being immune, for the person in question, comes to nothing more and nothing less than having those antibodies. The antibodies do not cause the immunity, as we say, they constitute it.

The relationship between people's freedom as nondomination and the institutions that would support that freedom in the ideal republic—assuming that an ideal republic is attainable—is going to be constitutive in the same sense. If freedom is nondomination, if freedom consists in the status of being more or less immune to arbitrary interference by others, then the institutions that ensure that immunity will relate to it neither in a definitional, nor in a causal way. Not in a definitional way, because the understanding and definition of nondomination will not require a reference to the precise institutions that work in the circumstances on hand. And not in a causal way, because the relationship between the institutions in question and the immunity to arbitrary interference that they confer will be exactly like the relationship between the antibodies in our earlier example and the immunity that they give against a certain disease. If freedom is noninterference, then freedom is causally brought about by suitably protective and empowering institutions: it is a result of the inhibiting effect of the protection and empowerment, now on this potential offender, now on that. If freedom is nondomination, then freedom just is the protected and empowered status—the invulnerability or nondomination—enjoyed in the presence of the institutions and it exists prior to any potential offenders actually coming to be inhibited.

Liberty and republican virtue

We have seen that republican freedom just is nondomination and that if freedom in that sense is enjoyed by citizens, then it is constituted by the institutions that support it, not merely causally related to those institutions. The third element that I want to add is that, this being the case, we can also see a close connection between republican freedom and certain forms of civic virtue.

The connection comes of the fact, recognized throughout the republican tradition, that while the effective rule of law may confer freedom in the sense of nondomination, the laws themselves will only be effective in a society where they are supported by actively sustained norms.[59] Thus Machiavelli says: "just as good morals, if they are to be maintained, have need of the laws, so the laws, if they are to be observed, have need of good morals."[60] One argument for why the laws have need of good morals or customs—*buoni costumi*—comes in two stages. The first is that the laws will be effective in protecting and empowering each against others only so far as the laws command universal allegiance, in particular allegiance among those in power. And the second is that the laws will enjoy this command only so far as people are normatively committed to the laws, not just committed to them for fear of the penalty attending noncompliance or underperformance.[61] The background thought here, supported by contemporary criminology, is that fear of penalty is not a very effective motive, all on its own, in binding people to the law.

A second argument for why laws have need of morals—have need of civic virtue or civility—is that if the laws are to effectively track people's changing ideas and interests, and if they are to be guaranteed to remain nondominating, then there must be enough civic virtue in the society to ensure that those ideas and interests will be reliably represented in the forums of law-making and the regime of law made to answer to them. Think of the civic virtue evident in the environmental movement, or the women's movement, or the civil rights movement. Think of the virtue evident in people's being willing to give time to public affairs, to stand for office and to exercise office punctiliously. Were such virtue not available in a society, then there would be no hope of keeping the law in line with people's attitudes and in ensuring that they remain the masters of the law, not just its subjects. Adam Ferguson was firmly of the view that the rule of law in Britain of the eighteenth century was a great force for republican freedom. But he emphasized the bedrock of virtue on which it must rest if it is to have that effect when he wrote: "it requires a fabric no less than the whole political constitution of Great Britain, a spirit no less than the refractory and turbulent zeal of this fortunate people, to secure it."[62]

A third reason why the rule of law depends on a regime of civic virtue is that there is little hope of ensuring compliance among ordinary people, or among public officials, unless people generally are prepared to remain vigilant in their inspection of one another and in their readiness to rebuke or report offences. The price of liberty, in the old adage, is eternal vigilance, in particular vigilance in looking at those in power and in challenging, where necessary, their claims and initiatives. A paradox worth noting is that the more people remain ready to rebuke and report in the manner envisaged, the less occasion there may be for their having to do that. To the extent that people know they are each disposed in this way they know that others will think badly of them for offending against the law and think well of them for complying with it. And to that extent they will become motivated towards compliance by the desire to avoid shame and win renown. Here is a familiar republican theme: where virtue fails, the saving vice may be a love of glory.

This case for the necessity of virtue, it is worth mentioning, ought also to be available to liberals who think of freedom as noninterference, not as nondomination, and who see the institutions designed to support freedom as causally rather than constitutively related to it. But as a matter of fact the emphasis on virtue does distinguish the republican from the liberal tradition. This is probably because the emphasis in liberalism on minimizing interference, including the interference of the state, has tended to argue against any moralistic interventions by the state as well as against interference proper. The ideal model of government for liberals has often been the government of the invisible hand that is allegedly exercised by the free market. The market takes people's preferences as given—it is not designed to be formative, in Sandel's phrase—and arranges things so that if people pursue their own individual preference-satisfaction there will still be a collectively satisfactory result: people will sell their services and their products at the competitive price. The holy grail of liberal politics has always been a mode of organizing government that would enable the state to be equally indifferent about the supply of virtue. The goal, to connect up with Sandel's main theme, has been a no-value neutralism.

3. Sandel's Reworked Narrative

Suppose we now go back to Sandel's narrative and read it under the assumption that the three ideas introduced in the last section are endorsed. What effect is this going to have on that narrative? I want to suggest that the reworking required will have little or no impact on the first three themes in Sandel's story and that, repairing the indeterminacies noted, it will make for a considerable improvement in the fourth and fifth. I will first consider how it can make for that improvement in the last two themes and then go back to look at how it sustains the first three themes.

Sandel's fourth and fifth themes

The indeterminacies that worried me in Sandel's account of America's lost republicanism bear on the nature of republican ideals, the nature of the civic virtue they require and the nature of the institutions and programs that those ideals, and that virtue, would mandate. As for the nature of republican ideals, a reworking around the elements I introduced would say, first, that the ultimate ideal is freedom as nondomination for the citizens of the republic, where citizenship is an inclusive category; and, second, that the freedom of citizens is constitutively tied to those participatory and other institutions whereby it is supported: the invulnerability of citizens to arbitrary interference, so far as that ideal has been achieved, is constituted by their being embedded in such protective and empowering practices. There is no secret about the nature or attraction of republican freedom, under this account, and there is no mystery about how it can be constituted for citizens by the public institutions under which they live. So far it should be manifest, then, that we have attained a clarity that is missing in Sandel's own formulations.

As for the nature of the civic virtue required by republican ideals, that also becomes unmysterious under the proposed reworking of Sandel's narrative. For we saw in the last section that, as republican wisdom has it, there are many ways in which the participatory and other institutions required to support republican freedom are going to depend for their existence and effectiveness on a supply of various sorts of virtue among the citizenry. Allegiance to and compliance with the practices in question; readiness to assume a public profile, even a public office, and to try and ensure that the practices continue to answer to the ideas or interests of relevant parts of the society; the vigilance and courage required to ensure that those who disrespect the practices, particularly those in power who do so, are called to account. These are salient examples of the sorts of civic virtue that republican institutions are bound to require. Again, no vagueness, and no mystery.

What, finally, of the direction in which republican ideals and republican virtue must be expected to take the state? What of the institutions and programs that they would support? Under Sandel's original narrative, we are offered little or no reason to identify any particular direction as presumptively attractive. Sandel himself is clearly of a decentralist, a reformist, and a progressivist inclination: he favors Tocqueville's mediating institutions over Rousseau's single assembly; he thinks that inequality should be reduced; and he believes that a republic would be tolerant of homosexuality and, more generally, would be inclined to uphold individual rights. But his remarks on these matters of policy are few and far between and they often seem to come of independent commitments, not of any firm sense of what republicanism requires.

As with the other indeterminacies, I believe that this all changes utterly—but still, from Sandel's point of view, congenially—under the reworking I propose. When Sandel sets up republicanism against liberalism—that is, against no-value neutralism—then it appears that he espouses a non-neutralism, welcoming into the public forum all the discontented, moralistic voices that are currently marginalized; that is inherent in the prospect of a self-governing community where nothing is taken off the agenda in the name of neutrality. Thus we are naturally left in some uncertainty about where republican government is likely to lead and in some doubt about Sandel's belief that it will lead in a decentralist, reformist, or progressivist direction. But such indeterminacy is banished once it is clear, as under the proposed reworking of Sandel, that while republicanism rejects no-value neutralism, it does this because of explicitly giving one overall value—freedom as nondomination—a guiding role for law and government, not because of wanting to let loose the dogs of moralistic enthusiasm.

If liberalism represents no-value neutralism, then republicanism represents what we might call a shared-value neutralism. For the idea long embraced in the republican tradition is that everyone is bound to cherish the prospect of freedom as nondenomination for themselves and so, forced to universalize, are bound to embrace the neutral value of freedom as a very important good. But though it is a good that ought to appeal from almost every perspective, freedom as nondenomination is something that can only be promoted for all on the basis of collective, political action. And so the public institutions of a good society ought to be designed with a view to advancing this value, if necessary in the teeth of opposition from more sectarian or sectional commitments.[63] What I think of as the republicanism of the commonwealthman tradition has been described, for this reason, as an old liberalism that stands in stark opposition to the new: as a shared-value, rather than a no-value, neutralism.[64]

Once we see republicanism as committed to the promotion of the ecumenical value of nondomination, but not independently associated with any particular value-position, then it becomes possible, in the light of empirical assumptions, to work systematically at elaborating the direction in which a republican government ought to go. Domination is a threat in our society on two broad fronts: in virtue of the private power or *dominium* that some individuals or organizations or groups exercise over others; and in virtue of the public power or *imperium* assumed by those in government itself. We can investigate where republicanism is likely to lead by looking at the measures of protection, empowerment, redistribution, and recognition that are required for combating *dominium*, and by reviewing the different controls, the different checks and balances, that are going to be necessary if the *imperium* of government is not itself to represent a dominating presence in our lives. There is a sensible research program here and, though the research clearly remains to be done, still there can be no serious complaint that the policy direction of republicanism lies shrouded in permanent mist.

So much for the way in which we can draw on the elements introduced in the last section and rework Sandel's narrative so that the indeterminacies I identified are repaired. This done, the fourth theme in that narrative assumes a new character: the republicanism to which he would direct us takes a firmer and somewhat different shape. The effect of the change is immediately apparent, as we turn to the fifth theme: the recommendation that we espouse republicanism as an alternative to our current liberalism. For there is no longer any need, with the doctrine we now discern, to rest our case for embracing it on the revulsion that we should allegedly feel for the liberal alternative. There is clearly much to be said for the value of freedom as nondomination—much of it continuous with the things that are often said in support of liberalism—and there is room for exploring the advantages that argue for a republican as distinct from a liberal public philosophy.

Sandel's first three themes

What I recommend is a reworking of Sandel's narrative, so I claim, not a complete rewrite. But if I am to bear out that claim, then I need to show that the changes I have proposed in thinking about republicanism are consistent with the story that he tells in the first three themes identified earlier: in effect, with the story which most of his book is given to elaborating. I turn to that topic in concluding my discussion.

His first theme is that American constitutional law has become rights-based in a way in which it was not originally so and in a way in which it would not remain so under a republican renaissance. There is nothing in my proposed account of republicanism that undermines the historical story that Sandel tells; for all that that account implies, the story may be fundamentally correct. But would my account of republicanism sustain his sense that the no-value neutralist mode of constitutional thinking represents an infidelity to America's founding republicanism?

I say that it would, for reasons that are many and manifest. Take his remarks on the civic as distinct from the voluntarist approach to religious freedom, to freedom of speech, and to privacy. The fact that religion is an area of presumptive importance in social life, giving people an identity that is significant for them, implies that the state should protect people in this area in a special way, not just by way of honoring personal preference; for any exposure in this area to arbitrary interference on the part of others is going to have a very serious effect on people's freedom as nondomination. Again, the fact that some speech is essential to making one's voice heard in the public forum, and essential to seeing that the public authorities continue to track the interests and ideas of those in one's quarter, means that that speech calls for protection on quite a different basis from other sorts of speech; indeed other sorts of speech, such as that associated with pornography or even burning the flag, may be thought detrimental to others' freedom as nondomination, or to the infrastructure of that freedom, and may not call for protection at all. Or, finally, the fact that privacy in some matters is an essential protection against certain forms of domination, and privacy in other matters not so essential, means that privacy will not be defended on a blanket, voluntarist basis but in proportion to the way in which it serves the ultimate republican cause.

Take a particular issue like that which is raised by homosexuality, therefore, and consider the way in which the reworked version of Sandel's republicanism would support toleration. The support would not be of the liberal, neutralist kind that he criticizes: the kind that would say it is not the state's job to impose community values in a case like this and so that the neutral state has to stay its hand and respect the privacy of practicing homosexuals.[65] The republican state would argue for toleration of homosexual practices on the basis of the shared value of freedom as nondomination and would argue with those of more moralistic views that their opposition is inconsistent with espousal of that central ideal. Thus it would address those views, as Sandel requires, and would stand some chance of winning for homosexuals more than the "thin and fragile toleration"[66] that is all that that liberalism can offer.

Take again an issue like that of whether abortion ought to be available to those women who request it. Sandel is forthright in his claim that the neutralist approach is just no good here as a basis for toleration: that in face of the religious values that people so passionately invoke on the other side, the case for toleration cannot be effectively made in a neutralist key; the only effective route will be to fight fire with fire, and to combat value with value.[67] Sandel does not say where he thinks republicanism would lead on this issue—in my mind, a worrying silence—but it is worth noting that on the reworked republicanism I would have him endorse, the case for toleration can be defended in the manner for which he looks. For it is clear that making abortion unavailable would mean that women are dominated by the state—they are subject to a sort of interference that is not forced to track their interests and ideals—and it would clearly expose women to other forms of domination by partner and family and community. What, however, of the fetus? Here I must be controversial. I simply record that the most compelling view, as I see things, is that until the fetus is viable, it cannot assume the place of a citizen and cannot make a claim on the protection and empowerment that the republican state would offer to its citizens.

As the reworked republican narrative fits well with the first, major theme in Sandel's book, so it fits well—if anything, better—with the second. Sandel documents the concern of American republicans with industrial employment and the dependency that it introduces for employees. He is forced, because of his emphasis on self-government and the virtue it requires, to argue that this concern stems from a worry that dependent workers will not develop the character necessary in the citizens of a self-governing republic. But this argument always seems strained in the account he offers and is never really substantiated by his many quotations from the speeches and pamphlets of earlier republicans. They complain about dependency as such: about the plight of the "man whose bread and that of his children are dependent on the will of any other man, or who has no interest in his work except to please an employer."[68] And it seems artificial to construe the complaint as an expression of concern for the quality of the citizenry and the prospect for self-government.

There is no need to construe the complaint in this way, if we go over to my account of republicanism and take the concern with freedom as nondomination to have been at the heart of republican worries. For under this account, the dependency of employee on employer is almost bound to give the employer a certain power of arbitrary interference in the life of the employee—if only the interference implicit in the power of firing without good cause—and so employees are going to assume the profile of unfree, dominated agents. They are going to seem no better than slaves in the extent to which they live at the mercy of employers and in the degree to which they have to bow and scrape to "that haughty, overbearing disposition, that purse-proud insolence" that the Lowell protestors found in their masters.[69] They are going to be presented, as in fact they were recurrently described, as "wage slaves."

Not only would the reworked version of Sandel's narrative recast this concern with dependency in a more natural, more persuasive, manner; it would also enable us to sustain Sandel's sense that consumerism betrays republicanism. For if we are concerned about freedom as nondomination, then we are going to look to economic arrangements for much more than the satisfaction of whatever preferences consumers display. Conditions of production are going to be important since, as we have just seen, they can reduce employees to the status of dominated dependents. And issues of poverty and inequality are going to be significant to the extent that they can, and clearly do, make people vulnerable to the evil of domination against which the republican state must set itself.

It is worth noting here, in passing, that the republican state that I envisage would not only have reason to concern itself with dependencies and vulnerabilities that the liberal state typically ignores. It would also be proof against the standard liberal or libertarian argument that when the state does anything about problems of private interference it itself must interfere in people's lives—at the least it must tax people to fund its activities—and so everything depends on whether the interference perpetrated will be justified by the interference prevented.[70] From the republican point of view, the danger to be eliminated is domination—exposure to arbitrary interference—but the means adopted by the state in the attempt to eliminate such domination need not be themselves dominating: they will not be, if the interference involved can be effectively made out to be nonarbitrary. There will be significant limits on what the republican state should attempt, since it is clear that an excessively powerful state can easily become dominating. And there will be a recognition of the fact that even if law does not itself dominate, it does reduce the ease or range of choice in which people can enjoy nondomination.[71] But there will not be the same inhibition about state activity that libertarians would impose.

Finally, to the third theme in Sandel's narrative, which is implicit throughout his book but hardly gets any explicit mention. This is the idea that the interest-group pluralism that characterizes contemporary American politics is itself neutralist in having the stronger side win, regardless of the deliberative considerations or values that argue the other way. If freedom is nondomination, and if nondomination is not to be compromised by governmental activity, then there must be constraints in place which help to ensure that that activity will track the interests and ideas of every sector of the society: or, assuming that the sector wishes to belong to the society, at least those interests and ideas that are consistent with their wishing to live under a shared political arrangement with others. But it is surely clear that under interest-group pluralism, there is no hope of achieving this; such an arrangement would represent, not a nonarbitrary mode of decision-making, but the rule of naked preference and crude power.[72] If it is to hold out any chance of avoiding domination, the political system must come to represent a rule of reasons, and the democracy come to display a deliberative rather than a bargaining character.[73]

As the reworked republicanism would set us against a purely rights-based law and a purely preference-based economics, so therefore it would set us against the third, less salient of Sandel's demons: a purely interest-based politics. The reworking I propose for *Democracy's Discontent* is indeed just that. While it would certainly make for changes in some quite central claims about republican freedom, republican virtue, and republican policy, it would sustain most of the themes that the book puts on parade. The themes might march to a different drum but they would continue to march in the same direction.

II

Toward an American Public Philosophy

4

Political Economy and the Politics of Virtue: US Public Philosophy at Century's End

WILLIAM A. GALSTON

Introduction

IN this chapter, I will undertake four tasks: first, to define public philosophy as a general concept; second, to briefly describe the problems with which public philosophy in the United States must deal at century's end; third, to sketch some of the principal competing public philosophies that have emerged (or appear to be emerging) in response to these problems; and finally, to examine in somewhat greater detail the specific analysis and prescription offered by Michael Sandel in *Democracy's Discontent: America in Search of a Public Philosophy*.

I write as a committed though not untroubled partisan of liberal democracy, believing with Winston Churchill that it is the worst form of government and social life except for all the rest that have ever been tried. I do not believe that America's liberal democracy is in "crisis" (a word overused by academics and pundits in search of more drama than reality will admit). Rather, we suffer from a multitude of ills along many fronts—ills that cannot be traced to a single source.

Many of these ills represent advantages of liberal democracy taken to excess; their amelioration lies in a return to balance, moderation, and common sense. Others call for a greater measure of institutional and programmatic innovation. Fortunately, our public life has not lost its capacity for self-evaluation and correction.

The Concept of Public Philosophy

To begin, public philosophy should be understood in contradistinction to the classical conception of a universal or perennial philosophy that is addressed to all human beings at all times. A public philosophy is rooted in, and addressed to, a particular public in a specific historical situation. A public philosophy may include some universalizable claims, as did—for example—Abraham Lincoln's Gettysburg Address. But that speech was addressed principally to citizens of the United States who found themselves in the midst of a great war fraught with contested moral significance. The validity of Lincoln's assertions for other political communities raises a different set of issues altogether.

Second, a public philosophy consists in more than fundamental moral propositions such as "All men are created equal." Public philosophy links such abstract propositions with specific conceptions of socio-political institutions. In the US context, this institutional specification takes the form of liberal constitutional democracy, which encompasses at least the following familiar elements:

- a system of rights, fully and equally enjoyed by every individual, spelled out and secured against invasion by other individuals, social groups, and public authorities;
- a boundary, ever-shifting and contestable to be sure, between matters legitimately subject to public determination and those that are private;
- freedom of religion, expressed institutionally as nonestablishment and socially as a pluralism of faiths practiced without impediment;
- a market economy in which the influence of public command-and-control decisions is relatively confined;
- a zone, neither market nor state, in which individuals may freely belong to, enter, and leave a range of diverse groups and associations to pursue common purposes and express shared values;
- a society of "careers open to talents" in which every individual enjoys an equal opportunity to develop and use talents and in which no one is subject to discrimination;
- a government in which all legitimate authority is derived from the people and in which institutions of popular representation and direct participation are combined in a manner and proportion determined by the people; and
- the rule of law through settled and promulgated procedures rather than arbitrary whim or irregular decree.

In the United States, then, discussions of public philosophy can address two quite different kinds of questions: whether changing circumstances make it necessary to alter the manner in which we seek to realize these core elements of liberal constitutional democracy; alternatively, whether liberal constitutional democracy is itself adequate to achieve central public purposes.

Third, public philosophy goes beyond principles and institutions to specify general directions for public policy within a basic understanding of how the world works. Neoclassical economics is one example of such an understanding; the *Federalist's* emphasis on the scarcity and unreliability of civic virtue is another.

Fourth, a public philosophy represents an effort to solve specific public problems. In the United States, one of the most creative periods for public philosophy occurred between 1890 and 1920, as intellectuals and political leaders grappled with the challenges of an economy shifting from a agriculture/craft base to industrial corporations, a society in rapid transition from rural small towns, the large cities, a diversifying population swelled by unprecedented waves of immigration, and an increasingly corrupt and unresponsive political system. This period of intellectual development spawned the era of Progressive reform and culminated in the public philosophy of the New Deal, which dominated the US political landscape from the 1930s through the early 1970s.

The Public and Its Problems at Century's End

Over the past two decades, the basic principles of the New Deal approach have been called into question. Conservatives have challenged the presumption in favor of national government solutions to social problems, while a new generation of public intellectuals has sought progressive alternatives to an increasingly sclerotic bureaucratic-regulatory state.

These developments have been sparked by new conditions. I would single out three: the *economic anxiety* produced by the shift from a hegemonic national industrial economy to a global information economy; *the social disintegration* associated with the decay of traditional sources of stability and meaning such as nuclear families, neighborhoods, and voluntary associations, and with the rise of a social understanding focused almost exclusively on individual rights; and the *political dysfunction* that accompanies the decline of traditional parties and the rise of a politics dominated by the media and concentrated economic power.

Beyond these dominant features of the American landscape (some of which have their counterparts in Europe), there are problems common to virtually all the Western democracies. There is a dramatic imbalance between the social promises of the welfare state and the resources available to meet those promises; an increasing orientation toward present consumption at the expense of investments for future needs; increasing tension between the requirements of national unity and the centrifugal tugs of subnational identity groups based on region, ethnicity, or religion; an escalating citizen mistrust of government and established institutions in general; and the weakness of the voluntary associations of civil society that should discharge many of the functions that governments perform badly, or not at all.

Let me now return, somewhat more systematically, to public problems as seen from the specific vantage point of the United States.

Economic anxiety

As recently as a decade ago, economists and political candidates debated the prospects for the industrial economy. Today, most would agree that we are in the midst of a great transformation from an economy based on industrial mass production to one revolving around knowledge, information, and technological innovation. This transformation is every bit as sweeping as the shift a century ago from agriculture to industry as the basis of national wealth, from rural to urban life, and from individual artisanship to the giant corporation. And it is generating significant new problems not yet adequately addressed through public policy.

At the peak of the industrial economy in the quarter century after the Second World War, the fruits of economic growth were widely shared, and gross disparities of income and wealth tended to diminish. But over the past two decades, at an accelerating pace, those best able to function in the emerging information economy (a relatively small fraction of the workforce) have reaped nearly all the gains from growth while the incomes of the majority have stagnated or actually fallen. This is more than a statistical or normative/distributional issue. A strong middle class constitutes the social base for a stable liberal democracy. But the new economy is squeezing middle-class incomes.

The new economy is also shattering expectations. A generation or two ago, it was not unusual for workers (both blue-collar and managerial) to spend their entire working lives within a single large corporation. Unemployment tended to be cyclical and temporary. Individuals enjoyed a substantial measure of job continuity, and employers gradually increased their contributions to health and pension plans. Today, insecurity is the watchword. Technology is replacing blue-collars jobs. Waves of corporate downsizing have thinned the ranks of middle managers. Employers are reducing health care and pensions, and they are resorting more and more to temporary contractual relations that free them from these responsibilities altogether. Even in a society as entrepreneurial and risk-oriented as the United States, the resulting level of anxiety is dysfunctional. We need to create new structures of individual security for the information age.

In addressing these and other problems, we must now operate in a world in which individual nations have lost a substantial measure of control over their own economic destiny. Multinational corporations, technological diffusion, and unchecked capital flows have reduced the efficacy of traditional instruments of macroeconomic management. The restoration of the largely closed national economies in which these tools once operated is unlikely at best. If a global race to the bottom is to be averted, many believe that new transnational norms and institutions will have to be constructed. (The new World Trade Organization represents a small step in that direction.) But this strategy will encounter—indeed, has already triggered—anxiety verging on paranoia about the further loss of national sovereignty, especially among those who feel most threatened by the new economy.

Social disintegration

A vigorous network of nonstate, nonmarket associations ("civil society") has long been seen as a distinctive strength of American liberal democracy. They are widely regarded as the arenas within which we learn to trust and work with one another, accommodate rather than demonize difference, develop the rudiments of a shared civic culture across our differences, and cultivate the dispositions and traits of character a healthy liberal democracy requires. (Some theorists also see civil associations as bastions of resistance against totalizing state power and as arenas within which a variety of conceptions of the good—including many that deviate widely from the beliefs of the mainstream majority—may be freely enacted.)

Not surprisingly, signs of decay in civil society—weaker families, fraying neighborhoods, a decline of voluntary associations (whether real or apparent is a matter of intense debate), increased dependency and diminished regard for law, among others—have sparked widespread anxiety. We can argue about whether the dramatic increase in mistrust of government over the past three decades is warranted or unwarranted, good or bad. (For what it is worth, I believe that this development has pushed a classic American tendency well beyond reasonable and productive bounds.) But it should be difficult for anyone to view with equanimity the significant decline in our propensity to trust one another, as fellow citizens.

As one might expect, these phenomena have evoked a range of explanations. Many conservatives argue that civil society has become weak because government, especially the national government, has grown too strong. Many liberals (joined by some conservatives) counter that the dynamics of global economic competition are at war with stable and healthy social relations. Across the political spectrum, it is widely thought that television is also part of the explanation, because it reduces family solidarity, promotes consumption over civic engagement, and fosters a comprehensive, home-based privatism ("cocooning"). The expansion of rights-based individualism may corrode associational motives and capacities. The rise of "identity politics" based on characteristics such as race, ethnicity, and gender may diminish trust across these lines of division and multiply barriers to certain kinds of associational life. Whatever the causes, the status of civil society is clearly one of the central public concerns of liberal democracy in America at century's end.

Political dysfunction

Starting with the rise of the Progressive movement, and accelerating during the New Deal, a novel conception of liberal democratic governance took hold in America. Its basic elements included expanded functions for public institutions, political centralization at the national level to carry out these functions, bureaucracy as a key institution for command and control, and detailed regulation as a key means of control involving the restriction of administrative and local discretion.

Today, the Progressive/New Deal model of governance is under attack, and not just by conservatives. Many wonder whether government can possibly carry out all the tasks it has assumed during the past century, whether centralization has usurped responsibilities better discharged by states and localities, whether multilayered bureaucratic hierarchy is really effective in the information age, and whether the endless multiplication of regulations accomplishes public purposes efficiently and effectively. The federal budget has become the vehicle for questioning long-established institutions and programs.

These difficulties illustrate the contemporary vicissitudes of the rule of law. The core idea is compelling: equal concern for, and fair treatment of, every individual within a system of legislation and adjudication authorized by the people. No prejudice, no favoritism, no special exemptions; only the even-handed application of the rules in accordance with a publicly recognized truth. But since the New Deal, this has been expanded to the presumption that every aspect of life should be governed by law and administrative regulation.

Two difficulties arise. As law expands, the scope for discretion and judgment contracts, and decisions that are best made informally are enveloped in cumbersome rules. Moreover, if everything is to be subject to public law, then the classic liberal distinction between public and private collapses. It is one thing for law to define the boundary between public and private, or even a general framework within which private decisions must be made, quite another for law to determine, or review, the content of those decisions. The rectification of private unfairness frequently requires, and must be balanced against, the restriction of personal liberty. The mistrust of government we see today can be traced in part to a widespread sense that this balance has been poorly struck.

This mistrust is exacerbated by other unattractive features of contemporary governance. Let me mention just three. The political reach of special interests—organized lobbies and concentrated wealth—expands inexorably at the expense of average citizens and the common good. Existing mechanisms of communication and decision-making do not encourage public education and deliberation, turning our politics into a battle of dueling slogans and sound bites (witness the failed health care debate of 1994). And the terms of political combat tend to drive the established political parties toward extreme positions and uncivil discourse rather than sensible problem-solving built on common ground. The result is that most Americans feel shut out, ill-informed, unrepresented, manipulated, and politically homeless. The demand for fundamental political reform has intensified. And trust in government has collapsed, from roughly three-quarters of the population in the early 1960s to less than one-quarter today.

To be sure, a measure of mistrust can puncture the pretensions of public officials and thwart usurpations that threaten public liberty. But as I argued earlier, it is difficult to view the current level of mistrust as anything other than a sign of civic distress. One of the most important tasks before us is to restore the public's confidence in government as the instrument of their purposes rather than as what it now appears—an alien, intrusive, unresponsive power.

Public Philosophy in the United States: Recent Developments

As one might imagine, intellectuals and political leaders in the United States have begun to respond to these problems with efforts (some quite preliminary) to forge new public philosophies. Some of these represent efforts to realize the goals of liberal-constitutional democracy in changing circumstances; others strain against the limits of this institutional tradition. It may prove useful to array these proposals along various dimensions of disagreement.

The question of agency

A threshold question for public philosophy is the division of responsibilities among the public, private, and voluntary sectors. Contemporary libertarians such as David Boaz and Charles Murray argue that an expansion of markets and market-like mechanisms based on individual liberty and choice holds the key to the resolution of our ills. Not only will the economy function better under such circumstances, but also political corruption and disaffection will diminish as the state withdraws from politically contested regulation of economic and social life. Libertarians characteristically argue that social disintegration is in part overemphasized, and in equal measure misunderstood. If we agree on a stable (procedural) framework within which individuals may choose freely, we do not need a further (substantive) agreement on the content of those individual choices, or on the social pattern their aggregation may form. And as an empirical matter, the retrenchment of the state may well increase the propensity of individuals to band together into voluntary associations where shared purposes can be promoted without the coercion of the law.

Liberals and social democrats (many of whom are clustered at the journal *The American Prospect*) argue that at the root of today's problems is not the weakness, but rather the excessive strength, of market forces. The devotees of neoclassical economics have long acknowledged the existence of "market failures" that lead to the underprovision of socially valued goods. In contemporary circumstances, moreover, the market leads to increased inequality and insecurity, with deleterious social consequences. What is needed instead is a stronger state, capable of higher levels of public investment, economic redistribution, and social insurance. In the long run, it is claimed, this strengthened state will nurture rather than undermine a thriving market economy: public investment will increase productivity, while enhanced equality and security will bolster support for market-based outcomes.

Among those thinkers who continue to favor a strong state, disagreements have emerged concerning the design of public institutions and policies. Some believe that suitably updated versions of New Deal mechanisms remain workable today, especially for universal social insurance programs. By contrast, "neoliberal" critics of top-down, command-and-control mechanisms (David Osborne is a leader of this school) argue that even the state sector can benefit from increased individual incentives, competition, and autonomy. Bureaucracy should be made smaller, flatter, and more flexible as layers of middle management are squeezed out and front-line workers are given expanded authority as well as responsibility. In place of regulatory micromanagement, government should specify broad public purposes and allow regulated entities far more discretion in the selection of means to achieve these purposes. This approach has deeply influenced the "Reinventing Government" project directed by Vice President Albert Gore, Jr. Analysts clustered at the Progressive Policy Institute have offered proposals for choice-oriented programs within the framework of a strong state in areas such as social security, health insurance, and education. A comprehensive statement of neoliberal public philosophy was advanced in the *New Progressive Declaration*, published by the Progressive Foundation in 1996.

Another important axis of disagreement concerns the most appropriate geographic scope for public authority. The debate over "devolution" now occurring throughout Europe is intensifying in the United States, where federalism is an integral element of the basic constitutional structure. In the half-century after the beginning of the New Deal, power flowed from the states to the national government. This transfer, sparked by a wide range of domestic and international policy concerns, was supported by the judiciary, which reinterpreted constitutional language so as to nullify restraints on the growth of the central state. Starting in the 1980s, however, the Supreme Court began rebuilding these restraints, a development that has accelerated in the 1990s. As the national government has become the focal-point for public mistrust, pressures have intensified to devolve authority to states and localities. Specific policy debates have played a role as well, culminating in the 1996 decision to dismantle national welfare guarantees in place since the New Deal in favor of expanded discretion for the fifty states.

Proponents of devolution argue, first, that national legal and regulatory structures cannot cope with the variety of local structures; second, that the dispersion of power increases diversity and policy innovation; and third, that government closer to the people is more transparent and more trusted by the people. Opponents counter (in a manner reminiscent of James Madison in the *Federalist*) that national power is needed as a counterweight to local injustice. They fear, as well, that competition among jurisdictions can lead to a "race to the bottom" that weakens programs designed to protect the poorest and most vulnerable citizens.

It may also be argued that the division of responsibilities between national and subnational jurisdictions should be viewed contextually rather than ideologically: as circumstances and public demands change over time, so will our understanding of which institutions are responsible for what. This sorting-out process, advocated by Federal Reserve Board vice-chair Alice Rivlin among others, seems to be proceeding piecemeal in late twentieth-century America. Some issues long considered predominantly national, such as welfare and low-income health care, are being shifted in the direction of states and localities; others long considered local, such as crime and education, are receiving increased attention at the national level. While it is not easy to predict the outcome of these processes, it is clear that US public philosophy in the early twenty-first century will be shaped in important ways by this latest round of the classic American debate concerning the scope and content of federalism.

Two decades ago, Peter Berger and Richard John Neuhaus advocated renewed attention to "mediating structures"—standing between individuals and the state, animated neither by economic self-interest nor by legal coercion—as key sites of social action. In recent years, interest in this topic has been reawakened by Robert Putnam's work—not only his famous essay "Bowling Alone," but also his neo-Tocquevillian analysis of Italian regionalism suggesting that the quality of official public life is shaped by the vitality of civil society institutions. This work has given rise to a vigorous debate on several fronts. Has US civil society been in decline since the 1950s, as Putnam suggests? And does the causal arrow really point from civil society to the state or (as Theda Skocpol has argued) in the reverse direction as well, with sustained state action catalyzing the formation of new civil society institutions? What is the capacity of voluntary-sector institutions to supplement, or replace, public-sector action? If the public sector retrenches, will civil society spontaneously flower or (as some conservatives are now arguing) will new forms of government support be needed to reinvigorate the voluntary sector? These civil conservatives are offering a wide range of proposals: changes in family law, efforts to reconnect parents with their children's education, changes in the tax code to encourage contributions to local voluntary associations, the transfer of resources and responsibilities for service delivery from governmental to civic institutions, more community control over, and responsibility for, economic development. While it is far too early to determine whether these and similar measures can have significant consequences, clearly efforts to redefine the relationship between the public and voluntary sectors will shape the future development of public philosophy in the United States.

The national economy and the global market

One of the fundamental fault-lines in contemporary American society and social thought divides those who celebrate from those who deplore the increased integration of the global economy. One school of thought sees the global economy as a source of growth and innovation. The mobility of capital and technology upsets monopolies and brings billions of new workers out of subsistence agriculture into market-driven production processes. Liberalized trade regimes—NAFTA, GATT, the recently struck telecommunications agreement—help free resources for their most efficient use and ultimately improve the well-being of even the least advantaged populations in trading nations.

Others are more inclined to see the global economy as a threat to the living standards of workers and the solidarity of communities. When capital and technology are able to move freely, the bargaining power of organized labor is reduced and wages decline. When corporations can pull up stakes without penalty, local communities organized around long-standing modes of production such as steel and textile mills are sent reeling. Individual countries lose their ability to sustain distinctive national economic policies; generous social democracies come under pressure to reduce social programs and protections.

From this standpoint, farsighted public policy will restrict rather than encourage mobility. Footloose corporations should be required to internalize the social costs of their decisions. Trade treaties should mute the perverse effects of competition by forcing up working conditions and environmental standards in less-developed countries. The international regime-building begun at Bretton Woods half a century ago should be completed with global structures capable of reining in unregulated capital flows. As a general proposition, the only way of creating a new balance between labor and capital, and between national states and international corporations, is to establish binding frameworks from which even mobile factors of production cannot exit and within which they must therefore negotiate.

It seems increasingly likely that competing conceptions of the global economy will move to the center of US politics before the end of this century. While most elites and elected officials within the Republican party favor the move to open markets, Patrick Buchanan's 1996 candidacy provided a rallying-point for the millions of culturally conservative voters who feel disadvantaged by economic restructuring. A majority of Democratic members of Congress opposed their own president during the 1993 struggle to ratify the North American Free Trade Agreement, and the party's presidential nominating process in the year 2000 could well revolve around a trade debate between Vice President Albert Gore, Jr. and House Minority Leader Richard Gephardt. Meanwhile, independent candidates such as Ross Perot continue to focus on this issue, which could gain increased public resonance in the event of an economic downturn. The outcome of this debate, which pits transnational corporations against beleaguered labor unions and upper middle-class professionals against downscale workers, will shape the governing philosophy of the United States well into the next century.

Unity, diversity, and the rise of "identity politics"

Beginning in the 1880s, waves of immigration from new sources dramatically increased the ethnic and religious diversity of the American people. Three responses emerged to this demographic diversification. The first was an effort to stabilize the demography of the United States by restricting immigration. The second was a program of vigorous "Americanization" centered in the public schools to forge unity out of diversity. The third was an intellectual movement, led by thinkers such as Horace Kallen, to legitimize a greater measure of cultural pluralism. By the mid-1920s, immigrations laws were tightened significantly, and an ideal of political and cultural unity had taken shape. During the next four decades, the forces of homogeneity were clearly dominant.

All this changed in the 1960s, on several fronts. Immigration laws were relaxed; the overall level of immigration rose significantly and (as in the 1880s) new sources came to dominate the mix. Domestic social changes were equally significant. The civil rights movement began to end the exclusion of African-Americans from the social and political mainstream. Jews and Catholics refused to accept the continuation of their quasi-marginal status. Other groups that had been subordinated in various ways (for reasons of gender, ethnicity, and sexual orientation, among others) demanded not only entrance into the mainstream but, more radically, a broadening of its definition. Some demanded the elimination of the ideal of a common culture, with its implications of inequality and hierarchy, in the name of egalitarian polycentricity.

Not surprisingly, late twentieth-century responses to increased diversity mirror those of the previous century. Efforts to restrict immigration are intensifying at the federal level as well as in states, such as California, that have received the largest numbers of immigrants. Scholars are debating whether the new immigrants, who have on average lower levels of education and training than did cohorts admitted between 1924 and 1965, impose greater burdens on society for longer periods than did their predecessors. During the 1996 presidential nominating campaign, Republican candidate Patrick Buchanan even raised the question of whether cultural proximity to mainstream American culture should serve as a basis for regulating immigration. (As the noted sociologist Seymour Martin Lipset has pointed out, all this is rather mild by the standards of the anti-Catholic "Know Nothing" movement of the pre-Civil War period or the anti-Italian and antisemitic nativism of the late nineteenth century.)

The deeper debate today is between those who wish to update the classic American motto *e pluribus unum* and those who see the very idea of common standards as inherently hierarchical and coercive. While this debate plays out in the political arena, it reflects an academic confrontation between the adherents of an Enlightenment "modernity" (roughly speaking, the descendants of Locke and Kant) and the partisans of a "postmodernism" rooted in Nietzsche and his contemporary followers such as Lyotard and Foucault. For postmodernists, every set of ostensibly rational standards is both an effect of power relations and a source of coercive domination against which oppressed groups are bound to struggle. Postmodernist politics can be understood as Marxism without the idea of a universal class whose interests coincide with that of the society as a whole. It is, then, an "agonistic" politics of inevitable and unending struggles for power.

It is in this context that (for example) the itinerary of the African-American civil rights movement over the past forty years can be understood. Martin Luther King, Jr. articulated the idea of a common standard, animated by the biblical passion for justice and specified in the fundamental charters of American politics—the Declaration of Independence and the Constitution. Integration was to be achieved on the basis of this standard, or not at all. King's critics argued that this standard (even if followed, which it neither was nor will be) reflected the specific culture of the white majority; some kind of separatism was the only option consistent with the integrity of the African-American community. Some contemporary arguments in favor of race-conscious congressional redistricting rest on similar premises: only minority-dominated districts could overcome the essentially antagonistic relations between the majority and the minority and make possible "authentic" (radical, uncompromising) race-based political representation.

During the past decade, most criticisms of identity politics have been associated with the right wing of American politics. In one of history's modest ironies, many who opposed King during his life have appropriated his unifying political credo for use against his political heirs. In recent years, however, some intellectuals on the left (Todd Gitlin and Michael Tomasky, among others) have denounced identity politics as a key obstacle to the construction of a grass-roots political coalition capable of opposing the conservative movement. For many progressives and social democrats, cultural politics represents an unaffordable diversion from what they consider to be the real task—constructing new policies that comprehend and effectively counter increasing economic inequality and the diminished bargaining power of average working families.

Liberal democracy and political unity

Identity politics represents a challenge, not just to a class-based united front, but also (and more fundamentally) to the unity of the American polity. After the formal disestablishment of religion in the early nineteenth century, the next hundred years of US history nonetheless witnessed an informal "cultural establishment" of the beliefs and mores of white Anglo-Saxon Protestants, typically male, but sometimes (especially in reform movements) female as well. Today and for the future, it is clear that no such establishment can or should serve as the basis of national unity. While it is true, for example, that African-American culture has penetrated the cultural mainstream during the past generation, deep differences remain and are likely to persist. The alternative to a common culture would seem to be a revitalized understanding of political unity—what the legal scholar Sanford Levinson has called a "constitutional faith." The late African-American Representative Barbara Jordan's profession of total faith in the Constitution electrified the nation, not only for the illumination it shed on the immediate issue of Watergate, but also for the hope it created in a future of shared and equal citizenship.

To the extent that public attention focuses on politico-constitutional unity, the US Supreme Court will retain its key role in defining the terms of that unity. For example, relations between minority groups and the majority will be defined by cases involving issues such as political representation and affirmative action. These and other cases bring to the fore competing conceptions of the constitutional meaning of equality. If equality is understood to require equal *results*, then some form of group-based proportional representation is bound to function as the operative standard. If equality is understood as equal *opportunity*, then attention shifts to the appropriateness of the standards by which social goods are competitively allocated and to fairness of the processes by which valued social competencies are developed.

Another example: while the Constitution establishes a norm of equal citizenship, the unequal distribution of resources means that some citizens can raise their voices louder in the political debate than others. For two decades, the Supreme Court has interpreted the constitutional guarantee of free speech in a manner that thwarts most government efforts to regulate the role of money in politics. Not surprisingly, the American public increasingly believes that their government is dominated by concentrations of wealth and special interests at the expense of average citizens, and public trust in government has plunged. Serious political figures, including former Senator Bill Bradley, have reached the conclusion that if the promise of equal citizenship is to be realized, the Constitution must be amended to make it clear that freedom of speech does not entail the untrammeled right to amplify one's voice at the expense of one's fellow citizens.

Further examples. As distinct from other kinds of democracy, a *liberal* democracy includes a sphere of rights that are not fully subject to majoritarian democratic decisions. The constitution of a liberal democracy exists in part to protect that sphere. Constitutional institutions, especially but not exclusively the courts, must define the contents of that sphere and the terms on which its claims can be overridden by democratic politics. This is the issue at stake in areas ranging from the rights of defendants in criminal cases to the ability of religious groups to act (sometimes controversially) on their deepest beliefs.

It is hardly surprising that a nation officially dedicated to securing the rights of individuals would have witnessed the expansion of spheres in which these rights are protected. The success of the civil rights movement a generation ago triggered an outpouring of pent-up demands throughout our society for the recognition of long-denied rights. While few question the appropriateness of this recognition, some public intellectuals are now expressing doubts about the general "culture of rights" to which it has given rise. These doubts reflect real issues:

Rights and rightness. There is a temptation to regard the language of rights, standing alone, as an adequate moral vocabulary. But of course it is not. The assertion "I have the right to do X," even if accurate, does not warrant the conclusion that "X is the right thing to do." The gap between rights and rightness can only be filled with a moral discourse that goes well beyond rights-talk.

Rights and responsibilities. Translating rights from talk to effective practice requires institutions sustained by social cooperation and contribution. The assertion of rights unaccompanied by the willingness to do one's fair share to maintain them leads over time, in practice, to the attenuation of rights. The canonical example of this contradiction is the insistence on one's right to trial by jury without the corresponding willingness to serve on juries. Survey data indicate rising concern about the decline of reciprocity in our social life.

Rights and deliberation. Rights stand in an uneasy relation to democratic deliberation. Typically, the assertion of a right is intended to end, not begin, a public discussion: if I have a right to something, then it doesn't matter what anyone else (or even everyone else) thinks. Of course, removing certain matters from democratic determination is a core function of rights. Still, as the sphere of rights expands beyond those needed to constitute and participate in democratic institutions, the sphere of democratic decision-making tends to contract. This is all the more true because the assertion of rights impedes the art of democratic compromise based on the balancing of legitimate interests. And in many cases, rights are asserted outside the legislative arena altogether, in courts insulated from public deliberation. Given the past forty years of our national history, it is easy to understand the attractions of a court-centered strategy for the recognition of rights. But taken to excess, the resort to venues so far removed from public authorization becomes self-defeating.

Rights and the common good. As the Preamble to the Constitution makes clear, the point of democratic institutions is to enable the people to pursue key public purposes—the common good—through collective action. As occasions for the assertion of individual rights are multiplied, the ability of the people to pursue public purposes is diminished. That is not to say that either moral theory or the Constitution authorizes a democratic majority to proceed in reckless disregard of basic rights of conscience, property, and personal security. It is to say that the repeated creation of new rights-regarding procedures giving powers of delay or veto to individuals and tiny minorities ends by diminishing the public's confidence in the capacity of democratic institutions to serve the public good.

Rights and groups. Individual rights can collide with claims made by, or on behalf of, groups. One type of conflict occurs when the simple fact of membership in a particular group serves as the basis for claiming social goods. A portion of recent debates over affirmative action revolves around the moral significance of group membership: should the children of an African-American lawyer receive any preferences over the children of a white coalminer in the distribution of educational and employment opportunities? Questions of this form are rendered even more perplexing by the complexities of contemporary ethnicity; consider the diversity among "Hispanics," or rising ethnic amalgamation through intermarriage.

Another kind of conflict occurs when publicly defined conceptions of individual rights run up against constitutive elements of a group's self-definition. Nancy Rosenblum has argued that the internal affairs of voluntary groups within a liberal democracy need not be wholly "congruent" with the polity's public principles; others have taken the view that basic racial, gender, and participatory rights must be enforced throughout the society—if need be, over the objections of dissenting groups.

The contemporary discussion of democracy in America goes beyond interpreting the meaning of rights-based, representative liberal democracy as guaranteed by the Constitution to question some of the basic decisions that shaped this document. Some thinkers influenced by Rousseau (Benjamin Barber is an example) challenge the constitutional preference for representative over direct democracy in the name of a more vigorous and engaged conception of democratic citizenship. Others challenge Madison's acceptance of interest-based politics in favor of a more deliberative conception of democracy in which individuals are expected to offer genuinely public reasons for their policy preferences.

It is not impossible to combine representation and deliberation. Indeed, Madison is sometimes interpreted as supporting representation and other "filtering" devices as ways of insulating the political sphere from the influence of narrow social and economic interests, facilitating deliberation among government officials. But those who favor more participatory citizens and stronger democracy cannot be satisfied with enhanced deliberation among elites. Theorists such as Amy Gutmann and Dennis Thompson have developed the outlines for the constitution of a deliberative democracy in this broader sense. Given most Americans' ambivalence about the place of political activities in their lives, it remains to be seen whether this ideal of a more engaged and demanding citizenship can gain public support and become the basis of an effective new public philosophy.

The politics of virtue

As recently as a decade ago, public philosophy in America hardly touched on issues of virtue. Social scientists emphasized well-designed institutions and processes as substitutes for good character; philosophers developed theories of justice applied to the "basic structure of society" (John Rawls's phrase) rather than to the structure of the human soul. Today, by contrast, discussions of virtue are in vogue. In the context of public philosophy, a pair of questions are central: what are the virtues relevant to the conduct of social and political life; and what are the means through which these virtues may be developed?

Much of this discussion revolves around questions of citizenship. For traditional liberals, virtues such as respect for the dignity and rights of others are key. Thinkers inspired by the "civic republican" tradition emphasize capacities and motivations needed for active participation in public life as well as devotion to the common good over private interests. Still others stress autonomous judgment and skillful deliberation.

Other schools of thought are less comfortable with citizenship as a point of departure. Many feminists call into question the very distinction between public and private and, by implication, the distinction between public and private virtues. If in our personal lives we think it right to focus on the particularity of individual cases and to take our bearings from the imperatives of care and connection, then why should our public life be shaped by norms of separation (such as autonomy) and abstraction (such as justice)? Environmentalists question not only the sustainability, but also the morality, of a society based on ever-expanding consumption and untrammeled individualism. They insist instead on the virtues of self-restraint, simplicity, and far-sighted concern for the consequences of one's acts.

Many religious denominations argue that genuine virtue is incompatible with the humanistic assumptions that man is the measure of all things or that the only binding law is self-imposed. These beliefs are manifestations of culpable pride; true faith counsels humility in the face of a higher power, and respect for commandments that are given from without rather than created from within. Because religious faith and observance are far more pervasive in the United States than in any other advanced industrial country, it is impossible to understand the American dialogue about public philosophy without taking religion into account.

To care about virtue is to care about the institutions and circumstances that tend to foster virtue. When Americans say (as they have repeatedly in opinion surveys over the past decade) that the United States is in the grip of a moral crisis, they mean in part that key formative institutions—families, neighborhoods, public schools, voluntary organizations, religious institutions—are weaker than they once were. They also mean that newer social forces, particularly the mass media, are stronger than they should be and tend to foster traits of character—greed, violence, lust, misogyny, disrespect, heedlessness, passivity—at odds with true virtue.

There is, however, vigorous disagreement over specific diagnoses and prescriptions. While many call for the revitalization of "family values," others see the traditional family as the locus of hierarchy, patriarchy, oppression, and violence. While many call for increased public regulation of the mass media, particularly when children and young people are involved, others see such limits as reflecting fearful narrow-mindedness and violating the spirit of liberty. Still, most parties to the debate would agree that public philosophy must give renewed attention to issues of character formation. It is in this context, I would suggest, that Robert Putnam's thesis concerning the alleged decline of civil society is to be understand. And Michael Sandel's call to rediscover the "political economy of citizenship" is a reminder that we are shaped by modes of material production and distribution as well as by patterns of familial and social connection. It is to the analysis of Sandel's thesis that I now turn.

The Politics of Virtue

Democracy's Discontent is an analytical history, guided by a distinction between two families of political philosophy—procedural liberalism and civic republicanism. Procedural liberalism is said to rest on (Sandel's now-familiar phrase) the unencumbered self, shorn of particular duties and constitutive identities, while civic republicanism reflects such duties and identities. The civic republic recognizes a need to form its citizens, through economic and civil institutions as well as formal education and the family, while the procedural republic is officially indifferent to the preferences and character of its citizens. Sandel's historical thesis—traced principally through the spheres of the economy and constitutional law—is that American life over the past two centuries has witnessed a replacement of the civic republic by the procedural republic and that this replacement explains many of the ills we now experience—specifically, the felt losses of agency, mastery, community, and trust. As Sandel summarizes his case:

> The procedural republic that has unfolded over the past half-century can now be seen as an epic experiment in the claims of liberal as against republican political thought. Our present predicament lends weight to the republican claim that liberty cannot be detached from self-government and the virtues that sustain it, that the formative project cannot be dispensed with after all. The procedural republic, it turns out, cannot secure the liberty it promises because it cannot inspire the moral and civic engagement self-government requires.[1]

In Sandel's view, these developments require a broad response. As a nation, we must return to a collective concern for nonneutral public morality and for the civic formation of citizens. And on the institutional plane, we must overcome the antipathy (rooted in the Progressive era) to both local political institutions and civil associations. Liberal Democrats will have to put aside their mistrust of intermediate communities as bigoted and repressive; conservative Republicans will have to acknowledge that big business, not just big government, can be the enemy of the civic republic: "If American politics is to revitalize the civic strand of freedom, it must find a way to ask what economic arrangements are hospitable to self-government and how the public life of a pluralist society might cultivate in citizens the expansive self-understandings that civic engagement requires. It must revive, in terms relevant to our own time, the political economy of citizenship."[2]

Sandel succeeds in making the historical case that the concern about civic character formation was once more central to public debate than it is today. This debate had focused not only on the formative role of civil and educational institutions, but also on the question of what economic arrangements are most hospitable to self-government.[3] With the rise of consumerism in the Progressive era and Keynesian economics during the New Deal, active interest in this question largely disappeared.

On Sandel's own account, however, proposals for a political economy of citizenship have been remarkably disparate; the general rhetoric of civic formation has proved compatible with almost any mode of economic organization. Thomas Jefferson was able to shift from staunch agrarianism to the acceptance of manufacturing without altering his civic convictions. Two generations later, both Whigs and Jacksonians used the vocabulary of civic formation but came to opposed conclusions about political economy. Two generations after that, the Progressives split into two camps: one, led by Louis Brandeis and Woodrow Wilson, arguing that economic and political centralization posed grave threats to democratic self-government; the other, led by Herbert Croly and Theodore Roosevelt, countering with an effort to decouple the formative ambitions of civic republicanism from its historic commitment to economic and political localism. By the 1920s it was even possible to invert the republican tradition and argue that large corporations formed better citizens than did small businesses![4]

On reflection, it is not hard to explain the protean quality of the political economy of citizenship. The content of civic virtue was left largely undefined throughout our history (as it is in Sandel's account). The objective of the "formative impulse" is thus hard to pin down. Even when civic virtues were specified, the empirical/causal connection between their cultivation and specific forms of political economy was never clarified. And there is an ambiguous relation at best between the noble vocabulary of civic virtue and the actual motivation of political agents. It is not implausible to understand the National Chain Store Association's civic defense of twentieth-century corner drugstore owners as the "yeomen of their day"[5] as a rhetorical cloak for economic self-interest and complacency.

As Sandel emphasizes, the political economy of citizenship is part of an even larger discussion of possible arenas for civic character formation. The drafters of the Constitution and authors of the *Federalist* papers did not regard the national government as the appropriate site for such activities. Throughout much of our history, the family, local public institutions, and civil associations were regarded as keys to the success of the formative enterprise. In his own account of civic formation, however, Sandel cannot escape a tension between the authority of the state to shape character and the kinds of "encumbrances" on which he dwells. To the extent that we take seriously particularist duties (for example, to family members) or group identification (for example, with faith communities), we may be inclined to resist rather than embrace public direction of civic character formation.

Sandel is well aware of the most deeply felt objection to civic republicanism: especially in modern circumstances of pluralism and inclusion, the formative project can shade over into unwelcome paternalism and can even threaten liberty. He concedes the risks.[6] But he invites devotees of procedural liberalism to ask themselves whether there are not risks in their stance as well. Like nature, politics abhors a vacuum. The "naked public square" is all too likely to be filled with intolerant fundamentalisms.

While Sandel's historical plot line depicts the rise of proceduralism and the decline of civic republicanism, it is more nearly accurate to say that civic and procedural strands of political thought have coexisted in American thought and practice from the beginning. The Declaration of Independence, which Sandel unaccountably ignores as a statement of American public philosophy, weaves together mutual civic commitment and the defense of individual rights.

Sandel himself provides some of the raw materials for this alternative account. He notes that the Founders pursued two tracks—the formative and the procedural.[7] While they sought to increase civic virtue, they also pursued institutional arrangements that would make virtue less necessary, and its absence less damaging. A century later, the Progressives responded to a perceived crisis of self-government and loss of community with a similar two-track strategy: on the one hand, proceduralism-management by neutral experts; on the other, moral and civic formation, especially through strategies of urban reform.[8]

Sandel does show that the civic republican strand of American thought had became attenuated by the mid-twentieth century. But throughout a strongly historical book, he offers a surprisingly ahistorical account of this development. For the most part, the rise of procedural liberalism, of the unencumbered self, of the ethic of voluntarism is presented as a free-floating episode in the history of (bad) ideas. An effort to relate this conceptual shift to concrete economic and social experiences (the flight from rural stultification and racial oppression, pell-mell urbanization, increased religious and ethnic diversity, the broadening of middle-class prosperity, and the spread of mass communication, among others) would have permitted a more nuanced and balanced assessment of the proceduralist impulse. It would also have enabled us to examine more precisely the varying sources of our current ills. As Sandel himself notes,[9] the procedural republic seemed to work well enough during the quarter-century "moment of mastery" after the Second World War. If real family incomes were still rising by 3 percent, year after year, would we be having the same discussion about the inner defects of voluntarism?

Beyond these historical doubts, difficulties also arise at the conceptual level. It is not the case that "procedural" or rights-based liberalism is generically indifferent to civic character and to the modes of its formation. Both John Rawls and Judith Shklar argue that there are forms of virtue and character necessary for citizens of modern liberal regimes. Indeed, Rawls insists that no citizen of such a regime can properly object to morally appropriate civic education: "For in agreeing to principles of right the parties in the original position at the same time consent to the arrangements necessary to make these principles effective in their conduct."[10] (Rawls surely disagrees with Sandel about the content of civic education, but that is another matter.)

Nor can one agree unreservedly to the conceptual shift—from a detached, unencumbered self to the situated particularized one—that underpins Sandel's critique of procedural liberalism. While it is true that the idea of the unencumbered self is inadequate to the full range of our experience, so is the idea of the encumbered self. An adequate account of morality must make room for particularist duties and for mutual commitments seen as constitutive of individual identity. Similarly, an adequate account of liberty must accommodate a conception of citizenship as permitting, and as unaffected by, changes of group membership—including religious identification.

Sandel's account of political liberty is puzzling. He begins by offering his version of Constant's distinction between the liberty of the ancients and the liberty of the moderns. The former (civic republican) conception sees liberty as the consequence of self-government; the latter (procedural liberal) conception sees it as a constraint on majoritarian decisions. Given Sandel's overall story, we would expect him to come down solidly in favor of civic republican liberty. Instead, he declares that each tradition highlights a potential deficiency in the other.[11] This points us in a sensible direction: both participation in government and protection from government are important goods whose relative weight varies with individuals, issues, and circumstances. Rather than a forced and artificial choice between two abstract concepts, the point is to reach a workable balance between participation and protection. That is the intention of, for example, the Bill of Rights and related constitutional amendments, whose provisions secure both the conditions of participation and the terms of self-protection. The problem with this commonsense, plural-valued stance is that it greatly complicates the overall contrast Sandel wishes to draw between civic republicanism (good) and procedural liberalism (bad).

This complication helps explain the odd combination of reticence and ambivalence Sandel displays when he turns to social policy. He traces the Supreme Court's *Roe* v. *Wade* decision and the rise of no-fault divorce to a procedural liberalism that moves unfettered individual choice stage center while trying (unsuccessfully) to maintain neutrality by bracketing controversial conceptions of the meaning and worth of life. But as far as I can tell, he never makes clear the conclusions he believes would flow from civic republicanism for the constitutional law of abortion. As for family life, he declares that "the liberal self-image [which detaches the self from fixed roles and duties] has had beneficial consequences as well as destructive ones."[12] We are left wondering whether civic republicanism represents a fundamental alternative to voluntarist legalism, or rather a circuitous new route to familiar procedural-liberal conclusions.

There is no ambiguity about Sandel's overall prescription for our ills—the reinvigoration of local political institutions and voluntary associations. Sandel points to signs that Robert F. Kennedy's 1968 campaign call for decentralization has found a small but sturdy and growing audience; he cites community-based economic development corporations, models of local political organization such as the Industrial Areas Foundation, and coalitions to protect local main streets against the depredations of Wal-Mart.

This strategy, however, is embattled on many fronts. The vitality of local communities is challenged, not just by entrenched procedural nationalism, but also by the rising influence of the global economy. There is a tempting historical analogy: just as new national political power was deployed against new national/corporate economic power during the Progressive era, now we must forge new international governance institutions to check the influence of global capital. Sandel is skeptical: at a time when citizens around the world are finding it harder to identify with units as large as nation-states, effective global institutions require a capacity for even wider identification that may not be possible, or wholly desirable (pp. 340 ff.). In the end, then, we are left with a proposal for reempowered local communities whose means of defense against transnational economic forces is at best unclear.

If anything, Sandel understates the scope of the problem. Many of the economic (let alone social) challenges to liberal democracy cannot be adequately addressed through markets alone. New forms of national public action will be required to mute disparities of income and wealth, enhance individual opportunity and security, and regulate the consequences of unchecked competition. But securing democratic authorization for these steps will be difficult at best in an era in which the competence and integrity of government are so widely questioned.

The economy is not the only obstacle to localism. The structure of the US Constitution reflects the fear that small homogeneous communities could threaten individual liberties. It is true that until the twentieth century, the Bill of Rights was interpreted to limit only the power of the national government. But as Sandel himself notes, James Madison was also in favor of constitutional protection for individual rights against state and local governments and included such protections in his original draft of the Bill of Rights. (The first

Congress rejected them.) Sandel rightly emphasizes the civic republican element of the civil rights movement.[13] But it was that very movement that fought for, and won, an historic expansion of national power *vis-à-vis* local communities in the name of individual rights.

As a general matter, the extent to which the power of the national state should be deployed against local communities and civil associations in the name of shared citizenship raises moral and prudential considerations that do not always favor enhanced localism.

Conclusion: Public Philosophy and the Challenge of Particularism

Not many years ago, with the fall of the Berlin Wall and the collapse of the Soviet Union, a certain triumphalism was in the air. Not only was liberal democracy the only regime whose legitimacy could be rationally and publicly justified; but also, surely, its superior merits would come to be widely, even universally, acknowledged. The mood is decidedly more sober today, and for good reason. Liberal democracy is many things, of course, but John Gray is more right than wrong to see a kind of universalist humanism at its core: universalist in the belief that what human beings have in common, their moral dignity, trumps what distinguishes and divides them; humanism in the sense of resting legitimacy on natural reason and consent (variously understood within the liberal tradition) rather than external revelation.

It should always have been obvious, and it is now undeniable, that two powerful and enduring forces, linked but distinct, obstruct the progress of liberal democracy, so conceived. On nearly every continent, millions of people resist membership in multiethnic states that seem to threaten the survival of their ethnic identity, or to impede its official public acknowledgment. In some cases this is a reflection of physical fear; more often, a sense that an intense desire for collective self-expression is in danger of being stifled. The ethnic self seeking expression is not experienced as a choice among "plans of life," but rather a destiny decreed by history or fate. And all too often, the difference it defines is seen as more important than whatever may be shared with nonmembers by virtue of a common humanity.

Alongside (and sometimes reinforcing) ethnicity is religious faith, typically fundamentalist, that locates legitimacy in divine law or decree rather than human authorization. Adherents of various fundamentalisms are bound to hear the liberal democratic call for tolerance of differences as a summons to abandon the serious practice of their faith. At best, a derivative tolerance may find a place within the structure of faith. To the liberal charge that intolerance means coercion and war, fundamentalists will typically reply that the very high value accorded to noncoercion and peace represents a commitment internal to the liberal tradition and not binding beyond its borders.

While alarmism is unwarranted, it would be foolish to assume that these conflicts are confined to the Teherans and Sarajevos of this world. Ethnic particularism and fundamentalism are elements of the contemporary American experience. The challenge is to persuade their adherents that they have more to gain than to lose from finding their place within the liberal democratic order. I believe, as I have argued elsewhere, that our best chance lies in limiting the demands of the common order to the essentials while allowing the maximum feasible scope for diversity within this frame. In my view, a liberal democracy should be prepared to allow wide though not unlimited scope for diverse group practices, with the understanding that membership in certain groups may involve the voluntary renunciation of certain otherwise enforceable individual rights. If we go farther, if we press too hard on moral ideals such as liberal autonomy, democratic individuality, or direct participation in public affairs, if we require subgroups to reorganize their internal affairs in accordance with liberal democratic principles, we run the risk of exacerbating the conflicts we set out to abate.

This is of course to describe the contours of the strategy, but not to specify it. For example, many liberals believe that the development of autonomy and critical reflection is an ineliminable part of the minimum common order. I yield to no one in my regard for these human capacities. The question is whether it is necessary, or useful, to regard them as essential to liberal democratic citizenship. I for one would be satisfied if citizens obeyed the law, did what they could to support themselves and their families, contributed their fair share to the support of our basic institutions, and refrained from violence and coercion as means of promulgating their vision of the good life.

These observations illustrate the central point I urged in my analysis of *Democracy's Discontent*: before we can speak with useful precision about formative institutions in general (let alone the political economy of citizenship), we must have some sense of the civic virtues we seek to promote. This understanding of the virtues will in turn reflect a specific conception of what is "common," to be required of every citizen, as opposed to those matters that can be left to individual, family, or group determination. Public philosophy risks overreaching whenever it loses sight of the limits of the public realm.

5

The Encumbered American Self

CLIFFORD ORWIN

IN *Democracy's Discontent*, Michael Sandel paints in broad strokes to establish the existence of a vanished consensus in favor of a civic-minded understanding of American democracy. This is both a strength and a weakness. On the one hand, he offers impressive evidence of both the ubiquity and the persistence of the American republican tradition, which turns up in the darnedest places. The book is full of wonderful quotations which are themselves worth the price of admission. On the other, so broad is Sandel's notion of republicanism that it becomes the big tent of the American political tradition. In his zeal to enlist every possible ally, Sandel invokes not only Jefferson's hope of fostering a natural aristocracy in the bosom of democracy but Hubert H. Humphrey's campaign to save the bacon of small-town pharmacists through resale price maintenance laws. His exposition thus leaves unresolved crucial questions of emphasis. True, both Federalists and Anti-Federalists agreed that republican virtue had a role to play in American life, as did Jeffersonians and Hamiltonians, Jacksonians and Whigs, but they disagreed as to the dimensions of that role and even as to the character of that virtue. Sandel does not suppress these disagreements, but neither does he explore them in depth. Was self-government to aim primarily at securing the rights of the individual or at some more general goal? Were the virtues of the citizen ends in themselves or means to some other end? How was American civic virtue to relate to those fostered by such earlier (and disparate) republics as Athens, Sparta, Rome, Geneva, and Holland? What was the relationship of civic virtue to Christian virtue, and to those virtues of frugality and enterprise appropriate to a polity sustained by commerce? In short, *what kind* of republic was America to be?

If Sandel adds relatively little to our understanding of past centuries of American life, he does illumine important tendencies of our own. He provides an intriguing account of the evolution of public policy from the Progressive era onward. Dwelling on judicial decisions and on the formation of economic and regulatory policies, he shows how private welfare has steadily usurped

Reprinted with permission, Clifford Orwin, "Michael Sandel's America," *The Weekly Standard*, 35 (May 1996), 37.

citizenship as the object of public action. He offers a provocative critique of judicial and policy milestones that many conservatives join liberals in praising as progressive.

Sandel brilliantly expounds the bankruptcy of what he calls the "procedural republic." Focussing on issues of religious liberty, freedom of speech, privacy rights, and family law, he shows that many of our reigning public dogmas flout not only common sense but the conditions of healthy republicanism. He demonstrates that professed judicial "neutrality" among human "values" has proved anything but neutral in practice. "The new law of divorce . . . by making dependence a dangerous thing . . . burdens the practice of marriage as a community in the constitutive sense. By bracketing moral judgments, celebrating self-sufficiency, and loosening the relation between the self and its roles, the law is not neutral among competing visions of married life, but recasts the institution of marriage in the image of the unencumbered self." "It is not neutral among conceptions of the good, but favorable to certain views of family life, inhospitable to others."

Procedural liberalism, then, typecasts us as "unencumbered selves," free agents for whom freedom of agency is the ultimate publicly recognizable good. In the name of defending that freedom, the law curtails the role alike of the polity and of private communities such as church and family. Deprived of a meaningful public life and thrown back on our individuality, we are to congratulate ourselves that the state keeps out of our bedrooms and that some anonymous agency out there protects our interests as consumers. Sandel thus explains the seeming paradox that precisely the vast expansion of the public sector in twentieth-century America has coincided with the increasing impoverishment of public life. He is certainly right, moreover, that any hope of improving our situation must begin from clarity concerning it, and that the ideology of "procedural liberalism" befuddles us by assuring us of our ever greater autonomy as individuals even as our communal power to shape our lives recedes ever further from us.

As a piece of social criticism, then, the book is of great value. Like many social critics, however, Sandel is more persuasive in stating problems than in finding solutions. He knows this, which is why he devotes only 10 pages out of 350 to specific practical proposals. These include community development corporations, sprawl busting (i.e. opposition to the proliferation of Wal-Mart department stores), the new urbanism, and community organizing. He is aware, I think, that it is hard to imagine these making much difference to the way that too many of us live now: overworked, overstressed, economically pressed, without deep roots in the places where we live, or the leisure and energy for local citizenship. All Sandel's proposals have been tried, and could doubtless be tried harder, but if the earth were to open to swallow every Wal-Mart, whom would that benefit except K-Mart? The people have made it clear that they would rather pay $8.49 to John Madden than $300 for the same wrench at whatever family-owned store the

Pentagon shops. By demanding competitive prices the public also supports free trade, downsizing, and ever greater economies of scale. Here as elsewhere Sandel's remedies resemble whistling in the dark, brave and earnest but not likely efficacious.

On the level of national politics, Sandel agrees with many conservatives in favoring a "New Federalism." But is he willing to pay the price for it, less fiscal dependence on the Federal government? This seems doubtful given his emphatic support for greater income redistribution ("less for the sake of distributive justice than for the sake of . . . forming the civic identity of rich and poor alike"). Indeed Sandel sees the welfare state and a renewal of public spiritedness as mutually reinforcing. Only a heightened sense of civic solidarity will sustain our willingness to pay higher taxes to underwrite civic equality, which is in turn a condition of true communal self-government.

It is hard to reconcile this call for more redistribution with that for a "dispersal" of sovereignty. Will increased public interference in the economy help us dig ourselves out from under big government? And how likely is such redistribution to benefit republicanism? However hard Sandel squeezes the republican tradition, he will find no encouragement to expect civic virtue from the economically dependent. He trusts too much in the power of rhetoric. Rechristen welfare as "civic identity payments" and you still won't find the underclass so dumb as to believe that they are standing on their own two feet.

Sandel is right the first time, in recommending community development as the proper approach to the problems of the poor—an approach incompatible with their continued reliance on a dole from above.

Another obstacle to the dispersal of sovereignty is the continued (and increasing) concentration of economic power in the hands of corporate behemoths. Indeed when Sandel turns to the problems for local self-government posed by the globalization of the economy and the emergence of transnational political authorities, he faces a daunting dilemma. He wants the public to retain enough power to curb large corporations on not just the national but the international plane, but he wants such public power dispersed rather than concentrated. (Whether ever more dispersed political power could hope to restrain ever more concentrated economic power remains a big and obvious question.) We are to think and act both locally and globally, not as "unencumbered individuals" but as members of overlapping communities. "[Self government today] requires citizens who can think and act as multiply situated selves."

Two objections suggest themselves here. The first is practical, namely the grave difficulty of devising effective strategies of the "dispersal" of sovereignty. On these would depend whether such dispersal would prove empowering or merely divisive. As a resident of Canada I find myself pessimistic on this score. Here we have dispersal of sovereignty aplenty, and it has chiefly profited the politicians and lawyers who haggle over which crumb of sovereignty belongs to whom.

Secondly, I'm a little dubious of the "multiply situated self" itself. If, as Sandel claims, the community constitutes us rather than vice versa—if we are truly "encumbered beings"—just how many different communities can encumber us at once? How many ways can our self be divided? Inevitably such a self must face the question of which of its several communities can claim its primary allegiance. There are no "multiply situated selves" in foxholes. A Spartan was a Spartan and a Roman was a Roman, but Sandel's "multiply situated self" resembles a joiner—an individualistic sort of self that chooses its identities and picks its situations. Perhaps Sandel is more of a liberal than he realizes.

In fact procedural liberalism has already come to recognize the "encumbered self." In this respect, at least, Sandel's analysis, while forceful, is also curiously one-sided. Lately liberalism so-called has wreaked at least as much mischief by deferring to "community" as by failing to do so. "Communities,"—the African-American, the gay and lesbian, the female (i.e. feminist), the Hispanic, etc., etc.—are all the rage among liberals today. Sandel's critique of the "abstract individual" is not a voice crying in the desert but the conventional wisdom of liberalism. Politically, however, it has sparked anything but a resurgence of republicanism. Rather it has helped judges and bureaucracies break new ground in encroaching on private life as well as on the political process. It has encouraged not renewed autonomy (individual or communal) but "victimology" and the culture of complaint.

Consider the policies that go by the names of affirmative action and multiculturalism. These enact the Sandelian premise that we are not primarily individuals but members of communities—and that we are to be publicly catalogued and treated as such. In all such cases not the politics of individualism but that of membership prevails. It is because we are claimed to be constituted by our communities that loyalty to communities overrides any broader patriotism. It is because we are claimed to be so constituted that there can be no such thing as science or history simply, only black, white, or female science and history; no such thing as reason simply, only black, white, or female reason. And then there is the backlash to all this, on the part of white males whom this very doctrine encourages to band together as such. The teaching that our identities are communal from the ground up has thus proved every bit as corrosive of the bond of common citizenship as the individualism blamed by Sandel.

Sandel sees clearly that America faces a moral crisis. In his critique of the "procedural republic" he even hints at the root of that crisis: the relativism that reduces human life to the strife of arbitrary values, with the state playing neutral arbiter. It is not, however, merely state action or inaction on the basis of this relativism but the doctrine itself that has subverted our communal institutions. Nor, however, is this relativism (as Sandel implies) simply individualist in its implications. In its assault on the notion of a common human reason, it equally encourages, as I have just suggested, an intransigent assertion of group particularity. Sandel seems to suggest that the "value" of community itself can help to resolve our present crisis. But this is to put the cart before the horse. Community (even if you call it "republicanism") cannot serve as a moral principle; rather our moral principles must furnish the basis of our community. The question that community poses is always the same, namely, community *of what*? The multiculturalists have offered one answer to this question; Sandel gropes for another, one that would unite Americans rather than divide them. Unfortunately, there cannot be a community of a tradition of community; nostalgia does not suffice to build communities.

I have noted that while Sandel stresses the republicanism of the American tradition, he fails to explore the question of what sort of republic America was meant to be. If he does us a favor by reminding us that America was originally republican as well as liberal, we can repay him by reminding him—that it has always been liberal as well as republican. (Here I mean "liberal" in the generic sense, to which most "conservatives" also subscribe, of beginning from the primacy of the freedom of the individual.) As Woodrow Wilson once put it, "our Constitution has thrown [the individual] upon his own resources, as if it honored him enough to release him from leading strings and trust him to seek his own rights." Its premise is that "no man must look to have the government take care of him, but that every man must take care of himself." Such a system, Wilson continued, does not merely presuppose but "elicits intelligence and creates independence of spirit."

So yes, Americans have always aspired to constitute a community, but one of free self-reliant individuals. While cherishing their country, their families, their churches, their associations of every sort, they have not viewed themselves as submerged by them. Sandel's "encumbered self," fully constituted by its communal environment, is not a homespun article but an imported Heideggerian one. These are two very different notions of the self and of what it owes to the community. We must not fudge this distinction; Heidegger certainly did not.

To the extent that we are encumbered selves, however, that very fact would imply that we dance with the community what brung us. If America is that community, it is republican but not "communitarian." We have all been raised as members of a community of liberals; as Sandel's own evidence confirms, this liberalism is anything but superficial. Its roots have sunk ever deeper in the past century even as its branches have risen ever higher. Only a liberal could regard this liberalism as something that we have chosen and that we are therefore free to reject. Paradoxically, to disown the individualistic strain of our tradition would itself amount to a declaration of unencumberedness.

We here reach what I regard as the ultimate problem with *Democracy's Discontent*. Sandel's rejection of individualism in favor of a communitarian republicanism is not just historically implausible; it fails to do justice to all the resources available to us as Americans. Because he acknowledges only grudgingly that our republicanism was from its genesis in the Declaration of Independence a liberal or individualist one, he does not explore the crucial question of the proper interaction of the two components. There is no doubt that the imbalances of "procedural liberalism" must be redressed. This, however, it seems to me, could be accomplished only on the basis of a more sympathetic understanding of liberalism as such than is available from Sandel. Such an understanding would seek to do justice to the communitarian elements not only of republicanism but of original liberalism. For me a model of such efforts of retrieval is Steven Kautz's *Liberalism and Community*.[1] If there is an appropriate response to Sandel's powerful call for the revival of American republicanism, it is that this last must depend upon the renewal of American individualism. Not until we are again willing to take responsibility for ourselves as individuals will we be fit to assume it as a community.

6

A Public Philosophy for the Professional-Managerial Class

MARK TUSHNET

ANY work praised, as *Democracy's Discontent* has been, by Social Democrat Eric Foner,[1] Christian Democrat Mary Ann Glendon,[2] and Tory George Will must be extremely wise, quite confused, or so abstract that each reader can find in it what she or he wants. *Democracy's Discontent* has been so well received, I believe, more because it expresses a mood than because it makes an argument.[3]

I suggest that Sandel should be taken as a "culture critic" who bases his interpretation of our culture more on his participation in it than on social scientific survey evidence and the like. With some diffidence, I take the same stance toward Sandel's work, and suggest that it responds to the discontent of today's professional-managerial class faced with reduced autonomy as corporate capitalism increasingly limits the domain in which professionals can exercise professional judgment and discretion.[4] Today's professional-managerial middle class is discontented with the procedural republic that it served well, and that served it well, during the period of sustained economic growth in the United States after 1945. The procedural republic was at least compatible with the self-conception of professionals and managers as social engineers, experts who designed the machinery that then operated to produce economic growth and social stability. As growth slowed, the economic position of professionals and managers changed. They were no longer experts offering professional and autonomous advice on how best to steer the economy. They became employees subject to the market forces they had believed they controlled. No wonder they are discontented, and thrashing around for a public philosophy for their class to replace the procedural republic that no longer satisfies them. Sandel offers an alternative with some elements that respond to the new position of the professional-managerial class. But his prescriptions do not in the end

Excerpted with permission, Mark Tushnet, "A Public Philosophy for the Professional-Managerial Class," *Yale Law Journal*, 106 (1997), 1571–610.

satisfactorily address the real source of their discontent: the apparently uncontrollable power of transnational corporations.

Sandel's proposed public philosophy evokes the Progressive era even as it departs from some of its prescriptions.[5] The Progressive movement, historians have argued, was basically a movement of middle-class professionals who sought to define public policy by combining an emphasis on efficiency with efforts to achieve moral uplift.[6] Efficiency was to be achieved by following the prescriptions of experts drawn from the movement's base of independent professionals. Moral progress was defined with reference to the standards of the professional class, and would be achieved sometimes by coercion and sometimes by creating institutions that would induce their participants to act morally.

Sandel's vision is striking because it restates the Progressive emphasis on moral uplift while eliminating the Progressive interest in efficiency and expertise.[7] By dropping deference to expert judgment Sandel shows himself to be a more committed democrat than were the Progressives.[8] His stance may also reflect the understanding of contemporary professionals that the bureaucracies within which they work do not actually value their expertise as professionals.

Subordinating efficiency is more problematic. Sandel describes the contemporary "anti-sprawl" movement as a revisitation of the anti-chainstore movement.[9] As Thomas McCraw has argued in detail, the Brandeisian program was not an obviously sensible one.[10] It sacrificed real economic benefits—lower prices for goods—in exchange for speculative benefits in the form of greater civic participation by people of the type caricatured in Sinclair Lewis's novels.[11] Sandel's contemporary example is an activist opposing the location of a Wal-Mart, who declared, "I'd rather have a viable community than a cheap pair of underwear."[12]

I do not know anything about that particular activist, but that is the sort of thing that can be said, or at least admired, only by people who do not have to worry that higher-priced underwear means sending their children to school in worn-out underwear or having less food on the table for dinner. So, one characteristic of the class to which Sandel's vision appeals is reasonable material security. Its members are less concerned with efficiency than were the Progressives because the marginal gains from more efficient operation would not significantly affect the material dimensions of their lives.

The procedural republic triumphed when "the performance of the domestic economy gave Americans a sense of command over their individual destinies."[13] Prosperity made credible the "consumerist vision" of a people united only in "the experience of consumption."[14] Contemporary professionals have lost the sense of control and mastery. "America's moment of mastery expired" in 1968,[15] after which "[a]t home and abroad, events spun out of control, and government seemed helpless to respond."[16] Despite this, middle-class professionals have not experienced substantial reductions in material well-being.

Unsurprisingly, they might be interested in recapturing some control at the expense of some slight reduction in *their* material well-being, even if the effects on the material well-being of less privileged groups might be more substantial.

Why might such a class fail to develop a vision in which expertise plays the role it did in the Progressive vision? Perhaps because today's professional class is not truly independent.[17] Engineers and doctors are increasingly employees rather than independent contractors. Perhaps too it is this lack of independence that makes Sandel's interest in developing a political economy of citizenship appealing. Until today's professionals become independent they know that they cannot impose policies in the name of their expertise; they would instead simply be acting on behalf of their employers. Like many jeremiads, Sandel's evokes images of a romanticized past that we have lost but might recreate.[18] He tells today's professionals that they once were independent and ought to be so again.

What is left is moral uplift. Sandel criticizes modern no-fault divorce law because it "bracket[s] the moral considerations that had traditionally governed the law of divorce."[19] Given the prevalence of divorce among today's professionals, however, he does not urge a return to a fault-based divorce regime. Instead, he seeks only "reforms giving greater attention to the economic conditions of women and children after divorce," reforms that he acknowledges might in some cases "be defended in terms consistent with procedural liberalism."[20] He is a bit more aggressive about using systems of public assistance to "form moral character or shape behavior or cultivate virtue," criticizing proposals made during the 1960s and 1970s for a guaranteed income on the ground that they would merely "enable recipients to choose their values and ends for themselves."[21]

Sandel nonetheless emphasizes "the civic case against inequality,"[22] because economic inequality "erodes civic virtue"[23] as the affluent secede from the public sphere. Sandel endorses a description of that secession appearing in a celebrated book by President Clinton's former Secretary of Labor Robert Reich.[24] Reich describes the proliferation of "private health clubs, golf clubs, tennis clubs, skating clubs,"[25] private schools, private garbage-collection services, and private security guards.[26] This secession is real, but Sandel and Reich perhaps overestimate it. I suspect that it describes more what middle-class professionals fear that they need but will be unable to afford, than the lived experiences of the bulk of that class.

Sandel discusses public policies committed to formative projects "aimed at cultivating citizens of a certain kind."[27] He occasionally hints at what seems obvious, that each formative project was connected to a particular social class.[28] Some of his historical actors are Jeffersonian agrarians,[29] Jacksonian artisans seeking secure property holdings,[30] wage laborers hoping "to rise to own productive property and to work for [themselves],"[31] and workers seeking an eight-hour day in part to give them time to participate in civic affairs.[32]

When we reach the procedural republic, however, the material basis disappears from view. Sandel offers no direct account of the material basis for the procedural republic, nor of the material basis for the rather vague formative project he urges as an alternative public philosophy.[33]

Sandel points out that the "sense of disempowerment" he attributes to Americans "arises from the fact that the liberal self-image and the actual organization of modern social and economic life are sharply at odds."[34] "Self-government . . . requires political communities that control their destinies," but "[i]n a world of global interdependence, even the most powerful nation-states are no longer the masters of their destiny."[35] Thus, "[i]f American politics is to revitalize the civic strand of freedom, it must find a way to ask what economic arrangements are hospitable to self-government."[36]

When Sandel sketches his way out, however, the suggestions seem ill-suited to the task. He admires community development corporations, the "New Urbanism," and community organizing.[37] He acknowledges, though, that "[i]n a world where capital and goods . . . flow across national boundaries with unprecedented ease, politics must assume transnational, even global forms, if only to keep up. Otherwise, economic power will go unchecked by democratically sanctioned political power."[38] But how can we "cultivate the civic identities necessary to sustain those institutions, to supply them with the moral authority they require"?[39]

The problem is one Progressives confronted early in the twentieth century.[40] Sandel describes two dimensions of the Progressive project. The more familiar involves the expansion of national political power to control the expanded power of corporations.[41] Less familiar is the Brandeisian vision. As an example, Sandel describes anti-chainstore legislation following the First World War as an expression of a public philosophy seeking to preserve small businesses whose owners made important contributions to their communities' public life—at added expense to consumers, of course.[42] The chainstores won:

> While local grocers and druggists had presented themselves, not wholly convincingly, as the yeomen of their day, the last bearers of republican virtue, the chains stood instead for good products at low prices. In the face of these alternatives, the political economy of citizenship was losing its capacity to inspire.[43]

Similar alternatives present themselves today. We might seek to expand the capacity of supranational institutions to control supranational corporations, while simultaneously remedying the democratic deficit that notoriously afflicts such institutions today.[44] But, Sandel suggests, creating transnational institutions that "can inspire the identification and allegiance—the moral and civic culture—on which democratic authority ultimately depends" may be impossible.[45] Historical experience is discouraging, for "even nation-states find it difficult to inspire the sense of community and civic engagement self-government requires. Political associations more expansive than nations, and

at most that one particular identity—womanhood—take precedence over another—nationality. Even Greens can be understood to be asking that our identities as consumers be subordinated to our identities as citizens or, more narrowly, as citizens of particular nations, states, or even neighborhoods.[58]

Further, Sandel acknowledges that some aspects of the cosmopolitan ideal are "attractive."[59] I am puzzled by his insistence that cosmopolitanism is an all-or-nothing identity. Why cannot our political identities, and therefore our public philosophy, be fluid, sometimes expressing the valuable aspects of cosmopolitanism and sometimes expressing our more particular commitments to family, friends, neighbors, nations, ethnic groups, and religious confreres? I admit that these different identities might sometimes conflict, but I do not see why a public philosophy that acknowledges the possibility of internal conflicts, and treats such conflicts as an occasion for political deliberation and struggle, could not inspire the allegiance that Sandel requires. In particular, Sandel's own account suggests that some *economic* dimension of identity—as farmer, as artisan, as professional—may be essential to the construction of an overall public philosophy adequate to deal with the global economy. It seems clear that the identity "consumer" will not do, but it is not clear to me that no alternative identity is possible. Indeed, economic identities in a world of transnational economic arrangements may themselves transcend national boundaries: Farmers in the European Union may have more in common with farmers in the United States than they do with professionals in Germany, for example.[60]

On the penultimate page of *Democracy's Discontent,* Sandel writes that, "[t]he civic virtue distinctive to our time is the capacity to negotiate our way among the sometimes overlapping, sometimes conflicting obligations that claim us, and to live with the tension to which multiple loyalties give rise."[61] The New Social Movements in their transnational forms may satisfy Sandel's description. He can dismiss cosmopolitanism only because he treats it as insisting on the primacy of a universal personhood in all circumstances.

A complex cosmopolitanism, it seems to me, is necessary to eliminate what otherwise seems to be a dramatic mismatch between Sandel's desire to diffuse sovereignty and his acknowledgment of transnational economic power.[62] Simply put, we need an explanation of how diffusing sovereignty downward, for example, to the Kurds and Quebecois, will generate allegiance to transnational institutions, such as the European Union and its equivalents, with enough power to control transnational economic actors. Sandel writes, "In the age of NAFTA, the politics of neighborhood matters more, not less. People will not pledge allegiance to vast and distant entities . . . unless those institutions are somehow connected to political arrangements that reflect the identity of the participants."[63] It remains unclear to me, however, how people are "connected to" transnational institutions except through aspects of the cosmopolitanism that Sandel thinks inadequate. Perhaps the experience of politics in a neighborhood will help shape political character in a way that will make people better participants in the politics of supranational institutions that have become both more democratic and more powerful. But to exercise effective control over transnational corporate power, I would think, people must participate in such institutions as *democrats,* not as Kurds or Quebecois—and to that extent, as cosmopolitans.

No one should be surprised that *Democracy's Discontent* has been as well received as it has been. After all, book reviews in elite newspapers and journals of opinion are written by and for members of the professional-managerial class to which Sandel's analysis would naturally appeal. As a member of that class, I am hardly in a position to say that the anxieties Sandel describes have no foundation whatsoever. If any institutions will ever be able to take control of supranational corporate power, they will need to have the support of the professional-managerial class. Sandel's vision of "multiply encumbered citizens" may allow members of that class to become political allies of the New Social Movements or other more cosmopolitan efforts. His interest in federalism provides an opportunity to examine how that might occur.

7

Notes of A Jewish Episcopalian: Gender as a Language of Class; Religion as a Dialect of Liberalism

JOAN C. WILLIAMS

COMMUNITARIANS have long been intrigued by republicanism as an alternative to a liberalism that is neutral with respect to competing visions of the good life. Michael Sandel's *Democracy's Discontent*[1] is devoted to a rewrite of the American tradition that places republicanism rather than liberalism at the center of our heritage. Sandel's message is that we have fallen from the true path and need to "recover republican ideals."[2]

This romance with republicanism has an odd ring to someone who has already seen it come and go in two different fields: first in history, then in the law reviews. Now it shows up again in political theory. Why the inexorable attraction?

If republicanism had never existed, we would have had to invent it. It is rediscovered with such regularity because it is the only mainstream political vision to offer a historical reference point for those dissatisfied with the flattened version of liberalism that has dominated the last twenty years of US politics. Among US historians, the republican revival was a response to Louis Hartz's picture of the American tradition as an unbroken line of Locke.[3] Law professors in the 1980s turned to republicanism to challenge the image of government as rent-seeking with an image that promised a deliberative conversation on the common good. Sandel turns to republicanism to advocate a communitarian agenda as a return to republican ideals.

Ironically, republicanism helps Sandel but little in his only two chapters on concrete issues. He mentions republicanism infrequently in chapter 3 on the relationship of religion and free speech and in chapter 4 on privacy and family.[4] Indeed, historical republicanism has little to offer on issues of free speech, religion, family responsibilities, and sexual mores.

Special thanks to my colleague Jim May, whose encyclopedic knowledge helped orient me to the historical literature.

It has a lot to offer on another issue Sandel identifies but does not fully develop: whether the sharp, recent increase in income disparities in the USA is compatible with self-government. This is a major issue. Ten percent of Americans now own fully 70 percent of the nation's wealth. The top 1 percent owns about 40 percent of the wealth; in Britain the equivalent number is 18 percent. The lowest-earning fifth of the US population earns roughly 6 percent of all after-tax income; in Finland the equivalent number is nearly twice that high. Japanese manufacturing-company CEOs make an average of ten times more than their workers; top US executives earn 25 times more. "We are the most unequal industrialized country in terms of income and wealth, and we're growing unequal faster than other industrialized countries," according to one noted economist.[5] As the 1980s ended, wage-and-salary earnings were divided more unequally than at any time since 1939.[6]

The traditional language to address such issues is the language of class. But there is no socialism in the United States and no viable language of working-class solidarity. As we delve deeper into American history for a resonant language to protest the unequal distribution of wealth and income, republicanism is an obvious candidate.

This chapter will first contest some aspects of Sandel's description of republicanism, including his contention that it died out. The egalitarian strain Sandel seeks to revive is alive and well and delivering huge mortgage interest deductions to the rich. Republicanism in the contemporary USA has transmuted into the mystique of homeownership, which is extraordinarily strong and generally anti-redistributive. One step in reviving republicanism's redistributive potential is to separate citizenship from homeownership. Another is to highlight republicanism's linkage of character with economic independence—a point Sandel notes, but does not fully focus. A third is to revive attacks on corporate corruption, associated with populism, Progressivism, and other rhetorics that attack misuse of corporate power.

What we need is not a return to the True Way, but a new public discourse that melds republicanism with themes from two sources that are not in the canon of political history. The first is religion: Sandel's initial defense of religion is followed by an eerie silence. The second is domesticity. In an age when "family values" is one of the strongest political rhetorics around, Sandel overlooks the potential of gender as a language of class. While Americans rarely feel entitlements as *workers*, they do feel entitlements as *parents*: domesticity embeds a felt entitlement to a middle-class standard of living that has important potential.

This proposal to meld republicanism with themes from domesticity and religion is controversial, for both religion and domesticity are the subject of strong taboos. Many feminists object that the rhetoric and ideology of domesticity perpetuates stereotypes about women. Using religion as a language of politics is even more risky. Is this legitimate in a multicultural society? I will argue it is, from my viewpoint as someone who believes in religion though not in God, and who sees many liberal themes as thinly secularized retreads of precepts originally stated in religious terms.

Republicanism and Redistribution

> The rich man in his castle,
> The poor man at his gate,
> God made them, high or lowly,
> And ordered their estate.[7]

Because classical republican theory predates Enlightenment liberalism, it assumed the Great Chain of Being most Europeans took for granted before all men were declared equal. In the Great Chain, "angel is set over angel, rank upon rank in the kingdom of heaven; man is set over man, beast over beast, bird over bird. . . : so that there is no worm that crawls upon the ground, no bird that flies on high, no fish that swims in the depths, which the chain of this order does not bind in most harmonious concord."[8] The harmony of society depended on the stability of the Great Chain over time; virtue was defined as fulfilling the obligations of one's "station." Just as men were viewed as physically, mentally, and morally superior to women, the propertied were considered mentally and morally superior to the "mean." The original link between property and character stemmed from the logic of the Great Chain.

Sandel's interpretation of republicanism is not always attuned to its links to hierarchy. The republican tradition "taught that a certain distance between the people and their government was unavoidable, even desirable"[9] not because of their concern for the mediating institutions communitarians rightly value, but because they believed in leaving government to a small subset of the republic's inhabitants ("citizens"). The original elitist republicans sought to preserve the republic by limiting citizenship to the propertied, who had the virtue to pursue the common good. (This was the theory behind the property qualifications of the early republic.)

An alternative strategy is to preserve the republic by distributing property so widely that a broad band of citizens has independence, and therefore the virtue, to pursue the common good. In contrast to the elitist assumption that the poor man's lack of both property and character were evidence of his proper estate, egalitarian republicans stressed how *the lack of property itself* robbed men of the independence they needed to pursue the common good. Sandel tends to stress the theme that, for self-government to work, citizens need a certain moral character. But the profound point of this strain of republicanism is that the widespread distribution of property is a prerequisite for creating the character necessary for self-government.

How true: one need only look at our disenfranchised poor. Whose fault is the "concrete nihilism"[10] of an underclass whose only life options are a lifetime of flipping hamburgers at minimum wage or a short (and often fatal) career in the drug trade? Neither path offers the kind of stable stake in society required for people to act like citizens. When the law professors were celebrating republicanism's potential to promote deliberative conversations in the 1980s, all I could think of was a teenage drug-dealer telling a high-paid law professor that he would join him in selfless deliberation just as soon as society offered him something other than a dead-end job in a violent neighborhood. Civic virtue stems from the reasonable expectation of a respected place in a viable community.

"Dependence begets subservience and venality and suffocates the germ of virtue," wrote Thomas Jefferson.[11] Note the shift away from the Great Chain. The propertyless lack character, Jefferson asserts, only because they lack sufficient property to give them independence. The solution to their lack of virtue is not to bar them from politics but to give them property. Sandel is right to spot the potential power of this argument: it evades a dynamic constructed in the late nineteenth century, in which economists intimated that the only alternative to a capitalist vision of property was socialism, demonized as foreign and subversive.[12] This demonizing strategy has triumphed virtually completely. The charge of socialism is a conversation-stopper; republicanism offers a native American alternative.

It is often said that Thomas Jefferson, along with most other republicans, opposed outright redistribution: after all, property could not provide men with sustained independence if it could be redistributed at will. This is true, but irrelevant. Jefferson opposed redistribution because he felt it unnecessary in a country without the extremes of wealth and poverty that existed in Europe. Said Jefferson in France in 1785:

> Whenever there is in any country uncultivated lands and unemployed poor, it is clear that the laws of property have been so far extended as to violate natural right. The earth is given as a common stock for man to labour and live on. If, for the encouragement of industry we allow it to be appropriated, we must take care that other employment be furnished to those excluded from the appropriation. . . . It is too soon yet in our country to say that every man who cannot find employment but who can find uncultivated land, shall be at liberty to cultivate it, paying a moderate rent. But it is not too soon to provide by every possible means that as few as possible shall be without a little portion of land. The small landowners are the most precious part of a state.[13]

Today we have such extremes that some citizens sleep in their own urine on the streets of one of the richest societies of the world.

Although Jefferson opposed outright redistribution, that approach is not feasible in the USA today, even assuming it to be desirable. The two feasible approaches take less direct methods of the sort Jefferson envisioned. One is a return to openly redistributive taxation; according to historian Stanley Katz, Jefferson floated an early proposal for a progressive income tax.[14] The other is a redesign of tax and inheritance laws that now allow massive accumulations of wealth—the contemporary equivalents of the legal rules Jefferson abolished in Virginia (primogeniture and the fee tail), which had provided the legal infrastructure for intergenerational transmission of the Great Chain.

The egalitarian republicanism Sandel seeks found later expression in the Homestead Act of 1862, designed to carry out Jefferson's principle of equality: that every time the government is involved in land distribution it should distribute land in "small portions." Surely its most poignant expression was the freedmen's cry of "forty acres and a mule." Why did the former slaves assume that full citizenship would include the means to achieve economic independence? This republican vision was still part of the vernacular. It transmuted into populism and (in a very different way) into Progressivism.[15]

Sandel overlooks contemporary work with republican resonance. Take a recent *New York Times Magazine* article in which the economist Lester Thurow starts with economic data documenting the sharp rise in inequality in the USA. He notes that the net worth of the richest Americans rose sharply between 1983 and 1989, and that by the early 1990s, the top 1 percent of Americans held about twice as much of the national wealth as they had held between roughly 1929 (when the progressive income tax was introduced) and 1974. He asks:

> When 1 percent of the population owns 49 percent of wealth, where is our sense of community? When the 45 percent of the people on the bottom own only 2 percent of the wealth, what do we mean by democracy?[16]

He concludes: "These are uncharted waters for American democracy," and argues that the skewed distribution of property is incompatible with self-government.

A more explicit use of the republican themes appears in one of the most cited law review articles ever written, Charles Reich's "The New Property." Writing in 1964, Reich argued that "new property" such as government benefits and licenses should be accorded the constitutional protection traditionally granted to "old" property like cash and land. To justify his radical widening of the concept of property, Reich mixed the liberal language of privacy with language from the republican egalitarian strain, as he advocated a move "Towards Individual Stakes in the Commonwealth":

> The aim of [the new property] is to preserve the self-sufficiency of the individual, to rehabilitate him where necessary, and to allow him to be a valuable member of a family and a community; in theory they represent part of the individual's rightful share in the commonwealth. . . . Above all, the time has come for us to remember what the framers of the Constitutions knew so well—that "a power over a man's subsistence amounts to a power over his will." . . . Just as the Homestead Act was a deliberate effort to foster individual values at an earlier time, so we must try to build an economic basis for liberty today—a Homestead Act for rootless twentieth century man.[17]

The most resonant republican theme today is the mystique of homeownership, which is imperfectly redistributive to say the least. When Americans talk about homeownership, they project their feelings about the linkage of ownership and citizenship onto a single, very expensive type of housing. "No greater contribution could be made to the stability of the Nation, and the advancement of its ideals, than to make it a Nation of homeowning families." (Calvin Coolidge). "[T]oo much cannot be said about the value of stimulating home ownership because of its effect on good citizenship and the strengthening of family ties." (President Hoover's Conference Report on Home Building and Home Ownership). "A nation of home owners, of people who own a real share in their own land, is unconquerable." (Franklin Roosevelt).[18] A recent study by FNMA found that "Americans would sacrifice just about anything to own a home—it is one of their highest priorities in life."[19] The huge subsidies for single-family housing after the Second World War are another expression of this cultural fact of life: the USA has one of the highest rates of homeownership in the world, in significant part because of VA and FHA loans and the huge and continuing mortgage interest deduction. [20]

Americans use republican language to explain why they are so fixated on single-family homes. The FNMA survey found that, for many Americans, homeownership "is a metaphor for *personal* and *family* security. . . . the sum total of the findings in this survey suggest that owning one's home is, in essence, an empowering act, giving people a stake in society and a sense of control over their own lives. Put differently, homeownership strengthens the social fabric." Clearly, the mystique of homeownership carries on republican themes, such as the notion that property offers a stable stake in society, and the notion that owners make good citizens. The special place of homeownership also emerges strongly in American case law on public and private land use controls, where, by and large, it serves the cause of exclusion—upholding owners' rights to keep their neighborhoods homogeneous. The republican instinct to protect the best by excluding the rest emerges in clear focus.

Republicanism is alive and well and delivering huge subsidies to the rich; the question is how to mobilize it for nobler goals. One key lies in linking republican themes with themes from domesticity.

The Redistributive Potential of "Family Values"

The ideology of domesticity traditionally is dated to between 1780 and 1830—although, like so many other secular themes, it probably began much earlier, as a religious one.[21] It replaced the (Great Chain) ideology of gender inferiority with the notion that men and women were equal in their separate spheres: men in the public sphere of market work; women in the private sphere of the home. In place of the old image of women as morally inferior, domesticity asserted that women in fact were *more* moral than men. Whereas men were the self-interested actors of liberal individualism, women were the Moral Mothers whose selflessness was a model for their families and for the world.

Ruth Bloch has documented the complex process by which virtue ceased to be associated with the manly *virtú* required for citizenship in the virile republic, and was associated instead with feminine virtues in the private sphere of the home. Bloch corrects the view that the demise of republican *virtú* led to a culture bereft of virtue. Instead, the virtue republicanism associated with the public sphere was relocated in family life.[22]

The mystique of homeownership blends the republican themes with themes from domesticity: recall the Hoover Conference report extolling homeownership's "effect on good citizenship *and the strengthening of family ties*" (emphasis added). During the course of the nineteenth century, domesticity emerged as a language of politics that linked the future of the republic with good citizens raised in stable homes. The current fervor for "family values" is only the most recent expression of domesticity as a language of politics. A key force behind Progressivism and the beginning of social welfare programs in the USA were women who argued they were doing "social housekeeping."[23]

Domesticity's political role stems from its "*cri de coeur* against modern work relations."

> In accentuating the split between "work" and "home" and proposing the latter as a place of salvation, the canon of domesticity tacitly acknowledged the capacity of modern work to desecrate the human spirit. Authors of domestic literature, especially the female authors, denigrated business and politics as arenas of selfishness, exertion, embarrassment, and degradation of soul. These rhetoricians suggested what Marx's analysis of alienated labor in the 1840s would assert, that "the worker . . . feels at ease only outside work, and during work he is outside himself. . . ."[24]

Women's role was to provide a refuge from "that bank note world": "women's self-renunciation was called upon to remedy men's self-alienation." To this day, domesticity offers an internal critique of capitalism that avoids the perceived stridency of radical discourse: it is a Marxism you can bring home to mother.[25]

The most common political use of domesticity is to defend traditional notions of family life as crucial to the survival of the republic. But domesticity can also function as a language of class entitlement. From the beginning domesticity had ties to class. Indeed, it crystallized in early nineteenth-century America as the gender strategy by which the middle class differentiated itself from the working class.[26] Keeping an Angel in the Home cost money: what made it possible was a middle-class salary.

In the nineteenth century, the reasons for keeping mothers home were openly classist. "Ladies" did not work, so any married woman who did jeopardized her own status as a lady and her husband's status as a stolid bourgeois. Middle- and upper-class women did not stay home for lack of child care, which was delegated to the servants who were another signal of middle-class status. Instead, they stayed home as a signal of their social status. Today the rationales have changed for domesticity's pattern of the man-in-the-market/women-at-home. At-home mothers today typically give two reasons for domesticity. One is that they value caregiving over the "rat race"; this translates directly back into nineteenth-century Angels valuing selflessness more than "that bank note world."[27] The other contemporary rationale is new: they do not want their children "raised by strangers."[28]

Upon reflection, this is an odd formulation. The person who takes care of your children every day is certainly not a stranger, either to them or to you. What the formulation signals is that children *should* be taken care of by family members, a central norm of contemporary domesticity I have called the norm of parental care.[29]

The radical potential of this norm is that, although American workers often do not feel many entitlements as *workers*, they do feel entitlements as *parents*. Partly these relate to time: witness GM strikes protesting too much mandatory overtime.[30] Workers complain they have no time for family life: the sense that children are entitled to see their parents becomes the basis for challenging the great American speed-up employers use to amortize benefit dollars over the maximum possible number of hours.

It would not have occurred to industrial workers in the nineteenth century that they were entitled to an ideal of family life that was, at that time, still overtly identified with the middle class. But today domesticity has been democratized, so it can be used by workers to demand an entitlement to a standard of childrearing once reserved for the relatively privileged.

Women workers are insistent that their employers should accommodate their "needs as mothers."[31] This can translate into resistance to mandatory overtime, demands for personal time off to care for infants or sick children, for doctors' appointments or the school play. It may even translate into demands for health benefits and decent wages, on the grounds that someone who works hard is entitled to a decent standard of living for her children. In addition, women's sense of children's needs and their own vulnerability, in our system of providing for children's care by marginalizing their caregivers, makes them far more willing to demand a significantly larger role for government in providing social benefits. What political analysts call the "gender gap" contains a profound message: the "fact" that Americans don't like big government is a more accurate description of American men than American women. "Over the past sixteen years men have become much more antigovernment; women have not."[32]

Public opinion surveys find acute concern over the impact of working conditions on family life. When the respondents to one survey were asked to rate the accuracy of thirteen descriptions of the economy, the most widely endorsed concerned pressures on the family. Nearly three-fourths of all respondents said that "reducing stress on working families with policies like flexible hours and affordable child care" would be a very effective way of improving their economic situation. Concerns over the pressures on families outweighed even people's desire for increased salaries and concerns over layoffs.[33]

Unions are beginning to use gender as a language of class both in organizing and in their efforts to turn out the vote in national political campaigns. Consider the following ad:

> SOME POLITICIANS DON'T KNOW MUCH.
> THEY DON'T KNOW WHAT IT'S LIKE SAVING FOR BOTH AN EDUCATION
> AND AN ELECTRIC BILL
> THEY DON'T KNOW SECOND MORTGAGES, SECOND SHIFTS OR SECOND-HAND
> THEY CERTAINLY DON'T KNOW THE PRICE OF
> MACARONI AND CHEESE
> OR HOW TOUGH IT IS TO FIND A GOOD JOB.
> OR HOW TOUGH IT IS TO LOSE ONE.
> AT THE END OF THE DAY, THE HEALTH CARE PROBLEM ISN'T CRYING IN THEIR LAPS.
> THE ECONOMY ISN'T ASKING THEM FOR
> A NEW PAIR OF SNEAKERS. . .
> PLEASE VOTE[34]

Note that two of the three items in big type (i.e. electric bill, macaroni and cheese, sneekers) are explicitly related to children. The ad shrinks down traditional political issues and rhetoric (health care, the economy) and pops out the message that voters should vote a redistributive agenda to protect their children. Family values have tremendous redistributive potential.

Religion and Redistribution

The use of domesticity as a political language will be controversial. Some feminists argue that any use of the gendered imagery of domesticity perpetuates its claims about the special role and responsibilities of mothers. They are probably right.

But consider the alternative. If feminists do not use the rhetoric of domesticity, its extraordinary power will be used *only* to target gays and keep women in the home. The grip of domesticity is so profound that the only realistic strategy is to transform it from within, to turn arguments for why women should remain in the home into demands to employers and the government to spread the costs of childrearing instead of privatizing them onto the women and children who represent 77 percent of those in poverty.[35]

Using religion as a language of politics is even more controversial than using domesticity. Is it appropriate to bring religion into the public square? The recent resurgence of religious rhetoric in political discourse is nothing new: religion has long functioned as a language of politics. Examples range from the abolitionists to the Gettysburg Address, the biblical imagery of Martin Luther King to the social gospel of Walter Rauschenbusch and Jane Adams, to the recent sanctuary movement for Salvadorian refugees.[36]

The only instance in American history of an open and immediate redistribution of property—the abolition of slavery—stemmed from the religious argument that slavery was a sin; they burned the Constitution because of its compromise on slavery.[37] Another rare moment where an American advocated immediate redistribution was when Thomas Skidmore melded egalitarian republicanism with religious language in early nineteenth-century New York. Skidmore was a machinist, one of the working-class "mechanics" who appropriated republican arguments, to argue that craftsmen like themselves were citizens with the independence to think and act free of the restraints of others. "Each competent master appeared, in his workshop relations, as the quintessence of independence, free to exercise his virtue uncorrupted. . . ."[38]

Skidmore, who enjoyed brief political success as the leader of the Working Men of 1829, married republican egalitarian language with language from religion. Starting from the premise that souls had an identical relationship with "the Creator," he reasoned each had an equal claim to the Creator's endowment.

> Is the work of creation to be let out on hire? And are the great mass of mankind to be hirelings to those who undertake to set up a claim, as the government is now constructed, that the world was made for them? Why not sell the winds of heaven, that man might not breathe without price? Why not sell the light of the sun, that a man should not see without making another rich?[39]

Skidmore argued for immediate redistribution, after which, according to historian Sean Wilentz, "men and women, of all races . . . would be permitted to labor as they chose, in splendid cooperative independence, each with an equal stake of property."[40]

The equality rhetoric Skidmore used usually is associated with liberalism. In Skidmore we see it in its original religious form. Locke himself derived the "self-evident truth" that all men are created equal from the principle that all are God's servants: "For Men being all the workmanship of one Omnipotent, and infinitely wise Maker; All the Servants of one Sovereign Master, sent into the World by his order and about his business. . . . And being furnished with like Faculties, sharing all in one Community of Nature, there cannot be supposed any such *Subordination* among us."[41]

Locke secularized the principle of the equal dignity of souls to undercut the Great Chain. Today the language of equality coexists in two dialects: one secular, one religious. What appears in modern analyses as "the political use of religious language" is often the use of equality rhetoric in its religious rather than its liberal formulation.

Carrying through with this analysis yields some intriguing results. A central Western impulse is to model ethical thought around the heuristic of "putting yourself in someone else's shoes." The single most influential formulation is the Golden Rule to "Love your neighbor as yourself." (Mark 12: 31).[42] Kant's categorical imperative to "act according to that maxim by which you can at the same time will that it should become a universal law" can be viewed as a thinly secularized retread; as can Rawls's original position, which proposes the ground rule that no one will know in what social position he will end up, presumably on the theory that such a rule will encourage one to treat one's neighbor as oneself.[43]

This is the kind of "analysis of deep structures" that has all the strengths and limitations of the structuralism that was popular in the 1970s. While the parallels are instructive, we need not forget the marked differences between the Gospel of Mark, the categorical imperative, and the original position. The point is not that each formulation is the same, but that "the moral intuitions of those who are not religiously committed have been influenced by centuries of Christianity . . ."[44]

The legal literature on the use of religious language in political discourse starts from the assumption that a sharp distinction exists between religious and other forms of political argument. For some purposes they *are* very different: the golden rule and the categorical imperative, for example, rest on very different kinds of justifications. In other contexts religious and secular language seem like dialects of the same language. Equality rhetoric provides one example.

Another is a theme I call the liberal dignity strain, the argument that property rights should be limited to the extent they sully human dignity. This strain emerges in landmark law reform cases that abruptly limit landlords' rights where property is used to sully the dignity of tenants. One example is *State* v. *Shack*, in which the New Jersey Supreme Court held that a landowner could not bar entrance to government workers offering medical and legal help to farmworkers.[45] The court's opinion uses the language of human dignity and cites the Golden Rule (!) to hold that the government workers did not trespass because the farmer had no right to exclude them in the first place. *Hilder* v. *St. Peter* is another example.[46] There the Supreme Court of Vermont required a landlord to refund all rent previously paid, and awarded future tenants punitive damages. The opinion uses thick description to show graphically how Mrs. Hilder's apartment stank so of sewage that she felt humiliated, and was in such a dangerous condition that her children and grandchildren were placed at risk.

The liberal dignity strain also emerges strongly in the commodification debates over whether to replace the current adoption system with a market for babies and to allow the sale of human organs.[47] Opponents of commodification often argue that both proposals constitute an affront to human dignity. Though intellectuals typically frame this in liberal, Kantian terms,[48] nearly a decade of teaching the commodification debates to a large, first-year property class has shown me that many Americans articulate this intuition in religious rather than liberal language. One student attacked the proposal for a market for human organs on the grounds that "you don't own your body." When I asked who does, he silently pointed up.

Why silently? As we all know, speaking in openly religious terms in intellectual contexts is embarrassing at best, and intellectually discrediting at worst. Historians of religion have studied the process whereby religious language went from being a lingua franca of educated people to a taboo among them.[49] This taboo remains strong; it affected Sandel's book. Consider his response to the libertarian argument that redistributive policies use some people as means to others' ends. "What egalitarian liberalism requires, but cannot within its own terms provide, is some way of defining the relevant community of sharing, some way of seeing the participants as mutually indebted and morally engaged to begin with. It needs a way of answering Emerson's challenge to the man who solicited his contribution to the poor—'Are they *my* poor?' "[50]

Sandel overestimates the resources of republicanism in providing an answer to this question. While republicanism does not, Christianity does. "For the poor shall never cease out of the land: therefore, I command thee, saying, Thou shalt open thine hand wide unto thy brother, to thy poor, and thy needy, in thy land" (Deut. 15: 11). "For I was hungry, and ye gave me food. . . . [A]s ye did it not to one of the least of these, ye did it not to me" (Matt. 25: 35–45). Jesus spent his time consorting with lepers and prostitutes precisely to send the message that the poor are our poor.

According to a survey conducted by *The Nation* (of all places), two-thirds of those active in social movements in the USA draw principally on religious motivation for their involvement.[51] "How we treat the least among us—the least important, the least appealing, the least wanted—is the most important test in the Judeo-Christian tradition."[52]

"No one may claim the name Christian and be comfortable in the face of hunger, hopelessness, insecurity, and the injustice found in this country and around the world," said the National Conference of Catholic Bishops in a pastoral letter to guide those "trying to live their faith in the market place." Every economic decision and institution, they argued, "must be judged in light of whether it protects or undermines the dignity of the human person." Said another religious leader during the recent health-care debate, "Jesus didn't say *some* of you will be fed. Jesus said *all* of you will be fed. . . . 'Have they no knowledge, all the evildoers, who eat up my people as they eat bread?' "[53]

One context where lawyers have thought a lot about the power of religious language is in death-penalty cases. "Most Americans . . . define life's ultimate moral questions in religious terms and in terms of virtue and personal moral responsibility," said leading death-penalty lawyer Kevin Doyle.

> For those of you who have yet to locate the gift of faith, I am not suggesting you have to return to your church or synagogue. I am suggesting that you cheat your client when you kid yourself about the moral language your jurors speak or refuse to learn it yourself. So go out and study a children's Bible or try to remember what your parents taught you as a kid. But meet the jury in the moral world it occupies.[54]

An upper-middle-class woman, separated from her husband in the situation that clearly spelled domestic violence, received a visit from her neighbor, a devout middle-aged black woman with seven children. Her neighbor told her, unsolicited, that she had left her husband despite her seven children and no visible means of support, because Jesus had come to her in a vision and told her that she needed to leave, because she loved her husband more than herself. She left.

From a postmodern perspective where all is metaphor, it makes no sense to refuse to use the metaphoric that works best. In a culture with few viable redistributive rhetorics, religion has tremendous potential for building cross-class and cross-race coalitions.

Is this manipulative? To me it feels not cynical but respectful. As a nonfoundationalist who believes "it is turtles all the way down," to embrace the Judeo-Christian tradition as a metaphoric rather than as literal truth is not to rank it second-rate. It is a key source of the metaphors we live by; it has helped make us who we are. Indeed, it seems profligate to throw away the metaphoric through which Bach and Schubert accessed spiritual life. Though I do not accept the transcendental claims of Christianity, I feel about them much the way I feel about most other transcendental claims, from the picture theory of knowledge to the ideal speech situation. They simply do not interest me. They seem beside the point.

Many near-misses with embarrassment have taught me that this approach feels odd to most Christians. The reason it feels so right to me contains a message about the complex patterns of loyalty and betrayal that characterize our relation to tradition.

Although my father was an Episcopalian, my maternal grandfather was a reform rabbi (German-Jewish: I joke I am Episcopalian twice). I have found that, though most Christians have trouble understanding my relationship to religion, many Jews do not. The idea of being loyal to a tradition and an identity but uninterested in its transcendental claims makes sense to many intellectual Jews. To them—as to me—it reads as loyalty, not betrayal.

If one approaches religion in this spirit, it is easier to see a role for religious rhetoric in public life. This is particularly true when one combines this viewpoint with the notion that our moral intuitions are shaped by rhetorics that often coexist in religious and secular form. To be sure, one must make sure that the values one is tapping do exist in both formulations: this may be a good first test for determining whether it belongs in the public square. "[M]any elements and aspects of a religious ethic . . . can be presented in public discussion in ways that do not presume assent to them on the specific premises of a faith grounded in revelation."[55] Michael Perry has called this the test of "public accessibility."[56]

A new rhetoric of redistribution could meld republican and domestic themes with the liberal dignity strain and the sense that the poor are our poor. A final religious form with redistributive potential is the jeremiad.

Why do Americans feel so financially pressed that they readily respond to "no new taxes"? Different classes do for different reasons. But it is clear that Americans of all social groups have a bad case of consumerism. Once I asked a public defender why her clients stole. "Simple," she said, "they have a bad case of the wants." So does the rest of American society. Recent studies show that the standard of material goods Americans now expect far exceeds what they did thirty years ago.[57] When John Kenneth Galbraith called us the "Affluent Society" in 1958, less than 10 percent of US households had air conditioning, about 4 percent had dishwashers, and fewer than 15 percent had more than one car. By 1980, when Ronald Reagan won the presidency based on the pervasive sense that people were suffering economically, the percentage of homes with air conditioning had quintupled, the percentage with dishwashers had increased more than 700 percent, and the percentage with two or more cars had nearly tripled.[58]

This expanded sense of material "needs" is a major component of the dynamic of rich and poor in the USA. To address it, we need a jeremiad against materialism. Religious rhetoric is effective, although the most effective contemporary jeremiads need not be religious. Juliet Schor's *The Overworked American* is a classic jeremiad in secular form. Her diatribe against "the insidious cycle of work and spend" argues that Americans are caught in "capitalism's squirrel cage" where they work sharply longer hours than they did a generation ago, only to "shop til they drop" of stress and sheer exhaustion. Her message is not framed in explicitly spiritual terms. Instead, the focus is on the price Americans pay in terms of their own health—and their children's well-being: the norm of parental care reemerges again.[59]

Schor's analytical frame of reference is the Marxist tradition, but she deftly uses a religious form and a gendered norm to avoid Marxist language. The result was a bestseller excoriating contemporary capitalism, and arguing in favor of the "rational, and humane solution—reducing hours to spread the work."[60] Schor's jeremiad has been joined by another recent bestseller extolling the virtues of the stripped-down life. *Your Money or Your Life*, by Joe Dominguez and Vicki Robin, has the peppy tone and format of a self-help book, but the authors recommend a "A Spiritual Discipline" in cutting down on expenditures by deflating material "needs."[61] The authors urge their readers to live a spiritually fulfilling life they will not regret upon their death, not trading off serenity for more Nikes. The advantage of an openly religious jeremiad, as death-penalty litigators have recognized, is its ability to tap profound emotions and spiritual aspirations, to offer something more filling than is available in self-help form.[62]

Jeremiads, whether explicitly religious or not, can be melded with populist protests against the abuse of corporate power, long part of the American republican tradition. Sandel discusses Jacksonian and Progressive variants but omits the strongest contemporary forms, which carry on Populist excoriations of "big business" and fat corporations.[63] A recent issue of *Newsweek* showed mug shots of some of the nation's top CEOs who have cut thousands of jobs to raise their stock prices, with the caption "Corporate Killers."[64] This is a powerful rhetoric: think of the impact it has had in tort law in redistributing the costs of product defects from individual accident victims to the deep pockets of manufacturers. Thus far, its potential has not yet been fully realized.[65]

Republicanism in Solution

Sandel's book begins the important work of identifying plausible redistributive rhetorics to help in achieving communitarian goals. But he missed an important point: that republicanism has always existed in solution, not as a pure precipitate.[66] The revival Sandel seeks can best be accomplished by melding republican egalitarian arguments linking self-government with the widespread distribution of property, with arguments that enable the working poor and working class to claim domesticity's middle-class ideals of family life, and arguments (in either religious or secularized variants) that insist that the poor are our poor, that property rights should be limited where they present a threat to human dignity, and that Americans need to reassess their microwave lives.

III

Liberal Republicanism

8

A Defense of Minimalist Liberalism

RICHARD RORTY

MICHAEL SANDEL'S *Democracy's Discontent: America in Search of a Public Philosophy* is an instructive and insightful account of some of the tensions within our political history. But I have doubts both about the philosophical assumptions which frame Sandel's historical narrative and about his diagnosis of our present troubles.

I shall first take up some passages in his book at which these philosophical assumptions emerge, grouping them under four headings: liberty, selfhood, truth, and sentiment. Then I shall briefly describe the difference between his and my ways of viewing recent American political and social history.

Liberty

Sandel sees liberals and republicans as disagreeing about the nature of freedom, or liberty. Republicans believe that liberty "depends on sharing in self-government."[1] Liberals believe that it consists in "the capacity of persons to choose their values and ends." On Sandel's account,

> The voluntarist conception of freedom promises to lay to rest, once and for all, the risks of republican politics. If liberty can be detached from the exercise of self-government and conceived instead as the capacity of persons to choose their own ends, then the difficult task of forming civic virtue can finally be dispensed with.[2]

The way Sandel sets up the quarrel between liberals and republicans seems to me factitious. Most people nowadays believe *both* that a free society is one in which citizens participate in government, *and* that it is one in which people are, within the limits Mill defined, left alone to choose their own values and ends. They see no need to choose between these two definitions. Any society that does not meet *both* requirements, they think, hardly deserves to be called "free."

Another problem I have with the passage I have quoted is that I cannot think of a liberal who would want either to "detach liberty from the exercise of self-government," or to "dispense with the difficult task of forming civic virtue." Kant, Mill, and Dewey do not fit either description. Rawls, I assume, wants the state to do its best to inculcate the civic virtue of taking the right to be prior to the good. I cannot imagine any of these thinkers claiming that the risks of republican politics can ever be avoided.

My main reaction to this passage, however, is that the level of abstraction at which we pose questions like "in what does liberty consist?" or "what does 'freedom' really mean?" is too high to do us any good. I think that philosophers and political scientists should resist the temptation to ascend to that level. Unlike Sandel, I do not think that America is "in search of a public philosophy." It is certainly in search of a moral identity. But I do not think that such an identity can be acquired by getting clearer about the meanings of terms like "liberty."

The Self

I am what Sandel calls a "minimalist liberal." As he says, "minimalist liberalism frees politics from moral philosophy."[3] We minimalists, as he also says, "argue that the case for liberalism is political, not philosophical or metaphysical, and so does not depend on controversial claims about the nature of the self."

By contrast, Sandel thinks that you cannot get very far in political theory without thinking hard about the nature of the self. The philosophical portions of his new book revolve around a distinction between encumbered and unencumbered selves. An encumbered self has built-in ends, needs, wants, and purposes. An unencumbered self sits back and chooses those ends, needs, wants, and purposes. It is "prior" to them.

According to Sandel, "if the self is not prior to its ends, then the right is not prior to the good."[4] In other words, unless there are unencumbered selves, Rawls is wrong. Sandel argues that there are no such selves, and I entirely agree with him. But I think that this admission leaves Rawls unscathed.

One reason I am a minimalist is that I think liberals should not allow themselves to be encumbered with the idea of a self which is prior to its ends—an existentialist, Californian, self which can somehow sit back and choose ends, values, and affiliations without reference to anything except its own momentary pleasure. This existentialist self seems to me as much a myth as the Kantian noumenal self, the one which can hear nothing but the unconditional call of duty. Both myths presuppose the triad of faculties (reason, will, and appetite) which has unfortunately become canonical, a triad which goes back to Plato's mischievous hierarchy of parts of the soul.

If liberals allow Sandel to saddle them with the notion of a naked will—one which chooses ends and affiliations just because they take its fancy—then they will of course look light-minded and unreflective. But we minimalist liberals do not need a theory of the self to make a distinction between more reflective and less reflective people. We can just say that you get more reflective people, people better suited for the responsibilities of self-government, whenever you provide more education, security, and leisure. This is not a philosophical point, but just the empirical observation that people who enjoy more of these three goods are better able to consider alternative scenarios for their personal futures, and for the future of their societies. They are more patient, tolerant, and imaginative, and so are better citizens of a democracy.

On my view, there is no need to break the self down into faculties. It suffices to view the self as a network of beliefs and desires. All selves are always already equally encumbered, but some of them are encumbered with good beliefs and desires and some with bad ones. None of them are more willful or more rational or more appetitive than others, but some of them have affiliations which make them more apt for democratic citizenship than would other affiliations. An affiliation with a fundamentalist church, for example, makes them less apt for such citizenship than does an affiliation with an extended family, a trade union, or a bowling league. That is why Rawls had to exclude religious fanatics from the original position.

I agree with Rawls that the right should, for political purposes, be thought of as prior to the good. But I think that the argument for doing so—for preferring what Sandel calls "procedural republics" to other regimes—is merely historical, not philosophical. Procedural republics are those in which as few answers to substantial moral questions—as few views about the Good for Man—are built into political institutions as possible. Such republics have the best track record among the regimes which we have tried so far.

Truth

The topic of truth comes up when Sandel says that liberals who want to put everything up for political compromise sometimes try to "bracket" questions about the existence of witches, or about whether human life begins at conception. They do this, Sandel says, because "one way of assuring the priority of the practical is to deny that any of the moral or religious conceptions it brackets could be true." "But," he rightly objects, "this is precisely the sort of controversial metaphysical claim the minimalist liberal wants to avoid."

I quite agree, and that is why I think we minimalist liberals should never deny that any intelligible statement can be true. We should not try to divide culture up into the cognitive part, where there is a fact of the matter, and the noncognitive part, where there is not. James and Dewey did yeoman service in fuzzing up the cognitive-vs.-noncognitive distinction, and we should continue to keep it fuzzy.

Sandel, however, thinks that if we minimalist liberals do not take refuge in noncognitivity we shall have a big problem. He states the problem in a rhetorical question:

If the liberal must . . . allow that some such conceptions might be true, then what is to assure that none can generate interests sufficiently compelling to burst the brackets, so to speak, and morally outweigh the practical interest in social cooperation?[5]

The answer to that question will be the same no matter what one says about truth: namely, *nothing* could possibly guarantee that there may not be interests, beliefs and desires sufficiently compelling to outweigh the practical interest in social cooperation. We should stop hoping for such guarantees, and for philosophies which will somehow provide them.

Beliefs about transubstantiation or miscegenation, or about the legitimacy of slavery or of abortion, may indeed, for certain people at certain times, outweigh their practical interest in social cooperation. Sometimes people cannot live with themselves unless they draw a line in the sand. Their moral identity demands that if their community begins to tolerate heresy, or to permit slavery, then they must emigrate, or foment a revolution, or otherwise break off their participation in the political process. Sometimes a whole segment of society needs to draw a line in the sand. Then we get civil war, or secession.

I take the pragmatist, minimalist liberal, position to be: try to educate the citizenry in the civic virtue of having as few such compelling interests, beliefs, and desires as possible. Try, for example, to get them to change the subject from "When does human life begin?" to "How can some unprincipled and wishy-washy consensus about abortion be hammered out?" Try to get them to be as flexible and wishy-washy as possible, and to value democratic consensus more than they value almost anything else. Try to make them as little inclined to emigrate or secede as possible, by encouraging them to tolerate compromise on matters which they previously thought uncompromisable.

Notice that this position has nothing to do with the nature or the extent of truth. It does not say that there is no truth about moral and religious questions. It does not say that they are matters of opinion rather than knowledge. It says instead: try to raise as few moral and religious questions as you can manage. Try to replace as many such questions as possible with political questions. Minimalist liberalism does not say that morality and religion are noncognitive, or somehow epistemologically or metaphysically second-rate. It just tries to deflect attention from all questions other than "what sort of compromise might we be able freely to agree upon?" The procedural republic tries to instill in its citizens the virtues of compromise and tolerance, and to educate them out of other virtues (those of the warrior or the nun, for example)—the kind of virtues which might get in the way of compromise and tolerance.

Sandel is of course right that there are some questions, such as slavery, about which we twentieth-century Americans cannot tolerate compromise. Rawls would agree that any procedural republic has to have some moral backbone: agreement on procedure cannot be all that keeps the community together. But Rawls wants this moral backbone to be, so to speak, as thin and flexible as possible. We minimalists think that there is no point in asking philosophers to figure out how thin is too thin, nor how flexible is too flexible. For those too are practical questions. Democracies make political decisions about what principles to compromise. Philosophers then clean up the mess by formulating new principles which justify having compromised the old principles.

Sentiment

Sandel says that:

> It is sometimes argued, in defense of the liberal view, that loyalties and allegiances not grounded in consent, however psychologically compelling, are matters of sentiment, not morality, and so do not suggest an obligation unavailable to unencumbered selves. But it is difficult to make sense of certain familiar moral and political dilemmas without recognizing obligations of solidarity, and the thickly-constituted, encumbered selves that they imply.[6]

To illustrate this latter point, Sandel says of Robert E. Lee's decision to fight for Virginia rather than for the Union that:

> one cannot make sense of his dilemma as a *moral* dilemma without acknowledging that the call to stand with his people, even to lead them in a cause he opposed, was a claim of moral and not merely sentimental import, capable at least of weighing in the balance against other duties and obligations.[7]

As a pragmatist, and as an opponent of faculty psychology, I reject the "merely" in the phrase "moral and not merely sentimental import." I reject the Kantian suggestion that sentiment is too low down on the scale of human faculties to impose moral obligations. I entirely agree that we have obligations which spring from solidarity, but I think that solidarity is created by educating our sentiments. As I see it, a procedural republic instills virtuous habits in its citizen by arranging for them to experience what Hume called "a progress of sentiments" (a phrase recently revived by Annette Baier). So when Sandel says that we liberals who have a merely "cooperative" vision of community cannot meet Nozickian objections to redistributivist policies, I should reply that we meet them by telling sob stories about what happens to the poor in nonredistributivist societies. The answer to Nozick is not Aristotle or Augustine or Kant, but, for example, the writings of William Julius Wilson, and the autobiographies of kids who grew up in urban ghettos.

I agree with Sandel that it is not enough to reply to the libertarian that "social and economic rights are required as a matter of equal respect for persons." Sandel is right that "the question remains why *these* persons, the ones who happen to live in my country, have a claim on my concern that others do not." I think that this is a general objection to all Kantian accounts of moral education, all attempts at moral education which propose to rely on what Kantians like to call "reason alone," and to abjure an appeal to sentiment. Moral education, I think, is sentimental or nothing.

I agree with Sandel that Kantian talk about equal respect for persons cannot create the necessary solidarity. Utilitarian talk about the advantages for each egotistical individual of social cooperation cannot do it either. As far as I can see, only soppy sentimentality can. Annette Baier seems right in suggesting that it would be better to use "justified trust" rather than "obligation" as the basic moral concept. Doing so would help us to stop distinguishing between heavyweight selves, encumbered with moral obligations, and lightweight selves, blissfully free of such encumbrances. We would instead distinguish between distrustful (and therefore somewhat untrustworthy) people and trusting (and therefore somewhat trustworthy) people. Trustworthy and decent people and untrustworthy sociopaths are equally encumbered. But the former are encumbered with a more desirable set of beliefs and desires than the latter.

I agree with Sandel that we admire people like Lee for "the quality of character their deliberation reflects," and that the quality at stake is the disposition to see and bear one's life circumstance as a reflectively situated being—claimed by the history that implicates me in a particular life, but self-conscious of its particularity, and so alive to other ways, wider horizons.[8] It was precisely this quality that I called "irony" in my *Contingency, Irony and Solidarity*. It is a quality which is fostered, as it was in Lee's case, by education, security, and leisure. I do not think that the state can do much to instill irony in its citizens, apart from creating these fostering conditions. But there is a lot that sentimental films, novels, and TV shows can do.

I agree with Sandel that the desirable quality Lee exhibited is unlikely to occur in "those who think of themselves as "unencumbered selves", and who construe their agency as a choice that is "purely preferential" or "radically free."[9] But, apart from a few philosophically minded twits, I have never met anybody who thinks of himself like that. I suspect that such people exist only in the imagination of existentialist philosophers, and perhaps in the fantasies of the authors of self-help books. Whatever else may be wrong with Rawls's doctrine that the right is prior to the good, it is not a doctrine that has any existentialist presuppositions or implications.

To urge that the right be made prior to the good is, among other things, to suggest that trust in people wishy-washy enough to make tactful, unprincipled, political compromises is often, ironically enough, preferable to trust in one's initial moral and religious convictions. Obviously, it is not *always* preferable. But no amount of theoretical sophistication will help you decide when it is preferable and when not.

American History

So much for philosophy. I turn now to recent American history. Sandel writes that:

In the course of the twentieth century, the notion that government should shape the moral and civic character of its citizens gave way to the notion that government should

> be neutral toward the values its citizens espouse, and respect each person's capacity to choose his or her own ends. In the decades following World War II, for example, the voluntarist ideal figured prominently in justifications for the welfare state and the judicial expansion of individual rights.[10]

He goes on to say that:

> Despite its achievements . . . the public life informed by the voluntarist self-image was unable to fulfill the aspiration to self-government. Despite the expansion of individual rights and entitlements in recent decades, Americans find to their frustration that their control over the forces that govern their lives is receding rather than increasing.[11]

I am not convinced by either of these passages. I am unable to spot anything plausibly called a "voluntarist ideal" which has come to the fore since the Second World War. I do not think that we Americans feel more subject to uncontrollable forces now than in 1890 or 1930, or than Europeans felt in 1800. Nor do I see that our aspirations to self-government have gone unsatisfied. Nor do I see that, as Sandel says a bit further on, "the absence of a common life at the level of the nation motivates the drift to the procedural republic."[12]

Let me start with this last point of disagreement. The United States, in the decades after the Second World War, offered one of the very rare peacetime examples of a huge industrialized democracy living a very intense "common life at the level of the nation." For those decades witnessed the rise and the triumph of the civil rights movement. Limited as that triumph was, it amounted to the greatest single set of changes in the manners and morals of the Americans ever accomplished by peaceful political consensus. Each of these changes was intensely discussed in almost every bar, union hiring-hall, boardroom, and locker-room in the country. If, as Sandel says, "the republican tradition taught that to be free is to share in governing a political community that controls its own fate,"[13] then republicans should rejoice in what America accomplished between 1950 and 1970.

Sandel does, in fact, rejoice. He describes the civil rights movement as "the finest expression of republican politics in our time."[14] But I do not see why it could not equally well be described as the finest expression of *liberal* politics in our time. Certainly we who call ourselves "liberals" think of it that way. It seems to me that only Sandel's attempt to encumber political liberalism with philosophical voluntarism prevents him from accepting this alternative description.

If thirty years ago the USA was still capable of pulling itself up by its own moral bootstraps, can it be accurate to describe postwar America as gradually coming to despair over its ability to govern itself? Sandel thinks of postwar America this way partly because he thinks that "the liberal self-image and the actual organization of modern social and economic life are sharply at odds." But, once again, I do not think that what he calls "the liberal self- image," the image of the self as pure unencumbered will, exists outside the minds of philosophers and political theorists. I do not think that the average American's self-image has shifted from republican to liberal. The farthest I can go toward agreement with Sandel's sense that things are getting worse is to agree that Americans were more trusting, tolerant, and self-confident during the King years than they are now.

But this seems explicable by the fact that during those years the gap between rich and poor was narrowing, whereas more recently it has been widening. In the last twenty-five years, most Americans have lost the sense of economic security which the previous twenty produced. The change in national mood seems to me sufficiently accounted for by economic facts. I see no need to appeal, as Sandel does, to changes in moral sensibility. Sandel thinks that:

> The sense of disempowerment that afflicts citizens of the procedural republic may reflect the loss of agency that results when liberty is detached from self-government and located in the will of an independent self, unencumbered by moral and communal ties it has chosen.[15]

I think that notions like "loss of agency" and "the will of an independent self" are much too abstract, much too philosophical, to explain what is going on.

More concrete stories than Sandel's are told by Edward Luttwak and Michael Lind. These stories are about what Lind calls the "Brazilianization" of America: the increasing power of a conspicuously consuming oligarchy, the increasing social and cultural distance between that oligarchy and everybody else, and the consequent loss of assurance that most American children can look forward to a satisfying and secure future. The stories Luttwak and Lind tell, concentrating on money rather than self-image, seem to me more plausible than Sandel's. Granted that nowadays there is a lot of disenchantment with politics and a lot of fear for the possibility of self-government, I do not think this is because of an increasingly voluntarist self-image. I suspect that it has the same banal causes as gave rise to disenchantment with politics during the Gilded Age: the rise of a self-enclosed oligarchy, increasing economic insecurity in the bottom half of the population, and the increasing shamelessness of elected officials in accepting bribes.

I have no idea whether we shall see, in the next century, the sort of re-enchantment with politics that gave us the Progressive era and, later, the civil rights movement. Maybe this time around the oligarchs will win, and democratic government be reduced to a farce once and for all. But in trying to estimate the chances that this tragedy will occur, I do not think it helps to look for changes in our understanding of the nature of liberty or of selfhood.

Conclusion

By way of conclusion, let me say that I quite agree with Sandel when he says that "a politics that brackets morality and religion too completely soon generates its own disenchantment."[16] But I think it important to remember that what emerges from Rawlsian attempts to put the search for consensual compromise above moral and religious conviction is not an *absence* of morality and religion, but new moralities and new religions. The morality of America was different after the King years than before, but it was no less a morality, and no less cohesive a bond between citizens. The religion of many American Protestants became different in the decades after the theologians of the Progressive era proclaimed the Social Gospel. But the resulting version of Protestantism—a version that paid less attention to sex and more to love—was still a religion, and was no less efficacious in the lives of believers.

Politics will always be bound up with morality and religion, but morality and religion are as much subject to historical mutation as is politics. In the past it was assumed that they provided a framework within which to discuss politics. I read Dewey, and try to read Rawls, as taking democratic politics as a framework within which to discuss morality and religion.

9

Michael Sandel and Richard Rorty: Two Models of the Republic

RICHARD SENNETT

IN the last few years many students of politics have turned away from the study of political institutions to the analysis of citizenship. This academic shift parallels the public's belief that government is increasingly out of touch with the needs of citizens, and the public's demand that government be more responsive to economic distress, family breakdowns, religious conflicts, and other social ills. In Britain and America, these demands have produced a paradox: many citizens want the government to shrink in size but expand in scope.

Michael Sandel's *Democracy's Discontent* is an inspired and deeply disturbing polemic about citizenship. It asks if our very ways of thinking about political activity can address these expanded demands, particularly in the economic realm, and answers that our political understanding is too impoverished and arid to do so. Sandel's book has aroused great debate in the United States, most trenchantly an attack by the philosopher Richard Rorty. But the issue Sandel raises is so basic that it transcends the confines of scholarly argument or indeed of American society. (As a reader's weather advisory, I should note that both writers are known to me; in this chapter, I want to make clear, as impartially as I can, why they are in conflict.)

Sandel's target is liberal politics, not in its ordinary American sense as championship of the welfare state, but in the more classical usage of the word "liberal" in political theory; this is a tradition which begins with Locke, follows one path in the writings of Kant, another, utilitarian direction in the work of John Stuart Mill and finds one denouement in such modern philosophers as John Rawls.

In Sandel's view, this liberal tradition has erred in imagining citizens ideally as "unencumbered selves," members of the genus *citizen* without, in Sandel's words "any special obligations to their fellow citizens, apart from the univer-

Reprinted with permission, Richard Sennett, "And for the Pursuit of the Common Good," *The Times Literary Supplement*, 18 Oct. 1996, 15.

sal, natural duty not to commit injustice."[1] Such a view seems to Sandel wrong in principle:

> It fails to capture those loyalties and responsibilities whose moral force consists partly in . . . understanding ourselves as the particular persons we are—as members of this family or city or nation or people. As bearers of that history. As citizens of this republic.[2]

Such a minimalist view of citizenship, he maintains, cannot provide people with the will and energy they need to fight for the common good, particularly when that shared well-being is challenged, as it is, today, by economic forces which threaten to crack apart community and isolate people in individual struggles for survival. The "encumbrances" of religious faith, family feeling, communal identity are instead the ingredients of the political will to fight for a better common fate.

For Sandel, formal politics ought to orchestrate these social relations. It can only perform this sovereign task if it makes substantive judgments of value: rather than affirm the right of homosexuals to live in a married state, for instance, the polity has to affirm that homosexual unions share family virtues kindred to heterosexual ones; rather than simply affirm the private right of a woman to choose, the polity in dealing with abortion has actually to decide when life begins.[3]

Sandel's is a politics of commitment. He calls it "republican," again not to identify his views with the American Republican Party—if that institution has any firm views beyond the sponsorship of greed—but in order to make common cause with American political leaders like James Madison or Abraham Lincoln who believed the State should serve as the place of judgment for society, rather than more passively as society's umpire. Sandel thus does not dwell in Clintonia, that other America in which words speak louder than deeds. Sandel's version of republican democracy focuses on surmounting the hesitancy that impedes acting together; democracy means making and keeping mutual commitments. More largely, *Democracy's Discontent* affirms the pursuit of the common good in republican democracy in contrast to the pursuit of procedural rights in liberal democracy.

Most of Sandel's critics have attacked this general account of liberalism and republicanism, but it occupies only the first third of his book. The last two-thirds of *Democracy's Discontent*, called "The Political Economy of Citizenship," explores with great historical acumen just how these two principles have become manifest in the real world of labor, class, and capitalist development. Sandel earns his theory by this history.

At the risk of brutally simplifying, this history could be summarized as the unintended triumph of liberal democracy in the course of capitalism's evolution in America. As the modern economy took form, the recurrent impulse of our citizens was to search for some form of republican government which would tame the economy's ills. Jefferson sought that recourse in the *Notes on the State of Virginia*, wherein he advocates the republican cohesion of rural yeoman facing the first challenges of urban commerce; Lincoln in his debates with Stephen Douglas sought to affirm a republican ideal not only in the face of slavery as a social practice but as an economic system; Herbert Croly sought to rescue the republic from a virulent capitalism by recourse to notions of a common American community, as did many of the advocates of the New Deal and the Great Society.

Yet at each stage of capitalism's development, the concepts of the liberal, "procedural" republic proved better at rationalizing economic growth. Sandel knows too much history simply to identify liberalism with economic individualism. In his discussion of the history of free labor versus wage labor in the United States, for instance, he shows how communal relations among workers were gradually eroded as wage labor advanced; all unions could do was attempt to regulate the conditions of work, a pursuit which became ever more procedural, concerned with labor hours or seniority. Collective action grew through these efforts, but not a solidarity which would challenge the source of workers' ills.

In his discussion of the 1930s' New Deal, he similarly shows how some of the precepts of Keynesian economics gradually supported a view of welfare based on individual entitlements and rights rather than on grounds of moral duty towards the poor, the infirm, or the elderly. Again, he is much too sophisticated to fall back on a devil's theory of capitalism, as though Keynes were in cahoots with Henry Ford. Rather, he wants to show how the economy forced us, even in creating a welfare system, to fall back on procedural, minimalist views of the common good; the American Keynesians, public-spirited as they were, still were constrained to make Ford's world workable.

Given this history of failed republican democracy, why does Sandel want to try again? Because now the political economy is cracking apart society in new ways; the contradictions of capitalism, as Marxists used to say, open up a new chance for collective politics. The modern economy is, we know, uprooting large numbers of people who now labor at short-term tasks rather than pursue long-term careers; it's hard to be loyal to corporations which do not practice loyalty in return, harder to take seriously the current hand-wringing about corporate responsibility on the part of institutions compulsively oriented to their quarterly earnings reports. Concomitantly, the welfare state is in the process of shrinking the very guarantees and entitlements which rescued the economic order in an earlier generation. What citizens want is for government to respond to these human fissures.

Democracy's Discontent argues that the polity can only respond by rethinking the moral and social foundations of the economy itself, rather than by thinking up more rights or protections against the economy; economic practice has to submit to a higher principle of sovereignty. All well and good—we used to call this socialism. But Sandel's insight is that we cannot speak of the duty economic institutions owe those who labor for them if we fight shy of the concept of duty itself. In the same way, we are incompetent politically to demand that corporations act responsibly, if we have no idea of how families are to be conducted responsibly; unable to define corporate loyalty if we have not yielded to loyalty's demands in communal life.

"Commitment", "loyalty", "duty"—those words may sound a jarring note to those of us who, like Sandel, grew up in the wake of the 1960s, when these code words asked us, as we thought, to submit to political evil. Perhaps Sandel picks up on a certain element of bad faith in that youthful resistance. In reading Sandel, I hear the echo of the voice of friends who were conscientious objectors to the Vietnam War but still went East as medics, of whites who went South as freedom riders, of college drop-outs who went to work in poor communities. It is a voice of conscience convinced that to dwell on one's rights alone is to dwell in a state of luxury, that only the blindly privileged could imagine they could shed the "encumbrance" of the distasteful views or actions of their fellow citizens. One must give something back to them. One has no choice about whether to do so, only in how to perform that duty.

But words like "duty" and "loyalty" do contain in themselves a coercive undertow, and it is that current in Sandel's thinking which his most serious critics, such as Richard Rorty, have contested. Rorty's politics are as left-leaning as Sandel's, but he leans in that direction from a different position.

First, Rorty does not think the public is "in search of a public philosophy," as Sandel's subtitle proclaims, because for Rorty, there is no need to choose between liberal and republican goals. The public wants both rights and common goods; it deserves both, and it gets too little of each.

Second, Rorty rejects the characterization of liberalism in terms of its belief in a "minimalist self," at least liberalism of a pragmatic sort. "All selves are always already equally encumbered, but some of them are encumbered with good beliefs and desires and some with bad ones."[4] For instance, Rorty argues, membership in an American fundamentalist church makes a person less apt to search for the common democratic good "than does an affiliation with an extended family, a trade union, or a bowling league."[5] Take your own views seriously, he says to Sandel, and you really will have to judge between good and bad, or even more perilously, true and false beliefs; your polity will shrink radically once you start to do so, the Christian Coalition will be expelled beyond the pale, the local trade union and bowling league within it. The anti-democratic character of this ultimate judgment is why Rorty wants to change the subject, in the case of abortion, "from 'when does human life begin?' to 'how can some unprincipled and wishy-washy consensus about abortion be hammered out?' "

Finally, the two disagree about what Richard Rorty calls "sentiment" but what seems to me a much broader intellectual issue.

One of the most moving passages in Sandel's book is his depiction of the Southern general Robert E. Lee on the eve of the Civil War, torn between fighting in the name of his native Virginia or for the principle of the American Union. Sandel contemplates Lee's moral dilemma in deciding to "stand with his people, even to lead them in a cause which he opposed."[6] For Sandel this is a telling instance of the sense of obligation which creates commitment. When he writes of Lee as an example of "the disposition to see and bear one's life circumstance as a reflectively situated being,"[7] the key word in that phrase is "bear." Politics is not about the pursuit of happiness; it addresses shared experiences which weigh heavily on those who do their duty by one another. Sandel's use of the word "encumbered" evokes this same weight. Lee's plight resonates with other forms of republican sentiment; the necessity of making commitments to a particular collective good, if not always tragic, more often than not entails an arduous, painful sacrifice.

Rorty looks at Lee's dilemma as an instance of what he calls "irony." By this he does not intend any frou-frou lightness. Rather, he means the capacity for distancing oneself from circumstances so as to judge well whether and how to act; Lee was possessed of that ironic distance, though I imagine Rorty believes Lee's tragedy lay in accepting the more local rather than the larger common good. But the capacity for ironic distance seems to Rorty a genuine moral sentiment, and it leads him to a particular political credo: "I do not think that the state can do much to instill irony in its citizens . . ."[8] That moral temper has more to do with culture and the habits of everyday life.

So this debate is really about the relation between civil society and political activity. Sandel sees civil society culminating in political action—or it should move in that direction if we are to do battle with an ever more corrosive capitalism. For Rorty, civil society, whether strong or weak, ironic or blind, stands beyond the reach of politics. Moreover, the "network of beliefs and desires" that Rorty calls the self is too complicated a map to have a single destination. While, for Sandel, the more weighted, encumbered with commitment, the more consequent and dignified the self becomes. As a result, what I detect in this debate is that Sandel is more likely, and Rorty less likely, to believe political activity is cathartic.

This is a philosophical disagreement about the nature of citizenship, but one with historical resonances and practical consequences. John Winthrop's arguments in favor of a Puritan commonwealth eerily foreshadow Michael Sandel's views on democracy, while colonial Quakers sounded a more Rortian note. Those Quakers worried about "the immoderate desire for the good," in William Sharples' words, fearing the personal disappointment and political confusion that immoderate desire for the good inevitably produces. So does Richard Rorty. But Sandel, like Winthrop, sees matters differently. Both the Puritan and the republican-socialist have worried about the lack of will and energy in the polity—if only our difficulties lay in an excess of fervor. Michael Sandel's is the most compelling, if troubling, account I have read of how citizens might draw on the energies of everyday life and the ties of civil society to reinvigorate the public realm.

10

Liberal Egalitarianism and Civic Republicanism: Friends or Enemies?

WILL KYMLICKA

MICHAEL SANDEL'S *Democracy's Discontent* presents us with a domestic equivalent of Samuel Huntington's "clash of civilizations" thesis. Huntington argues that international relations should be understood as driven by a clash between rival and incommensurable worldviews—e.g. Christian, Islamic, and Confucian—each with their own conception of the person, society, and polity. Sandel argues that within the Christian West—or at least within the United States—domestic politics should be understood as a clash between two rival and incommensurable worldviews—civic republicanism and procedural liberalism. According to Sandel, procedural liberalism has increasingly displaced civic republicanism, with disastrous consequences for American democracy.

Presenting American politics as a clash of two worldviews makes it seem rather more exciting than an old-fashioned view of politics as a clash of innumerable and cross-cutting interests and values. But I doubt it is the most accurate or helpful way to understand politics. Since I am not an expert on American history, I will not dispute Sandel's account of the historical interaction between these two worldviews. I will instead focus on the contemporary situation, and ask whether civic republicanism and procedural liberalism are allies or enemies in confronting the "discontent" that Western democracies currently suffer from. I will argue that they are—or should be—allies, and that exaggerating their differences is philosophically suspect and politically counterproductive.

I will start by specifying more clearly what sort of procedural liberalism I wish to defend—namely, the sort of left-wing liberal egalitarianism associated with Rawls and Dworkin (Section 1). I will then explain why I think Sandel exaggerates the differences between this version of procedural liberalism and civic republicanism (Section 2). This is not to deny that the two approaches will sometimes generate conflicting recommendations. But in these (relatively rare) cases, I will argue that we should prefer procedural liberalism to civic republicanism—that is, promoting the collective good of self-government does not justify the unjust treatment of individuals (Section 3).

It seems to me that Sandel has two different criticisms of procedural liberalism. In some places, he seems to say that procedural liberalism is wrong in principle, in the sense that it gets the wrong answer on a variety of issues, independent of its long-term sustainability. But in other places, he seems to be saying that it is desirable in principle, but unsustainable in practice. That is, it gets the right answer on issues, taken one by one, but the cumulative effect of these decisions is to undermine the viability of liberal democratic institutions.

I will focus on the first principled objection, but I will return at the end of the chapter to the second practical objection. I think this second objection raises an important issue which liberal theorists have not adequately addressed, but reflecting on it helps to clarify why liberalism and republicanism should be seen as allies, not enemies (Section 4).

1. What is Procedural Liberalism?

As Sandel notes, procedural liberalism can take many forms. At one end of the political spectrum, there is the right-wing libertarianism associated with Robert Nozick and David Gauthier, which affirms the sanctity of property rights, and which is hostile to all forms of state enforced redistribution; at the other end of the spectrum, there is the left-wing liberal egalitarianism associated with John Rawls, Ronald Dworkin, and Bruce Ackerman, which affirms the necessity of rectifying undeserved inequalities, and which gives moral priority to the well-being of the least well-off.

At first glance, these appear to be very different—even diametrically opposed—theories. But Sandel insists that at a deeper level, these different forms of procedural liberalism share certain key assumptions—in particular, a conception of the unencumbered self, and of the neutral state. And it is these shared assumptions which underlie and explain the inability of procedural liberalism, in either its right-wing or left-wing form, to deal with democracy's discontents.

I agree that there are important assumptions which are shared by right- and left-wing versions of procedural liberalism. However, the political implications of these assumptions may—and I think do—differ dramatically between right-wing and left-wing liberalism. Assumptions which have disastrous political consequences when combined with a belief in the sanctity of property rights may have quite different consequences when combined with a belief in giving moral priority to the least well-off. To properly assess the impact of procedural liberalism, therefore, we need to pick a particular version of procedural liberalism, and see how these assumptions about the individual and state play themselves out in that context.

Since I endorse the left-wing version of procedural liberalism, I will focus in the rest of the chapter on the relationship between civic republicanism and liberal egalitarianism.[1] What then is (left-wing) procedural liberalism? Sandel uses a number of terms to describe this theory—e.g. in some places, he describes it as a "proceduralist" or "neutralist" theory; in other places, he describes it as giving priority to the right over the good; in yet other places, he talks about unencumbered selves, autonomy, and the priority of the self over its ends. All of these terms and phrases are ambiguous and potentially confusing, so let me specify what exactly I understand by liberal egalitarianism. I would characterize it in terms of three main claims about the self, the state, and fairness respectively. The first two are common to both left-wing and right-wing liberalism, the third is distinctive to left-wing liberal egalitarianism:

(1) Rational Revisability Individuals are not assumed to have fixed and unchangeable conceptions of the good. Rather each individual should have the capacity to rationally reflect on the ends she currently endorses, and to revise these ends if they are no longer deemed worthy of her continued allegiance. The state must make it possible for individuals to develop and exercise this capacity for rational revisability. The state does this in part by providing children with a suitable liberal education which develops this capacity, and in part by prohibiting attempts by other individuals or groups to prevent people from exercising this capacity. (This commitment to rational revisability is the claim which Sandel sometimes refers to as the "unencumbered self," or as "the priority of the self over its ends.")[2]

(2) The Nonperfectionist State The state should be neutral amongst conceptions of the good, in the sense that it should not justify its legislation by appeal to some ranking of the intrinsic worth of particular conceptions of the good. The role of the state is to protect the capacity for individuals to judge for themselves the worth of different conceptions of the good life, and to provide a fair distribution of rights and resources to enable people to pursue their conception of the good. The state tells people what is rightfully theirs, and what rightfully belongs to others, and insists that people adjust their conception of the good to respect the rightful claims of others. But if someone's conception of the good does respect the rightful claims of others, then the state should not be assessing the intrinsic merits of her (justice-respecting) way of life. The state does not justify its actions by reference to some public ranking of the intrinsic worth of different (justice-respecting) ways of life, for there is no public ranking to refer to. As Rawls puts it, government is neutral amongst different conceptions of the good "not in the sense that there is an agreed public measure of intrinsic value or satisfaction with respect to which all these conceptions come out equal, but in the sense that they are not evaluated at all from a [public] standpoint."[3] (This is the claim which Sandel sometimes refers to as the "neutral state," or as the "priority of justice to the good.")

These first two claims are common to all forms of procedural liberalism. The third, however, is distinctive to left-wing liberal egalitarianism:

(3) Rectifying Morally Arbitrary Inequalities Inequalities which are "morally arbitrary"—that is, inequalities which are not chosen or deserved—are unjust, and should be rectified. A liberal theory of justice will insist that individuals can come to have different holdings as a result of different choices that they have made about how they wish to lead their lives (e.g. different choices about the trade-off between work and leisure; or between current consumption and long-term savings; or between aversion to risk). However, if people have unequal holdings as a result of their *circumstances*—rather than their own choices—then these are morally arbitrary and unjust. Sources of morally arbitrary inequalities include not only social circumstances (e.g. being born into a disadvantaged family), but also natural endowments (e.g. being born with fewer physical or mental natural talents). As Dworkin puts it, on a left-liberal conception of distributive justice, distribution should be "choice-sensitive" but "circumstance-insensitive"—it should allow for differences in holdings due to people's choices, but rectify inequalities due to people's natural endowments or social circumstances.

These three claims constitute the core of left-wing procedural liberalism.[4] While I have not used precisely the same terminology that Sandel uses to describe this theory, I think (and hope) that he would agree with this basic characterization. What I now want to argue is that this left-wing version of procedural liberalism is an ally of civic republicanism on most issues, and that Sandel's attempt to paint procedural liberalism as an enemy is philosophically misguided and politically unhelpful.

One reason for my skepticism about Sandel's approach is that it fits uncomfortably well into the long and unfortunate tradition of left sectarianism. People on the left who agree on 95 percent of the actual issues confronting our society spend all of their time arguing with each other about the 5 percent of issues we disagree about, rather than fighting alongside each other for the 95 percent of issues we have in common. My sense is that these internecine debates are often unnecessary and counterproductive. Sandel, however, insists that liberal egalitarianism is the cause of, not the solution to, democracy's discontents. According to Sandel, progress can only be made by diminishing the hold of liberal egalitarianism on the popular imagination and popular discourse. This is what I want to challenge.

2. Is Liberal Egalitarianism the Cause of Discontent?

The heart of Sandel's objection to procedural liberalism can be put this way:

(1) Americans today are feeling discontent because of a loss of a sense of community, and a loss of a sense of mastery over their fate;
(2) this sense of discontent can only be solved by attending to issues of communal identity and civic virtue;
(3) procedural liberalism cannot attend to either communal identity or

civic virtue because of its commitment to rational revisability (the "unencumbered self") and the non-perfectionist state ("state neutrality").

I will accept, for the moment, claims (1) and (2), and focus on claim (3). Is it true that liberal egalitarians cannot attend to issues of communal identity and civic virtue? It is true that the core principles of liberal egalitarianism, as I have described them above, do not say anything about these issues. It is fair to say, I think, that while liberal egalitarianism has an intrinsic and foundational commitment to a particular conception of individual agency and social justice, it has no similar intrinsic or foundational commitment to a particular conception of communal identity or civic virtue. From a liberal egalitarian point of view, communal identities and civic virtues can play only a secondary role, to be judged by the extent to which they are consistent with, or promote, foundational values of individual agency and social justice.

But to say that communal identities and civic virtues can play only a secondary role within liberal egalitarianism is not to say that they can play no role at all. On the contrary, it may turn out that they play a vital and indispensable role. It may be that liberal egalitarian values can best be achieved, or indeed can only be achieved, within societies which have certain sorts of communal identities and civic virtues. If so, liberal egalitarians would have the strongest possible reasons, from within their own theory, for attending to issues of communal identity and civic virtue. From a liberal egalitarian point of view, this is an open question, to be evaluated empirically, on a case-by-case basis.

Some critics might think that treating communal identities and civic virtues as secondary values, to be assessed in terms of their impact on liberal justice, is inadequate. Some critics will insist that they should be accorded intrinsic value, and should be promoted as such, even at the expense of liberal values of individual agency and social justice. This is indeed what classical civic republicans have often claimed, and I will return to this question below. But Sandel himself makes the rather different—and quite puzzling—claim that liberal egalitarianism cannot address these issues at all, even as secondary values. According to Sandel, procedural liberalism is precluded *in principle* from using state policies to promote any conception of communal identity or civic virtue.

I think Sandel is simply mistaken here. It seems to me that he has seriously misunderstood what the liberal commitments to rational revisability and non-perfectionism entail. According to Sandel, procedural liberalism is unable to deal with issues of identity and virtue because of its underlying commitment to state neutrality. His argument, insofar as I understand it, is that if the state is committed to neutrality amongst conceptions of the good, then it must also be neutral amongst conceptions of communal identity and civic virtue, since these are inextricably tied to particular conceptions of the good life.

Sandel never actually defends the claim that conceptions of communal identity and civic virtue are inextricably tied to particular conceptions of the good, and it is not clear what exactly is the relationship he sees between them. He often simply conflates them, as if they were one and the same thing. At times, he seems to be making a definitional claim—i.e. that conceptions of identity and virtue just *are* conceptions of the good life. But in other places, he seems to be making more of an argument by analogy—i.e. that whatever reason liberals have for being neutral amongst conceptions of the good are also reasons for being neutral amongst conceptions of identity and virtue.

Since I am not sure what exactly Sandel is claiming here, I am not sure how best to respond to it. But let me start with the definitional claim. It is clearly not true that promoting a conception of virtue is *by definition* promoting a conception of the good. It all depends on *why* one is promoting a conception of civic virtue. If the state promotes certain virtues on the grounds that possessing these virtues will make someone's life more worthwhile or fulfilling, then clearly it is promoting a particular conception of the good. However, if the state is promoting these virtues on the grounds that possessing them will make someone more likely to fulfill her obligations of justice, then it is not promoting a particular conception of the good. It has made no claim whatsoever about what makes her life go better, or about what ends in life are rewarding or fulfilling. It may well be that possessing these virtues is actually a burden to some people. For example, people who possess a willingness to remedy the disadvantages of others may perceive the exercise of this virtue as involving a sacrifice of their own well-being for the sake of others.

Of course, some people will find the exercise of these virtues inherently rewarding and fulfilling. Moreover, insofar as the liberal state insists that people abide by the requirements of justice, then it is likely that people will try to find ways to make the fulfillment of their obligations of justice as rewarding as possible. But personal gratification need not be—and in a liberal society is not—the basis on which the state promotes civic virtues. Civic virtues are promoted because, and insofar as, they enable us to achieve liberal principles of individual agency and social justice.

In short, a virtue is not a conception of the good unless it is justified on the basis that it enriches the life of the person who possesses it. But that is not the only possible justification for promoting civic virtues, which can instead be defended as a precondition of justice to others.

The same applies to questions of communal identity. Promoting a particular communal identity need not involve promoting a particular conception of the good life. It all depends on what sort of identity it is, and why it is being promoted. If the basis for the communal identity is a shared conception of the good, then promoting such an identity will obviously involve promoting a particular conception of the good life. However, this is not the only basis for communal identities. In many cases, the basis for communal identity is not a shared conception of the good, but rather a more diffuse sense of belonging to with fewer cultural traditions and historical memories to draw upon, may find the task of cultivating commonality more difficult still."[46]

Sandel notes that some "commentators of the 1990s saw in international environmental, human rights, and women's movements the emergence of a 'global civil society' that might serve as a counterweight to the power of global markets and media,"[47] but he finds the cosmopolitan ideal that animates this suggestion "flawed, both as a moral ideal and as a public philosophy for self-government in our time."[48] As Sandel sees it, advocates of the global civic society urge that "universal identities must always take precedence over particular ones";[49] but this position implausibly requires that we subordinate our friends and neighbors to humanity in general. On the political level, even national sovereignty is "challenged . . . by the resurgent aspirations of subnational groups for autonomy and self-rule."[50] Thus, "[g]iven the limits of cosmopolitan politics, the attempt to save democracy by globalizing citizenship . . . is unlikely to succeed."[51]

The alternative, reminiscent of Sandel's interest in federalism and the anti-chainstore movement, is to "disperse" sovereignty by ensuring that there is "a multiplicity of communities and political bodies—some more, some less extensive than nations—among which sovereignty is diffused."[52] In some settings, "dispersing sovereignty may entail according greater cultural and political autonomy to subnational communities—such as Catalans and Kurds, Scots and Quebecois—even while strengthening and democratizing transnational structures, such as the European Union."[53]

Again, this is a rich but puzzling account of the possibilities for a better public philosophy. It suggests a path by which the now inadequate procedural republic might come to embody a public philosophy that would better serve the interests of the professional-managerial class.[54] Dispersing sovereignty may create communities whose local commitments allow them to resist economic transformations that global capitalism describes as mere interregional capital flows. With such a base, the professional-managerial class might turn its attention to the real source of its discontent, the transnational corporation. But how can that resistance succeed?

Begin with the vision of a "global civil society."[55] As Sandel notes, its advocates have welcomed the development of transnational social movements—the so-called New Social Movements—encompassing the environmental movements typified by Greens in many countries; women's movements exemplified by the nongovernmental organizations associated with the United Nations conferences on women; and the international human rights movement. Except for the last, it does not seem to me that these movements demand that "universal identities . . . always take precedence over particular ones."[56] True, the human rights movement seeks minimal human decencies, universal in their application but rather restricted in their scope. It allows a substantial range of particular practices within a framework of minimal human rights.[57] The transnational women's movement rather evidently asks an intergenerational society, having a common past and sharing a common future.

This, indeed, is how national identities typically operate in modern Western democracies. Citizens think of themselves as "American," for example, and identify with other Americans, without sharing a conception of the good. They may automatically think of other Americans as "one of us," without knowing anything about others' conception of the good. Americans disagree with each other (sometimes violently) about the good life, but they still recognize and identify each other as Americans, because they share a sense of belonging to an intergenerational society which has some historical reference points, and a common future. They may disagree about how to interpret their past, and may have very different hopes for the future, but they recognize each other as belonging to the same society, and this sense of shared belonging underlies their national identity.

Liberal states have historically promoted this sort of "thin" national identity. And they have done so, not in order to promote a particular conception of the good life, but rather to increase the likelihood that citizens will fulfill their obligations of justice. We know that people are more likely to make sacrifices for others if these others are viewed as "one of us," and so promoting a sense of national identity strengthens the sense of mutual obligation needed to sustain liberal justice.[5]

If the state promotes such "thin" communal identities on the grounds that possessing them will make someone more likely to fulfill her obligations of justice, then it is not violating liberal neutrality. The identity it is promoting is not grounded in a particular conception of the good; and it is not saying that a life with this particular identity is more rewarding than a life with some other identity. It is not saying anything about what ends in life are rewarding or fulfilling. It is simply saying that we are more likely to fulfill our obligations of justice if we view others as members of "our" society.

As these examples show, I hope, the key distinction in procedural liberalism theory is between "the right" (or justice) and "the good." A liberal state upholds principles of right, but it is individuals who judge the good. Sandel knows this, of course. He emphasizes it himself at the beginning of his book. But he then misjudges where this dividing line falls. He assumes, without any explanation or argument, that virtues and identities automatically fall on the side of "the good" rather than "the right," and hence assumes that promoting particular virtues or identities is a matter of promoting a conception of the good, rather than upholding principles of right. He writes as if issues of rights and resources fall on the side of "the right," whereas issues of virtues and identities fall on the side of "the good."

But this is a mistake. The line between the good and the right is orthogonal to the distinction between identities/virtues and rights/resources. The distinction between the good and the right is a distinction between two kinds of *justifications* for public policies, not a distinction between two kinds of *objects* of public policy. Liberals insist that whatever the object of public policy—whether it is legal rights, economic resources, political institutions, civic virtues, or communal identities—the aim of state policy should be to promote principles of right, not to promote particular conceptions of the good. By contrast, a perfectionist state would decide all issues of public policy—whether rights, resources, or virtues—on the basis of how best to promote a particular conception of the good life which has been judged to be the most rewarding or fulfilling.

Rawls himself makes this point quite clear. In an important passage on the role of virtues within procedural liberalism, Rawls distinguishes between what he calls "classical republicanism" and "civic humanism." According to classical republicanism, certain political virtues must be promoted amongst citizens in order to prevent the degeneration of liberal democracy into tyranny or religious/nationalist fanaticism. Rawls notes that this justification for promoting civic virtues is entirely consistent with procedural liberalism, since they are defended as preconditions for liberal justice. By contrast, "civic humanism" asserts that political virtues should be promoted because our "essential nature" is realized in political life which is the "privileged locus of the good life." As Rawls notes, there is a "fundamental opposition" between procedural liberalism and civic humanism, since civic humanists defend virtues on the basis of a particular conception of the good life, not on grounds of justice.[6]

So there is no reason in principle why liberal states cannot promote certain conceptions of virtue or identity. It all depends on what the virtues and identities are, and why they are being promoted. If these virtues and identities encourage individuals to fulfill their obligations of justice, while still leaving them free to rationally assess and revise their own conceptions of the good, then they are fully consistent with foundational liberal values of individual agency and social justice. If civic virtues and communal identities help individuals to identify and fulfill their obligations to others, then they are consistent with, and indeed promote, liberal egalitarianism.

And these are precisely the sorts of virtues and identities which liberal states (and liberal theorists) have always endorsed. Liberal states have always promoted certain virtues of responsible citizenship and certain national identities—indeed, the promotion of these virtues and identities was perhaps the key justification liberal theorists gave for mandatory education.

Sandel often writes as if the term "conception of the good life" covers all normative beliefs. But a conception of the good life is just that—i.e. a conception of what makes one's life good, of what makes one's life go better. It is a conception of what makes one's life worth living, of the activities, relationships, and goods which make one's life fuller and richer and more rewarding and satisfying. And so when liberals say that the state should be neutral amongst conceptions of the good life, they mean that the state should not rank the goodness of different ways of life. The state should leave judgments about the good life to individuals, and should seek instead to ensure a free and fair context for individuals to make these judgments.

This does not preclude the promotion of certain virtues or identities so long as they are defended as identifying the limits within which we can pursue our conception of the good life. Possessing certain virtues and identities can help us to recognize when our pursuit of our own good is violating the rightful claims of others. These virtues and identities do not tell us where our own good lies; rather, they tell us how far we can go in pursuing our own good. As Rawls puts it, "justice draws the limit, the good shows the point."[7] Liberals can endorse state promotion of those virtues and identities which help us "draw the limit," but will not endorse state promotion of virtues and identities which reflect a particular conception of "the point" of human existence.[8]

3. But Is It Enough?

There is an obvious objection to what I have argued so far. Someone might argue that even if procedural liberalism can endorse *some* virtues and identities, it cannot endorse the right ones, or perhaps cannot endorse them strongly enough. This objection could be developed at either a theoretical level, in terms of what liberalism is capable in principle of endorsing, or at a more practical level, in terms of what liberalism is likely to lead to in practice.

Let me start with the theoretical level. As I noted earlier, liberalism treats issues of virtues and identities as dependent values, to be assessed in terms of, and constrained by, deeper liberal principles of individual agency and social justice. Perhaps Sandel would argue that we should view them as intrinsic values, and endorse them even if they conflict with the requirements of liberal justice. For example, perhaps he would argue that we should not only be Rawls's "classical republicans," who promote political virtue in order to sustain just institutions, but also civic humanists, who promote political virtues because our "essential nature" is realized in political life which is the "privileged locus of the good life."

This, I think, would be an interesting argument to pursue. Unfortunately, Sandel never really tackles this question. He spends so much time defending a platitude—namely, the view that politics must attend to issues of virtues and identities—that he does not get very far in developing the details of his preferred account of virtues and identities. Which virtues and identities would he promote, and how would they differ from the sorts of virtues and identities which liberal egalitarians promote?

For example, liberal theorists working on the topic of citizenship education have typically emphasized the importance of promoting virtues of civility, public reasonableness, a sense of justice, and a critical attitude towards government authority.[9] These are all defended on the grounds that they are needed to create and sustain just institutions (rather than as constituents of a particular conception of the good life). They are defended as consistent with liberal commitments to rational revisability, and with liberal prohibitions on state perfectionism. How would Sandel's conception of citizenship education differ? Are there additional virtues that he would add? And if so, would he defend them on grounds of justice or the good?

Similarly, liberal theorists working on the topic of political community have typically emphasized the importance of promoting a variety of political identities, from the local (local self-government as a school in democracy) to the national (the nation as the largest feasible unit of redistribution), and also including special protections for minority ethnocultural identities.[10] Here again, the justification for state recognition of these identities is that they help to sustain just institutions, and to rectify injustices. They are defended as consistent with liberal commitments to rational revisability, and with liberal prohibitions on state perfectionism. How would Sandel's conception of identity politics differ? Which additional identities would he promote, and would he defend them on grounds of justice or the good?

Without a more detailed answer to these questions, it is impossible to judge whether Sandel's conception of republican politics is superior to, or even genuinely different from, the liberal egalitarian politics he claims to be objecting to. In fact, I could not locate a single instance where Sandel clearly and explicitly endorses the promotion of particular virtues or identities even when it conflicts with liberal egalitarian justice.

One can imagine cases where promoting civic humanist virtues as part of a conception of the good life (rather than as a way of sustaining just institutions) would come at the expense of liberal justice. Indeed, Sandel himself cites an example from American history, although it is not clear whether he endorses it. In the nineteenth century, many Americans argued that their conception of the good life, which viewed republican political participation as uniquely and intrinsically valuable, could only be sustained by westward expansion—that is, by conquering and displacing the American Indians. Without the promise of new land and a unifying national project of expansion, these intrinsically valuable forms of republican political participation would diminish, replaced by more mundane and instrumental forms of politics. Let us assume that this claim were true, and that an intrinsically valuable way of life bound up with political participation could only be sustained by unjust treatment of Indians. Does the promotion of a civic humanist conception of the good life justify this injustice?

Similarly, imagine that the most effective way to mobilize people to participate in politics and to think about the collective good is to create some perceived threat to national survival, either from inside the country (e.g. illegal immigrants, homosexuals, communists, drug addicts), or outside (e.g. the Soviet Union, Islamic terrorists). Imagine, in other words, that the best or only way to mobilize people to participate in republican self-government is to declare war on some invented enemy. This is not a fanciful example. Sandel himself notes that xenophobes are often quite successful in mobilizing people, and warns us against this danger. But what if this sort of mobilization in fact creates more of what Sandel calls "republican freedom," or the "collective good of self-government," for a greater number of people? What if it increases most people's sense of community and collective mastery, and reduces their feelings of discontent with democracy? What if we face a trade-off between promoting republican freedom for the many, and upholding justice for the few? What if promoting civic humanism as a way of life reduces the discontent of the majority, albeit at the expense of oppressing a minority?

My guess is that in all of these cases, Sandel would side with liberal justice. However much he describes republican freedom as an alternative to liberal justice, my guess is that he would not promote the former at the expense of the latter, and that he (tacitly) views principles of justice as setting constraints on the promotion of republican freedom. I suspect that in the end he shares the liberal belief that political institutions are not to be judged primarily by how satisfying they are to participants, but by how just their results are.

Perhaps Sandel would disagree with this. Since he never explicitly addresses the question, it is difficult to say. But if so, he has provided no real argument why we should abandon the liberal view that justice is the first virtue of political institutions. Suppose we face a choice between, on the one hand, political institutions which are just but which provide few opportunities for intrinsically rewarding participation, and, on the other hand, political institutions which are unjust to the minority but which provide intrinsically rewarding participation to the majority. Faced with this choice, liberals would choose just political institutions. Political institutions which claim coercive power over all citizens should not be seen as an arena for the majority to pursue intrinsically valuable ways of life. The raison d'être of political institutions is to secure justice for all citizens, and the promotion of republican virtues must operate within this constraint.

Of course, in many cases, enhancing the quality of political participation would not require sacrificing liberal justice. On the contrary, most plausible suggestions for how to improve collective self-government would also involve improving liberal justice—that is, they would involve reducing undeserved inequalities in people's social status, economic resources, and political influence. And that indeed is just my point. On virtually all real-world issues, civic republicans and liberal egalitarians should be allies. There is so much that can be done to promote both liberal equality and republican democracy that it is almost idle speculation to ask what we should do when the two conflict. But if Sandel insists that we declare where we would stand in the event of such a conflict, then I would side with the liberals, and I do not see that he has provided any argument in the book to challenge this.

But perhaps Sandel would make a more practical objection to my argument so far. He might argue that, whatever the theoretical resources of liberal egalitarianism, the fact remains that in practice procedural liberalism has failed to deal satisfactorily with issues of virtues and identities. According to Sandel, the triumph of procedural liberalism in the United States has gone hand-in-hand with an increasing reluctance to deal with issues of virtue and identity. Whether or not procedural liberalism can in principle deal with such issues, it has failed to do so in practice, and this is surely no accident—there must be some internal obstacle or inhibition within procedural liberalism which makes it difficult to address these issues.

But here, I think, we need to be cautious in talking about "the triumph of the procedural republic," as if there were a single version of procedural liberalism which has conquered American jurisprudence and political discourse. On the contrary, as I noted earlier, there are at least two very different forms of procedural liberalism—right and left—which have different implications for issues of virtue and identity. Insofar as procedural liberalism has triumphed in the USA, it is predominantly the right-wing version. The United States has a higher (and growing) level of inequality amongst citizens than other Western democracies, and the lowest (and declining) level of redistribution. Insofar as the USA has been influenced by liberalism, it has been influenced by the right-wing view which rejects the principle that inequalities should be rectified (and a fortiori rejects the idea that the state should promote the sort of virtues and identities which would encourage people to fulfill obligations of egalitarian justice).

Since left-wing liberalism remains a voice in the wilderness in the USA, at least compared to other Western democracies, we have no clear idea what effect it would have were it to triumph politically. Moreover, insofar as right-wing liberalism has triumphed, it is at least in part because it has formed an alliance with other, non-liberal, strands of American political thought. Sandel notes that republicanism in the United States has historically been influenced by and distorted by racism, nativism, class prejudice, sexism, fear of big government, etc. But the same is true of liberalism, and the sort of right-wing liberalism which has triumphed in the United States is a strange amalgamation of ideologies and convictions. (Consider the unholy alliance of right-wing liberals and cultural conservatives under Reagan.)

It is quite misleading, therefore, to talk as if current American institutions, or current Supreme Court jurisprudence, reflects the triumph of any one particular political theory. I agree with Sandel that political theories—what he calls "public philosophies"—are important. They do influence political institutions. But they also influence each other, to the extent that it becomes implausible, if not impossible, to describe any particular institution or decision as the pure and unalloyed consequence of a particular political philosophy.

How then can we assess the impact of left-wing liberal egalitarianism in practice, given that it is relatively weak on the ground in the United States, and always influenced and distorted by other political theories and cultural trends? It seems to me that there are two possible routes, neither of which

Sandel really pursues. The first would be to engage in cross-country comparisons. We know that other Western democracies have also been increasingly influenced by "procedural liberalism," and for the same reasons as the United States—e.g. increasing diversity, secularization, autonomy, mobility, etc. Moreover, in most of these countries, the left-wing version of procedural liberalism is considerably stronger than in the United States. (Indeed, the influence of Rawls on public discourse has been much greater in many Western European countries than in the USA.) Public opinion polls have shown that citizens in most Western democracies express greater support for liberal egalitarian values than in the United States.

Of course, in each of these countries, left-wing liberal egalitarianism has been influenced by other political ideologies and cultural characteristics. So none of them provides a pure form of left-wing liberal egalitarianism in practice. But many of these local influences get filtered out if we focus on the general cross-country trends. And so far as I can tell, the evidence suggests that left-wing procedural liberalism in these countries has not prevented governments from adopting successful policies to promote both civic virtues and communal identities, and, more generally, from sustaining not only higher levels of political participation than in the United States, but also higher levels of satisfaction with this participation. I would hypothesize that the more influential liberal egalitarianism is in a country, the more likely it is that citizens have not only a strong sense of national identity, but vibrant local politics, and recognition of minority ethnocultural identities; also, I expect they are more likely to exhibit a willingness to make sacrifices for co-citizens, have a more equitable level of political participation, and a higher sense of efficacy regarding political participation. I do not have the evidence at hand to confirm or refute this hypothesis, but this is the sort of evidence which I think would actually be needed to properly evaluate the impact of liberal egalitarianism in practice.

This raises a concern I had about the parochialism of Sandel's book. His concern is primarily with the American experience. There is nothing wrong with this, of course, and indeed I think that the best works of political theory are always grounded in a deep understanding of a particular society. But I also think that, having studied one's own society intensively, it is important to raise one's eyes and see if the conclusions one has drawn from one's own country are validated in other countries. It is important to consider the experience of other countries, not necessarily because one has an intrinsic interest in them, but because their experience provides a way to assess the merits of one's analysis of one's own country. For example, one way to test Sandel's hypothesis about the impact of procedural liberalism on issues such as gay rights or hate speech would be to examine how other liberal democracies have dealt with these issues. If other countries which have a strong commitment to procedural liberalism have dealt with these issues in a different way—as indeed they have—that suggests Sandel's hypothesis may be mistaken.

Sandel's claim is that the triumph of procedural liberalism, in both its left-wing and right-wing versions, generates discontent with democracy. But if the experience of other countries suggests that the influence of left-wing liberalism has not had this effect, then perhaps Sandel has misdiagnosed the real causes of discontent in America.

This leads to the second possible strategy for evaluating the impact of liberal egalitarianism. Rather than examining the impact of liberal egalitarianism in other countries, one could study American liberalism more closely, to see how it has been influenced or distorted by its interaction with other public philosophies and other cultural characteristics of American society. In order to identify the specific impact of liberalism, we need to understand the cultural forces which have been mixed in with liberalism in practice, and which make American liberalism distinctive from liberalism in other countries.

Many people think that what makes American liberalism distinctive is that it is highly proceduralist, and that this proceduralist liberalism is highly influential in public life. I would argue, however, that these are not particularly distinctive to America. Liberalism in many other Western democracies is equally proceduralist, and equally influential. What makes American liberalism distinctive, I would argue, is that it is disproportionately right-wing—that is, the balance between right-wing liberalism and left-wing liberalism is strongly tilted to the right in the United States. I would also argue that this right-wing American liberalism is itself strongly influenced and distorted by other non-liberal forms of right-wing ideology.

Consider various areas of policy in which the United States differs from all other liberal democracies—e.g. the lack of gun control or comprehensive public health care or laws against hate speech; the presence of capital punishment; the requirement for active voter registration; and laws criminalizing homosexuality. From my point of view, and I suspect Sandel's as well, these are all failings of American democracy. But what explains American distinctiveness on these issues? Sandel wants to argue that in at least some cases, the fault lies with procedural liberalism. But that cannot be the explanation for most of these issues, since most of them clearly violate liberal norms. Moreover, other countries, where liberal egalitarian norms are stronger, have dealt quite differently with these issues.

I suggest that what underlies these issues is something else entirely—namely, a distinctively American attitude which is close to Social Darwinism. Many Americans not only admire success, but are contemptuous of failure—they admire people who rise above their circumstances, and dislike, even fear, those people who are unable to do so. This of course is the very opposite of a liberal egalitarian impulse, which says, not that people should be able to rise above their circumstances, but rather that circumstances should be equalized.

This Social Darwinism is exacerbated by another distinctively American attitude—namely, distrust of big government. This too is in conflict with liberal egalitarianism, since the government's responsibility to rectify unequal circumstances amongst citizens can only be fulfilled by major government programs (e.g. health care). The combination of these two attitudes, I think, helps explain many of the distinctive characteristics of American politics, including the dominance of right-wing liberalism. But, as I see it, right-wing liberalism is not the cause of these attitudes—on the contrary, right-wing liberalism is often the rationalization of underlying cultural attitudes, which are themselves often rooted in various forms of racial and class prejudice. It is these attitudes which are the most important obstacle to meaningful political and social reform, since they corrode a sense of national identity and solidarity, and rationalize highly inegalitarian political structures.

Consider the recent Supreme Court cases striking down the redrawing of Congressional boundaries in order to create Black-majority electoral districts.[11] Sandel typically presents the Supreme Court as making a good-faith effort to promote basic liberal principles. If the Supreme Courts rejects the redrawing of political boundaries, even in order to help disadvantaged groups, then it must be because liberalism is unable to deal with issues of group membership. It seems clear to me, however, reading the decisions, that the Supreme Court made no attempt whatsoever to consider or apply liberal norms to this case. The Court has said, in effect, that electoral boundaries can be redrawn to increase the voting power of any social group (e.g. farmers, religious groups, suburbanites), *except Blacks*—the one group which has suffered most in the past from gerrymandering, and the one group which was most under-represented in Congress. And the Court has said that their position—i.e. that boundaries can be redrawn to help any group except Blacks—is required by equality! Now it seems clear to me, reading the decisions, that the Justices personally opposed the creation of Black-majority districts, and were aware that an increasingly conservative electorate also opposed them, and so looked around desperately to find some rationalization for rejecting them. The resulting decision is, I think, nonsensical. But in any event, it obviously was not motivated at all by liberal impulses. Whether or not they are a good idea, from a policy point of view, creating Black-majority districts clearly does not violate any basic liberal principle—it does not restrict rational revisability of ends, or involve state perfectionism. Indeed, from a liberal egalitarian point of view, such policies which assist the disadvantaged without restricting individual liberty are not only permissible, but in fact required. The opposition to creating Black-majority districts is rooted, at bottom, in a set of nonliberal attitudes, including race and class prejudice.

It seems clear to me that, in this case at least, right-wing liberalism is simply providing a vocabulary which the Court used to rationalize nonliberal opposition to policies which benefit Blacks. And if one agrees that this is at least a possible interpretation of the gerrymandering cases, then it is worth rereading other recent Supreme Court decisions, to see whether they too fit this pattern. And indeed I would argue that the Court's decisions on many issues—gay rights, hate speech, abortion, affirmative action, welfare—reflect the same pattern. Right-wing liberalism may be providing the vocabulary, but it is being used to rationalize cultural attitudes which are opposed (often for nonliberal reasons) to policies which benefit the disadvantaged or minorities, and thereby to legitimate inegalitarian social, economic, and political institutions. Perhaps I am exaggerating this phenomenon, but any analysis of American liberalism which does not take into account the way it has been influenced and distorted by illiberal cultural conservatism is bound to be seriously misleading.

From my point of view—admittedly as an outsider to American politics—Sandel's claim that liberal egalitarianism is one of the causes of America's discontent seems multiply bizarre. Left-wing liberalism has been far too weak to have such consequences, and the real causes of discontent lie in cultural attitudes which are independent of, and in contradiction to, liberal egalitarianism. While right-wing liberalism has been influential, its influence has often been to rationalize nonliberal opposition to progressive policies. And the reason it has been able to do so is that it is right-wing (i.e. because it opposes redistribution), not because it is liberal (i.e. not because of its commitment to revisability and its rejection of perfectionism).

And the solution to this is surely not less liberal egalitarianism, but more. If enough Americans really believed in the liberal egalitarian principle that unequal circumstances should be rectified (rather than feeling contempt for those who cannot rise above their circumstances), then there is nothing in liberal norms of revisability and neutrality which would prevent Americans from strengthening their sense of common identity, and from enhancing the fairness and efficacy of their political system, at both the local and national levels, and from dealing in myriad other ways with their discontents.

So I see no reason to endorse Sandel's claim that we should replace liberal egalitarian arguments with civic republican arguments. But I hasten to add that I would equally oppose efforts to replace all civic republican arguments with liberal arguments. As a strategic matter, different arguments are likely to be convincing to different people. Some people who cannot be motivated to make sacrifices in the name of justice might be motivated to do so in the name of enriching the good of democratic life. Others, who do not view political participation as a privileged locus of the good life, might be untouched by republican arguments, but would be motivated by considerations of justice. Since the two approaches will generate similar conclusions on most issues, there is no reason not to invoke both arguments. From a liberal egalitarian point of view, one of the likely beneficial side-effects of promoting justice is to enrich the quality of political participation; from a civic republican point of view, one of the likely beneficial side effects of promoting the quality of political participation is to achieve greater social justice. In the overwhelming majority of cases, these arguments are complementary, and there is no reason to insist that only one be made.

Of course, as philosophers, we may want to know which is the "real" argument—i.e. which takes precedence should they conflict. But this is a philosopher's question, which would rarely arise in the minds of everyday political agents. It is true that in some rare circumstances, these two arguments may come apart. Promoting an intrinsically rewarding form of political participation for the majority may exacerbate an injustice to the minority. If so, then I believe that liberal egalitarianism should take precedence. But it is unnecessary, and unwise, to extrapolate from these rare moments of conflict to the conclusion that liberal egalitarianism and civic republicanism are inherently in conflict.

4. Long-Term Sustainability

I noted earlier that Sandel could be interpreted, not as objecting to the principles of liberal equality, but rather as arguing that it is unsustainable over the long term. In particular, Sandel rightly notes that liberal egalitarianism requires some sense of bounded community—i.e. some basis for deciding to whom we have obligations of justice—and he doubts that liberal egalitarianism can sustain the underlying sense of solidarity and identity that this requires. Most of the time, he argues that liberal egalitarianism is incapable in principle of addressing the issue of identity. I have tried to show why that principled objection to liberal egalitarianism is mistaken. Liberal states have consistently, and actively, and indeed successfully, promoted a sense of national identity as a response to this problem, without undermining their foundational commitment to individual agency and their opposition to state perfectionism.

But Sandel has a second argument, I think—namely, that this liberal nation-building strategy is no longer viable, due to economic globalization and internal cultural differentiation. He argues that the nation is no longer a viable unit for the purposes of liberal justice, and that we need to develop new forms of political community and political participation.

This is a complicated issue, on which we have lots of armchair speculation but relatively little well-established evidence. For what it is worth, my own sense is that the alleged decentering of national identities is vastly exaggerated, at least in most Western democracies. There is no evidence that I can see to support the claim that the primacy of national identities is being seriously challenged by either external globalization or internal cultural differentiation.[12] On the contrary, in most countries, there remains a fierce commitment to the principle that the nation should remain the primary forum for collective self-government and social justice.[13]

Of course, this is an empirical question, and perhaps down the road the nation will lose its place as the privileged locus of political identity and social justice. If so, then liberal egalitarians will need to create or strengthen just institutions at the supranational and subnational levels, in order to fill the vacuum. And then they will have to adjust their conceptions of virtues and identities accordingly, so as to make these new institutions viable. Some of this is already going on, particularly in Europe. Much of Habermas's work can be seen in this light. And as his work shows, there is nothing in the basic liberal egalitarian commitment to rational revisability, state neutrality, and egalitarian redistribution which precludes this rethinking.

In any event, none of this involves a conflict between liberal equality and civic republicanism. If the traditional liberal commitment to national institutions as the site of collective self-government and distributive justice is no longer viable, then liberals will need to create new forums of self-government, new institutions of redistribution, and corresponding new forms of identity and virtues. All of this is perfectly consistent with, and indeed required by, liberal egalitarian justice. Liberal egalitarian justice remains the criterion for assessing political institutions and policies, but liberals should have an open mind about what institutions and policies, at what levels, will best serve those principles. And on this, as on most issues, liberal egalitarians and civic republicans can and should work together to find imaginative proposals that promote both social justice and participatory democracy.

11

Moral Status and the Status of Morality in Political Liberalism

ANDREW W. SIEGEL

1. Introduction: Law, Politics, and Metaphysics

In *Democracy's Discontent*, Michael Sandel's diagnosis of the ills of contemporary American constitutional law centers in large measure on the liberal ideal of neutrality and the conception of the person which underwrites that ideal. The leitmotif of Sandel's account is that the Supreme Court's interpretation of the Constitution as a framework of rights which is neutral between competing views of the good is premised on the Kantian picture of persons as autonomous agents who transcend their desires and purposes and who are capable of freely choosing their ends. For Sandel, the problem with this mode of representing the self is that it fails to capture the experience of encumbered selves, who conceive of their moral identities as constituted by their ends. We cannot rely upon legal doctrine fashioned in the image of the free and independent self to adequately protect the interests of persons who view themselves as claimed by aims and attachments which are not the result of an exercise of free will. Moreover, according to Sandel, the liberal ideal of neutrality and toleration which the Kantian concept of the self supports provides an impoverished form of respect for individual rights because "it seeks respect for persons without winning respect for the convictions they hold or the lives they live."[1] The corrective Sandel proposes to these problems is that we purge constitutional law of its liberal metaphysics and the ideal of neutrality which that metaphysics sustains. This will allow the law both to reflect the moral experience of encumbered selves and to supplant liberal toleration with a value-laden discourse which can affirm conceptions of the good.

Now while Sandel insightfully indicates some problems with the metaphysics of contemporary constitutional law, the rejection of this metaphysics does not necessarily undermine the liberal enterprise. For there is a version of

I would like to thank the Greenwall Foundation for fellowship support during work on this chapter.

liberalism, championed in the recent writings of John Rawls, which seeks to expel all metaphysics from its account of justice.[2] This form of liberalism—"political liberalism"—aims to specify the conditions under which a fair and stable system of social cooperation can exist given the plurality of reasonable but often conflicting ethical, religious, and philosophical viewpoints which characterize modern democratic societies. Political liberalism asserts that, in light of the fact of reasonable pluralism, the principles of justice which govern the basic social structure cannot be founded on a set of doctrines which some reasonable persons would not accept. The imposition of a comprehensive philosophical or religious doctrine on persons who reasonably reject it is, according to the political liberal, an oppressive use of state power. Political liberalism thus "applies the principle of toleration to philosophy itself,"[3] and seeks to construct an account of justice on which citizens who adhere to opposing philosophical and religious doctrines can reach an overlapping consensus.

The political liberal can thus endorse Sandel's critique of liberalism insofar as it is directed against the dominance of the Kantian view of the person in law and politics. From the standpoint of political liberalism, the institutionalization of the Kantian conception of the person itself constitutes a failure to be sufficiently tolerant of competing views of the self. The political liberal would affirm Sandel's view that encumbered selves should not be disadvantaged in constitutional adjudication. But where the political liberal must part company with Sandel is at the point at which Sandel presses for abandoning the ideal of neutrality and permitting constitutional argument to appeal to controversial doctrines of the good. The political liberal's concern is that relinquishing neutrality would place citizens at an unwarranted risk of oppressive uses of state power. For the political liberal, Sandel's critique of the pervasiveness of the unencumbered self in legal discourse shows that we need to raise neutrality to a higher level, not that we need to relinquish it. Political liberalism promises a higher-order neutrality which both avoids marginalizing encumbered selves and protects against the risks of coercion which communitarianism poses.

Sandel argues, however, that political liberalism cannot deliver on its promise. He maintains that "a political conception of justice must sometimes presuppose an answer to the moral and religious questions it purports to bracket."[4] Sandel's suggestion is that controversial assumptions about morality and religion are an ineliminable feature of legal and political decisions. If Sandel is right about this, then political liberalism fails to satisfy its own criterion of legitimacy. The political liberal cannot herself escape the charge of acting in a coercive manner; and thus she cannot, without creating a Pecksniffian stench, continue to decry the communitarian's wish to inject contentious moral doctrines into politics and constitutional law.

In what follows, I will assess Sandel's arguments against political liberalism. I will maintain that he does not successfully demonstrate that political liberalism is incapable of preserving the neutrality which its account of justice demands. While we will discover that sometimes the costs of sustaining the level of neutrality required by political liberalism exceed what many liberals are prepared to incur, this finding will not advance the communitarian cause. Indeed, the considerations which lead us to this point will draw our attention to some important problems with Sandel's game plan for dethroning liberalism.

2. Abortion and Slavery: Political Justice and Moral Status

Sandel invokes the abortion and slavery debates to support his position that the political conception of justice sometimes relies on implicit answers to the moral and religious controversies which it claims to bracket. He presents two related arguments. His first argument is that the political liberal must make certain moral or religious assumptions in defending the right to abortion and the right not to be enslaved. Sandel holds that those who believe that toleration requires that we leave the abortion decision to women presuppose that the fetus does not have the moral status of a person: "The case for respecting a woman's right to abortion depends on showing that there is a relevant moral difference between aborting a fetus at a relatively early stage of development and killing a child."[5] Similarly, he suggests that one cannot oppose slavery on the grounds that it violates individual rights without appealing to a view about the moral status of slaves:

> Present-day liberals will surely . . . want national policy to oppose slavery, presumably on the grounds that slavery violates people's rights. But it is doubtful that liberalism conceived as a political conception of justice can make this claim without violating its own strictures against appeals to comprehensive moral ideals. For example, a Kantian liberal can oppose slavery as a failure to treat persons as ends in themselves, worthy of respect. But this argument, resting as it does on a Kantian conception of the person, is unavailable to [political] liberalism.[6]

Sandel's second argument against political liberalism is that what counts as bracketing the moral and religious issues associated with abortion and slavery is itself controversial; and "this controversy may require for its solution either a substantive evaluation of the interests at stake or at least a conception of the self that [political] liberalism resolves to avoid."[7] On the abortion issue, the Supreme Court can seek to remain neutral on the morality of abortion either by allowing individual women to decide the matter for themselves or by leaving the question to the people of the states to vote on. Sandel maintains that those who want to promote neutrality by leaving the abortion decision to women are committed to a Kantian view of the self: "If liberals want to bracket controversial moral questions in a way that assures individual choice . . . they must affirm after all a conception of the person on which the self is prior to its ends."[8] On the slavery issue, Stephen Douglas, in his debate with Lincoln, argued that national policy should be neutral on the question of the morality of slavery, and that the matter should be left to the people of the territories to decide. Again, according to Sandel, the political liberal can reject this position only if she takes a substantive position on the morality of slavery.

I believe that neither of these arguments is successful in showing that political liberals must decide legal and political issues in a manner which violates the tenets of their own theory of justice. Against Sandel, I will argue that one can oppose slavery and defend abortion rights while remaining neutral on moral and theological questions. I will also argue that the political liberal can specify criteria for choosing between different modes of bracketing moral and religious issues without relying on an implicit position on those issues. I do not think, however, that most liberals will find themselves emerging from my analysis unscathed. In responding to Sandel's argument on the abortion issue, we will find the political liberal faced with a situation which is likely to evoke some nostalgia for metaphysics.

Slavery: Moral vs. *Political Conceptions of the Person*

Political liberals can readily handle Sandel's objection that their commitment to a purely political account of justice leaves them without the resources needed to oppose slavery. While Sandel suggests that the liberal's opposition to slavery must appeal to a moral conception of the person which rules out the institution, the political liberal in fact has a political conception of the person which yields the same result.

In Rawls's political account of justice as fairness, "the idea of the person as having moral personality with the full capacity of moral agency is transformed into that of the citizen."[9] Political liberalism does not operate with a metaphysical view of the person, but rather defines persons in relation to its goal of identifying a fair system of social cooperation. The conception of the person which serves this goal is that of a citizen, namely, a person who can respect and exercise the rights and duties of social life and thus function as "a normal and fully cooperating member of society over a complete life."[10] In order for a person to function as such, she must both have ends which she wants to advance by fair cooperation and be willing to recognize the validity of the claims of others. According to Rawls, it follows that the political account of justice regards persons as free and equal. Persons are free inasmuch as they possess both the capacity to form, revise, and pursue a conception of the good and the capacity to act from a sense of justice. Persons are equal inasmuch as they possess these capacities to the minimum degree required to be fully cooperating members of society.

Slavery is impermissible on the political conception of justice because it fails to recognize the political status of individuals who possess the properties of citizens and because it violates the principles which govern the fair terms of social cooperation among citizens. Since slaves have the capacity for a conception of the good and a sense of justice, they possess the attributes which define political personhood. Slavery falsely represents citizens as nonpersons, as socially dead. Moreover, once we recognize slaves as citizens, it is clear that the political liberal's principles for the legitimate exercise of power exclude the possibility of slavery. A governing principle in the political liberal's account is the "criterion of reciprocity," according to which "[o]ur exercise of political power is proper only when we sincerely believe that the reasons we offer for our political action may reasonably be accepted by [all] other citizens as a justification of those actions."[11] There can be no doubt that slavery is an institution which fails to satisfy this condition.

It is evident, then, that the political liberal can oppose slavery without appealing to moral or religious doctrines. The idea of society as a fair system of cooperation and the political conception of the person which goes with this idea are sufficient to generate principles which bar slavery. These considerations also reveal that the political liberal can choose between different modes of bracketing moral and religious controversies without taking a position on the controversies. In this instance, the essential bracketing of moral and religious doctrines occurred at the point at which the political liberal formulated her principles of political justice. These principles include a specification of basic liberties designed to ensure that citizens can flourish as free and equal persons. The political liberal's principles of justice support a constitution which forbids states from restricting citizens' political freedoms. Douglas's stance that we should bracket the moral issues of slavery by leaving the matter to the territories is incompatible with this constitutional framework because it allows citizens to exercise power in a manner which undermines political freedoms. Sandel's invocation of the slavery debate therefore does not ultimately thwart political liberalism.

Abortion

Sandel's claim that political liberalism cannot furnish neutral grounds for deciding the abortion issue presents political liberals with far more vexing problems than those posed by the slavery debate. The central problem Sandel raises is that one cannot defend abortion rights without making assumptions about the value of fetal life. Sandel cites the Supreme Court's decision in *Roe* v. *Wade* to illustrate this problem. In *Roe*, Texas argued that its law prohibiting abortion was justified because the State has a compelling interest in protecting life from the moment of conception. The Court struck the law down, asserting that it did "not agree that, by adopting one theory of life, Texas may override the rights of the pregnant woman that are at stake."[12] However, while the Court professed to be neutral between competing theories of life, its decision relied on a controversial view about the value of fetal life: "With respect to the State's important and legitimate interest in potential life, the 'compelling' point is at viability. This is so because the fetus then presumably has the capability of meaningful life outside the mother's womb. State regulation protective of fetal life after viability thus has both logical and biological justifications."[13] The Court's characterization of its opinion as grounded in logic and biology masks the value judgments which inform its decision. The Court can hold that viability is the point at which the state has an "important and legitimate interest" in protecting fetal life only through an implicit rejection of the thesis that the fetus has the moral status of a person at all points in its development.

Rawls similarly relies on a view about the value of fetal life in his discussion of the abortion issue:

> Suppose . . . that we consider the [abortion] question in terms of these three important political values: the due respect for human life, the ordered reproduction of political society over time, including the family in some form, and finally the equality of women as equal citizens . . . Now I believe any reasonable balance of these three values will give a woman a duly qualified right to decide whether or not to end her pregnancy during the first trimester. The reason for this is that at this early stage of pregnancy the political value of the equality of women is overriding, and this right is required to give it substance and force.[14]

It is clear that Rawls's perception of what constitutes a reasonable balance of political values in the abortion case is colored by certain assumptions about the moral status of the fetus. For one who believes that aborting a first-trimester fetus is morally equivalent to killing an innocent person will almost certainly—and I think it is fair to assume Rawls would—hold that the value of due respect for the fetus's life outweighs the value of the equality which abortion rights advance for women.

Given that both the Supreme Court and the most prominent political liberals presuppose a view about the moral status of the fetus in their support of abortion rights, Sandel's claim that there do not exist neutral grounds upon which to defend the right to abortion might seem unassailable. However, Sandel's analysis overlooks that there are liberals who have argued that we can divorce our judgment about the permissibility of abortion from our beliefs about the value of fetal of life. I think that at least one of their arguments attenuates Sandel's critique of political liberalism, though it also has some consequences which most liberals will find disquieting.

Equal Protection One line of argument for detaching the case for abortion rights from judgments about the status of the fetus states that even if we concede that the fetus is a person with a right to life, its right to life does not give it a right to use a woman's body to sustain its life.[15] To compel a woman to carry through with an unwanted pregnancy would be tantamount to imposing upon her a duty to rescue the fetus. But since the law does not require that we allow other persons to exploit our bodies for sustenance, it would violate equal protection to force pregnant women to make this kind of sacrifice. Whatever one thinks about the moral status of the fetus, a pregnant woman is under no obligation to save its life.

This argument is, however, problematic. There are a number of features of the abortion case that seem to importantly distinguish it from standard instances of refusals of aid. First, a woman typically bears partial responsibility for placing the fetus in the position in which it needs her aid. Second, a woman's intent in having an abortion is generally not so much to be free of the burdens of pregnancy as it is to avoid the burdens of being a parent.[16] Arguably, most women who choose abortion are seeking to deny the fetus an existence altogether.[17] Third, an abortion requires an assault on the fetus which results in its demise. Although it is true that the right to life does not give a person a positive right to aid, it does entail a negative right not to be killed.

These considerations taken together make it difficult to defend abortion where one concedes that the fetus is a person. If there were a case in which (a) a parent acted in a negligent or reckless manner which resulted in his or her child needing aid; (b) the parent wished to refuse the child aid in order to avoid being a parent; and (c) denying aid required an attack on the child, we would likely hold that the parent does not have a right to refuse aid to the child. The general rule that we do not have a duty to save the lives of others thus does not appear to be applicable in the abortion case when we assume that the fetus has the moral status of a person.

Religious Freedom Ronald Dworkin's observation that our beliefs about the value of fetal life are "*essentially* religious beliefs" provides the foundation for a different approach for preserving neutrality on the abortion issue.[18] Dworkin argues that those who oppose abortion do so on the religious (or at least quasi-religious) grounds that the act insults the sanctity of human life. He suggests that the defense of abortion rights need not be premised on a rejection of this view about the intrinsic value of life. Instead, he argues that we can defend abortion rights on the grounds that it would be a violation of the religious freedom which the First Amendent guarantees for states to impose a particular conception of the sacred on everyone. Dworkin believes that once we understand the abortion issue as one which fundamentally concerns religious tolerance, we can overcome the polarizations which plague the current abortion debate.

Dworkin's argument shows that Sandel is mistaken when he speaks of the "impossibility of bracketing the moral-theological question of when human life begins."[19] One can defend abortion rights on neutral grounds if one adheres to the principle that a state may not curtail a person's liberties through the imposition of a controversial religious view. As long as one deems laws prohibiting abortion unconstitutional on the sole basis that they enforce a controversial conception of the sacred, one can successfully defend abortion rights without taking a position on the status of the fetus.

But while we can enlist Dworkin's argument to refute Sandel's claim that a liberal *necessarily* presupposes a view about the moral and religious questions which she asserts we must bracket, there are logical extensions of the neutral standpoint Dworkin offers which I think few liberals would be prepared to accept. Imagine, for example, a religious group which believes that (painlessly) sacrificing their own newborn infants is required for the salvation of the members of the group. Surely, almost all liberals would consider such a practice atrocious and hold that we should not permit it. But how can a liberal deny this group the right to engage in infanticide without imposing a particular view of the sacred on them?

It is true, as Dworkin would claim, that newborn infants have interests which early-stage fetuses do not because newborns are sentient. However, while sentience may be sufficient for a right to be spared pain (which I have stipulated the religious group in question respects), we do not regard it sufficient to ground a right to life. This is amply demonstrated by the fact that the animals which we regularly slaughter are sentient. It is also worth noting that many of these animals possess greater cognitive capacities than newborn infants. Of course, a newborn has the potential for higher cognitive capacities than other creatures. But this potential is shared by the early-stage fetuses which liberals think it permissible for women to abort.

It seems doubtful, then, that a liberal can reconcile her opposition to the religious group's right to infanticide with her (typical) stance on abortion and animal rights by appealing to some demonstrable properties of newborns which crucially distinguish them from fetuses and animals.[20] The more plausible explanation for the liberal's opposition to infanticide is that she believes infants have an intrinsic value which is inviolable. It seems most liberals would be willing to interfere with the hypothetical religious group's practice precisely because it is so at odds with their own conception of the sacred.[21] But it follows that the liberal defense of abortion rights is in fact generally premised on a rejection of the pro-life view of the value of fetal life. The liberal who opposes a right to infanticide in the above case would not permit abortion if she believed that fetuses and newborns had the same moral status.

Thus, *pace* Sandel, a political liberal can advocate a constitutional right to abortion on a neutral foundation. But it appears she can do so only if she is prepared to accept the logical consequences of Dworkin's analysis. Because it is unlikely that most political liberals would embrace these consequences, the political liberal cannot in good faith subsume abortion rights under the basic liberties which her political conception of justice supports. It seems the political liberal cannot promote a constitutional right to abortion without administering a fatal dose of metaphysics into her account.

Nevertheless, the political liberal can provide a neutral resolution of the abortion issue. Although it appears that the political liberal must, in order to ward off metaphysics, denounce a constitutional right to abortion, she can preserve legal neutrality by leaving the issue of abortion rights to the states to decide. Rawls notes this option: "[D]isputed questions, such as that of abortion, may lead to a stand-off between different political conceptions, and citizens must simply vote on the question."[22] Sandel is mistaken when he claims that one cannot choose whether to leave the issue to the states without taking "a substantive view about the moral and religious interests at stake."[23] If political liberals were to make this choice based on their moral and religious views, it is evident that most would promote a constitutional right to abortion. The political liberal must be prepared to leave the issue to the states *despite* her moral and religious beliefs.

Of course, given the fervor with which liberals defend the constitutional right to abortion, it is not at all clear that we can expect many wholehearted conversions to political liberalism. Liberals will no doubt be strongly inclined to cling to their metaphysics if its expulsion from the law entails a denial of constitutional protection of abortion rights.

Thus, while Sandel has not demonstrated that a "political conception of justice must sometimes presuppose an answer to the moral and religious questions it purports to bracket,"[24] maneuvering around his objections leads us down a road which most liberals will not want to travel. The question with which we ultimately have to come to terms is whether the tolls which political liberalism would exact in raising tolerance to new heights are worth paying. Though we cannot resolve this matter here, we can strengthen the case for political liberalism by exposing some problems with the alternative path which Sandel's communitarianism offers.

3. Communitarianism and the Limits of Morality

In his discussion of constitutional law, Sandel maintains that, even where liberalism can sustain the neutrality which its theory of justice demands, the kind of toleration which liberalism provides is problematic: "Given its aspiration to neutrality, it brackets the value of the practices it tolerates . . . The toleration that results does not cultivate appreciation for the ways of life it permits, only respect for the selves whose lives they are."[25] Sandel believes that we should abandon the liberal ideal of neutrality and allow moral argument to play a role in constitutional adjudication. It is only in this way that we can "realize the higher pluralism of persons and communities who appreciate and affirm the distinctive goods their different lives express."[26]

There are, however, several difficulties with Sandel's proposal. First, moral argument in constitutional adjudication can do as much damage as it can good. It is true that we can use moral argument to strengthen our defense of certain rights. Sandel points out, for example, that a moral argument which "articulate[s] the human goods that homosexual intimacy may share with heterosexual unions" has advantages over the neutral case for tolerating homosexual rights, which "leaves wholly unchallenged the adverse views of homosexuality itself."[27] But one can—and many would—deploy moral argument to demean and undermine these same rights. Though liberal neutrality does not offer affirmation and appreciation of the practices which it tolerates, it does shelter individual rights from the menace to which Sandel's approach exposes them.

Second, it is far from obvious that moral argument in constitutional law is necessary for cultivating an appreciation for different ways of life. It might well be that we can accomplish this end through moral persuasion in nonstate forums. Sandel's riposte is that we cannot expect to succeed in this because the kind of moral and political dialogue which occurs outside of the law mirrors that which occurs in the constitutional arena: "Assumptions drawn from constitutional discourse increasingly set the terms of moral and political debate in general."[28] But Sandel's suggestion here rests on unsupported causal assumptions. While Sandel establishes that liberal notions of the self and the state are pervasive in both law and society, he does not show that the liberal ideas embodied in the social sphere originate from constitutional discourse. It seems just as plausible, given the evidence he provides, that the liberalism of constitutional law is an epiphenomenon of the liberalism of other aspects of our culture. Sandel thus offers no compelling reason to think that changing the nature of constitutional discourse is a necessary condition for changing the kind of moral and political dialogue which takes place in other spheres.

Finally, Sandel's faith that moral argument in law can help us to realize a "higher pluralism of persons and communities who appreciate and affirm the distinctive goods their different lives express" seems blind to the depth of the divisions which mark the pluralistic society in which we live. As we have seen, the moral disagreements which surround issues like abortion are so fundamental that the affirmation of one moral stance entails a rejection of competing views. The Court cannot defend or gainsay a constitutional right to abortion through a set of judgments about the morality of the practice without displaying a lack of respect for the (reasonable) convictions of certain groups. Where the divisions run this deep, Sandel's call for a form of respect superior to that which liberalism provides is self-defeating. The poverty of the respect political liberalism affords is an unavoidable product of the elixir which permits a rich diversity of beliefs and practices to flourish.

12

Sandel's Liberal Politics

BRUCE FROHNEN

FIRST I should state what I am not attempting in this chapter. By discussing the liberal nature of Michael Sandel's vision of politics and the self, I do not intend to engage in sterile intellectual gamesmanship, "catching" Sandel in an inconsistency by proving that he is a liberal despite himself. Such an endeavor would add nothing to our understanding of Sandel, liberalism, or communitarianism. What is more, a number of political philosophers have written with great insight concerning the essentially liberal character of contemporary communitarianism.

For example, Charles Taylor argues that the liberal-communitarian debate is actually one between liberals "who believe that the state should be neutral between the different conceptions of the good life espoused by individuals, on the one hand, and those who believe that a democratic society needs some commonly recognized definition of the good life, on the other."[1] Communitarians are liberals who want to reestablish a common sense among the people of what the nation is for—of what its people share in their history and what they should strive together to accomplish.

I believe that this is a useful starting point for a study of a self-professed communitarian like Sandel. Why? Because my goal is to understand better the nature of both the suppositions and the good toward which Sandel, communitarianism, and liberalism would have us strive. And I have become convinced that the good is individual flourishing, the self-directed development of the choice-making self. I also have become convinced that the suppositions concerning the self on which this vision of the good relies, and the politics by which Sandel and other communitarians would have us achieve that good, guarantee that real, substantive community will never be achieved on liberal/communitarian grounds.

Older, conservative communitarians such as Robert Nisbet and Russell Kirk sought to revive families and other fundamental associations in the belief that only forceful institutions and traditions, ones which we cannot "choose" to discard, can provide the structure we need. Without them individuals cannot act in accordance with transcendent standards of good conduct, and societies cannot maintain their internal order and coherence. On this view, we must combat the centralized state to make room for mediating institutions so that we and our communities again can strive to live up to permanent standards beyond our power to choose or refuse.[2]

On first look, Sandel's critique of liberal individualism seems to have much in common with the demands of older communitarians. After all, Sandel has focused on the sense in which many of our attachments are not products of our individual choice, yet shape our characters. On this view, liberalism's mistaken emphasis on the primacy of individual voluntary choice has undermined both community and individual character development.[3]

But I will argue here that to accommodate the liberal self's attachments, to situate it, is not to eliminate or even displace it. Indeed, in my view Sandel's project is calculated to save the liberal self from its unnecessary and in the end illogical emptying out, a process that began with Kant and increased dramatically in recent decades. John Locke, arguably the thinker most responsible for the formation of liberalism, did not posit an individual that was reduced to a disembodied will. Locke's individual had rights based on the property it held in its own body and the talents and character traits it developed over time—through its relationships with other individuals and groups.

In this light we can see that Sandel's recognition of the encumbrances all individuals pick up over the course of their lives merely makes more sensible his vision of individual flourishing. At no time does he go beyond the idea of individuals forming and breaking commitments in accordance with their own self-view to a vision recognizing the role of permanent standards of good conduct that transcend human will. Sandel's self remains liberal because it remains the center of attention.

Sandel retains the primal liberal attachment to individual flourishing as the proper end of life.[4] He seeks to promote a self that fulfills its authentic nature, making morally meaningful choices on the basis of its own attachments. His attempt relies on maximizing society's obligation to accommodate individual choices, rather than imposing a hyper-individualist, morally empty life on individuals. To implement social accommodation to individual attachments or encumbrances, Sandel prescribes a public life characterized by toleration, equality, and political activity—all liberal political goals. Thus he merely completes the modern liberal vision of the good life.

I first examine Sandel's critique of the liberalism espoused (following Kant) by John Rawls, and in particular Sandel's rejection of disembodied will. I next reconstruct Sandel's own vision of the self, showing its critical similarities to a proper reading of Locke. Finally, I analyze Sandel's political vision to show its attachment to fundamentally liberal goals. Sandel's early work focused on making a distinction between the Rawlsian and his own communitarian or constituted self. As such, the bulk of the first two sections of this chapter concentrate on that early work. Sandel's most recent book, *Democracy's Discontent: America in Search of a Public Philosophy*, is an attempt to construct a political vision capable of doing justice to the self he posits in opposition to Rawls. I deal with that book in the third and final section of the chapter.

Sandel vs. Rawls

Sandel's career began in explicit opposition to liberal individualism.[5] His first book, *Liberalism and the Limits of Justice,* was a critique of John Rawls's *Theory of Justice.* Of particular concern to Sandel was Rawls's prioritization of the just over the good, of the bases on which goods and status would be distributed, over any common goals, including that of promoting individual virtue.[6] As important, for Sandel, was the theory of the self on which this liberal prioritization rested.

To justify prioritizing the right (justice) over the good, according to Sandel, Kant, and following him Rawls, had to separate the individual from the world of experience. Only a disembodied self, one not subject to the demands of the material world, could be truly free. And only a truly free individual could be worthy of being treated as an end in itself—as properly demanding just treatment. The subject of experience, rather than the object of experience, was the only self capable of supporting the claims of justice to priority over the good. According to Sandel, for Kant

> *Qua* object of experience, I belong to the sensible world; my actions are determined, as the movements of all other objects are determined, by the laws of nature and the regularities of cause and effect. *Qua* subject of experience, by contrast, I inhabit an intelligible or super-sensible world; here, being independent of the laws of nature, I am capable of autonomy, capable of acting according to a law I give myself.
>
> Only from this second standpoint can I regard myself as free, "for to be independent of determination by causes in the sensible world . . . is to be free." Were I wholly an empirical being, I would not be capable of freedom, for every exercise of will would be conditioned by the desire for some object. . . My will could never be a first cause, only the effect of some prior cause, the instrument of one or another impulse or inclination.[7]

Thus, also for Sandel's Kant,

> the basis of the moral law is to be found in the subject, not the object of practical reason, a subject capable of an autonomous will. No empirical end but rather "a subject of ends, namely a rational being himself, must be made the ground for all maxims of action." Nothing other than "the subject of all possible ends himself" can give rise to the right, for only this subject is also the subject of an autonomous will. Only such a subject could be that "something which elevates man above himself as a part of the world of sense" and enables him to participate in an ideal, unconditioned realm wholly independent of our social and psychological inclinations.[8]

On Sandel's view, Rawls's largely Kantian theory of justice rests on an emptying out of human nature. Kant's individual attained the status of "subject" by dispensing with its attachments and goals. It achieved priority over any particular social end by becoming a universal; by jettisoning all its unique, distinguishing characteristics so that it could encompass all possible choices of ends or, rather, embody the universal notion of free choice.

This abstraction of the self precluded a common good toward which all of us might aim. It made choice, rather than any substantive end, the determining characteristic of humanity. Thus, "Society is best arranged when it is governed by principles that do not presuppose any particular conception of the good, for any other arrangement would fail to respect persons as beings capable of choice; it would treat them as objects rather than subjects, as means rather than ends in themselves."[9]

According to Sandel, freedom from the restrictions of a preconceived notion of the good is purchased at a heavy price. The self's reduction to subject separates each of us from the crucial attachments and characteristics that make us human. To begin with, the separation of the self from its assets—including talents and character traits such as hard work—makes the Rawlsian self incapable of desert. The self's traits and talents are the result of mere chance, on this reading. It deserves no reward for any proper or useful conduct because it did not truly produce this conduct; its unearned attributes did.

Because the self cannot deserve its own attributes, society has a prior claim to them, and can reward or punish them in accordance with its own desires. Thus, "either my prospects are left at the mercy of institutions established for 'prior and independent social ends,' ends which may or may not coincide with my own, or I must count myself a member of a community defined in part by those ends, in which case I cease to be unencumbered by constitutive attachments."[10]

Rawls cannot allow an encumbered self into his system because this would undermine his prioritization of the right over the good. His self must be rendered subservient to his goal-less society, and so "is less liberated than disempowered." Stripped of its attachments, Rawls's self loses control over its destiny and even its day-to-day circumstances as society takes control over "its" pool of assets and character traits.[11]

Even within its own limited purview, the Rawlsian self is in a sense powerless because its lack of attachments leads to a loss of identity, self-reflection, and the possibility of moral choice. Because it is a "subject," Rawls's self is preconstituted; it is not affected by life-experiences or attachments. No matter what its experiences, the subject remains disembodied will, the universal, unencumbered choice-maker. The self's lack of substantive attachments undermines

> those loyalties and convictions whose moral force consists partly in the fact that living by them is inseparable from understanding ourselves as the particular persons we are—as members of this family or community or nation or people, as citizens of this republic. Allegiances such as these are more than values I happen to have or aims I "espouse at any given time." They go beyond the obligations I voluntarily incur and the "natural duties" I owe to human beings as such. They allow that to some I owe more than justice requires or even permits, not by reason of agreements I have made but instead in virtue

of those more or less enduring attachments and commitments which taken together partly define the person I am.

To imagine a person incapable of constitutive attachments such as these is not to conceive an ideally free and rational agent, but to imagine a person wholly without character, without moral depth.[12]

The Rawlsian self is not a full human being. It cannot make moral choices, but instead merely follows discovered preferences. And its lack of moral depth extends to its relations with others. A self without character cannot forge lasting, mutually enriching relationships. It is incapable of friendship because it can only act according to the formalities of distributive justice. Justice becomes the form and substance of a self rendered empty and shapeless by its search for autonomy.

Sandel's Self

Luckily for us, according to Sandel, the Rawlsian self contradicts reality. Our "selves" are not wholly independent, predetermined, and radically separated from our assets, ends, and attachments. We are, in fact, partly constituted by the connections we form with others.

Sandel points out that close relations form intimate attachments. They affect the individuals taking part in them precisely because they require more than mere justice. Family ties and close friendships would be harmed or even destroyed if one of the parties held the others to contractual formalities—no matter how just.[13] Justice ought to have, and in practice has, priority over the good only in those circumstances in which individuals lack ties more intimate and important to their lives than contracts. Indeed,

we can readily imagine a range of more intimate or solidaristic associations in which the values and aims of the participants coincide closely enough that the circumstances of justice prevail to a relatively small degree. As Hume himself observes, we need not have recourse to utopian visions or the diction of poets to imagine such conditions, but "may discover the same truth by common experience and observation."[14]

Most fundamental, for Hume (and following him, Sandel) is the family. In Hume's words "between married persons, the cement of friendship is by the laws supposed so strong as to abolish all division of possessions; and has often, in reality, the force ascribed to it."[15] Sandel continues:

While the institution of the family may represent am extreme case in this respect, we can easily imagine a range of intermediate cases of social institutions, a continuum of human associations characterized in varying degrees by the circumstances of justice. These would include, at various points along the spectrum, tribes, neighborhoods, cities, towns, universities, trade unions, national liberation elements and established nationalism, and a wide variety of ethnic, religious, cultural, and linguistic communities with more or less clearly-defined common identities and shared purposes, precisely those attributes whose presence signifies the relative absence of the circumstances of justice.[16]

On Sandel's reading justice is a remedial virtue, needed only when the shared goals and aspirations of a group crumble and are replaced by conflict over the distribution of necessary goods. "Justice is the first virtue of social institutions not absolutely, as truth is to theories, but only conditionally, as physical courage is to a war zone."[17] Instead of justice, according to Sandel, properly constituted communities are held together by benevolence, by spontaneous affections based on shared circumstances.[18] Rawls's self lacks these attachments because Rawls has stripped them from it in order to give justice a priority not properly its own. "For to have a character is to know that I move in a history I neither summon nor command, which carries consequences nonetheless for my choices and conduct. It draws me closer to some and more distant from others; it makes some aims more appropriate, others less so."[19] In the place of Rawls's disembodied self, Sandel offers one that is at least partially constructed by its attachments. Sandel's self is changed by its relations with others. Its experiences in dealing with other individuals and groups cause it to form habits, and gain or lose character traits such as honesty or dishonesty.

Sandel argues that it is the capacity for change that makes meaningful moral choice possible.

> When I act out of more or less enduring qualities of character . . . my choice of ends is not arbitrary in the same way [as for Rawls's self]. In consulting my preferences, I have not only to weigh their intensity but also to assess their suitability to the person I (already) am. I ask, as I deliberate, not only what I really want but who I really am, and this last question takes me beyond an attention to my desires alone to reflect on my identity itself.[20]

Self-reflection requires context. One must know something of one's attachments or encumbrances (and perhaps consult those to whom one is attached) to know of one's self. And this knowledge is necessary to set one free. "While the notion of constitutive attachments may at first seem an obstacle to agency—the self, now encumbered, is no longer strictly prior—some relative fixity of character appears essential to prevent the lapse into arbitrariness which the deontological self is unable to avoid."[21]

Only if we have a character, a set of habits and attachments put at risk by our moral choices, can those choices be meaningful. And only by making meaningful choices can we exercise our full capacities, exercising and developing our individual, authentic self. According to Sandel, it is by interacting and forming attachments with others that we learn how to make authentic choices. We are not born with the ability to make moral choices. We must develop this ability, becoming autonomous, moral choice-makers over time.

By noting the requirements for genuine choice, Sandel continues a long tradition of liberal thought. For example, John Stuart Mill argued for authenticity—but only for those with the capacity to exercise it properly: "If a person possesses any tolerable amount of common sense and experience, his own mode of laying out his existence is the best, not because it is the best in itself, but because it is his own mode."[22] For Mill anyone *not* possessed of a tolerable amount of common sense and experience should not be allowed to lay out his own existence. His choices, because they would be nonsensical, would also be useless, or even harmful. Only if we have the right character can we make coherent choices and so be truly, authentically free.

John Locke also saw the individual's need for proper education if it is to exercise meaningful autonomy. Indeed, Locke saw the family, Sandel's own prototypical constitutive community, as the center of learning, the font of character and authentic choice. Locke argued that families developed from the natural, innate desire to procreate and the requirements of child-rearing.[23] The family forms naturally, according to Locke, and its educative function—the natural (and naturally recognized) duty of parents to care for their offspring until they can shift for themselves—is essential to its nature (para. 79).

Ruth Grant has argued that Locke sought to free the individual's reason from the confines of often irrational and unnatural social custom.[24] But this freedom is acquired only after the individual has been taught, in the family, how to be rational and therefore autonomous.[25] The rational faculties do not spring fully developed from the wilds. As Alex Neill argues, for Locke reason is acquired through an education which instills the proper habits of mind and the proper control over desires so that self-interest will be tamed and led to become dispassionate and farsighted.[26]

A child cannot reason properly as yet, so his parents must reason for him, providing him with "the necessities of his life, the health of his body, and the information of his mind" (para. 61). While their child is not yet rational, parents have the natural duty to preserve his life and train him so that he will become autonomous—able to exercise his natural liberty[27] (para. 61).

Once the defects of weakness and undeveloped reason are supplied, the power of parents over their children ceases, leaving the children obligated to honor the parents for their services. But these encumbered children owe honor only in proportion to the care received. Uncaring parents deserve no honor (para. 70). What is more, the continuing authority of the parents is based on the continuing propriety of their actions.

Opposing Sir Robert Filmer's defense of hereditary patriarchy, Locke argued that fathers became rulers only by exercising, nurturing, and building on the natural benevolence spawned in the family. A trusted father is allowed to exercise increasing authority as the family and its territory and concerns grow. Children allow their father to settle disputes between them because they are accustomed to trusting in the fairness and "tenderness" of he who raised them (para. 75).

Sandel also sees benevolence as the glue holding fundamental relationships together. Only friends and loved ones can share the mutual knowledge and regard necessary to look out for one another's interests. Only friends and loved ones can help one develop the self-knowledge needed for genuine moral choice.[28]

Attachments, for Locke and for Sandel, are necessary because they are the natural means by which we become capable of meaningful choice. Intimate associations are necessary to give the individual the context and character traits necessary to make moral choices. But the authentic choice of the individual self remains primary. Intimate relations, while natural, are good only because and to the extent that they promote independent, rationally-based moral choice. And, as I argue below, politics remains, for Sandel as for all liberals, at the service of the individual, intended to maximize its opportunity for autonomous choice.

Republican Liberalism

Sandel's latest work, *Democracy's Discontent,* is an attempt to apply his critique of individualist theory to the practice of public life in America. Much of this work attempts to outline a "republican" tradition in the United States opposed to radical individualism. Republicanism, according to Sandel, is the belief that true freedom resides in communal self-rule. But it is the self that is to be made free; free to make autonomous choices and flourish through participation in politics. Sandel's politics, like his psychological view of the self, does not promote some amorphous alternative to liberalism; it promotes a more robust and activist form of liberalism.

Sandel's self remains a self-actuating, liberal self. Government must provide it with the opportunity to fulfill itself through voluntary action. Only now the "encumbrances" of that self—including religious beliefs drawn from its upbringing—are to be respected and not judged good or bad. For Sandel, as for all liberals, it is development of the authentic self, with all its commitments, that is the goal, rather than any substantive common good. Sandel has merely added to liberalism the claim that individual commitments must be respected by government and that politics is the primary sphere in which self-fulfillment takes place. Thus Sandel's just society is one in which individuals join numerous political causes to carry on a persistent public debate over the nature and requirements of the (never fully agreed-upon) common good.

While he identifies good government with pursuit of the common good, Sandel opposes any "unitary and uncontestable" view of that good as likely to breed coercion. Indeed, he defends republicanism in part on the grounds that it "is not necessarily exclusive or coercive. It can sometimes find democratic, pluralistic expression."[29]

Why, then, does Sandel want a politics dedicated to pursuit of the good? To maximize meaningful, autonomous choice. Sandel praises "Those in the 1990s who spoke of virtue and soulcraft emphasiz[ing] the moral and cultural prerequisites of self-government," and also those who "emphasized the economic prerequisites." All of these people sought to bring back "a political economy of citizenship."[30] By demanding increasing economic equality and supporting formation of a tutelary state, these people sought to foster individual capacity for self-government. They sought to make individuals capable of making moral choices for themselves and to participate in moral decision-making in their communities. And for Sandel it is only by participating in such decision-making that we become fully autonomous individuals.

One result of this vision of politics is strident opposition to visions of the good that close off debate. Sandel's self is fulfilled through choice-making. Thus visions of the good that preclude constant choice-making are in his view stultifying. He defends reinfusion of moral issues into the public square on the grounds that it is necessary to keep that square open to continual choice: "A politics that brackets morality and religion too completely soon generates its own disenchantment. Where political discourse lacks moral resonance, the yearning for a public life of larger meaning finds undesirable expression. Groups like the Moral Majority seek to clothe the naked public square with narrow, intolerant moralisms. . . . Fundamentalists rush in where liberals fear to tread."[31]

By abandoning the public square, according to Sandel, liberals have left it to bad groups like the (in actuality long-disbanded) Moral Majority. Government must recognize the self's natural attachments so that it may preserve the public square from the assaults of substantive morality. It must allow individuals to express themselves there, while preventing any one vision from gaining primacy. It must enforce liberal toleration.

Sandel's public rejection of contemporary liberalism rests in large part on his claim that that ideology has insufficient concern for the social attachments individuals carry into their public lives. His review of Supreme Court decisions is intended to show how liberal jurisprudence, insisting on the primacy of the individual's voluntary choice, ends by undermining the ability of the individual to lead a full, autonomous life. This has been particularly true, Sandel points out, in the area of religion. Justice Stevens's claim that "religious beliefs worthy of respect are the product of free and voluntary choice" in Sandel's view shows insufficient respect for authentically held beliefs growing out of the self's upbringing.

"If all religious beliefs are matters of choice . . . it is difficult to distinguish between claims of conscience on the one hand and personal preferences and desires on the other."[32] We must see individual beliefs as fundamental, self-constituting choices. The state must treat such choices as "encumbrances"—as parts of the individual's identity much like the other attachments, such as the family, that form it into a full, autonomous choice-maker.

Religious beliefs, like other involuntary attachments and disabilities, like prior choices of all kinds and like character itself, are literally "encumbrances." They impinge on the self's ability to choose freely its modes of conduct. The state's duty is to see to it that the public square accommodates individual encumbrances as much as possible, without changing its morally neutral character (and thereby imposing a unitary vision of the good). The self is not to be pressured into any action that might reduce its autonomy. Instead it is to be provided with the chance to participate, with all its encumbrances, in public, political life.

In true liberal fashion, Sandel would have the government accommodate individual encumbrances by, for example, allowing the wearing of yarmulkes in the military, conscientious objection to military service, and even sectarian schooling.[33] Each of these allowances is, for Sandel as for all liberals, a trump against state action. The state may not interfere with the carrying out of private choices in the public square. But private religious conduct will not be allowed to take on a public character. Indeed, because communitarian actions such as public displays of nativity scenes are so important, because they convey a serious religious message concerning the beliefs of the community as a whole, they must be banned.[34] Such communal expressions constitute coercion and may harm the self-esteem of selves encumbered by different religious beliefs. Because this self remains the center of concern, and may be inhibited from autonomous action by wounds to its pride, such harmful conduct cannot be allowed.[35]

Sandel ignores the numerous state promotions of, and disabilities on, certain religious practices even into this century.[36] He also ignores any and all arguments for judicial restraint—including those based on respect for majority rule. Instead he merely asserts that the courts should allow individual religious expression in the public sphere while placing even more onerous restrictions than it already does on communal displays of belief.

Religion must be respected in the individual. It is an encumbrance which the state must accept and for which it must make allowances. But religion must be opposed if it might limit the extent to which politics is an unending debate over the nature and requirements of the public good.

What, then, does Sandel want? He posits as the proper response to our current radical individualism a return to Alexis de Tocqueville's understanding of the public sphere as a collection of many associations. Individuals must join with others in various local organizations, and thereby develop a concern for the well-being of their neighbors and community. Tocquevillian institutions

> include the township, schools, religions, and virtue sustaining occupations that form the "character of mind" and "habits of the heart" a democratic republic requires. Whatever their more particular purposes, these agencies of civic education inculcate the habit of attending to public things. And yet, given their multiplicity, they prevent public life from dissolving into an undifferentiated whole.[37]

The "Tocquevillian" institutional pattern does not promote coercion or stasis because the sites of individual concern and socialization are many and varied. But it teaches all of us to care for our fellow citizens.

Sandel does not, however, seek a return to the highly religious townships of Tocqueville's day. Nor does he wish to revive the distinction between strictly political associations like political parties and the far more important social institutions in which Tocqueville saw the bulk of public life taking place.[38] Instead Sandel seeks to promote a variety of overtly political associations debating largely economic issues, resting on a consensus concerning the primacy of political participation as the good of life.

Sandel's fear is that his republican politics will be seen as undemocratic and intolerant. He states his first concern thus:

> If sharing in self-rule requires the capacity to deliberate well about the common good, then citizens must possess certain excellences—of character, judgment, and concern for the whole. But this implies that citizenship cannot be indiscriminately bestowed. It must be restricted to those who either possess the relevant virtues or can come to acquire them.[39]

All must be included in republican activity, Sandel says, or it is flawed. It seems clear that the flaw in an "exclusive" republicanism for Sandel lies in its failure to treat individuals as ends, to respect the autonomy of each self. But the demand for universal participation need not preclude republican politics. The tutelary state can train us all to be good, autonomous republicans.

The assumption that the capacity for virtue is incorrigible, tied to roles or identities fixed in advance, is not intrinsic to republican political theory, and not all republicans have embraced it. Some have argued that good citizens are made, not found, and have rested their hopes on the formative project of republican politics. This is especially true of the democratic versions of republican thought that arose with the enlightenment. When the incorrigibility thesis gives way, so does the tendency of republican politics to sanction exclusion.[40]

As for Locke, for Sandel no individual is inherently capable of political participation. It must be trained. According to Locke, this training takes place principally in the family. For Sandel the tutelary state is crucial to the process.

Unfortunately, the rise of the tutelary state brings to the fore another problem: the possibility of coercion. "But," Sandel argues, "civic education need not take so harsh a form." He explicitly separates himself from that part of Jean-Jacques Rousseau's vision of community that attacks individual autonomy in the name of the general will. For Rousseau, "the more the individual will is 'dead and obliterated,' the more likely he is to embrace the general will."[41]

Rousseau sought a community in which everyone explicitly agreed on the good toward which their community must move, and for which each individual must sacrifice. And Sandel, liberal that he is, has no such vision. For him it is the individual's good that is paramount. Politics is crucial to him, not as the means toward a specific, communal good, but as the means by which individuals flourish. Political conduct itself—debate and disagreement—is at the center of Sandel's liberal project.

According to Sandel, "The civic conception of freedom does not render disagreement unnecessary. It offers a way of conducting political argument, not transcending it." This is why Sandel attacks "unitary" conceptions of the good. Such conceptions render further choice-making and further public disagreement more difficult. Consensus itself is a problem for Sandel, save on the fundamental belief that democracy, inclusion, and toleration are essential to human flourishing, and that individual flourishing is the proper goal of life.

In seeking a renewal of public life Sandel recommends a number of structural reforms. He opposes strip malls in favor of preexisting downtown areas, in which citizens can linger and meet with one another. He recommends replacing suburban sprawl with traditional, mixed-use neighborhoods that even out traffic flow and allow for pedestrian traffic. Most importantly, however, Sandel emphasizes the need for a rebirth of 1960s style political activism. From politicized "community development corporations" to associations like the Industrial Areas Foundation (IAF)—"a network of community-based organizations that teach residents of poor communities how to engage in effective political activity"—Sandel wants us to commit ourselves to overtly political organizations.[42]

We must join organizations that teach us to define the public good in egalitarian terms. That is, proper, tutelary organizations will form habits in the people conducive to continuous political action—aimed at bringing economic and other institutions under political control. Politics offers the means by which individuals may flourish, so all should be exposed to it as much as possible.

Like Sandel, the IAF recognizes the importance of traditional mediating institutions. Also like Sandel, it sees them as "points of departure for political activity."[43] Local affection, the little platoons of life, are facts, in Sandel's view, that cannot be ignored. But they are facts that can be overcome through political education. Beginning from traditional institutions, political organizations can liberate individual selves from their involuntary encumbrances, or at least minimize the importance of these encumbrances, by getting individuals involved in the exciting world of political activism.

Sandel's liberalism recognizes the self's rootedness in community and belief. Taking these into account, even "respecting" these encumbrances through public accommodation, he hopes the government can use them to help it create activist citizens engaged in a perpetual debate over the common good. Of course not all notions of the common good deserve a hearing. Those who look to God and tradition for the norms of behavior are, on this view, both coercive and uncommunitarian because they value the permanent things more than the majority view of the moment or the ultimate liberal good, tolerance. By failing to see the individual's flourishing as the goal of life they fall outside the confines of modern liberalism. Precisely because he refuses to question the self's centrality, Sandel remains safely within these liberal confines, unwilling or unable to question the validity of liberal suppositions.

As a result, Sandel's liberal self remains the measure of all things. Commitment remains a choice of temporary attachments subservient to the individual's whim. And religion and tradition, the customs and habits that give structure to truly communal life, remain impotent. They are undermined by a government and an intellectual class hostile to rules and even public professions that may harm the individual's self-defined self-esteem.

Sandel's vision of the individual and of political life does not seem conducive to the institutions, beliefs, and practices on which any substantive community must rely. For that vision we must look beyond even the encumbered liberal self. We must look to other suppositions, recognizing that no philosophical argument can be made without them. We must look to the possibility that not all attachments can be freely broken; that some attachments, such as the family, must be seen as sacred, unbreakable bonds if we are to find meaning again in our communities.

Only if individuals forgo satiation of their appetites, whatever they may be, in order to perform their duties can the fundamental structures of social life be reconstituted. Only if the attractions of sex, career, and other achievements of the flourishing individual are subordinated to the proper ends of family, church, and local association can individual and community be reconciled. Only if we again consider the possibility that there are standards outside ourselves that tell us how we ought to live—not how we can best achieve our full potential, not how we can best lead a comfortable life, but how it is proper that we live—can we again live with one another rather than beside or even against one another.

IV

Living with Difference

13

Michael Sandel's America

MICHAEL WALZER

I

DEMOCRACY'S DISCONTENT is a wonderful example of immanent social criticism, which is to say, of social criticism as it ought to be written. It criticizes a certain tendency in American life (by looking closely at some of its consequences), and at the same time claims to find in that same American life a different possibility, a better expression of our political culture. Its search for a public philosophy is, in the first instance at least, more historical than philosophical: a reflection upon experience rather than a reflection upon ideas. Sandel gives us a double narrative, part constitutional, part socio-economic, with a single message: that a certain kind of procedural liberalism has supplanted a more substantive republicanism, with effects that we ought to regret, and that it is still possible to turn back, to recapture important elements of republican America.

With much of this argument, above all, with its critical thrust, I am in substantial agreement. But I have a somewhat different view of the history; I would want to tell (here I shall only try to evoke) a somewhat different story. The major part of the critique that follows is concerned with that difference, but I shall begin with a smaller point about the social logic of communitarianism.

II

Communitarianism comes in two versions. The first is a kind of civic republicanism, where the whole country is conceived of as one community of citizens, men and women whose virtue (commitment and responsibility) is something, so we are told, that we have to worry about; the republic depends upon it. Republican politics is a formative project, producing and reproducing the citizens it needs. The second communitarianism is a kind of pluralism, where the country is conceived of as a community of communities (nation of nationalities, social union of social unions), a whole constituted by its parts.

Now citizens are educated in the parts of the republic as well as in the whole, so that engagement and responsibility are mediated and indirect (but we still need to worry about them). The great strength of Michael Sandel's argument in *Democracy's Discontent* is that it draws freely on both versions of communitarianism. Its weakness is that it fails to acknowledge the tension between the two.

The tension is itself of two sorts. I am more interested in the second, though the first may well cut closer to the core theory of Sandel's earlier book, *Liberalism and the Limits of Justice*, which provides us with an extended philosophical account of the "unencumbered self." His second book raises the question of how we are to find or produce men and women who bear the particular encumbrances of citizenship. But his most illuminating and perceptive discussions of encumbered selves in this second book do not deal with citizens at all but with the members of religious communities—and religious communities of a fairly narrow and sectarian sort: the Amish, orthodox Jews, the Native American Church (whose rituals famously involve the use of peyote), and a few others. The sociologist Lewis Coser has described communities of this kind as "greedy," which is to say that they aim at absorbing as much as possible of the energy and commitment of their members. These members are indeed "encumbered," and Sandel is entirely right to argue that they do not experience the obligations that their membership imposes as matters of individual choice. He is also right to suggest that most liberals will have difficulty understanding these obligations and difficulty, too, respecting and then tolerating the obligated men and women; he offers some telling examples.

But how does Sandel himself propose to respect and tolerate these same people? His criterion is a hard one: "What makes a religious belief worthy of respect is not its mode of acquisition [as liberals commonly think] . . . but its place in a good life or, from a political point of view, its tendency to promote the habits and dispositions that make good citizens."[1] Greedy communities will mostly fail this political test. Their members do not make good citizens because they are only marginally interested in the political community; their sense of the common good is determined mostly by their religious beliefs and not by their membership in or allegiance to the state—some of them refuse, on principle, to declare their allegiance to anything as secular as a state. Indeed, the compromise arrangement worked out for the education of Amish children (allowing them to spend less time in public schools than other Americans), which Sandel supports, depends on the commitment of the Amish community as a whole to its permanent political marginality. If the children were going to grow up to be active citizens, we would (rightly) be more insistent on the full scope of their education.

There is a more general point here, and it is Rousseau's point: if the republic needs citizens in the strong sense of that word, then it cannot tolerate "secondary associations" that are primary for their own members. Encumbered men and women do not make good citizens of the republic unless their first encumbrance is, in John Adams's words, quoted by Sandel, "a positive passion for the public good." This argument applies also, I think, to the case of Robert E. Lee, to which Sandel devotes some eloquent lines. He sees Lee as a man torn between his loyalties, deliberating on them, and making a reflective choice. But I doubt that description. Lee was a Southern aristocrat for whom the commitment to kinship and land was almost certainly indefeasible; his military oath and his political allegiance never had a chance. Blood and faith are alike in this respect, that they very often fail "to promote the habits and dispositions" of good citizens.

III

Historically and psychologically, what makes for citizenship is the loosening of these other, earlier social bonds. This is probably the point of Rousseau's argument that if there are to be secondary associations in the republic, there had best be a lot of them: plurality makes for weaker ties. But then it is a little unclear whether the members of the many groups are usefully called "encumbered selves." The first tension between civic republicanism and pluralism is focused on the conflict of strong obligations, and it raises the question whether the state can (or should, given Sandel's test) tolerate "greedy" groups that, so to speak, over-encumber their members. The second tension has to do with the effects of under-encumbrance or communal weakness. I will turn to the second now, and remain with it for the rest of this chapter, for it is the more common of the two; encumbered aristocrats and religious sectarians are few in number compared to the mass of ordinary men and women who, for better or worse, carry their obligations more lightly.

In the United States, this mass has been formed by an historically specific experience that is almost entirely passed over in *Democracy's Discontent*—the experience of immigration. The omission of this experience from the book seems to me astonishing, since any attempt at explaining the growing dominance of liberal individualism in American life must deal with the effects of immigration on the "obligations of loyalty and solidarity" that liberalism, according to Sandel, cannot explain. Perhaps it can't, but perhaps it doesn't have to. Immigration is an individual (or familial) decision, a free choice, for even in cases of extreme poverty and persecution, there are many people who choose to stay behind. The decision to leave represents a break with those Old World communities whose members were, in Sandel's exact sense, encumbered selves, that is, men and women whose obligations were given. The immigrants, once they have arrived in their new country, do not have obligations in quite the same sense. Givenness has been given up (or lost). Old communities are indeed reconstituted in America, but they do not have the same hold on their members, for the members know themselves now as agents of the reconstitution. They know that they have framed the community this way rather than that way—while other immigrants across town or down the street have framed it that way rather than this.

Consider the experience of American Jews, which both Michael Sandel and I know intimately. In Eastern Europe, say, the encumbrances of Jewish orthodoxy had been loosened somewhat by (a radically incomplete) emancipation, but they were still essentially given. In America those same encumbrances could only be chosen—and were in fact chosen by only a small minority of immigrant Jews. Reform and Conservative Judaism offered alternative choices (and there were other alternatives too), almost on a Protestant model: arriving in a new city, American or soon-to-be-American Jews literally had to choose which congregation to join and which religious commandments to fulfill. It was an open question how engaged in or disengaged from the community they "should" be, and it seemed perfectly plausible to give a liberal answer to that question: they should be as engaged or disengaged as they choose to be.

I do not mean to argue that these people were entirely unencumbered or thought of themselves in that way. Most of them believed that they had to make their choices within a relatively narrow range of possibilities. Self-respect as well as individual conscience and the bonds of family set limits to the range. Still, Sandel's account does not fit the experience that I am trying to describe. He imagines choice as a matter of deliberation about one's different encumbrances or one's multiple identities. Here I am, a Jew, a socialist, and a new American, let us say, and in any given case I must reflect on "which one [of these identities] is properly engaged"[2]—as if the content of the identities is given and all that I have to decide is whether that content fits or does not fit a particular social occasion. But in fact what I have to reflect on, and decide, is what that content is for me: what does it mean in my situation, with my family and friends, to be an X? And this is exactly the kind of "free" decision that liberalism claims to validate and defend.

In an immigrant society, there are many different ways of being what one "is". A single identity offers many possible identifications, and as a result of this pluralism, communities are very loosely organized. They have the form that John Higham has described: a center (or a couple of centers), whose activists have agreed more or less on a platform or doctrine, and a spreading periphery (or an overlapping set of peripheries) of people who either care less or disagree more and who are only marginally committed and intermittently engaged.[3] And citizenship is likely to be similarly organized . . . or disorganized. In the political community too there are activist cores and largely passive or only occasionally active peripheries. To attend to public affairs, to vote, to keep track of one's representatives, to join a party or movement: we can describe these as the duties of citizens, but they are experienced as matters of individual choice, not as moral encumbrances. If I join the movement, then I acquire obligations; and if not, not.

Sandel argues that a citizenship so attenuated, so dependent on individual choice, cannot provide the commitment necessary for democratic self-government or the solidarity necessary for the welfare state. Maybe not, but are there any examples of the relevant kinds of commitment and solidarity being provided by a *politics* of citizenship alone? The strongest republics (I mean the most Jacobin-like republics, where active citizenship is the norm) and the strongest welfare states (I mean the most generous ones) in the world today exist in, or were first established in, religiously or ethnically homogeneous countries—and I suspect that it is this homogeneity that grounds the commitment and solidarity. It is not an accident, as they say, that radically heterogeneous societies, like our own, have so far produced mostly inactive citizens and incomplete and shoddy welfare states. Does it make any sense to accept this heterogeneity, as Sandel seems to do, and then demand civic virtue and republican citizenship?

The difficulties here are a little obscured by the fact that the reference point for Sandel's pluralism is Tocqueville's America. But this is America before the great immigrations, where pluralism is not so much the product of diversity as of federalism and decentralization. Tocqueville celebrates local governments, town meetings, and juries—and the other associations that he notices are, almost all of them, versions of Protestant religion and politics. It probably makes sense to say that all those institutions and groups served to educate the citizens of the early republic. But if Tocqueville's America was a heterogenous society, its heterogeneity was remarkably homogeneous: everywhere one looks (except, perhaps, North and South), the republic's citizens look and sound very much alike; the groups that were different—Blacks and Indians—were not citizens.

Sandel's America, and ours, is nothing like Tocqueville's republic. But Sandel does not seem sufficiently aware of the differences—or sufficiently willing to explore their meaning. After the great immigrations (including the Black immigration from South to North), heterogeneity is racial, religious, ethnic, and linguistic in form and radical in character. The groups and their organizations are extraordinarily diverse, internally divided, relatively undisciplined, subject to strong centrifugal forces. To what degree, and in what ways, do they serve to educate citizens? These are questions that no longer invite easy Tocquevillian answers. Maybe the new groups serve republican ends—I believe that they do—but they also serve to change the nature of republicanism. The looseness of the bonds they foster has the effect of loosening also the bonds of citizenship. Hence the plausibility of the standard liberal understanding of political activity: it is one possible choice among the many that individual men and women can make.

IV

Nonetheless, Sandel's critique of this understanding and of the social world that it reflects seems to me largely justified. I will not rehearse the critique here, just point to some of its themes: declining participation in political life, alienation from democratic institutions, distrust of political leaders, growing inequality. America seems in need not only of a public philosophy but also of a political program. What ought to be done?

Sandel is not prepared to mourn the great immigrations; nor is he in favor of stopping immigration now—even though opposition to it has often been associated with republicanism: there was, for example, a strong Rousseauan element in the Know-Nothing party (along with some less attractive elements). Sandel lists "nativism" as one of the pathologies of republican politics, so, though he says nothing more about it, he presumably means to avoid it in any republican revival. But how can we generate a revival in the world the immigrants have made—and still are making? Even to begin to answer this question would require joining the "multiculturalism" debate, which I am a little reluctant to do. The word does not appear in Sandel's index, though his critique of the neutral state and his discussion of religious liberty would seem to bring him close to a (certain kind of) multiculturalist position. On the other hand, his strong republicanism would seem to distance him from that same position, for the plurality of cultural commitments, if they are strong commitments, will pull people away from the republic, while if they are weak, they will weaken republicanism in turn. So: what *can* be done?

My own inclination would be to (try to) answer this question as concretely as possible, with as little reference as possible to the ideologies of civic virtue and cultural identity. That would require us to begin with the actual heterogeneity of contemporary America and to look closely at the various groups and organizations that make it up: the religious communities and the various ethnic-religious combinations (Irish Catholics, German and Scandinavian Lutherans, Jews, Black Baptists, White Pentecostals, and so on), the class organizations (labor unions and professional associations), interest groups (farmers, retired persons, the growers or manufacturers of this or that commodity, the victims of AIDS, cancer, diabetes, and so on), social movements (feminist, environmentalist), and even political parties, though these are only barely present in American life today. We need to know how these groups work—and, again, in the most concrete sense. How do they govern themselves? How do they recruit members and mobilize them for particular activities? What activities do they mobilize them for? How do they accumulate and distribute resources? What kind of training and discipline do they provide for their more active, and for their less active, members? How do they relate to rival or simply neighboring groups and organizations? How do they deal with the agents of the state? An American public philosophy has to begin with the answers to these questions, critically reviewed and reflected on. I do not think that there is any other possible beginning.

One of the things we would find from a review of this sort—so, at any rate, studies by contemporary political scientists and sociologists suggest—is that the more active members of these groups (though not of the greediest among them) are also the more active citizens of the republic.[4] These are the people who come closest to the civic commitment that Sandel wants to encourage, though I doubt whether the old republican model would resonate much with their own sense of what they are doing. For a substantial part of what they are doing—and they probably understand it this way—is representing particular interests, bargaining for a place on "balanced" tickets, negotiating compromise arrangements, getting as much as they can from the state. And the representing, bargaining, negotiating, and getting are made possible by demonstrations of group strength: marching in the streets; contributing time, energy, and money to particular political campaigns; bloc voting. Deliberating on the common good is a small part of this kind of politics, though when the politics is working well, its participants must at least talk about the common good, and so it will come to figure, also, in their thinking. It is unlikely ever to dominate their thinking.

Insofar as we can find a way to strengthen these groups and to increase the number of active members, we will presumably also strengthen American citizenship (in its actual rather than its ideal republican version). But the groups are not only relatively weak when compared to older, more encumbering communities, they are also unevenly weak. The gross inequalities of American society, which Sandel rightly criticizes, are in large part the products of an increasingly unregulated capitalist economy. But these inequalities are, in complex ways, mediated by group difference—where the most relevant groups are racial, ethnic, and religious. Well-being and poverty in America today, and activism and passivity too, are group-linked. So any program for strengthening the groups must also aim at making them more equal—above all, in their capacity to accumulate and distribute resources. (I have elsewhere called this argument "meat and potatoes multiculturalism.")[5] This kind of program, however, can only succeed in a civic community marked by commitment and solidarity; liberal proceduralism does not generate the bonds that make redistributive policies possible: this is one of Sandel's central claims. And then we seem to be in a bind, for only a program like this can create such a community, insofar as it is possible at all in an immigrant society where, clearly, it does not yet exist.

But perhaps we can at least aspire to political commitment and civic solidarity—and the function of a public philosophy, Sandel would say, is to cultivate the aspiration. And then the hope for commitment and solidarity might motivate the activities through which the two are realized. That is plausible enough, so long as public philosophers understand that the more immediate motive of the activists, and perhaps the more effective one, will be to strengthen the bonds of this or that local community and enhance the resources at its disposal. And this motive is likely to be explained and defended in terms of distributive justice, which is (as Sandel argues) a liberal and not a republican language. But a mediated, group-focused version of distributive justice might be exactly what an immigrant society like ours needs. Justice here is a kind of recognition, and individual men and women who are recognized in their communities and empowered by them may be the most likely citizens of the community of communities.

Maybe the liberalism that Sandel criticizes, when it is given a genuinely pluralist turn, can serve the republican ends he advocates. Maybe. And that possibility might suggest a public philosophy more adequate to the conditions of an immigrant society than any version of civic republicanism focused on an earlier America. The immigrants have made, are making, a difference, and a difference that requires philosophical as well as practical acknowledgment: they have produced a society where citizenship is mostly a mediated experience, and they have produced a very specific form of mediation, where groups of lightly and diversely encumbered selves provide the critical basis for solidarity. Sandel worries too much, it seems to me, about the primary fact of American life today: that these selves are free to choose what they will be (or how they will be what they are). But he is right to argue that we all have an interest in helping them choose well.

14

Moral Dialogues: A Communitarian Core Element[1]

AMITAI ETZIONI

COMMUNITARIANS maintain that democratic societies require a core of shared values; that if democracy is conceptualized and practiced as merely a procedure that enables individuals who hold different values to work out shared policies on pragmatic, self-interested, or ad hoc grounds then these policies, and the polity in general, will lack in legitimacy. Michael Sandel agues that we will not want to be neutral on some issues of grave moral standing with which the state deals, such as abortion.[2] Moreover, on some issues at least, it is doubtful that the state can be neutral no matter what position it embraces—including if it chooses not to take one. Finally, if policies are only supported on pragmatic grounds, this support will be fragile and unreliable because it is liable to be lost if circumstances change (as they often do).

Once one recognizes the need for shared values (or social formulations of the good), then one faces the question of how such sharing may be achieved, assuming it is not naturally present nor can simply follow from the values handed down from previous generations. I argue here that reasoned deliberations, often expected to provide the needed forum, in themselves do not suffice; that moral dialogues are also needed; and that these can follow rules of engagement that will protect them from deteriorating into culture wars.

Reasoned Deliberations versus Culture Wars

The literature that explores the ways collectives formulate public policies is deeply influenced by the liberal way of thinking that argues that the way a democratic people ought to proceed (or/and does proceed) is for them to dispassionately discuss the facts of the situation, explore their logical implications, examine the alternatives that are available, and choose the one that is the most appropriate as determined on the basis of empirical evidence and logical conclusions. The process is often referred to as one of *deliberation*.[3] The overarching image that is reflected in this concept is that of a New England town meeting or of the ancient Greek polis.[4]

Jack Knight and James Johnson write:

> Deliberation involves reasoned argument. Proposals must be defended or criticized with reasons. The objective is to frame pressing problems, to identify attractive, feasible solutions to them, and to persuade rather than compel those who may be otherwise inclined to recognize their attractiveness and feasibility. Here the crucial point is that parties to deliberation rely only on what Habermas calls the "force of the better argument"; other forms of influence are explicitly excluded so that interlocutors are free to remain unconvinced so long as they withhold agreement with reasons.[5]

James Kuklinski and his associates also frame this concept well: "From Kant to Rawls, intellectuals have unabashedly placed a high premium on deliberative, rational thought and by implication, rejected emotions and feelings as legitimate (although unavoidable) elements of politics."[6]

The reasonableness of deliberations is often contrasted with an irrational and harmful, if not dangerous, way of attempting to chart a new course following one's passion. As James Q. Wilson writes, "The belief in deliberation is implied not only by the argument for an extended republic but also by the contrast Madison draws between opinions and passion, since opinion implies a belief amenable to reason whereas passion implies a disposition beyond reason's reach."[7]

Others have contrasted deliberations with culture wars, a term used to suggest that the public is profoundly divided in its commitments to basic values, and that segments of the public confront one another in unproductive manners instead of dealing with the issues at hand.[8] In culture wars two or more groups of the same community or society confront each other in a highly charged way, often demonizing one another and turning differences into total opposition to the other's fundamental commitments.[9]

Such culture wars tend to make reaching a shared course more difficult and they often invite violence (from bombing of abortion clinics to outright civil war). James Hunter writes that:

> Culture wars always precede shooting wars. . . . Indeed, the last time this country "debated" the issues of human life, personhood, liberty, and the rights of citizenship all together, the result was the bloodiest war ever to take place on this continent, the Civil War.[10]

Factors Pointing to a Third Model

There are at least two powerful reasons the purely deliberative model needs to be replaced. First, participants in charting a shared communal course do not command the information and computing capacity rational decision-making requires or the ability to distinguish between factual and normative statements, as has been shown in the work of Charles Lindblom[11] as well as the work of numerous psychologists. To illustrate the point: it has been repeatedly pointed out that it is impossible to decide in a chess game what is the optimal (most rational) move because the permutations are too numerous, although computers seem to be close to overcoming this limitation. Note though that compared to real-life decisions, chess is a very simple choice space. In chess, there are only two players, immutable rules, all the needed information is right in front of the actors, power relations among the pieces are fixed, and the rules of engagement are fully established. In communities and societies, the number of players is large and changing, rules are modified as the action unfolds, information is always much more meager than what is needed, relative power of those involved and those affected is changing, and the rules of engagement are in flux. As a result, participants in all decision-making must rely on much humbler processes than the ones of the rational decision-making school that are part of the deliberation model's core assumptions.[12]

Second, and most important, the issues under discussion are, to a significant extent, normative and not empirical or logical matters. This is clearly the case when issues of public policy concern such highly charged matters as abortion or slavery, as Sandel indicates. Actually normative issues arise very often, including when members of the polity debate the extent to which the USA should grant foreign aid on humanitarian grounds, return to fault divorce, allow mandated prayers in school, modify Affirmative Action, change the progressivity of the tax system, require corporations to notify communities before they close a plant, and for numerous other public policies.

Even considerations of many issues that seem technical are often deeply influenced by normative factors. For instance, the question of whether or not to inject fluoride into a town's main water supply brings into play values of those who oppose government "paternalism";[13] and questions concerning the best way to teach English to immigrant children raises values issues concerning the commitment to one's heritage versus the one to a new nation. There seem to be few if any significant decisions that are value-free. And hence most if not all formulations of a shared course require processes through which shared normative formulations can be found, or at least normative differences can be narrowed.

I am not arguing that when public policies are examined by communities and societies information and reason play no role. Indeed, Amy Gutmann and Dennis Thompson in their new book, *Democracy and Disagreement*,[14] go a long way to show how to include ethical considerations in deliberations, thus building a bridge between reason and values. I am pointing out that they play a much smaller role than the deliberation model assumes, and that other factors play a much larger role. I turn to discuss these "other" processes that are not deliberative in the usual sense this term is used. I suggest that an examination of the actual processes of sorting out values that take place in well-functioning communities and societies shows that rather different processes are taking place,[15] and that these processes are fully legitimate.

The Core Processes of Moral Dialogues

Moral dialogues occur when a group of people engage in a process of sorting the values that will guide their formulations of the social good. Such dialogues take place constantly in well-formed societies, and when they are successfully completed they lead to the formulation of a new shared direction for the respective societies (albeit sometimes only after a prolonged and painful discourse). For instance, moral dialogues led in the 1960s to a broadly shared understanding that legal segregation had to be abolished, and in the 1970s to the idea that the society must conduct itself in a much more responsible manner toward the environment.

Society-wide moral dialogues occur in two basic forms: The piecing together of a myriad of local dialogues through organizations that have local chapters, including numerous ethnic, religious, and political associations; and on national media such as call-in shows, televised town meetings, and panel discussions.

Moral dialogues have their own procedures that are distinct from those of the deliberative model.[16] One often-employed procedure in moral dialogues is the appeal to an overarching value shared by the various parties. Robert Goodin in effect is using this device when he seeks to pave the road for a community that must sort out a course between the rights of nonsmokers and those of smokers.[17] At first, this may seem to be a typical clash between two values: the rights of one group versus those of another. However, Goodin points out that both groups are committed to the value that one's liberty does not allow that person to violate the "space" of the other. In familiar terms, my right to extend my arm stops when my fist reaches your nose. (Actually quite a bit before that.) Goodin points out that because nonsmokers do not penetrate the smokers' space, while smokers do violate the space of nonsmokers when both groups are commingling in public spaces, nonsmoker rights should take priority. Thus, employing an overarching value (in this case, liberty) helps sort out conflicts between two or more "lower" level values. The same basic procedure or gambit is used when members of a community argue that a certain measure under consideration is not compatible with a free society, a self-respecting society, or a caring people.

Another often-used procedure is to bring into play a third value—albeit not a superordinate one—when two other values diverge or clash. For instance, those who recently sought to restore the Black-Jewish coalition of the 1960s have argued that both groups share a commitment to liberal causes.[18] These causes do not trump whatever distinct values Jews and African-Americans embrace, but to the extent that they are shared values, they have some normative halo effects that might help the two groups to conduct constructive moral dialogues on other issues.

I turn next to examine various rules that one encounters in examining moral dialogues. One notes that the more these rules are followed, the more productive are the dialogues, the more likely they are to lead to a truly supported closure, and the less likely they are to turn into culture wars (all other things being equal). The participants are not necessarily aware of these rules, such rules nonetheless affect their conduct.

Rules of Engagement

A major characteristic of moral dialogues is that they abide by rules of engagement that reflect the basic tenet that a participant's words and actions should be based on the recognition that the conflicting parties are members of one and the same community. Hence, groups and members should fight for their causes with one hand tied behind their back, rather than completely unrestrained. This issue has been much discussed in recent years as the question arose, "What makes for a civil dialogue?"

It is widely agreed that in a civil dialogue the contesting parties should not "demonize" one another or engage in *ad hominem* attacks; that they should refrain from depicting the other side's values as completely negative, "satanic,"[19] reflecting the anti-Christ, or treasonous. For instance, after the GOP won the 1994 elections in a landslide, the ebullient new Speaker of the House Newt Gingrich referred to his side as being supported by "Godfearing" Americans faced with an opposition of "Godless" people;[20] even discussions in academia are reported to have become "too vituperative."[21] In Israel, it is widely believed that the comparison of Prime Minister Rabin to Hitler as well as the depiction of him as a traitor by several religious groups egged on his assassin. It also bolstered the culture war between extreme religious groups and secular ones. In Britain, a negative advertisement that literally depicted Labour Party leader Tony Blair as a red-eyed devil was ruled inappropriate by the Advertising Standards Agency, the country's most powerful advertising watchdog.[22] This ruling was strongly supported by public opinion and several key members of the Tory party.

Another rule of moral dialogues is to not evoke wantonly the darkest moments in the collective memory of one's opponent. Thus, to confront a German with the horror of the Holocaust whenever one discusses a specific normative difference, or to provoke Jews by suggesting that they were involved in the slave trade, undermines the chance of a successful moral dialogue.[23]

A related but far from identical rule is not to affront the deepest-held beliefs of the other group, or so to speak push their emotional buttons. Thus for instance in dealing with the religious right, it would be inappropriate to mock their commitments to the text of the scriptures.

Another rule of constructive dialogues is developed by Mary Ann Glendon in her study of "rights talk." She states that using less of the language of rights and more of that of needs, wants, and interests makes dialogues less contentious, less likely to escalate into confrontation, and generally more effective.[24] As Glendon puts it, "For in its simplest American form, the language of rights is the language of no compromise. The winner takes all and the loser has to get out of town. The conversation is over."[25] Rights tend to lead one to think in absolute terms and to shun compromises; they often lead parties to invest themselves emotionally in what they consider their right, and point to litigation that is typically adversarial in nature. In contrast, discussion of one's needs does not necessarily cast doubt on the merits of the other side's needs and makes working out compromises or other shared positions more likely.

Another important rule is to agree to leave some issues out of debate to narrow the area of contest and to draw on an existing shared foundation. This is one reason Americans have been careful not to reconvene a constitutional assembly and have made it rather difficult to amend the Constitution. By leaving those matters ensconced in the Constitution off the negotiating table, the realm of conflict remains less pervasive than it would be otherwise. For instance, questions relating to the basic notions of the separation of state and church, the right to privacy, and freedom of speech need not be considered.

The less one views both the other side's and one's own side as monolithic the more opportunity one recognizes for normative, and not merely interest-based, give and take. For instance, at the height of anti-communism ideology in the United States, the Soviet Union was depicted as monolithic, and conservative Americans were highly resistant to any notions that there might be different brands of communism (that of Tito's Yugoslavia or Nyerere's Tanzania, for example) and were also hesitant to believe that Communist China and the USSR were following different courses. Over the last decade, as this ideological polarization gave way to recognition of a much more pluralistic and nuanced world, the tendency to engage in culture war subsided and working out our shared positions on subjects ranging from the Middle East to the environment improved.

Closely related but not identical are attempts to find ways to legitimate one's position in the other side's normative terms, rather than to seek to make the other side endorse, at least initially, one's whole normative paradigm. Thus, Daniel A. Bell argues that Western and Muslim intellectuals would be closer to closure if, instead of attacking on moral grounds the Islamic justification of *hudud* (the amputation of the right hand of thieves), Westerners should instead point out that according to Islamic religious law many conditions must be met before such amputations are justified.[26] These conditions are rarely met, yet the practice of *hudud* continues. It is on these grounds, then, that Westerners can show that this practice is morally unacceptable by Muslims' own standards, rather than relying only on their own ones.

In contrast, culture wars unfold by all parties typically assuming that good is on their side and that its opposition is "evil" (the actual term President Reagan used to describe the Soviet Union). There is no room for conceding that the other side may have some valid normative points, nor for drawing on those to move toward shared values or using them as part of a search for ways that will not require normative humiliation of the other side.

Another difference between culture wars and moral dialogues is that in the latter one does not seek to prove the other side totally wrong—as heretical. Those who engage in moral dialogues are quite content to allow those who are won over a way out by justifying a change in policy or mores in the other side's moral terms. For instance, in the debate about the moral standing of female circumcision, an Islamic scholar suggested such a way out for those Muslims who were willing to forgo the procedure because they accept the Western notion that this procedure constitutes a serious violation of human dignity and free choice. The ritualistic need, he suggested, could be satisfied with a small pinprick for girl infants about the same time boys are circumcised. Westerners, keen to promote human rights, may still find this acceptable. This is not a "compromise" because the two sides do not meet midway or even part of the way; one side's normative position prevails. But the other side gets more than face-saving; it receives respect for its general moral position while foregoing a specific, morally challenged ritual.

A different rule of moral dialogues is followed when one side accepts a symbolic gesture or ritual that allows the other side to respect its values, but nevertheless enables the first side's values to prevail in the shared course that is being charted. This rule is illustrated in a compromise that was reached between Orthodox Jews and the civic authorities in Israel on matters concerning the paving of roads that run into burial grounds. At first, Orthodox authorities demanded that when buried bones are found and the terrain excavated to make way for the roads, the bones should remain buried where they are and the roads detoured. Civic authorities insisted that such detours are too costly. A compromise was reached that would allow the Orthodox authorities to rebury the bones according to rituals; but the ossuaries in which the bones are found, which are of great national cultural interest, would be turned over to archaeologists. This compromise allowed one side to abide by its religious dictates and the other to fulfill its cultural and transportation needs. This compromise broke down as a culture war raged between civic right and religious groups, leading the religious authorities to declare that they will no longer abide by the previous agreement that was in place for decades. These conservative authorities either refused to rebury the bones or insisted that they should be reburied in their ossuaries, which they demanded to have enclosed in cement, thus destroying their archaeological value.

Finally, those who seek to engage in moral dialogues must realize that one does not face a slippery slope whenever one legitimates a part of the other side's view. When a rather moderate Israeli civil libertarian was asked why she objected so strenuously to the request of religious groups to close a major traffic artery (Bar Ilan) that runs through a densely populated religious neighborhood in Jerusalem, she responded that if this street were to be closed, the religious groups would soon demand to shut others ("Give them a finger and they will ask for the whole hand"). The fear of a slippery slope is an argument often employed by groups that oppose even small modifications in their initial stance, which often hinders a successful conclusion of moral dialogues.[27] The fear that one concession will open the door to others is one reason that reproductive choice groups oppose bans on partial birth abortions; that conservatives argue against the decriminalization of even those controlled substances that have few proven negative effects; and traditionalists oppose any changes in the liturgy, such as praying in the vernacular rather than in Latin. The record, though, shows that while on some occasions such changes do lead to slippages, in many they do not (not every girl who kisses a boy before marriage becomes promiscuous, and not every one who smokes a joint becomes a crack addict). Note also that if one truly accepts the "slippery slope" logic, one cannot tolerate any adaptations or changes, however badly needed. Above all, one can "notch" the slope to indicate a commitment by the opposing parties that the community or society shall realign only to a given point.[28] In the case of the Bar Ilan road in Jerusalem, one may indeed wish to close all arteries that go through major religious areas but not agree to close many others.

Understanding the rules of moral dialogues, along with the ways in which moral dialogues take place and can be enhanced, is a subject of great importance. Such dialogues sustain one of the key elements required for a good social order, one largely based on the sharing of values rather than the exercise of power: the charting of a normative course on specific issues without this resulting in major centrifugal side effects for the society. It is a subject that requires much more study and is likely to intensify once both the inability even to approximate the ideal of deliberation and the importance of moral dialogues, as distinct from culture wars, are more widely recognized.

Megalogues

The question arises if it is possible for a large society to engage in a dialogue that will lead its members to affirm a new, renewed, or some other set of values, the way a small community might. The answer is that societies do engage in megalogues in several ways. One main process involves linking together millions of local conversations (between couples, in neighborhood bars or pubs, in coffee or tea houses, next to water coolers at work). This is achieved by networking that takes place during regional and national meetings of many thousands of voluntary associations in which local representatives participate in dialogues; in state, regional, and national party caucuses; and increasingly via electronic links (such as groups that meet on the Internet).

Another way megalogues are advanced is through public focal points such as call-in shows, debates on network television, and in nationally circulated newspapers and magazines. Several associations, including the Council on

Foreign Relations, National Issues Forum, the Public Agenda Foundation, and the League of Women Voters, are explicitly dedicated to nourishing both local and nationwide dialogues. They hold that they are dedicated to the sharing of information and clarification of thinking; actually, they play a considerable normative role. The Council on Foreign Relations, for instance, has a strong anti-isolationist slant. The Forum and the Public Agenda have a firm progressive and civic slant.

National megalogues are often nourished, accelerated, and affected by public events such as public hearings (Clarence Thomas–Anita Hill focused discussion on what constitutes sexual harassment and the morally proper response to it), trials (the 1925 Scopes trial challenging the teaching of evolution), demonstrations (undermining the normative case for the war in Vietnam), and marches (which had a major effect in the 1960s in changing the country's view on racial discrimination). While fireside chats and other speeches from the bully pulpit of the presidency play much less of a role than is often attributed to them, especially when one expects that a president could change the direction of a country with a few well-honed speeches, they do serve to trigger, focus, and nourish megalogues. For example, in the aftermath of the Oklahoma City bombing in 1995, President Clinton succeeded in calling attention to the violation of the rules of engagement by some of the more virulent hosts of radio call-in shows, and more generally to the need for a return to a "common ground."

Both local moral dialogues and society-wide megalogues are often extensive, disorderly (in the sense that there is no clear pattern to them), and lack clear beginnings and clear or decisive conclusions. Nevertheless megalogues can lead to significant changes in core values. A few brief illustrations follow.

Until 1968, a person was considered dead when his or her heart and lungs stopped functioning.[29] Movies perpetuated this notion by depicting a person holding an ear to a dying person's chest or a mirror to the mouth to determine if it fogged over. As technology made extension of life by these criteria rather common (to well beyond the point where a person's chances of regaining a meaningful life were nil), a group of scientists and ethicists developed a new definition of death: brain death. But the community continued to demand that doctors do "all that could be done for loved ones" well after their hearts and lungs had stopped functioning under their own power. At this point various scholars primed a megalogue about the definition of death. The issue was dramatized by the Karen Quinlan case in the 1970s. The ensuing megalogue gradually led to a change in the public perception and the movie images of death. Although the change is still not complete, it advanced sufficiently to establish new social and legal mores. In recent decades, similar megalogues about the deficit, sexual harassment, women's rights, and the scope of the state have occurred, all leading to a change in normative direction.

Another example of megalogue is the environmental movement that crystallized in the early 1970s. Until then the environment was not considered a shared core value in Western societies, nor in many others. This is not to suggest that there were not studies, articles, and individuals who saw great value in its preservation; but society as a whole paid it little systematic heed, and protecting the environment was not listed among America's core values.[30] As is often the case, a book—Rachel Carson's *Silent Spring*[31]—triggered a nationwide megalogue. A massive oil spill, the ensuing protests in Santa Barbara, California, and the Three-Mile Island incident further impressed the subject on the national normative agenda. Thousands of people gathered in New York City to listen to pro-environment speeches and to pick up garbage along Fifth Avenue. Two hundred thousand people gathered on the Capitol Mall in 1970 to demonstrate concern for the environment on "Earth Day."[32] As a result, concern for the environment became a core shared value. There continue to be disagreements about the proper level of commitment to this cause, and the best ways to proceed, but not about the basic value. A conservative President, Richard Nixon, founded the Environmental Protection Agency during his Presidency; and many environmentalist policies, such as recycling, were introduced at this time. The extent to which this value sharing was breached in the mid-1990s is not yet clear, but it has held for twenty-five years and is now found in many other societies.

The same can be shown for values issues raised by the civil rights movement in the United States in the early 1960s, leading to broad-based agreement that legal segregation in the South had to be eliminated, and in the debate about excessive government intervention in the economy, leading by the early to mid-1990s to considerable consensus that such intervention needed to be curtailed. For two more examples of megalogue, consider the rise of clear consensus regarding the ban on smoking in public places and the emerging agreement surrounding driving while under the influence of alcohol.

In Conclusion

Deliberations do not provide a sufficient model for communities and societies to form shared, normatively laden courses. However, it does not follow that the only other alternative for social interaction and collective decision-making is culture wars. Moral dialogues are not merely possible and necessary, but do often occur in societies that fit the communitarian paradigm of balancing autonomy and order. Better understandings of the rules of engagement that communities and societies need to adhere to, if they are to prevent moral dialogues from turning into culture wars (rather than relying merely on deliberation), have been articulated in this chapter. Moreover, further development of these rules can serve both as an entry point into the dialogues themselves and as a pillar for sustaining them when social breakdowns are looming or the current normative course leaves certain groups feeling disassociated or disaffected from social processes.

15

Can This Republic Be Saved?

JEAN BETHKE ELSHTAIN AND CHRISTOPHER BEEM

DEMOCRACY'S DISCONTENT is a rare sort of book—rare not least because it seeks to restore the role of the political theorist within the broader public debate. In a society confronting a sea of troubles, Sandel connects, or, more properly, reconnects, the exigencies of social criticism (capaciousness, timeliness, accessibility) with the burdens of rigorous historical and theoretical analysis. *Democracy's Discontent* seeks to diagnose and prescribe treatment for what Sandel calls "the anxiety of the age," namely, "the loss of self-government and the erosion of community" (p. 3).[1] We think that is an apt description of our social woes. We also think he is right to call these anxieties a problem of political theory; more specifically, Sandel argues, they constitute a problem with how we understand freedom.

In our contemporary social world, Americans believe that freedom "consists in the capacity of persons to choose their values and ends" (p. 5). While this view is, of course, fairly constitutive of liberal thought, Sandel claims that it has of late come to prevail over any and all alternative understandings of what freedom is or what it requires. In present-day America, freedom means nothing but this. We can imagine freedom only as the extension of an individual's compass. We are voluptuaries of "free choice." As a result, we Americans have come to believe that the fundamental role of government is to secure our capacity to choose, through a system of individual rights, while staying neutral about the content of any such choice. "The liberal state therefore does not discriminate; none of its policies or laws may presuppose that any person or way of life is intrinsically more virtuous than any other. It respects persons as persons and secures their equal right to live the lives they choose" (p. 13).

Sandel contends that this conception (or, better, the unrivaled ascendancy of this conception) is both new (40 to 50 years old) and faulty. It does not accurately describe human beings or their commitments,[2] nor does it foster among the citizenry the kind of civic behavior upon which free society depends. "[D]espite its appeal, the liberal vision of freedom lacks the civic resources to sustain self-government . . . The public philosophy by which we live cannot secure the liberty it promises, because it cannot inspire the sense of community and civic engagement that liberty requires" (p. 6). So Sandel thinks that we Americans have developed a bad understanding of freedom. As a result, we endanger nothing less than our ability to sustain a well-ordered and free society. We are left disconnected from each other and from any common enterprise, and it is this condition which accounts for our anxiousness.

Sandel seeks to identify and reinvigorate another, more substantive American political tradition: namely, civic republicanism. Civic republicanism says that freedom is not simply or even primarily a matter of individual choice, but self-government. Thus, we Americans are free insofar as we struggle together to decide who we are, what is important, what is desirable, and how we want to live together. Under this conception, neutrality is impossible and its pursuit illegitimate. Argumentation about what the common, civic, social good is, and a common sense of responsibility for what that good is, is constitutive of a viable democratic society. What is more, this understanding of freedom depends upon, indeed, it is not understandable without, each individual to some degree attending to this good or having some such animating aspiration. Therefore, the moral character of individual citizens is a central public concern. The pursuit of freedom as the pursuit of self-government demands that we seek, through governmental and social institutions, to train or at least encourage citizens to care about what this common good is.

Living as we do in a procedural republic, this civic republican conception appears so distant, so unfamiliar, as to seem almost un-American. The bulk of Sandel's book is to show that that is not the case. He wants to remind us of our own history, of our former and long-standing concern for the obligations of American citizenship, and to show how we got to this sorry state of affairs: how we replaced one understanding of freedom with another, a replacement so complete that efforts to outline alternatives to this present construal evoke cries of alarm or labels of nostalgia. Sandel undertakes a magisterial tour of constitutional law and political economy, drawing these disciplines together within a single conceptual frame. By transgressing disciplinary fiefdoms, Sandel is singularly effective at showing us what happened—showing us, that is, that the civic republican tradition failed to carry the day, and why, as a result, we often do not even recognize that things could be otherwise.

Yet Sandel is not content to leave matters there. He goes on to affirm a growing and ever more articulate sense among the body politic that we are in rather big trouble. His analysis is obviously born of his desire to make things better: a perennial aspiration of political theory. *Democracy's Discontents* thus argues that we need to understand the past if we are to have any hope of recapturing the lost felicities of a former way of life.

> [F]or all its episodes of darkness, the republican tradition, with its emphasis on community and self-government, may offer a corrective to our impoverished civic life. Recalling the republican conception of freedom as self-rule may prompt us to pose questions we have forgotten how to ask: What economic arrangements are hospitable to self-

government? How might our political discourse engage rather than avoid the moral and religious convictions people bring to the public realm? And how might the public life of a pluralist society cultivate in citizens the expansive self-understandings that civic engagement requires? If the public philosophy of our day leaves little room for civic considerations, it may help to recall how earlier generations of Americans debated such questions (p. 7).

We disagree with none of this. But we judge the matter as yet incomplete. In light of what is at stake, it is not enough to outline the slow and steady diminution of civic republicanism in American public life. If we are to restore some version of that which has been lost, we need to know not only what happened, but why it happened. Therefore, in what follows, we intend to investigate a few of the animating reasons that might help to account for the central themes of Sandel's historical narrative.

To begin with, we want to consider just what this civic republicanism is and where it comes from. Sandel's genealogy of the term draws most explicitly from Aristotle, quoting the latter's famous summary that "The end and purpose of a polis is the good life, and the institutions of social life are means to that end" (p. 7). Yet unlike many advocates of contemporary liberal theory, Sandel explicitly denies that civic republicanism *necessarily* involves unanimity or the concomitant need for coercion.[3] What's more, his historical analysis confirms the point. He ably shows that, in America, calls for citizenship and appeals to the common good rarely took on the Rousseauan demand that individuality submerge itself in a general will, and that any and all idiosyncratic tendencies shrink before *"la nation une et indivisible."* For Sandel, Benjamin Rush's words of thundering excess—that the polity must "teach each citizen 'that he does not belong to himself, but that he is public property' "(p. 319)—is the exception that proves the rule. Even in the passionate afterglow of the Revolution, Americans operated predominantly under the conviction that politics was "more clamorous than consensual" (p. 320), and that most of the work of government was best done hands on, through a cacophonous collection of local municipal associations and institutions, including churches, unions, granges, a rich mulch of overlapping memberships in multiple groups, pluralistic rather than univocal. Government might help or hinder but it did not and should not supplant these self-starting expressions of self-government.

This describes the world of American civil society, and it is critically important to the discussion. For like so many in the contemporary debate (indeed, like ourselves), Sandel looks to these institutions because of the role they have played and continue to play in fostering the commitments he wants to celebrate and reinvigorate. "American democracy," he concludes, "had long relied on associations like these ['families and neighborhoods, cities and towns, schools and congregations'] to cultivate a public spirit that the nation alone cannot command." By bringing democracy down to a face-to-face level, civil society afforded Americans the opportunity to learn how to be citizens. It is thus little wonder that the contemporary "erosion" of those very associations is largely responsible for our nation's "rising discontent" (p. 314).

We concur with this general claim. But with respect to religious institutions, and their standing within American civil society, we would present the matter somewhat differently. We support Sandel's contention that the procedural republic wishes to turn religion into something it is not: it is neither private, nor is it just one more consumer decision. But there is more that must be said. Because he stresses the civic republican roots of our democratic robustness, we believe Sandel pays less attention than he should to the religious sources and energy of the American democracy.

For in what did self-government historically reside in the United States? What were the sites of civic formation? For most Americans, intense sectarian commitments embodied in congregations were central and helped to fuel the penchant for *political* liberty. Against the centralizing impulses of Cotton Mather, Congregationalist John Wise argued in 1717 that democracy was the form of *church* government most commensurate with the will of God. Christ himself desires for his church a form of government "as should least expose his people to hazard, either from the fraud or arbitrary measures of particular men. And it is as plain as daylight, there is no species of government like a democracy to attain this end."[4] According to church histotian Sydney Ahlstrom, "So clearly did he [Wise] anticipate later revolutionary attitudes that his tracts were republished in the 1770s to bolster the Patriot cause."[5] Such influence was not limited to the ideological realm. Out of congregationalism came town meetings and these, in turn, or in tandem, with constitutionalism, forged over time that sturdiness we have come to associate with our democratic foremothers and forefathers. These institutions, that is, fostered the enlivening, bracing idea that Americans could rise to new challenges, fashion a common vision, and shape vast forces to democratic purposes.[6]

Nor is it correct to see the preeminence of religious institutions as solely an historical phenomenon. In their voluminous study of American civic life, *Voice and Equality: Civic Voluntarism in American Politics*, Sidney Verba, Kay Scholzman, and Henry Brady present findings which show that among the institutions of civil society, churches remains *primus inter pares*. While Verba et al. acknowledge that there is normally a significant correlation between political activity and social-economic status, churches stand as important exceptions to this rule. They provide a uniquely powerful means for citizens who are less well-off, less well-educated, to develop the skills of political participation. Just as importantly, churches and church organizations often exemplify a democratic ideal; they provide one of the few remaining opportunities in which people of different economic and education levels can actually intermingle as equals. The authors conclude that "The domain of equal access to opportunities to learn civic skills is the church."[7] Finally, not all forms of civil society are equally effective in achieving desired social ends. Even jaded observers must acknowledge that salutary interventions on behalf of the most marginalized members of our society require a level of patience, commitment, and individual attention that is (to say the least) most commonly associated with religious faith. In John DiIulio's words, "When you look at the gutbucket stuff, the everyday, in-your-face working with troubled kids in these neighborhoods across the country . . . almost all of it is being done by people who are churched."[8] All of this leads us to insist that churches are not just one more manifestation of American civil society. They are not functionally on a par with the Youth Soccer, or a Neighborhood Watch group. Sandel, and anyone similarly concerned about the condition of American democratic society, should be explicit about the pivotal role and unparalleled status of religious institutions.

In any event, Sandel looks to the institutions of American civil society in the hopes of averting our cultural decline (pp. 328–9). This hope reveals a Tocquevillian spirit. Of course, by taking up this and other Tocquevillian themes, Sandel is hardly unique among contemporary social critics. Tocqueville is clearly the man of the hour. But we believe the connection goes deeper than that. This is the way it works: on a number of occasions, Sandel notes that the rise of the procedural republic has left us in a kind of paradox: the triumph of an individualist version of autonomy, a radically voluntarist conception of freedom, can be seen as consolation for the rise of state control, and the loss of agency—in Sandel's words, "the loss of mastery" (p. 294)—within the political and economic order. In other words, we now are more free because we have relinquished an alternative understanding of freedom. Thus, the issue is not, as is often assumed, freedom versus constraint, but rather, which freedom, for what, and in the name of what? We have made a political bargain with the state: we have paid for the establishment of an atomizing conception of freedom by sacrificing a measure of civic autonomy: the very dynamic Tocqueville foresaw. Thus, "the eclipse of the civic strand of freedom" has fueled a "gnawing fear that, individually and collectively, Americans were losing control of the forces that governed their lives" (p. 275). For all our pining for community, we want to be left alone; most importantly, we want no one to tell us what to do. Indeed, we covet this form of autonomy so strongly that we are willing to give up self-government to get it.

One hundred and fifty years ago, Tocqueville despaired of his ability to describe the benign despotism that he anticipated for democracies in an age of equality, but Sandel's description comes very close, disturbingly close in fact, to what Tocqueville had in mind. Tocqueville said that equality of conditions leads to two dangers: individualism and materialism. These constitutive, not contingent tendencies (well constrained within aristocratic society) lead people to value creature comforts above all else, and to ignore other aspects of their freedom. So long as their more basic and even base desires are fulfilled, the citizenry would one day permit the state to quietly dismantle political liberty, and to become "an immense, protective power which is alone responsible for securing their enjoyment and watching over their fate."[9]

Citizens would become subjects confronting that "powerful stranger" called government.

Now it is interesting that where Tocqueville sees the payback primarily in terms of the accumulation and undisturbed enjoyment of consumer goods, Sandel is more inclined to say that the state becomes ever more despotic, or at least ever more antidemocratic, by feeding people's egoistic impulses. Again, the new conception of liberty centers on "our capacity as persons to choose our values and ends for ourselves" (p. 275). We have become little sovereigns over a diminishing, and diminished, domain. While this is an interesting difference, we think it is more important to recognize a dramatic underlying similarity. For can one not read Sandel's analysis as confirmation of Tocqueville's darkest fears? Can one not summarize his discussion in very Tocquevillian terms? Namely: political liberty is not easy; it institutionalizes a set of demands for citizenship, and once the ardor of the revolution dies down, these demands, along with the innate urgencies of equality, leave citizens ever more willing to give away political liberty for the sake of furthering their all-too democratic vices. Leveling supplants excellence.

This might help to account for the recent turn in our political discourse to domestic language and intimate and familial metaphors as nigh obligatory rhetorical tools. Sandel notes this shift, recalling Mario Cuomo's metaphor of the nation as a family at the Democratic national convention in 1984. (He gives a few other examples.) He goes on to reject it, but he does so only because this "ideal of national community has lost its capacity to inspire . . ." (p. 314). Reading Sandel through Tocqueville, however, we are left with a more dire assessment.

Let us grant the decent intent behind this turn to familial metaphors. But to call a modern state a family in the interest of connecting us to one another should be faulted not just because it is ineffectual, but because it too easily gets played out in practice as solidifying a shift from we Americans as citizens to we Americans as big children. As Tocqueville has it, this new form of benign despotism would "resemble parental authority if, fatherlike, it tried to prepare its charges for a man's life, but on the contrary, it only tries to keep them in perpetual childhood."[10] Government, in this scenario, becomes a benevolent, sometimes chiding caretaker and protector.

The replacement of citizenship with a state-sanctioned, consumerist-driven, perpetual childhood also explains our willingness, even eagerness, to orient our politics according to the dictates of pity—that is, the uncritical embrace of the victim. For the trend Sandel attributes to Cuomo has continued unabated. Look at how cuddly and caring both parties tried to appear at their last presidential conventions. Babies on parade. Human ailment and affliction thrown down as trump cards in political advocacy. Of course, neediness and suffering make claims on us—including political claims—but in these examples, our emotional response is not meant to inform or set forth debate, but to replace it. Petitioners wrap themselves in the mantle of goodness that ostensibly inheres in the unmediated claims of victimhood and then insist that policy judgments turn on that status alone. For anyone wanting to make a political appeal, the lesson drawn from these recent exercises is readily apparent: establishing victimhood, rather than presenting an argument, is the price of admission. For the citizens, too, the lessons are clear: we can be moved to respond to these pleas, and as a result, feel good about ourselves, while sparing ourselves the very adult burden of considered judgment. We have spared ourselves, in other words, the burdens of justice, the burdens of democratic government.[11]

What we are seeing in this child-mindedness, this domestication of political imagery, is the reversal of the old standard *in loco parentis*. That rule was straightforward. For those not-yet-fully adult, other adults (or as the law would have it, the state) played the temporary role of guardians, arbiters, and perhaps disciplinarians. The situation now is almost completely reversed—parents are to follow a quasi-therapeutic regime, at times under the state's tutelage, or they are, de facto, bad parents. In the arenas of mental health, sexuality, values, we are all at sea, it seems, until others have clarified matters for us. Much as we have reversed the logic of the *in loco parentis* doctrine, we have forsaken the core dictum that democratic politics, as the common business of the people, is not there to make us feel good but to help us do right and to honor and to recognize a notion of civic goods. Because children, by definition, are not citizens, the deepening depiction of us as kids in a big family depletes citizenship, undermines legitimate democratic authority—which relies on the notion that people grow up and can be held accountable—and ultimately demeans us all.

Sandel may well accept our claim that he let the "domesticators" off too easy. But he would surely rebuke the idea that his book is primarily an explication of the underlying belief that Tocqueville, after all, was right: that is, that democracy will one day collapse under the sheer weight, and irresistible, rushing force, of human equality, and we are simply witnessing its inevitable decline into a new, comparatively benign, but predictable form of despotism. Throughout the book, the history Sandel offers can be read as the slow but perhaps foreordained death of the civic republican tradition. The strains continue to be heard, but they are ever less effectual against the dominant liberal understanding. They are echoes in the empty air. Yet for all this, Sandel finds some room for hope. He argues, in effect, that things have gone full circle. While the procedural republic still rules the day, it has "lost energy" (p. 324), and its undergirding theory is starting to collapse under its own weight. It can no longer sustain the absence of a moral and epistemological framework, and, therefore, citizens are and will be driven to resuscitate the features of the civic republican tradition.

Perhaps he is right. But we are not the only ones to suggest that Sandel's reasons for optimism (civic architecture, community organizing, along with the revitalization of American civil society) are fairly thin. We celebrate these examples as well. But not only are they thin reeds against the forces of atomization and apathy, their very nature, and what counts as success given this nature, precludes their becoming significantly more powerful. To ask them to do more than they are is to inevitably make them into something they are not, something which would surely undo the very reasons for their effectiveness. The civic benefits associated with a community meeting, for example, are primarily indirect. They result from the face-to-face interaction of individuals who share a common goal, but who otherwise would never have reason to associate. A larger meeting, a coalition of such groups, perhaps, might well achieve a greater political status, but the opportunities for informal interaction and personal dialogue would be gravely compromised. As Robert Putnam notes, the Environmental Defense Fund does not fill the gap left by declining PTAs.[12] Just as importantly, these civic initiatives and institutions do not appear to be any different from stalled efforts in the past. The call for protests against Wal-Marts in New England, for example, can be responded to in exactly the way Sandel himself accounts for the failure of antitrust laws many decades hence. "[W]e are by now too enamored of the fruits of consumption, too far down the path of economic concentration to speak realistically of restoring" (p. 245) the former economic order. Similarly, calls for civic architecture reflect the long-forgotten dreams of Chicago's Daniel Burnham, among others. One can celebrate these expressions as noble stands against the siege, but why would today's efforts be more effectual than past experiments?

We may identify here another explanation for what happened. Perhaps the problem is not just a problem of, and for, political theory. Perhaps it is a problem of civic epistemology. Historically, civic republicanism involved more than just a concern for a common good. When we say something is good, and that we think that we should organize our laws and procedures in such a way as to foster that good, then we are obliged to answer two accompanying questions: On what basis do we say that this is good? And: Can we make that basis intelligible to others? If this is so, then could one not argue that the explanation of the loss of the civic republican tradition is that, over the course of American history, calls for civic republicanism—i.e. calls for civic virtue and attention to the common good—have slowly detached themselves from the moral and epistemological realism which formerly supported such claims?

The Founders called their grounding commitments "self-evident" truths. If that is how you understand your beliefs, it is fairly easy to see how a civic republican polity might be constructed. A set of beliefs afforded that kind of epistemological status, to the extent that this status is shared, could readily enable Americans to reject pornographic theaters in their neighborhood; to afford greater respect to religious identity; to empower the courts to distinguish between Nazis marching in Skokie and Martin Luther King, Jr. marching from Selma to Montgomery—all examples drawn from Sandel's text. But as the history of the past thirty years or so demonstrates so palpably, the viability of such truth claims have become ever more suspect. As the epistemological status of civic claims has declined, it has become ever more difficult to counter the ethos of the "neutral" state. For unless we can say that we understand that the good we seek reflects a truth, and that the grounds for that belief are universally accessible to all persons of good will, then there are no grounds for avoiding the counter-charge of coercion. Unless there is an answer to the question, "Who are you to say I am wrong?" in a pluralistic society, there is nothing else left for the state to do but to secure rights while ignoring how those rights are exercised. Here, then, is the second hypothesis to the question why the change: transformations in constitutional law and profound shifts in the political economy are representative of an underlying atrophy in the assurance with which Americans once professed their ostensibly common civic beliefs.

Early on Sandel mentions that within the civic republican tradition there are two ways of understanding the relationship between virtue and liberty: intrinsic and instrumental. The intrinsic understanding is the stronger of the two. It argues that "given our nature as political beings, we are free only insofar as we exercise our capacity to deliberate about the common good, and participate in the public life of a free city or republic." The instrumental understanding, on the other hand, claims merely that "even the liberty to pursue our own ends depends on preserving the freedom of our political community, which depends in turn on the willingness to put the common good above our own interests" (p. 26). Of course, this distinction centers on Aristotle's question of whether the virtues of the good citizen are wholly commensurate with the virtues of a good person. This problem has haunted liberalism, indeed, the tradition of western political theory, from its inception. Sandel never engages the question directly, but it lurks in the interstices of his work.

Sandel has long regarded John Rawls as an exemplar of the theory which undergirds the procedural republic. It is, therefore, worth noting what Rawls has to say about the republican tradition Sandel wishes to revive. Rawls maintains, on the one hand, that Aristotle's conception of political life, along with those outlined by Plato, Thomas, and Augustine, all fall outside the liberal conception of justice. For each begins with the premise that there is "but one reasonable and rational conception of the good."[13] He goes on to note, however, that if and insofar as classical republicanism is limited to the claim that, "The safety of democratic liberties requires the active participation of citizens who possess the political virtues needed to maintain a constitutional regime,"[14] then he (Rawls) sees no opposition between it and his conception of political liberalism. The operative question is whether Sandel is, or should be, willing so to limit his conception of civic republicanism. Sandel does not hit this question head-on because he wants to have it both ways: he wants to restore a civic republican understanding of freedom as self-government without elaborating on some of the central questions about what such a restoration would, or must, entail. Sandel is not alone in this, of course. It is not just an intrinsically difficult question, it is also the case that civic republicans and communitarians and participatory democrats cherish and value many of the features of a rights-based, liberal society.

In light of the epistemological concerns raised above, however, that response leaves us dangling. One could, of course, see the virtues of citizenship as instrumental to a well-functioning democracy. But how would such a claim fit with any call for a renewed civic republicanism? Is the reason for reinvigorating a different conception of freedom and civic virtue limited to combating our contemporary anxieties and gnawing sense that all is not well, that we have gone off the right track somehow? We grant that democratic government requires a modicum of what is usually labeled civic virtue. Even the most ardent defenders of the procedural republic accept that. But can one celebrate the idea of freedom as self-government without claiming that self-government and its exercise is good *for its own sake;* indeed, that it conforms to a basic understanding of human flourishing? Would Sandel hold that the Americans who operated according to a civic republican ideal (that is, the citizens Sandel wants us to admire and emulate) saw themselves or should have seen themselves as operating according to a merely instrumental understanding—as furthering a "policy end" by contrast to realizing a human good?

For if the virtues sought here are not merely instrumental, it follows that democracy must concern itself with determining and institutionalizing intrinsic claims about the human good, about the dignity of human persons. If that is the case, how does one avoid the epistemological questions outlined above? To affirm civic republicanism is to affirm both that there is a civic good, and that the best way to determine that good is through reasoned debate and robust political constestation, all within a framework that both animates yet limits the meaning and worth of "the political." To be sure, democrats accept that one can never know the complete contents of an overarching human good. We also must surely accept the fact that the limits of legitimate and justifiable human expression are vast. Indeed, the claim that self-expression is one aspect of the *human* good demands that, for the purposes of our collective self-rule, the contents of the *civic* good are and ought to be both minimal and capacious. But if one is to prescribe civic republicanism—that is, prescribe a form of self-government in which equal citizens deliberate in order to pursue and establish a common good—then one cannot beg the question of whether or not such a common good actually exists and how we might come to know it if it does.

Yet again, there is an important echo in Tocqueville's thought. For Tocqueville did not believe civil society could effect a civic spirit through its own operation. He took it as a general rule that "for society to exist and, even more, to prosper, it is essential that all the minds of the citizens should always be rallied and held together by some leading ideas."[15] Tocqueville drew a distinction between political associations in America and Europe to show that the benign operation of civil society required that the citizens already accept and affirm a shared set of mores, values, and beliefs.[16] He thus recognized that while civil society inculcates and nurtures those mores, it does not produce them. In order for pluralistic institutions to invigorate a concern for the common good, those institutions require the presence and vitality of a set of overarching mores. Tocqueville's celebration of religion in America—and his advocacy for Roman Catholicism within the democratic order—confirms the point. The beneficent effects of civil society must operate within the context of a minimal yet universal, capacious yet authoritative, set of moral beliefs. Put differently, if the institutions of civil society are mediating institutions which stand between the individual and the state, then they must mediate something of the state back to the individual.

If the decline of democracy's epistemological prerequisites explains our discontent, then what do we do? Even if one were ready to accept that the state inevitably acts as a moral pedagogue, fostering—willy-nilly—some shared conception of values, norms, and expectations, it is another question entirely whether the state performs this role well. We share Sandel's enthusiasm for the work of San Antonio's COPS (Communities Organized for Public Service) and its leader, Ernesto Cortes. But Cortes and other similarly placed community leaders think that government most of the time is at best inept, at worst, a barrier to the civic. In its bureaucratic managerial forms, government itself is a civically depleting force. If we are right, then the state's task is not merely to foster a concern for the common good, but rather to help citizens to come to know that good when they see it: to recognize and to know goods in common and to distinguish these from what we possess or claim as individuals. In the face of widespread and often well-founded cynicism toward government, how are the government institutions to take on the delicate task of civic education? How can the state affirm certain values, norms, and beliefs, yet simultaneously sustain the free and multitudinous expressions of American civil society? Similarly, even if we were able to somehow ameliorate the state's ham-handedness in such matters, it is by no means clear that the actions of state institutions could help to restore civic republicanism's epistemological prerequisites. As Mary Ann Glendon has noted, "we are all post-modernists now."[17] If this is true, then the "boats against the current" feeling which Sandel's work evokes may be inescapable; the battle may already be over; civic republicanism may be gone for good.

We suspect that the difficulties associated with these questions are what lead so many of us to embrace civil society as the cure for what ails us or the name for much of what we have lost. Again, we do not dispute the idea that the many associations of civil society remain the singular mechanisms by which we Americans can cultivate republican virtues—including possibilities for commonalties and for solidarity (or solidarities). If we are to chasten the notion that our political and social identity is limited to our status as consumers, if we are to countermand the chimera of the sovereign self, if we are to remind ourselves that we are creatures as well as creators, and that there are limits to our visions of self-transcendence, we must restore robustness to these formative institutions, or some version of them. But civil society alone cannot instantiate (let alone restore) a commitment to the common good without an abiding sense that there is a common good out there—one which can be discovered and which ought to be both sustained and conveyed. We would not claim that identifying reasons for the decline of civic republicanism in America makes the matter of proposing even provisional solutions any easier. But we would say that if civic republicanism is to be revived, the matter of democratic epistemology is where the battle lines will be drawn.

16

Civic Republicanism and Civic Pluralism: The Silent Struggle of Michael Sandel

WILLIAM E. CONNOLLY

MICHAEL SANDEL is a cultural conservative with a generous soul and an economic liberal with a grudge against the voluntarist conception of self that governs some forms of liberal doctrine. He challenges the political alternatives with which we are most familiar. His first book spurred American liberals into a flurry of defensive activity just now beginning to abate.

In Sandel's second book liberalism is defined in the same restrictive terms. More consequently, that brand of liberalism (there are other brands) still provides the single point of contrast against which Sandel measures his own doctrine. But despite this flat staging of the adversary, Sandel's own vision has been enriched. The critique of Rawlsian philosophy has become a detailed excavation of historical debates between civic republicanism and liberal voluntarism in several domains of American life; the initial ideal of "community" has been translated into a somewhat more spacious "civic republicanism"; and perhaps most importantly, the promise of an American politics of the common good has devolved into the more modest search for a "public philosophy."

There are, however, tensions in Sandel's diagnosis of contemporary America, exemplary tensions that may also repay our attention. Consider his sanitary presentations of cultural conservatives such as William Bennett, Newt Gingrich, and George Will. Sandel appreciates the willingness of Bill Bennett to reinvigorate the institutions and virtues needed for citizenship.

Sandel's proclivity for ignoring the divisive political agenda that inspires Bennett also dampens his awareness of risks and cruelties implicit in the larger republican vision. In *The Devaluing of America,* whenever Bennett invokes "the

Revised and reprinted with permission, William Connolly, "Democracy's Discontent: America in Search of a Public Philosophy," *Raritan* (Fall 1996), 140–50.

American people," "our culture," "our children," "the Judeo-Christian tradition," "family values," "real people," and "common sense," he summons a spiritual image of an American nation in which each regular individual is a microcosm of the unified nation and the nation is a macrocosm of the regular individual. The endlessly reiterated phrase, "the American people," invokes this cultural imagination perfectly: it simultaneously summons a yearning for identity between individual and nation and identifies a diverse host of individuals, perhaps even a majority, falling below this threshold of tolerance in one way or another. What drug users, many inner-city residents, welfare recipients, most state bureaucrats, homosexuals, liberal churchleaders, secularists, atheists, feminists, most liberal arts academics, and liberal journalists share, according to the Bennett formula, is a series of corrupt deviations from the essential virtues of the nation. Dramatic public interventions into the life of the church, the family, the university, the military, the school, and the media are necessary to reinstate the appropriate fit between the character of the regular individual and the health of the nation. The Bennett political formula is skeptical of the state in economic life, but it is strongly disposed to use the state to recover a lost nation of regular individuals.

Michael Sandel is no William Bennett; he is a gentle man. He resists the logic of cultural war. Moreover, he, unlike Bennett, would encumber voluntarism, when it comes to corporate economics, in the interests of reducing inequality and reinvigorating the city. And Sandel does note briefly that "groups like the Moral Majority," acting in the space left vacant by the default of liberal voluntarism, "seek to clothe the naked public square with narrow, intolerant moralisms. Fundamentalists rush in where liberals fear to tread."

But limitations in Sandel's two-slot model of political analysis—civic republicanism versus liberal voluntarism—do take their toll in his reading of Bennett. Abstractly drawn to Bennett's invocation of national unity, civic virtues, and the reformation of mediating institutions, Sandel skates too lightly over the connection between Bennett's quest to reinstate old unities and his conversion of republican virtues into contemporary weapons of cultural war in the domains of race, ethnicity, religion, gender, and sexuality. This critical reticence, I think, expresses Sandel's ambivalence: he is attached to a model of civic republicanism out of touch with irreversible dimensions of late-modern life, and yet he also is attracted to an alternative model, as I would call it, of civic pluralism.

Thus we hear a lot about the early virtues of an agrarian republic but too little about specific virtues appropriate to the contemporary world. And we receive a sanitized history of republicanism disconnected from some of the evils in which it has been implicated. If Sandel, in the early pages of this book, pursued pluralist reservations about the republican vision he expresses in the last chapter, he would be required to rework significantly his history of the republican impulse in America. He would, for instance, review Madison's support of "westward expansion to preserve access to land" not only in terms of a republican concern to secure land ownership for a growing population but also with respect to the genocidal effects such policies had on Amerindians. Similarly, his celebration of Alexis de Tocqueville would be curbed by attention to the explicit exclusion of Indians and harsh devaluation of atheists generated by Tocqueville's placement of Christianity at the vital center of the American republic. Sandel is caught in the snare created by his two-slot model of analysis. Only his generosity allows him eventually to loosen the springs of a trap he has set for himself.

Consider the effects of the contest between doctrine and soul in the realm of sexuality, a realm which I emphasize because it is significant in itself and paradigmatic of Sandel's posture on a variety of issues. He skirts the voluntarist defense of sexual diversity by contending that sexual affinity, like religious conviction, is often an "encumbrance" of the self that precedes choice. He also resists (without citing it) the Vatican reading of same-sex desire as an objective disorder, a diseased encumbrance of desire the individual is morally obligated to control through self-mastery. He concedes that the court's civic concerns for the welfare of the family and heterosexual normality previously functioned to criminalize homosexuality. But a voluntarist defense of legalization, as Sandel reads it, supports sexual freedom in private without interrogating the larger cultural tendency to demean homosexual unions. "As the New York case suggests, the analogy with *Stanley* tolerates homosexuality at the price of demeaning it; it puts homosexual intimacy on a par with obscenity—a base thing that should nonetheless be tolerated so long as it takes place in private."

Sandel then issues a possible republican defense of sexual diversity. "But by refusing to articulate the human goods that homosexual intimacy may share with heterosexual unions, the voluntarist case for toleration . . . makes the ridicule difficult to refute. . . . A fuller respect would require, if not admiration, at least some appreciation of the lives homosexuals live." Thus both homosexuality and heterosexuality are compatible with long-term relationships; and each is congruent with unions that lend strength and dignity to both parties. These "shared goods" allow Sandel to modify and soften the republican tradition in this domain.

It is fitting to commend Sandel's appreciation of the encumbrances of faith and desire. The voluntarist language of choice is too flat, here as elsewhere. Still, Sandel's defense of homosexuality remains pretty straight. It proceeds by aligning the pleasures and risks of sexuality with a narrow range of republican virtues. What about single people who find adventurous sex with numerous partners at the core of their hearts' encumbrances? What about serial relations of intimacy that lend dignity to the parties involved?

The defense of sexual diversity can never stray too far from the rights of the parties involved to forge their own lives. But Sandel seems right to me in augmenting these arguments with a civic defense. It is just that if you diversify the ends of republicanism, you also open up the terms of augmentation. Thus, it is indeed important in civic terms that same- and different-sex couples who raise children commit themselves to stable relationships. But in an era when population growth is far from imperative, it is also civically constructive to appreciate multiple alternatives to univocal ideals of sexual relations and household organization. Cannot a powerful *civic* case be made that, since desire often precedes choice (or, better, because the relation between desire and choice is so dense and uncertain), since the ability to act without secrecy upon several of one's nonviolent and heartfelt desires contributes significantly to self-esteem, and since self-esteem is crucial to responsive citizenship, a strong cultural presumption must operate in favor of considerable variety in affectional affiliation and household organization? For besides the sharing of commonalities between citizens, there is an equally important engagement of differences between them. When the latter occurs without cultural demonization of either party by the other, each is placed in an improved position to appreciate elements of contingency (genetic, cultural, or both) in the organization of its own identity. This latter experience disrupts the destructive temptation to treat what you already are in each domain of identity as the paradigm of morality itself; that effect, in turn, helps you to cultivate the responsive civic sensibility needed for citizenship in a democracy marked by considerable diversity of class, region, religious belief, irreligion, ethnicity, sexuality, gender performance, and household organization. Certainly, civic limits must be set to avoid degradation and exploitation. But Sandel has not begun to touch that boundary; and, partly because of that, he has not yet identified the cardinal virtues of citizenship appropriate to a culture of civic pluralism.

Sandel first connects diverse encumbrances of sexual preference to the pursuit of a unified ideal of civic life. He then deftly bypasses the fundamental question of whether affectional affiliations are complex, entrenched formations—cultural, genetic, or both—within which the operations of choice are fixed, or diverse responses to a normal pattern of sexuality from which numerous individuals unfortunately or perversely fall away. If you acknowledge the first as a real possibility, if you then explore a variety of patterns through which intimate relations of dignity might be established, and if you thereby affirm the positive value to democratic citizenship itself of such plurality, you augment the voluntarist justification of sexual diversity. And you are also on the way to translating civic republicanism into a more timely vision of civic pluralism. For we humans acquire diverse dispositions, in this domain as in others; such variety strains the explanatory models through which we currently account for it and surpasses the simple categories in which public discussion of sexuality now transpires. It is consequential to the health of a pluralist culture that several such possibilities be valorized publicly so that as many people as possible can live dignified lives while participating openly (to the degree *they choose*) in marriage, child-rearing, church, education, the media, public office, public election, and military service, upon which a robust civic pluralism rests. Sandel takes a step down this path when he acknowledges encumbrances of desire while resisting the Vatican type of analysis of them. Further steps need to be taken.

In the last chapter Sandel confronts profound changes in contemporary life that impel revisions in the republican ideal he has recovered. Finally the voluntarist adversary recedes, and the struggle within Michael Sandel appears more vividly:

> But even a politics that engaged rather than avoided substantive moral discourse, that attended to the civic consequences of economic inequality, that strengthened the mediating institutions of civil society—even such a politics would confront a daunting obstacle. This obstacle consists in the formidable scale on which modern economic life is organized and the difficulty of constituting the democratic political authority necessary to govern it. (*Democracy's Discontent*, 338)

It turns out that even if the excesses of liberal voluntarism were curbed the republican ideal would no longer be sufficient unto itself in "constituting the democratic political authority necessary" to governance. If you add to Sandel's recognition of the political effects of economic globalization the impact on public life of the dramatic acceleration of *tempo* in so many domains of life, the insufficiency of republicanism to itself becomes even more profound. One implication now becomes difficult to deny. Nostalgia for a republicanism of self-contained islands of political action cannot hope to consolidate itself today; such an ideal can only foster melancholy or the angry translation of traditional republican virtues into weapons of cultural war against vulnerable constituencies held responsible for failure to attain the impossible end. Sandel does not put the point in such bald terms. But he now revises the picture of civic republicanism enough to disentangle himself from the culture wars. Thus, he says that today "even nation-states find it difficult to inspire the sense of community and civic engagement self-government requires." This is so because of the "mobility of capital, goods, and information across national boundaries" and a resurgence of subnational groups.

Sandel resists a cosmopolitan response to the globalization of contemporary life on the grounds that the identifications it enables are too vague and disconnected from available institutional bases of action. Instead he contends that "self-government works best when sovereignty is dispersed and citizenship formed across multiple sites of civic engagement." Such a politics "requires citizens who can think and act as multiply-situated selves."

"The republican tradition has viewed self-government as an activity rooted in a particular place." With this sentence, offered late in the book, Sandel waves goodbye to the classical dogma of civic republicanism. Its time has passed. A tone of regret is discernible in his prose as Sandel begins the search for a public philosophy appropriate to the new circumstances of political action. Such melancholy, while expressing a widespread mood, may inhibit

Sandel's opposition to the agents of cultural war (for they play upon such moods) and limit his ability to explore affirmative potentialities lodged in these very conditions. One might ask, for instance, about the degree to which the accelerated tempo of contemporary life might improve possibilities for people to become more alert to contestable assumptions and contingent elements in the identities they love the most. How might such a cultural effect, if it became generalized, *enable* "multiply-constituted selves" to collaborate effectively with numerous others in general assemblages of democratic action? Sandel bypasses these questions. He concedes that contemporary citizens are situated along several planes of action, but he does not yet address the distinctive virtues needed to negotiate relations upon and between these planes.

Contemporary civic pluralism needs citizens who affirm comparative elements of contingency and contestability in those identities—those "encumbrances"—that define them most dramatically; who establish relations of agonistic respect with faiths, even those of a philosophic and nontheistic bent, that challenge their own sources of moral inspiration; who cultivate critical responsiveness to surprising social movements that propel new identities into being out of old injuries, differences, and energies; and who acknowledge the state to be but one site of political identification and action among several others in the late-modern age. These civic virtues—each of which offers support and sustenance to the others—provide enabling conditions for a cultural pluralism of democratic governance appropriate to contemporary life. When they find expression in family life, schools, churches, military organizations, political speeches, public elections, corporate structures, and city politics they enable cultural pluralism to be. When such a pluralism is in place it creates the most impressive possibilities obtainable in contemporary life to build general political coalitions in support of its own economic and educational conditions of existence.

Today political action in support of the mediating institutions of democratic life flows neither from a single concept of the common good nor from a simple aggregation of interests between ethically unencumbered constituencies. The former promotes cultural war between dogmatic contenders to occupy the cultural center while the latter fosters neglect of the mediating institutions upon which a robust pluralism rests. Such political action in concert emerges—if and when it does—out of a dense plurality in which many constituencies fold the cardinal virtues of civic pluralism into the relations they establish with others. Gays and straights are more likely to agree on education and health care, and the religious and the nonreligious are more apt to bond together to reinvigorate their cities and reduce economic inequality, when none of these groups constructs its identity through demonization of the others.

The silent struggle of Michael Sandel between civic republicanism and civic pluralism is more fundamental than the explicit debate he stages between republicanism and voluntarism. For the most urgent task of political thought today is to pursue the agenda Sandel belatedly sets in the last chapter: to articulate a vision of civic pluralism appropriate to the distinct conditions of contemporary life.

17

Living with Difference

CHARLES TAYLOR

I

THIS chapter attempts to embroider and embellish the main line of argument in Michael Sandel's admirable *Democracy's Discontent*. I share Sandel's belief that procedural liberalism has done American democracy a grave disservice. I believe, however, that we need to go beyond negative criticism and try to articulate an alternative model of living together as equals. Sandel's book does a wonderful job in laying out the basic difference between two rival theories of liberal democracy, only one of which has arrogated the term "liberal" today. In fact, liberalism is a much broader church than Sandel's dichotomy acknowledges. *Democracy's Discontent* gives us some distance from the immediate present, and allows us to see how an alternative to the reigning vision once was important in the United States. It rescues the civic conception from oblivion, and where not forgotten, from the "enormous condescension" of posterity, if I can invoke Edward Thompson in this context.

A democracy focused on choice, on individual freedom, versus one centering on participation and shared self-government. Both have been there throughout the last two centuries of liberal democracy; and are there even today. Only the balance has shifted so strongly in one direction that the civic definition risks being forgotten altogether.

What has the focus on choice had going for it? A number of things, some of them tendencies in our philosophical tradition. I think we can see and understand the drift away from ethics of the good life towards ethics based on something allegedly less contentious and easier to carry general agreement. This partly explains the popularity of utilitarianism and Kantian-derived deontological theories. Both manage to abstract from issues of what life is more worthy, more admirable, more human, and to fall back on what seems more solid ground. In one case, we count all the preferences, regardless of the supposed quality of the goals sought. In the other, we can abstract from the preferences, and focus on the rights of the preferring agent.

The act of abstraction here benefits from three important considerations.

First, in an age of (at least menacing, if not actual) skepticism about moral views, it retreats from the terrain where the arguments seem the most dependent on our interpretation, the most contentious and incapable of winning universal assent; whereas we can presumably all agree that, other things being equal, it is better to let people have what they want, or to respect their freedom to choose. Second, this refusal to adopt a particular view of the good life leaves it to the individual to make the choice, and hence it fits with the antipaternalism of the modern age. It enshrines a kind of freedom. Third, in face of the tremendous differences of outlook in modern society, utilitarianism and Kantian deontology seem to promise a way of deciding the issues we face in common without having to espouse the views of some against others.

Now the first two considerations are based on philosophical arguments—about what can and cannot be known and proved, and about the nature of freedom, respectively. They have been much discussed, debated, and often refuted by philosophers. But the third is a political argument. Regardless of who is ultimately right in the battle between procedural ethics and those of the good life, we could conceivably be convinced on political grounds that the best political formula for democratic government of a complex society was a kind of neutral liberalism. And this is where the argument has mainly gone today. The shift between Rawls I and Rawls II is a clear example of this. His theory of justice is now presented as "political, not metaphysical." This shift perhaps comes in part from the difficulties that the purely philosophical arguments run into. But it also corresponds to the universal perception that diversity is a more important and crucial dimension of contemporary society. This comes partly from the actual growth in diversity in the population, through say, international migration; and partly from the growing demand that age-old diversities be taken seriously, put forward for instance, by feminists.

So the issue now could be: what conception of freedom, of equality, of fairness, and of the basis for social coexistence are, not right in the abstract, but feasible for modern democratic societies? How can people live together in difference, granted that this will be in a democratic regime, under conditions of fairness and equality?

The procedural republic starts right off with a big advantage. If in your understanding of the citizen's roles and rights, you abstract from any view of the good life, then you avoid endorsing the views of some at the expense of others. Moreover, you find an immediate common terrain on which all can gather. Respect me, and accord me rights, just in virtue of my being a citizen, not in virtue of my character, outlook, or the ends I espouse, not to speak of my gender, race, sexual orientation, etc.

Now no one in their right mind today would deny that this is an important dimension of any liberal society. The right to vote, for instance, is indeed accorded unconditionally; or on condition of certain bases of citizenship, but certainly in a way which is blind to differences of the range just quoted. The question Sandel poses is whether this can be the *only* basis for living together in a democratic state, whether this is the valid approach in *all* contexts, whether our liberalism approaches perfection the more we can treat people in ways which abstract from what they stand for and others do not.

Now it can look right off, that whatever other reasons there might be for treating people this way, at least it facilitates our coming together, and feeling ourselves to be part of a common enterprise. What we do all have in common is that we make choices, opt for some things rather than others, want to be helped and not hindered in pursuing the ends that flow from these options. So an enterprise that promises to further everyone's plan, on some fair basis, seems to be the ideal common ground. Indeed, it is hard to see what else could be.

Here I think we suffer in modern philosophy from an absence of alternative models: models of how people can associate and be bonded together in difference, without abstracting from these differences. But there is another important such model, which I myself adhere to, and I would like to spell it out a bit more here. It has been invoked, among others, by Herder and Durkheim—thinkers who were rather divergent in other respects. The crucial idea is that people can also bond not in spite of, but because of difference. They can sense, that is, that the difference enriches each party, that their lives are narrower and less full when they are alone than when they are in association with each other. In this sense, the difference defines a complement.

This can be the basis of a powerful theory of individual freedom, as we see in Humboldt's *On the Limits of State Action*. The argument is not the classical negative libertarian one that freedom is a right, in virtue of an inalienable claim on the part of each person to be able to choose his or her ends or goals. Rather Humboldt argues the crucial moral interest that each one of us has in the authentic development of the other. Since each life can only accomplish some small part of the human potential—Humboldt accepts Goethe's principle that we have to narrow ourselves to achieve anything—we can only benefit from the full range of human achievement and capacity if we live in close association with people who have taken other paths. To attempt to force conformity is to condemn ourselves to a narrower and poorer life.

One of the historical sources of this is a certain theological understanding of human life, emerging particularly from Christianity. Humboldt probably no longer drew on this directly, although I would argue that Herder clearly did. It is the idea of humanity as something to be realized, not in each individual human being, but rather in communion between all humans. The essence of humanity is not something which even in principle a single person could realize in his or her life. And this is not because of the finitude and limitation of this life, since we couldn't make up for the limitation of one by laying other lives, as it were, alongside it, until human variety is exhausted. The fullness of humanity comes not from the adding of differences, but from the exchange and communion between them. They achieve fullness not separately but together. The image Herder used was of a chorus, or we might say, orchestra.

The ultimate richness comes when all the different voices or instruments come together. It is something they create in the space between them. (The theology behind all this finds its sources in certain crucial Christian doctrines, e.g. the Trinity and the Communion of Saints.)

II

Having laid out this background, I want to look at some particular issues and cases where the two models of what it is to create an associative bond confront each other. My general claim will be that, while the difference-blind, or procedural model sometimes seems the obvious one, even the only one, in fact this may not be the case, and it may in the end be more of a source of discord. Perhaps I should repeat, in order to avoid misunderstanding: it is not at all my purpose to deny that this model is ever appropriate. On the contrary, it often is. What I am pleading for is a somewhat more complex and many-stranded version of liberalism.

But first I want to look at some pervasive differences in the way the two models encourage us to respond to difference. The procedural model asks us to abstract from difference in our political-legal dealings with others, and that on two kinds of grounds. On the political level, it is because taking account of difference would be invidious, or divisive, or unfair, or some combination of these. On the basis of the underlying philosophical anthropology—say, a Kantian one—it may be because what is really important about the person is what they share with everyone else, namely, the power to choose their ends, and direct their lives: their autonomy. This model does not encourage us to learn about other people's outlooks. Indeed, it may sometimes seem that the less we know, the easier it is going to be to treat people equitably, because their actual views are so offensive to us that it is hard to ignore them once we come to know them in all their repulsive detail.

Hate the sin, love the sinner. The Kantian saint will look away from the not very edifying actual outlooks that most people build for themselves, and keep firmly in view the autonomous agent ultimately responsible for them.

To the extent that we are operating out of the other model, on the other hand, there is a strong incentive to learn about the other. This is the powerful impulse, for example, behind Gadamerian hermeneutics, which in this respect is very Herderian. One of the principles of this hermeneutics is that there is no achieving understanding of the other which does not at the same time alter one's understanding of oneself. This is because what is preventing us from understanding the other initially is precisely the implicit and hence unwitting hold on us of our own too narrow horizon, the undisputed terms in which we understand our lives. The attempt to understand leads, if it is successful, to a "fusion of horizons," a broader set of basic terms in which the other's way of being can figure undistortively as one possibility among many. And of course, this means that our way too figures as one possibility among many, and this precisely constitutes the revolution in self-understanding.

Now this decentering could be seen as a loss, of course. It is most emphatically not seen as such by Gadamer. And that, I think, is a testimony to the way in which he stands in this Herder–Humboldt tradition I am arguing out of here. Put baldly, teleologically: we are meant to understand each other. This mutual understanding is growth, completion.

Now I have talked about two models here. But models are not people. Most of us operate to some extent on each. We treat different differences differently. No one is such a pure Kantian moral agent that he or she does not see some differences as complementarities, and act accordingly. So the issue is how we should respond to certain concrete cases. And here the different models of the associative bond, seen as overarching political formulae, dictate very different approaches.

III

So let us take one aspect of the "culture wars" now raging in the United States. Here I offer my interpretation, which is very contestable, and in addition, that of an outsider, and therefore doubly questionable. I think part of the anger of many of those cultural or "life-style" conservatives, which is directed against "liberals," and specifically what they see as highly educated, urban liberals, often in the media and the universities, comes from something like this: as they see themselves, what is of crucial defining importance in their lives are some religious commitments, and/or definitions of a good life, turning, among other things, on "family values," say. They are being told to bracket these, to remove them in various ways from the public square, e.g. through banning prayer in schools, or through redefining marriage to include homosexual unions.

Now they are not very happy with these measures as such. But I suspect that a good part of the anger comes not from the measures themselves, but from what they see as the attitude lying behind these measures. That is because they identify the "liberal" philosophy which has dictated these measures as in its very essence dismissive, and even sometimes contemptuous of what their lives are centered on. They are not only being asked to make a sacrifice, they are being told that they are barbarians even to see this as a sacrifice.

Let me take the school prayer case. I am willing to stipulate, for the sake of argument, that there actually are good reasons, in terms of creating an atmosphere where children from very different backgrounds and faiths could come together with minimum exclusion, to ban school prayer.

(I just want to enter a caveat here. Although there undoubtedly are urban schools which meet this condition, I cannot see the justification of a universal ban on prayer in all public schools everywhere. I think this is an unfortunate example of a rigidity which has entered into the American system of judicial review and rendered it largely dysfunctional, and indeed, a major source of divisions and culture wars. Having got this Canadian sentiment off my chest, I return to the main line of the argument.)

Let us say that this measure sits ill with certain long-established Christian communities. Now it is one thing to say to them: "We understand your feelings about prayer in the schools, but think what this means to the many children from Jewish, Muslim, Hindu, Buddhist, secular homes. Surely, we have to make some adjustment here?" Quite another to say: "The very desire for school prayer conflicts with the basic moral principles underlying liberal society, which principles are enshrined in our American constitution. You have to be either too primitive to see this evident truth, or else an enemy of our Constitution, in order to formulate this demand."

The first kind of discourse treats the commitments of the other side seriously. That is, they are neither branded as trivial nor just mistaken. It recognizes that there is an understandable desire here. Already this supposes that something has been taken in of what school prayer means to the people involved. But we can imagine the dialogue going on through even further exploration of the outlook. Once engaged in this kind of discourse, there is a premium on helping the other side toward a rearticulation of their outlook which can allow them to live with the new restriction; in this case, some way of conceiving their communal Christian life in which the absence of school prayer would not just be a truncation. But if we are to help with this, then we have to learn more about the outlook or faith in question. We get drawn into the process of mutual understanding, implicated further in a Gadamerian conversation.

The second kind of discourse cuts off all conversation from the start. Unless, that is, the other side is willing to bracket the faith that really matters to them, and enter onto the terrain of constitutional interpretation. Opponents of the judicial decisions may argue, for instance, from Founders' intent, like Judge Robert Bork. And the proponents of school prayer may be cheering them on. But this is just a stratagem. They in no wise think that Founders' intent is derived from the Gospel; but they think that prayer is. The views which really matter to them are not integral to the argument at this level.

Moreover, it not only cuts off the conversation, but it offers a very unflattering view of the objectors. In order to accept this decision so explained, to make their peace with it, they would have to undergo a total conversion, so that school prayer would cease to be a normal expression of their Christian way of life, and would become an unjustified imposition on others, in breach of the basic ground-tiles of the society they see as theirs. It is hardly surprising that this rankles.

Now my intent is not to portray the proponent of school prayer as ideal Gadamerian interlocutors, whose attempts at conversation have been brutally rebuffed. I am well aware that many of them, and particularly their self-appointed spokespersons, have themselves shown little desire to understand and accommodate the legitimate goals of their opponents. My point is rather to paint an alternative way of framing the debate, another terrain on which the political struggle could go forward. This is a way of going about arbitrating a difference, not by finding a procedural principle which will adjudicate it once and for all, but by confronting the identity needs and the demands of faith and principle that are here in confrontation, and trying to come to some defensible accommodation.

Behind these two ways of addressing disputes are the two models of the associative bond. If you think that the only way in which people of different outlooks can associate in fairness and comity is on the basis of difference-blind principle, then you will look for the most general and defensible such principles and decide all issues in conformity with them. If your model of associating across differences is closer to the Herder–Humboldt complementarity view, then you will seek the kind of accommodations which will allow people to live together and hopefully grow closer.

Now if you ask the further question, which model of the associative bond is actually going to work best to create a society of equals living together in comity, my bet is on the Herder–Humboldt model. I think that the example I have just cited, which touches on just one skirmish in a general culture war, certainly gives some color to my thesis. Deciding the issue of school prayer by one big meat-cleaver principle (here the famous "wall of separation" between church and state) not only creates all-out winners and all-out losers, but declares the losers as somehow beyond the pale of constitutional rectitude. It delegitimates their demands in principle, as against showing how they, alas, cannot be accommodated in practice, given other important such demands. Naturally, it breeds anger and alienation.

Of course, this is far from being the only source of alienation in the American political system today, as Michael Sandel's book amply demonstrates. But it is a not inconsiderable one. And one could argue that the divisions that it has created have made it harder to mobilize the majorities which might have dealt effectively with other, economic and social sources of alienation.

Here is where the argument for procedural liberalism tends to get confused. One could argue that it had failed here, especially in terms of one of its favoured self-descriptions. One of the most oft-cited principles is that one must accord everyone "equal concern and respect." But in this case, precisely what a lot of Christians did not see themselves as getting was respect. Quite the contrary.

What can one say to this? Well, if they had had the sense to stop being Christians, and to redefine themselves as agnostic Kantians, they would have seen that they were being equally respected, *qua* rational agents, or life-plan choosers. To take that as a modality of respect in a plural society sounds more like a bad joke than like good political philosophy.

So much so, that one is led to conclude that the real basis of holding to this liberalism is that it is seen in some deep philosophical way as being the correct view about human agency. Now I think this philosophical view is deeply wrong but what I want to point out here is that it is shifting the ground of the debate.

I said above that there were deep reasons in epistemology, and a theory of human agency and freedom, to go for a procedural ethics and politics. But the nature of the debate, in which the second Rawls is a key figure, the Rawls of *Philosophical Liberalism*, was meant to bypass metaphysics; to bracket the deep theories of epistemology and anthropology and propose a basis for fair political association.

Rawls's theory, of course, gives us the basis to reject some views, those which oppose a reasonable coexistence of difference in a plural society. For instance, we are all going to agree that we have to outlaw as incitement to murder, calls to carry out the infamous fatwa on Salman Rushdie. There are clear limits to what can be accommodated. So we could justify this quick way with the proponents of school prayer, provided we declare them to be unreasonable, in the Rawlsian sense, on all fours with aspiring executors of the fatwa.

But although intellectually possible, as a proposition for contemporary political theory, this would be ludicrous, and I do not know anyone who has proposed it. But then we are left with the paradox, that a theory which is meant to be based on equal respect ends up offering what many supposed beneficiaries cannot help seeing as the very opposite of respect.

The only way to defend the theory at this point would be to retreat to the philosophical level and say: dammit, this *is* respect, in virtue of the nature of human agency. You can like it or lump it. But beside being—I think—wrong, this is changing the subject, and abandoning the enterprise of finding a fair basis of coexistence which we could in fact hope to live by.

What all this shows, I think, is that the move to Rawls II, the move to a political not metaphysical theory, has been rather imperfectly carried out by procedural liberals. In fact, they seem still to be very much influenced by their epistemological and metaphysical views, and therefore are willing to stick to a position even when it is showing up very badly in the political arena. They seem somewhat too impervious to the way things are going on the ground to generate really convincing political theory. That is why Sandel's book is such a valuable contribution at this time.

The irony is that, seen from the Herder–Humboldt model, a crucial part of the self-perception of these liberals is reversed. They tend to see themselves as people who have broad views, and understand difference, while the grass-roots opponents of various liberal laws and judgments are narrow and exclusive. But in the light of the Herder–Humboldt model, the situation is pretty symmetrical. Neither side is listening very much to the other, or has much respect for it, and each has their principled reason in terms of their self-justification to shut their ears. And, of course, the intransigence of each encourages that of the other. This is a classical no-win situation for liberal democracy.

IV

I want to embroider another theme of *Democracy's Discontent* by spelling out a little how this situation is bad news for democracy. The crucial feature of a modern political society is that it has to be to as high a degree as possible what I will call a deliberative community.

I am, of course, speaking of democratic states, which are consequently founded in theory on popular sovereignty. For the people to be sovereign, it needs to form an entity and have a personality. This need can be expressed in the following way: the people is supposed to rule; this means that the members of this people make up a decision-making unit, a body which takes joint decisions. Moreover, it is supposed to make its decisions through a consensus, or at least a majority, of agents who are deemed equal and autonomous. It is not democratic for some citizens to be under the control of others. It might facilitate decision-making, but it is not democratically legitimate.

In addition, to form a decision-making unit of the type demanded here it is not enough for a vote to record the fully formed opinions of all the members. These units must not only decide together, but deliberate together. A democratic state is constantly facing new questions, and in action aspires to form a consensus on the questions that it has to decide, and not merely to reflect the outcome of diffuse opinion. However, a joint decision emerging from joint deliberation does not merely require everybody to vote according to his or her opinion. It is also necessary that each person's opinion should have been able to take shape or be reformed in the light of discussion, that is to say by exchange with others.

This necessarily implies a degree of cohesion. To some extent, the members must know one another, listen to one another, and understand one another. If they are not acquainted, or if they cannot really understand one another, how can they engage in joint deliberation? This is a matter which concerns the very conditions of legitimacy of democratic states.

If, for example, a subgroup of the nation considers that it is not being listened to by the rest, or that they are unable to understand its point of view, it will immediately consider itself excluded from joint deliberation. Popular sovereignty demands that we should live under laws which derive from such deliberation. Anyone who is excluded can have no part in the decisions which emerge and these consequently lose their legitimacy for him. A subgroup which is not listened to, is in some respects excluded from the "nation," but by this same token, it is no longer bound by the will of that nation.

For it to function legitimately, a people must thus be so constituted that its members are capable of listening to one another, and effectively do so, or at least that it should come close enough to that condition to ward off possible challenges to its democratic legitimacy from subgroups. In practice, more than that is normally required. It is not enough nowadays for us to be able to listen to one another. Our states aim to last, so we want an assurance that we shall continue to be able to listen to one another in the future. This demands a certain reciprocal commitment. In practice a nation can only ensure the stability of its legitimacy if its members are strongly committed to one another by means of their common allegiance to the political community. Moreover, it is the shared consciousness of this commitment which creates confidence in the various subgroups that they will indeed be heard, despite the possible causes for suspicion that are implicit in the differences between these subgroups.

In other words, a modern democratic state demands a people with a strong collective identity. Democracy obliges us to show much more solidarity and much more commitment to one another in our joint political project than was demanded by the hierarchical and authoritarian societies of yesteryear. In the good old days of the Austro-Hungarian Empire, the Polish peasant in Galicia could be altogether oblivious of the Hungarian country squire, the bourgeois of Prague, or the Viennese worker, without this in the slightest threatening the stability of the state. On the contrary, this condition of things only becomes untenable when ideas about popular government start to circulate. This is the moment when subgroups which will not, or cannot, be bound together, start to demand their own states. This is the era of nationalism, of the breakup of empires.

I have been discussing the political necessity of a strong common identity for modern democratic states in terms of the requirement of forming a people, a deliberative unit. But this is also evident in a number of other ways. Thinkers in the civic humanist tradition, from Aristotle through to Arendt, have noted that free societies require a higher level of commitment and participation than despotic or authoritarian ones. Citizens have to do for themselves, as it were, what otherwise the rulers do for them. But this will only happen if these citizens feel a strong bond of identification with their political community, and hence with those who share with them in this.

From another angle again, because these societies require strong commitment to do the common work, and because a situation in which some carried the burden of participation and others just enjoyed the benefits would be intolerable, free societies require a high level of mutual trust. In other words, they are extremely vulnerable to mistrust on the part of some citizens in relation to others, that the latter are not really assuming their commitments—e.g. that others are not paying their taxes, or are cheating on welfare, or as employers are benefiting from a good labour market without assuming any of the social costs. This kind of mistrust creates extreme tension, and threatens to unravel the whole skein of the mores of commitment which democratic societies need to operate. A continuing and constantly renewed mutual commitment is an essential basis for taking the measures needed to renew this trust.

What emerges from the above is that modern democratic societies are extremely vulnerable to citizen alienation, more than any form of authoritarian society, just because this alienation delegitimates, and that in virtue of the very underlying ideas of popular sovereignty. In particular, we can see two kinds of perceptions on the part of some group of citizens, which can create a gulf between them and the rest of the society. In one case, the members of the group feel that their views are not being heard, perhaps cannot really be understood by the majority, and that they are therefore not part of the community for deliberative purposes. In another, they may feel that the solidarity binding the members of the society does not extend to them. They are left out.

In a certain sense, these are two sides of the same coin. If they are not listened to, then already they are in a sense being ignored, and this certainly will mean that their needs and demands are not attended to. And if they are considered outsiders, then they will not be heard. But the sense of exclusion can arise from either side of this global sense of alienation. That is, the initial perception may be: they aren't listening to us, they can't recognize or hear us for what we are. Or it may be: the mechanisms of mutual aid and succor are no longer reaching to us.

In effect the United States suffers from both kinds of alienation today, and sometimes the same groups may have very strong perceptions of both of these types. (African-Americans living in urban ghettos are perhaps a case in point.) Alas, this is not an exceptional condition among Atlantic democracies. But some features of it may be exacerbated here. A perception of the second type, an abandonment of solidarity, may be arising today from the extreme polarization of income and wealth in the USA.

But a reaction of the first type, a sense of not being heard, seems to me to have arisen from the attempt to resolve some of the issues of family values, of religion in society, and the like, in a procedural liberal frame.

Now a sense of alienation of this kind may, in appropriate circumstances, give rise to a movement for separation. That is obviously the case that concerns me (obsesses me and my compatriots, would be a better expression). But there are other very bad consequences, even where separation is not on the cards. The sense "we're not being heard" is close to the sense: "we can't talk to those people; we can only defeat them." People engage in politics on issues which have aroused this reaction rather as though they were engaging in a war. The other side has to be wiped out or totally neutralized. The goal is not to go on living with them, but under a new arrangement. It is somehow to root them out, or subjugate them, so that one does not have to deal with what they stand for anymore.

This is carried on in languages on both sides which deny the other a legitimate place in the deliberative commmunity. On one side, the demands of the other are seen as against the fundamental morality of the constitutional order, and therefore as not to be countenanced in any form. On the other, the rhetorical turn is to define oneself as speaking for the people as against unrepresentative and arrogant elites, from whom usurped power has to be wrested.

Of course, some of the rhetoric is the good old knock-about stuff which has a long tradition in the United States. Think of the multiform history of populism there. But it seems to me that it is being carried to a rare and dangerous pitch in the present culture wars. In particular, this kind of polarization can make it very hard to address, and build majorities around other important issues, because the potential majorities lie athwart the division which is being thus absolutized.

Thus it appears to me that the United States is not destined by some immutable law of history to be as far away as it is from the Atlantic range of social democracies. It is hard, in any case, for this foreigner to see what are the overwhelming advantages in rejecting any mode of universal health scheme. But clearly the task of mobilizing a winning constituency for a plan of this kind has been greatly bedeviled by the deep divisions around values and religion.

V

Now my hypothesis above is that procedural liberalism has exacerbated differences and, in this way, has done American democracy a disservice. Here I am echoing the conclusions of Mike Sandel, with which I deeply agree. Moreover, I would argue that procedural liberalism is not a very good way of living with difference, principally because it calls on us to abstract from, to bracket, to look away from, so many differences. Once again, let me repeat, that I am not posing a stark choice between always abstracting from differences, and always taking them into account. My whole approach has been to steer away from these blockbuster universal principles. But the effect of procedural liberalism has been to push the difference-blind approach to unwarranted lengths.

But it might be protested, surely the really divisive moves are coming from people who reject procedural liberalism; from "postmodernists" and "multiculturalists." These are often blocked by conservatives along with "liberals," but nothing could be less fair, and the "postmodernists" themselves attack the unfortunate liberal with much greater gusto than they denounce the oppressive right.

Now there is some truth to this point. Indeed, there are highly destructive and divisive policies flying under the colors of "multiculturalism," alongside much that is very valuable. But where the policies are bad, I would like to argue that they are rooted in certain philosophical sources which are common with procedural liberalism. In particular, they share with it, either a commitment to negative liberty, that is, the voluntarist view of freedom, or/and a hostility to the Herder–Humboldt model of the associative bond. Otherwise put, policies framed in the languages of "postmodernism" usually share these properties with their procedural liberal enemies.

There is not room to argue this in detail. Let me take one example of a philosopher whose work is immensely influential in this field, Michel Foucault. Foucault was in an important sense a philosopher of freedom, in spite of his denials for a good part of his career. That is, he was a philosopher who claimed to unmask and lay bare domination, the interiorization of power relations by the victims of these—and although he often claimed that power had no subject, he certainly portrayed it as having victims. The moral thrust of these analyses, whether it was admitted or not in the text, was implicit in the language in which they were cast. They called for the opening of a line of resistance for the victim, a disengagement from the full grip of the current regime of power, particularly from its hold on our self-understanding. And Foucault's own interventions in politics and public life certainly bore out this interpretation.

Towards the end of his life, in the last volume of the *History of Sexuality*, and in the latest interviews, Foucault did make clearer his view of freedom, the building of an identity, relatively uncolonized by the current regimes of power. And it was plainly a negative conception, as he makes quite unambiguous in the interview a number of us had with him in Berkeley a year before his death.[1]

A Foucaultian influence, or at least an affinity, with this position is evident in important strands of feminist theorizing, of gay liberation, and calls for the recognition of "difference." The emphasis is on relations of oppression, and the undoing of them. The goal seems to be one in which the person or group concerned will have achieved full autonomy, will no longer be controlled or influenced. No place is allowed for another possible *telos* of this struggle, one in which the agents or the groups, previously related by modes of dominance might reassociate on a better basis. The invocation of the victim scenario is a very common move in a position of this type. The history is usually painted in such a way as to make it almost inconceivable that there could be a new mode of association, let alone that both sides need it to be complete beings.

This brings me to the other facet I mentioned above, the rejection of the Herder–Humboldt complementarity view. In a sense, this rather than the commitment to negative freedom captures better the basic structure of Foucault's position. Foucault never paints the interpenetration of identities as a potential gain. He is in this sense the most profoundly antidialogical thinker. It is not that he puts forward an express thesis rejecting a dialogical view. It is rather that the stories he offers, at the different stages of his writings, of the development of identity always represent the definition of identity through the other in the register of invasive power, the preferred response to which must be resistance.

Thus he discusses in *Surveiller et Punir*[2] the various modes of discipline which arise in the seventeenth and eighteenth centuries: parade square, asylum, prison; all forms of control. The development of modes of collective discipline by which people came to govern themselves, the modern reconstitution of civic freedom in puritan societies, for instance, all this remained completely outside his picture of our history. What Arendt defined as power, the increased capacity that people can create by associating in common action, and thus also the main theme of Sandel's book, remained completely off his map. He thought this kind of thing was an illusion, as he made quite clear in our interview in Berkeley.

On the contrary, what he defined as the only really healthy mode of identity formation, the definition of self in the aesthetic dimension,[3] was a completely solo operation, the achievement of lone virtuosi, who could learn from each other, but did not need to associate with each other. One could not be farther removed from the Herder–Humboldt perspective.

But it is perhaps only in this perspective that one can distinguish destructive from creative modes of multiculturalism. To put it oversimply, in judging different policies that fly under this title, the rule of thumb would be this: What is the *telos* of the policy? Does it aim to restore comity in which our need for each other can be met without the distortion of repression or exclusion? Or does the whole way in which the demand is framed point rather to a liberation into solitary self-sufficiency as the only adequate solution? Worse still, does it point this way even if this liberation cannot in fact be reached, so that the protest is doomed to be repeated forever in a ritual of endless accusation?

VI

I have dealt with a host of issues here, which all have to do with how to cope with, or live with difference. I have taken up from Michael Sandel the argument that procedural liberalism has often been a bad guide in how to do this, has in fact restricted our ability to deal with it. I am suggesting that we need to go beyond this negative criticism, and try to articulate an alternative model of the bond of association which can give an alternative answer to the question how to live as equals in difference. I see the model we need here as the one that we find in the Herder–Humboldt tradition, one whose key notion is complementarity, and whose basic idea is that we need each other, precisely in our difference, to be whole beings.

But if procedural liberalism is often not a good guide in this area, nor frequently is the family of views which offers itself as a major alternative, multiculturalism, in particular when this is informed by a "postmodernist" philosophy. What I wanted to argue here is that it is in taking up the

Herder–Humboldt perspective that we can begin to discern what is constructive and what is destructive within multiculturalism.

The issue of what model we adopt of the associative bond is thus a crucial one. It deserves much further exploration and discussion. My aim here has merely been to put it on our agenda.

V

Law, Morals, and Private Lives

18

Unencumbered Individuals and Embedded Selves: Reasons to Resist Dichotomous Thinking in Family Law

MARY LYNDON SHANLEY

LIKE many other thoughtful people in the United States today, Michael Sandel is worried about the family. Sandel believes that "the law increasingly treats persons as individual selves independent of their family roles."[1] He finds this trend harmful not only to our understanding of the meaning of family ties, but also to responsible behavior. His concern arises in the context of significant sociological and demographic changes affecting families. There is a sense that the family as we have known it in Western Europe and the United States over the past two hundred years has changed and is continuing to change in ways whose significance is hard to predict. By the 1970s, 50 percent of marriages ended in divorce; the percentage of mothers with preschool children who worked outside the home rose from 12 percent in 1950 to 45 percent in 1980; between the early 1960s and the l990s the percentage of children born to unmarried mothers rose from 5 percent to 25 percent; openly gay and lesbian households increased, some with children from prior heterosexual unions or from gamete donation; "blended families" created by the marriage of people with children became increasingly prominent.[2] These sociological changes seem consonant with what Sandel sees as a trend in both popular discourse and public law to regard family relationships as less important in establishing the self-understanding and legal obligations of family members than in previous decades.

Despite the fact that I share Sandel's view that individualistic models of family life and family relationships are both inaccurate and destructive of important social values, I find Sandel's view of family law misleading and likely to do harm if not qualified or amended. Sandel suggests that family law is fundamentally flawed because it rests on a false understanding of the individual, whom it views as a disembodied rather than as an embedded self.

Further, it regards the rights of such individuals as "trumps" in certain ethical and legal disputes. Finally, it abjures normative judgments about the proper ordering of family life in favor of state neutrality. In place of what he views as impoverished assumptions that underlie contemporary liberalism and United States law, Sandel would substitute an understanding of the individual as partially constituted by specific formative relationships. One of the goals of public policy and law would be to protect such relationships, abjuring neutrality in order to support and foster those relationships that citizens judged to be most valuable. Claims that an individual's rights were being abridged would then have less importance than they do now when weighed against the values of community or group cohesion or the fostering of social practices the community deems desirable.

I try to explain Sandel's dichotomous view and what I find problematic about it by looking at three issues in family law. First, I discuss Sandel's view that recent trends in divorce law treat family members primarily as individuals, and only secondarily as persons who in significant ways are defined by their roles in a family, and that this is deleterious to all family members, but perhaps particularly to women. Second, I examine Sandel's analysis of Justice Blackmun's dissenting opinion in *Bowers* v. *Hardwick,* the case that upheld a Georgia statute criminalizing sodomy. Sandel asserts that while Blackmun's dissent appears to support homosexual rights, by focusing on the individual and individual choice rather than on the value of homosexual intimacy Blackmun undermines the project of properly valuing the role of sexual intimacy in both heterosexual and homosexual relationships. This, Sandel contends, undermines the long-range interests of same-sex partners and contributes to the impoverishment of public discourse about values. Third, I look at an issue in family law that Sandel does not discuss, but that I find relevant to the question of whether and how models of "unencumbered" and "embedded" selves have influenced legal thinking about families: the controversy over whether race-matching or restrictions based on cultural identity should be allowed or prohibited in adoption law. US law and public policy has grappled with issues of race, cultural membership, and adoption in the Indian Child Welfare Act of 1978 and, with somewhat different results, in the Multiethnic Placement Act of 1994. I focus on the Indian Child Welfare Act in evaluating Sandel's view that rights talk and assertions of individual rights are necessarily in conflict both with a sense of self tied to group membership and with social and political respect for cultural diversity.

Consideration of these three issues reveals, I believe, that US law concerning families has not tipped as unequivocally in the direction of unbridled individualism as Sandel believes, and that, in any event, individualism and moral values are not diametrically opposed to one another. Sandel asserts that contemporary law and public policy must choose between a model of the "a priori" or "disembodied" self, the primacy of individual rights, and the necessity of state neutrality on the one hand; or a model of the "embedded" or "encumbered" self, the primacy of community over individual rights, and the necessity of state action in support of publicly agreed upon values on the other. But Sandel's insistence that a proper family law must reject individualism and the notion of the unencumbered self in order to embrace the notion of the embedded self and substantive moral values creates a misleading and potentially harmful dichotomy. Legal recognition of the individual rights of family members need not lead inexorably to the kind of exaggerated individualism with which Sandel and some other commentators on family law associate it, and believe it is undermining family life.[3]

The assertion of individualist values like autonomy and choice may expose relationships of domination and oppression, thus contributing not to atomism but to the reconstruction of relationships themselves. Similarly, an individual's rights may include the right to be in a relationship and to have others respect or preserve that relationship. Rather than seeing unencumbred and embedded selves, individualism and moral values, as pitted against one another, family law must be formulated to reflect the inseparability of individual well-being and human relationships, of autonomy and the moral life.

Sandel's Understanding of Self and Family

Sandel's concern about exaggerated individualism in both popular and legal discourse about families is an extension or application of the critique of liberalism and the liberal individual that he developed in *Liberalism and the Limits of Justice*.[4] In *Democracy's Discontent* Sandel argues that the objects of his criticism in *Liberalism and the Limits of Justice*—the deontological view of the self and the theory of justice to which it is inextricably linked—are not simply philosophical theories but are the ideological underpinnings of the procedural republic, one of two main strands of American political theory. Sandel reads the history of American political thought as an uneasy coexistence or struggle for dominance between the ideology of the procedural republic and that of civic republicanism. The procedural republic is characterized by acceptance of "the key features of contemporary liberalism—rights as trumps, the neutral state, and the unencumbered self." Sandel sees these characteristics as pervasive in American law in the latter half of the twentieth century; they "have come to inform the theory and practice of constitutional law and of family law in recent decades."[5]

Sandel's starting point in *Liberalism and the Limits of Justice* was a sustained critique of John Rawls's *A Theory of Justice*, particularly of Rawls's commitment to the Kantian understandings of the self as a subject who is prior to and independent of its objects, and of a notion that the right is prior to the good.[6] The kind of "deontological liberalism" to which Rawls subscribes "supposes that we can, indeed must, understand ourselves as independent," that is, "that we must stand to our circumstance always at a certain distance, conditioned to be sure, but part of us always antecedent to any conditions."[7] In the last analysis, Sandel argues, Rawls's theory rests upon (and encourages) an understanding of the individual that is abstract and atomistic, and that offers no coherent conception of community. Deontological liberalism puts the self "beyond the reach of politics"; it speaks the language of rights rather than of the good; it protects individuals rather than fostering the communities to which they belong; and it forgets that "when politics goes well, we can know a good in common that we cannot know alone."[8] The absence of any viable notion or theory of community in Rawls's and other liberals' works "marks the limits of justice and locates the incompleteness of the liberal idea."[9]

In both *Liberalism and the Limits of Justice* and *Democracy's Discontent* Sandel contends that changes in family law in the last half of the twentieth century have reflected the ascendancy of the understanding of the self that is characteristic of deontological liberalism. For David Hume, Sandel notes, the need for justice arose from imperfection, either from material scarcity or the want of a broad human benevolence. Hume found such benevolence or "enlarged affections" to be rare, but noted that in marriage "the cement of friendship is by the laws supposed so strong as to abolish all division of possessions; and has often, in reality, the force ascribed to it."[10] The family, then, provided a model of virtues that might make certain kinds of legal regulation and use of political power unnecessary.

Where traditional marriage law, like Hume, treated the family as more than the sum of its parts, a community of "mutual benevolence" and enlarged sentiment, the new family law, Sandel asserts, follows Rawls in treating the family as constituted by individuals who are properly regulated by precepts of justice rather than altruism or benevolence. Because we cannot know others' aims and desires, we need justice to tell us what is their due regardless of their specific ends. "Where for Hume, we need justice because we do not love each other well enough, for Rawls we need justice because we cannot know each other well enough for even love to serve alone."[11] Sandel is quick to point out that deontological liberalism's model of the self, which in his view underlies the new family law, does not assume that human beings are always, or even typically, governed by selfish or self-interested motives. Indeed, Rawls and thinkers like him are not making a claim about human motivations at all, but rather about the subjects who may have one motivation or another. Rawls's theory "assumes interests of a self, not necessarily in a self, a subject of possession individuated in advance and given prior to its ends."[12]

But, Sandel argues, individuals are not as distinct, nor as "opaque" (either to themselves or to others) as Rawls believes. It is a mistake to think of individuals as existing prior to their ends: "we cannot conceive ourselves as independent in this way, as bearers of selves wholly detached from our aims and attachments," some of which are "embedded in the story of those communities from which I derive my identity—whether family or city, tribe or nation, party or cause."[13] Individuals are members of one community or another (or several overlapping communities). Such a community is marked by a common vocabulary of discourse and a background of implicit practices and understandings within which the opacity of the participants is reduced if never finally dissolved. Insofar as justice depends for its preeminence on the separateness or boundedness of persons in the cognitive sense, its priority diminishes as that opacity fades and community deepens.[14]

Families are communities which are (ideally at least) the locus of some of the "central aspirations and attachments" of their members. The more family members love one another and see their fates as intertwined, the less family relationships will need to be regulated by the principles of justice. The point is not simply that members of loving families will turn to the courts less frequently than members of less harmonious households, but that law itself can promote family harmony. Because law shapes the way we conceptualize human relationships, we should make sure that "the tale told by law" reflects an understanding of the importance of communal interdependence to both individuals and society, rather than simply reflecting justice understood as the protection of individual rights. If the law tells the tale of selves "individuated in advance and given prior to [their] ends," spouses, parents, and children will have to struggle harder than they otherwise would to regulate their life together according to the precepts of love rather than justice. A great deal turns, therefore, on the conceptualization of the individual in liberal political theory and family law.

In what follows I analyze Sandel's depiction of the dangers of a family law that espouses a notion of the "unencumbered" individual, individual rights, and the neutral state. I examine his critique of the individualism reflected in contemporary divorce law and laws concerning homosexual relationships. I add to these a discussion of the Indian Child Welfare Act, legislation that corresponds to some extent to Sandel's idea that law should envision the individual (or at least members of Indian tribes) as embedded in the community. I hope my discussion of these issues will show that the dichotomous choice between grounding family policy in a view of either the unencumbered individual or the embedded individual is unnecessary and misleading. Recognition of the individual rights of those wishing to form families can coexist with an appreciation of the value of intimate association and group life; they are vital to the project of revisioning the human interdependence fostered and sustained in diverse families.

Issues

Individual or Spouse?: What Difference does Marriage Make?

Sandel regards contemporary family law as increasingly conceived in voluntarist terms, in which the exercise of free choice by each member is highly valued; this law differs in significant ways from earlier family law.[15] The "old family law" regarded marriage as a lifelong commitment between spouses to promote one another's welfare and that of the marital or family community. The law assumed that spouses had specific roles within that community, with corresponding obligations and claims. Husbands were expected to be breadwinners and to present the public face of the family in the larger business and civic communities. Wives were expected to do housework and to provide for many of the emotional and psychological needs of family members, particularly of children. In return for their labor, which was unpaid, wives were entitled to lifelong economic support from their husbands. While provisions for divorce varied from state to state, divorce was uncommon before the mid-nineteenth century, and until the mid-twentieth century one party had to prove the other had committed a grave "fault" against the marriage in order to obtain a divorce; a husband whose actions or "fault" caused the breakup of the marriage might be ordered to pay his wife alimony or economic support after divorce.[16]

The trend towards individualism in family law is, Sandel argues, reflected in the rise of "no-fault" divorce, initiated in the late 1960s.[17] The rejection of fault as grounds for divorce and property settlements meant that a marriage could be dissolved on the petition of one party alone, without either a finding of fault or the agreement of the other party. No-fault divorce was accompanied by the abandonment of the notion of marital roles tied to lifelong obligations, and an emphasis on self-sufficiency of each spouse after divorce. Where the old family law "treated persons as situated selves, whose identity as legal persons was tied to their roles as husbands, wives, and parents," the new family law emphasizes the individual and "loosens the relation between the self and its roles; it makes family roles easier to shed and relaxes the obligations that attach to them."[18] The new family law reflects the tendency of contemporary US law to regard individuals as unencumbered selves who have the right to enter and leave relationships almost at will, to bracket moral judgments, and to insure that law and government remain neutral with respect to differing conceptions of the good.[19]

The rise in individualism and the decline in the notion of a marital community of interests and of traditional roles affected the ways in which the law viewed obligations between ex-spouses. Where the old divorce law regarded divorced partners as "part of an ongoing community, in which the more financially fortunate member had a duty to respond to the needs of the less fortunate one," the new divorce law takes it as its purpose to allow the partners to make a "clean break" and go their separate ways. Many courts attempt to achieve this by dividing the assets accrued during the marriage as equally as possible, and perhaps requiring one spouse to help the other to economic self-sufficiency by paying for schooling, job-training, or vocational counseling.

The assumption that the purpose of the post-divorce financial settlement should be to move each person to economic independence as soon as possible has often resulted in serious hardship for many ex-spouses (mainly ex-wives).

Not only have many wives been out of the job market for some period of time, but they often have less education and fewer job skills than do their ex-husbands. The major asset of many marriages is the husband's earning power, but he carries this away with him when the marriage dissolves. The old marriage law that rested on a notion of lifelong community and commitment justified a wife's ongoing claim to a portion of her husband's income, but such a claim is much harder to justify under a model of marriage as a possibly temporary economic partnership.[20] Women who act as traditional homemakers and do not have their own source of income fare badly under the new marriage law's notion of a "clean break" which will return ex-spouses to their status as separate individuals.[21]

In promising wives long-term support if their marriage should end, the old marriage law provided some compensation to wives for their economic vulnerability, but it promoted an inequality in both the family and the larger society. The assumption that one member of the family would be the primary breadwinner while the other tended house and children, meant that educational and vocational training seemed less important for women than for men; this often deprived women of marketable skills and sometimes curbed their personal growth. Similarly, the wages attached to various jobs tended to be higher or lower depending upon whether the work was regarded as "men's" or "women's" work. And whole occupations were reserved for men (building trades, security officers) or for women (nursing, secretarial, domestic cleaning), with the wages for those occupations filled primarily by women being significantly less than those filled primarily by men.

The assumption that married women would (and should) be dependent on their husbands created relationships of super- and subordination both in some marriages and in the larger society.[22] As Susan Okin has pointed out, women's unequal status in the economic world, including the paucity of well-paying jobs for women, meant that women were often "trapped" in marriage in a way that most men were not. They could not leave, or even threaten to leave as a way of expressing discontent or exerting pressure for new behavior, because both they and their husbands knew such a threat was empty in the absence of marketable skills and work experience.[23] Many women also lacked the time and money to be active participants in public and political life. Traditional roles for married men and women, and marriage law based on those roles, did not always mean community and intimacy, it could mean oppression and subordination.

Sandel seems to understand this when he writes that where a "gain in justice" takes place because justice replaces injustice rather than benevolence, "the overall moral improvement is clear."[24] Yet the only concrete suggestion he offers to remedy the frequent unfairness of no-fault divorce and clean-break financial settlements is to revert to protections for vulnerable wives. Sandel observes that in making dependence during marriage dangerous to the dependent spouse should the marriage collapse, the new law of divorce "burdens the practice of marriage as a community in the constitutive sense. By bracketing moral judgments, celebrating self-sufficiency, and loosening the relation between the self and its roles, the law is not neutral among competing visions of married life, but recasts the institution of marriage in the image of the unencumbered self."[25] Sandel's alternative to the family of the unencumbered self, however, is not to suggest reforms that would create greater equality between men and women in both public and private realms of activity, nor to rethink the social and economic structures that make it so difficult for adults who are responsible for children to do remunerative work and care for those children at the same time. Protecting women who choose to stay home in the absence of broader reforms does not rectify the imbalance between the demands of the market and the demands of caregiving, and it places the costs of sustaining family relationships disproportionately on women.

There are, however, alternatives to Sandel's proposal that the law recognize the centrality of commitment (to the other spouse and to the marriage itself) by reinstating protections for a spouse who chooses to stay at home rather than enter the market place. As Milton Regan has argued, despite the fact that "in constructing the image of ex-spouses, we seem to assume that our only choices are to treat them as either spouses or as strangers, as inhabitants of either the family or the market domain," these are not mutually exclusive options between which social and legal discourse must choose. The complexity of divorce and its consequences is captured by neither of these models. "On the one hand, ex-spouses are persons whose lives have been intertwined in ways that cannot be instantly undone at divorce. On the other hand, they are persons who must seek to construct a new life that is distinct from the one that they previously had shared. Treating them as strangers is as unrealistic as treating them as spouses."[26] Only by treating divorcing partners under both rubrics can justice be approximated.

It is important to recognize that the model of the kind of voluntarist marriage that permits no-fault divorce does not preclude or necessarily discourage deep affection, mutual commitment, and personal transformation through the relationship. The possibility of no-fault divorce does not mean that spouses will necessarily hold one another at arm's length, but that they will not be forced to stay in a marriage when mutuality and commitment no longer exist. And it guarantees that each of them, and not the state, will make the judgment as to whether the relationship is viable or irreparably damaged.

While protecting displaced homemakers is a valuable short-term goal, it does not exhaust the measures the law might take to foster intimacy and recognize human interdependence, and to do so under conditions of equality for men and women.[27] In the long run, significantly more far-reaching measures will be necessary to foster respect for family life along with sexual equality in education and employment. Respect for families requires that business practices be changed to recognize that employees have important responsibilities to dependents that cannot be met if there is no accommodation for time off to care for children or the elderly, as proponents of the Family and Medical Leave Act rightly insisted. Respect for families requires that there be sufficient public support for children's needs that they do not have their life-chances severely curtailed because their parent(s) cannot afford adequate food, shelter, or medical care. Respect for families requires that men assume responsibility for the daily tasks involved in household maintenance and care of children. Sandel is right that a "clean break" has not and will not produce a just marriage law nor properly reflect the ongoing responsibilities of spouses for one another and for their children even after divorce. Yet that interdependence and responsibility must not be purchased at the cost of equality, as it will be unless financial protections are accompanied by deeper and more radical changes in the labor market, work place, and home. Above all, we must reject the temptation to think that equality and interdependence are incompatible. The "unified family" of nineteenth-century law rested upon conditions of severe legal, social, economic, and political inequality. The challenge for family law and family policy is to design measures that will allow deep affectionate ties to flourish while not locking some people—primarily women—into dependency.

Individuals and Relationships: Why Protect Homosexual Intimacy?

Sandel sees the same excessive attention to individuals in some legal thinking about homosexual sexual intimacy as he does in some legal thinking about divorce. As Sandel argues that homemakers are harmed by divorce settlements based on a notion that marriage is a (possibly temporary) agreement for cohabitation that does not fundamentally touch the self-definition or life-plans of the partners, so he believes that gay men and lesbians are harmed by the notion that their sexual relationships should be protected by the right to privacy understood as a guarantee for the expression of individual choice rather than as an acknowledgment of the value of intimate association.

Sandel sees this focus on individualism rather than relationship in Justice Blackmun's dissenting opinion in *Bowers* v. *Hardwick* (1986), a case in which the majority upheld the constitutionality of a Georgia statute outlawing sodomy. The majority contended that "homosexual sodomy" was not protected by the right to privacy enunciated in *Griswold* v. *Connecticut* in which the Supreme Court held that a state could not prohibit married couples from using contraceptives in part because of the valuable nature of the marriage relationship. By contrast, said the majority in *Bowers*: "No connection between family, marriage, or procreation on the one hand and homosexual activity on the other has been demonstrated."[28] Sandel notes that "[a]ny reply to the Court's position would have to show some connection between the practices already subject to privacy protection and the homosexual practices not yet protected." There are two ways of doing this, in his view. A voluntarist approach "argues from the autonomy the practices reflect," and "holds that people should be free to choose their intimate associations for themselves . . .

so long as they do not harm others." A substantive approach "appeals to the human goods the practices realize," and claims that "much that is valuable in conventional marriage is also present in homosexual unions" (Sandel 1996: 104). Of these two possible responses to the majority opinion, Sandel contends, "the dissenters in *Bowers* relied wholly on the first." He sees the core of Blackmun's dissent as the sentence declaring that the constitutional guarantee of privacy should protect "the freedom and individual has to *choose* the form and nature of these intensely personal bonds" (ibid. 100, quoting *Bowers*, emphasis in original). The dissent does not reflect or foster respect for homosexual unions, but simply toleration for "the fact that 'different individuals will make different choices' in deciding how to conduct their lives."[29]

In Sandel's eyes, the dissenters in *Bowers* missed an opportunity to articulate the possible goods to be realized by homosexual intimacy, and in doing so impoverished political discourse. The language of the dissent reflected the fact that "[e]ven . . . marriage and the family are increasingly conceived in voluntarist terms, prized less for the human goods they make possible than for the autonomous choices they express."[30] This relentless progression towards seeing all human relationships as simply voluntaristic, and the people in such relationships as "unencumbered selves" who "are conceived as prior to [their] ends," undermines the body politic and threatens self-government.[31]

Were this reading of the *Bowers* dissent fully accurate, it would indeed be disturbing, but Sandel overlooks passages in which Blackmun suggests that homosexual intimacy deserves the protection of privacy precisely because of the human relationship it reflects and creates. Throughout his opinion, Blackmun attempts to relate the importance to an individual of being a member of a family or an intimate association, and the ability to choose to establish or enter such a relationship. The relationship has value, but it loses some of that value if it is imposed or the result of coercion rather than choice. The inseparability in Blackmun's mind of the value of being in a relationship and of choosing to be in that relationship is strikingly clear in one of the early paragraphs of the dissenting opinion. Protesting the majority's contention that this case bears no resemblance to previous decisions affirming the right to privacy, Blackmun reminds the Court that certain rights associated with the family have repeatedly been accorded shelter under the Fourteenth Amendment's Due Process Clause.

> [W]e protect the decision whether to marry precisely because marriage "is an association that promotes a way of life, not causes; a harmony in living, not political faiths; a bilateral loyalty, not commercial or social projects." *Griswold* v. *Connecticut*, 381 U.S., at 486, 85 S. Ct. At 1682. We protect the decision whether to have a child because parenthood alters so dramatically an individual's self-definition, not because of demographic considerations or the Bible's command to be fruitful and multiply. Cf. *Thornburgh* v. *American Coll. Of Obst. & Gyn., 476* U.S., at *777*, n. 6, 106 S. Ct., at 2188, n. 6 (STEVENS, J. Concurring). And we protect the family because it contributes so powerfully to the happiness of individuals, not because of a preference for stereotypical households. Cf.

Moore v. *East Cleveland,* 431 U.S., at 500–506, 97 S. Ct., at 1936–1939 (plurality opinion).[32]

Individual identity is dependent upon being in relationships. This is both an empirical fact of psychological and social development, and a conceptual truth. Adults capable of leading self-directing lives do not spring full-grown from the ground, but form their identities through close relationships with parents, siblings, extended family, neighborhood, church, town, and other crucial associations.[33] Conceptually, although the individual and the relationship are distinct entities, no relationship can exist without its individual members, and no individuals can be who they are without the relationships that constitute them.

Twice in five pages Sandel quotes Blackmun's assertion that "much of the richness of a relationship will come from the freedom an individual has to *choose* the form and nature of these intensely personal bonds" in order to argue that Blackmun embraces a notion of unbridled individual volition cut loose from enduring human relationship. But this phrase occurs in the context of a paragraph in which Blackmun is defending a right asserted not by an isolated or atomistic individual, but by someone who is in a relationship and defending that human connection:

Only the most willful blindness could obscure the fact that sexual intimacy is "a sensitive, key relationship of human existence, central to family life, community welfare, and the development of human personality," *Paris Adult Theatre I* v. *Slaton,* 413 U.S. 49, 63, 93 S. Ct. 2628, 2638, 37 L. Ed. 2d 446 (1973); see also *Carey* v. *Population Services International,* 431 U.S. 678, 685, 97 S.Ct. 2010, 1016, 52 L.Ed.2d 675 (1977). The fact that individuals define themselves in a significant way through their intimate sexual relationships with others suggests, in a Nation as diverse as ours, that there may be many "right" ways of conducting those relationships, and that much of the richness of a relationship will come from the freedom an individual has to *choose* the form and nature of these intensely personal bonds. See Karst, The Freedom of Intimate Association, 89 *Yale L.J.* 624, 637 (1980); cf. *Eisenstadt* v. *Baird,* 405 U.S. 438, 453, 92 S. Ct. 1029, 1038, 31 L.Ed 2d 349 (1972); *Roe* v. *Wade,* 410 U.S., at 153, 93 S.Ct., at 726.

It is because of the centrality of sexual relationship (not choice alone) to the development of the person that Blackmun protests the Court's refusal to recognize "the fundamental interest all individuals have in controlling the nature of their intimate associations with others."[34]

The dissenters in *Bowers* made a strong case that same-sex as well as heterosexual relationships can be brought under the shelter of the privacy protections of *Griswold,* constitutional principles that protect not simply individuals, but relationships or intimate associations. The rights asserted in *Bowers* and endorsed in Blackmun's dissent do not focus on an isolated individual, but on an individual-in-relationship who seeks to protect that relationship from state scrutiny and criminal prosecution. Sandel's conviction that attention to protecting individual rights has diminished attention to human association blinds him to the blending of these perspectives in the *Bowers* dissent.[35]

Sandel's tendency to view rights as linked to individual volition overlooks another way in which Michael Hardwick's complaint does not isolate him in his desire but links him to others. In asserting that his constitutional rights have been abridged, Hardwick gives voice to the grievances of millions of gay men and lesbians that they have been denied the right to respect and to intimate association. The effort to strike down Georgia's antisodomy statute was an effort to remake the story of members of this larger group, specifically to change their status in law from persons who engage in criminal practices to citizens claiming constitutional protection.

One of the unfortunate consequences of Sandel's dichotomous vision of the self is that it leads him to reject strategies that assert individual rights but that nonetheless do not separate the individual from human association, community, or political movements.[36] One might expect Sandel to be more sympathetic to group rights than to individual rights, since the notion of group rights seems to reflect both the "embeddedness" of individuals and respect for cultural diversity and the value systems that often distinguish one group from another. Although Sandel does not talk about the Indian Child Welfare Act or group rights, a consideration of the provisions of the Act dealing with adoption provides another example of the ways in which it is misleading to assume that respect for individual rights entails abandonment of substantive moral values. On the contrary, reflection on the ICWA shows that while the claims of individualism and group membership may conflict in particular cases, autonomy—no less than solidarity—reflects values essential to the good life.

Individualism and Tribal Membership: The Unencumbered and the Embedded Self

Sandel believes that in order for serious discussion about how moral values should shape family law to thrive, a notion of the embedded self must replace that of the unencumbered individual contained in much writing on marriage and divorce law and on homosexual rights. Although I believe Sandel is right that people are "embedded" in moral obligations that they do not initially choose or that they cannot cast off simply at will, pitting the concept of an unencumbered self against that of an embedded self creates a misleading dichotomy: every person must be considered in two aspects, as a free-standing agent and as an individual-in-relationship with others, each of which carries with it important moral values.

The necessity for such a dual vision is evident in issues raised by the Indian Child Welfare Act of 1978 (ICWA), which regulates foster care and adoptive placement of Native American children.[37] Although Sandel does not discuss adoption, the ICWA seems to reflect and promote an understanding of Native Americans and Native American families that is consonant with Sandel's views.[38] The ICWA regards neither Indian infants nor their biological parents as unencumbered individuals, but rather suggests that they are embedded in a web of relationships they have not chosen, yet which in part constitute who they are and which justify particular legal stipulations regarding jurisdiction and placement in foster care and adoption cases. The ICWA also recognizes individual rights through provisions that allow for consideration of the wishes of the biological parents and of the best interests of a particular child. The Act has generated controversy however, because some state courts have sought to evade the provisions meant to foster tribal identity, and in response to these evasions some advocates of tribal rights have proposed eliminating parental choice concerning placement (the parent in such cases is usually an unmarried birth mother). A consideration of the issues raised by voluntary relinquishments of infants for adoption under the ICWA illustrates the values involved in regarding persons both as distinct individuals and as persons fundamentally involved in relationships of dependence, responsibility, and care.

Adoption law in the United States has historically reflected respect both for the freedom of individual volition and for family relationships. The rise of legally regulated adoption dates only from the mid-nineteenth century. Prior to 1850, the transfer of care of children from one family to another was not unusual; for example, orphans were often raised by their aunts and uncles while apprentices were brought up in their master's household. But these arrangements did not involve the formal transfer of legal custody from one family to another. Michael Grossberg has pointed out that legal adoption signaled a weakening of the patriarchal ideology that the family was a single entity under the rule of the husband-father, and of legal changes that accepted the independent legal standing of each family member.[39] Viewed in this light, adoption statutes incorporated an individualistic and voluntaristic understanding of family ties that permitted the legal bond between biological parent(s) and offspring to be severed, and another legal bond between adoptive parent(s) and child to be formed through the consent of both sets of parents. The practice of legal adoption, like compulsory schooling and child-labor laws, reflected not only individualism but also the strength of republican ideology which paid increased attention to the personality of children because it was intent upon making children into good democratic citizens. From this perspective adoption was a way of placing children into permanent and indissoluble relationships with non-biological parents, siblings, and other family members.[40] Infant adoption would seem to rest upon acceptance of the notion that infants, at least for a brief period of time after birth, can be regarded as unencumbered individuals who can be moved from one family to another and can be expected to take on an identity shaped by the roles, status, duties, and obligations that membership in the new family entails.

The ICWA was enacted in response to extensive congressional investigations of how Indian children fared in foster placement and adoption proceedings that found that Indian children were being removed from their homes and placed in non-Indian households by state courts and child-welfare agencies at extremely high rates.[41] In states with large Indian populations, for example, studies suggested that perhaps as many as 25 to 35 percent of all Indian children were removed from their homes by the state and placed in adoptive homes, foster homes, and institutions like the boarding-schools run by the Bureau of Indian Affairs. In most states, the vast majority of placements were in non-Indian homes, and in some states the proportion reached 90 percent. For many of these children, this resulted in a permanent separation not only from their family but from their tribe as well.[42] In some states the risk of Indian children being involuntarily separated from their parents was up to one thousand times greater than the risk for non-Indians.[43]

Congress intended the ICWA to reverse this trend. The Act declares it to be "the policy of this Nation to protect the best interests of Indian children and to promote the stability and security of Indian tribes and families by the establishment of minimum Federal standards for the removal of Indian children from their families and the placement of such children in foster or adoptive homes which will reflect the unique values of Indian culture . . ."[44] Two kinds of stipulations are meant to foster the interests of Indian children and the stability of the tribes. The first is jurisdictional. Tribes have exclusive jurisdiction over adoptions and foster placements of Indian children domiciled on the reservation. Furthermore, tribes have the right to be notified of any proceedings involving Indian children not domiciled on a reservation. The tribe may then intervene and request a transfer of jurisdiction to the tribal court; transfer of jurisdiction must be granted unless either parent objects or there is "good cause" not to do so.[45] The second outlines placement preferences that state courts are to apply in deciding custody matters. In an adoption proceeding involving an Indian child under state law, "a preference shall be given, in the absence of good cause to the contrary, to a placement with (1) a member of the child's extended family; (2) other members of the Indian child's tribe; or (3) other Indian families."[46] When appropriate, "the preference of the child or the parents shall be considered" in deciding on placement.[47]

Both the jurisdictional and placement provisions of the ICWA raise difficult issues concerning the role of race in determining placement of an Indian child.[48] In stipulating that in the absence of good cause, Indian children are to be placed with Indian adoptive parents, the ICWA differs markedly from the Multiethnic Placement Act of 1994 (MEPA) which prohibits the awarding of federal funds to any agency engaged in placing children for adoption that has prohibited or significantly delayed placement due to race. The line between those who favor race-blind adoption and those who favor racial or other "matching" in adoption is drawn most clearly in cases involving infants; most people acknowledge that older children have an interest in maintaining a racial, religious, or ethnic identity and so if possible should live with parents who share that characteristic. Infant adoption, however, raises the question of whether newborn infants have characteristics that partially define who they are and should set limits on where they may be placed.

Twila Perry has identified two approaches to the question of whether and to what extent race should be a relevant factor in the adoptive placement of infants. She calls these "liberal color-blind individualism" and "color and community consciousness," terms that suggest Sandel's contrast between individualistic and communitarian approaches to thinking about political life and law.[49] With respect to transracial adoption, proponents of liberal color-blind individualism tend to argue that race should not be a factor in adoption, or a factor of only minor significance. Proponents of community consciousness argue that race, ethnicity, or religion should be a factor in adoptive placements. The MEPA reflects color-blind individualism while the ICWA reflects community consciousness.[50]

The jurisdictional and placement provisions of the ICWA seems consonant with a Sandelian conviction that American politics and law should articulate greater respect for the group affiliations of citizens than is currently the practice. The jurisdictional provisions are intended to foster tribal self-rule and to protect the integrity of Indian culture and Indian families. The placement preferences reflect the judgments that the very existence of the tribes is threatened by assimilationist practices, and that tribes are communities that profoundly influence each tribal member's sense of himself or herself. The ICWA seems to incorporate the notion that individuals do not belong solely to themselves, but must be thought of as "obligated to fulfill ends we have not chosen—ends given by nature or God, for example, or by our identities as members of families, peoples, cultures, or traditions."[51] Unlike the government's ban on the wearing of yarmulkes while on active duty in the Air Force, or refusal to exempt peyote used in some Native American religious ceremonies from drug laws, in the ICWA it was recognized by Congress that different stipulations may be necessary to regulate practices for members of different groups. The ICWA rejects the universalism that Sandel contends is part of a commitment to the "unencumbered self,"[52] declares that the situation of Indian children is different than that of other children, and creates different legislative provisions to govern their adoption than those that apply to other children under US law.

The legal protection that the ICWA extends to Indian tribes in the name of cultural pluralism seems consonant with Sandel's judgment that "A pluralism that nurtures the distinctive expressions of community is better suited to citizenship, and so to self-government, than one that merely tolerates them."[53] Moreover, Sandel believes that cultural pluralism benefits not only groups that maintain their cultural integrity and self-governance, but enriches the rest of American society that benefits from the existence of vibrant Indian communities. "Respecting persons as unencumbered selves may afford a kind of social peace, but it is unlikely to realize the higher pluralism of persons and communities who appreciate and affirm the distinctive goods their different lives express."[54] A Sandelian approach might well view the ICWA as not only a way to halt the forced assimilation of Native American children into the dominant society, but also as a vehicle for preserving the benefits of cultural pluralism for all of American society.

The ICWA seems to me to reflect the claims of both individualism and community in American life and law. The requirement that all adoptions involving the children of tribal members domiciled on the reservation be heard by tribal courts is intended to foster tribal self-government, recognize the parents' "embeddedness" in the tribe, and establish a relationship between their offspring and the tribe. The tribes' claim to make decisions for these children is based partly on the imperative of group survival, and partly on the fact that it is on the reservation that their parents have been physically sustained and have developed many aspects of their cultural identity. Tribes that take up the responsibility of hearing adoption cases and providing adoptive homes for children certainly provide important service and care to their members. The provisions of the ICWA giving tribal and state courts concurrent jurisdiction in custody cases involving children of parents who do not live on a reservation, in turn, reflect the judgment that these parents may have a less clearly defined (and self-defining) relationship with the tribe. In such cases, concurrent jurisdiction allows a parent to request or to veto transfer of jurisdiction from state to tribal court.

Some courts, however, have been reluctant to turn certain cases involving Indian children over to tribal courts. For example, until the Supreme Court rejected such reasoning in *Mississippi Band of Choctaw Indians* v. *Holyfield*,[55] courts in several states held that the adoption of a child born to parents domiciled on a reservation but born off reservation did not need to be transferred to the tribal court. More recently, some state courts have attempted to avoid the jurisdiction and placement preferences of the ICWA either by invoking the "existing Indian family exception" to argue that the Act does not apply, or by holding that while the Act applies there is "good cause" not to follow the statutory placement preferences.[56] Such evasions of the provisions of the ICWA, in turn, have led some supporters of tribal rights to insist that only by curtailing the discretion of the state courts with respect to jurisdiction and placement can the purposes of the Act—and the preservation of Indian communities and cultures—be met. These critics advocate rejecting the "existing Indian family exception" altogether, and severely restricting the use of "good cause" to set aside the statutory placement preferences.

Critics of courts that evade the ICWA have proposed restricting circumstances under which a state court could find "good cause" to override the placement preferences of the ICWA. The Act states that courts may consider, "[w]here appropriate, the preference of the Indian child or parent" in determining good cause.[57] Erik Aamot-Snapp argues that "courts should rarely determine that the parent's request constitutes good cause to depart from the placement preferences." He proposes that "Courts should never consider a parent's placement preference when that parent's parental rights have been terminated. . . . When the court has terminated parental rights, it is inconsistent to give the terminated parent a measure of control over a child's placement."[58] But while a parent whose parental rights have been terminated should not *control* the placement of his or her child, it may make sense for the parent *to be heard* with respect to placement. Particularly in the case of voluntary relinquishment, the wishes of the biological parents (especially of the gestational mother in infant adoption) are not irrelevant to the child's placement simply because of the decision to surrender the child for adoption.[59] The majority of parents in voluntary adoption proceedings will be women, and off-handed dismissals of the relevance of their views and desires is disturbing. Parental authority (which includes the authority to make the decision to relinquish a child for adoption) properly derives from actual caregiving activity, and gestational mothers have a particularly strong claim to such authority because they provide most of a child's care prior to birth.[60] The decision to surrender a child for adoption should be regarded not as an act of abandonment that precludes any legitimate interest in the child's placement, but as part of an effort to provide care for one's offspring.

I think critics are right to reject the "existing Indian family exception" in issues of placement as well as of jurisdiction: there is no indication that Congress intended such an exemption; the issue of what constitutes an "existing Indian family" opens the door to tremendous individual subjectivity and cultural blindness concerning the nature both of "family" and of "Indian family"; and "the exception denies protection of any potential relationship between the child and the tribe."[61] But there is a clear need for better arguments and stipulations than those based on the genetic tie between male progenitor and his offspring to combat state courts' efforts to evade the provisions of the ICWA. Congress could advance a socially based rather than a genetically based understanding of parent–child relations while upholding the purposes of the ICWA by substituting new language in the statutory definition of "Indina child." The Act now says that an "Indian child" is "any unmarried person who is under age eighteen and is either (a) a member of an Indian tribe or (b) is eligible for membership in an Indian tribe and is *the biological child of a member of an Indian tribe*."[62] Changing the italicized material to "*the child of a legally recognized parent who is a member of an Indian tribe*" would reflect an understanding that "parent" and "child" are words connoting a social as well as a biological relationship. It would also make the definition of "Indian child" consonant with the definition of a "parent" under the Act, which includes any biological parent or any adoptive parent, but does not include an unwed father unless paternity has been acknowledged and established.[63]

The ICWA is notable for its commitment to striking an appropriate balance between the claims of both group membership and individual autonomy.[64] Reflection on the issues raised by the ICWA shows that regarding persons either as group members whose identities and commitments are exhausted by their affiliation with one group or another, or as "individuals" without group identities and commitments is inadequate. Just as parents' "embeddedness" as tribal members is reflected in strict application of the jurisdictional and placement provisions of the ICWA, so their right to be seen and heard as individuals is reflected in the statutory allowances that allow them to influence jurisdiction if they are not domiciled on a reservation, and to have their preference concerning placement considered by state courts.[65] In cases of differing perspectives between tribe and parents, even though one of these perspectives will win in the end, it is important that the "tale told by law" contain within it an acknowledgment of the complexity of preserving the self-governing ability and cultural integrity of different groups in a multicultural society; of respecting women's voices in reproductive decision-making; and of attending to children's needs both for stable nurturing relationships and for societal respect for their families and cultures of origin.[66]

Conclusion

Michael Sandel has argued energetically that family law is threatened by an exaggerated individualism that threatens the altruism and generosity and self-sacrifice that has traditionally characterized family life and made it a valuable counterpoint to the impersonal norms of public life. Sandel asks us to think of recent developments in family law as posing a struggle between two understandings of both the individual and the family, one of a kind of rootless individualism that disaggregates the family, rendering it an alliance (perhaps temporary) of individuals, and the other that of a collective entity that deeply engages and transforms its members. This dichotomous portrayal is, however, misleading; it affects Sandel's portrayal both of the poverty of liberal political theory and of family law. When Sandel argues that liberalism has bequeathed to family law a view of the self as prior to its ends, a self that is an empty and meaningless abstraction, he distorts the liberal commitment, which is not to a self prior to any ends whatsoever but to a self whose ends are neither imposed from without nor exempt from reexamination.[67] Liberalism understands that any person is simultaneously a situated individual (and thus shaped by particular group affiliations like religion, national origin, race) and a citizen to be treated similarly to fellow citizens. This same complex understanding that persons are alternately—even simultaneously—viewed as individuals and as members of groups is reflected in legal thinking about families as well.[68]

Despite his attentiveness to those aspects of human life that are linked to membership in a family, neighborhood, tribe, or nation, Sandel does not say much about how he would have the law take cognizance of and accommodate the claims group membership might create, much less develop a theory of group rights.[69] The Indian Child Welfare Act provides an example of legislation that recognizes the "embeddedness" of individuals by establishing a legally cognizable interest of the tribe in custody of an offspring of a tribal member. Yet even a brief consideration of the ICWA reveals the complexity, but not the impossibility, of framing measures that recognize the possible conflicts between group authority and individual autonomy.

What does it matter that Sandel tells a misleading story about individualism's corrupting effects on families and family law? Like Sandel, I believe that the stories we tell about our national life (and personal lives) are crucially important to the shaping of our civic life.[70] The stories we ensconce in law reflect and shape the values we espouse and encourage us to behave in one way or another. In attributing the risk of excessive individualism, anomie, and irresponsibility to assertions of individual rights in disputes about intimate associations, including families, Sandel risks depriving us of a vocabulary and conceptual framework with which to recognize and understand relationships of systemic subordination.

Intolerance and a lack of respect for diverse values and modes of family life are every bit as great a threat to contemporary American life as the excesses of individualism that Sandel fears. Many of those who suffer from intolerance, or from an indifference which renders them invisible, will find that talk about rights facilitates the articulation of their submerged narratives. Sandel espouses tolerance and diversity, but the false dichotomy between individual rights and communal attachment upon which he bases his discussion of family law undermines the possibility of realizing those laudable goals. One of the great tasks facing the American polity today is giving visibility and voice to those outside the structures of power, and rights talk is not simply the language of individualism run wild, but a vehicle by which the stories of those who have not shared in public power can be heard, including wives, gay men and lesbians, and birth-mothers. We need to construct the very complicated story of the role of rights and discourse about rights in family law with nuance and subtlety, or we will deny ourselves the intellectual and legal implements most useful in the never-ending construction and reconstruction of a just society and a just family law.

19

The Right of Privacy in Sandel's Procedural Republic

JAMES E. FLEMING AND LINDA C. McCLAIN

Introduction

IN *Democracy's Discontent: America In Search of a Public Philosophy*,[1] Michael J. Sandel critiques liberalism's Constitution of the "procedural republic" and calls for an alternative civic republican understanding, which we will call the Constitution of the "substantive republic." We will assess Sandel's search for a substantive republic through analyzing his approach to the problem of moral disagreement and political conflict in a pluralistic polity, in particular, by considering his criticism of constitutional law cases protecting a right of privacy or autonomy from *Griswold* v. *Connecticut* to *Planned Parenthood* v. *Casey*. Our basic contentions are that Sandel is in search of too thick a republican constitutional theory for a substantive republic and yet that, ironically, what he delivers is a form of procedural republic.[2]

The Constitution of the Substantive Republic

Sandel's Substantive Republicanism

Sandel calls for substantive moral argument in justifying and interpreting the Constitution. He argues that in interpreting constitutional freedoms courts should not bracket conceptions of the good, as they do in liberalism's procedural republic. They should move beyond liberal toleration or autonomy arguments, which justify protecting freedom to choose independent of the moral worth of what is chosen, to republican moral arguments, which justify securing freedoms on the basis of the substantive human goods or virtues or ends that they foster. Moreover, Sandel argues for viewing constitutional freedoms as preconditions for citizenship and self-government on a republican model.

Revised and reprinted with permission, James E. Fleming and Linda C. McClain, "In Search of a Substantive Republic," *Texas Law Review*, 76 (1997), 509–51.

Within the substantive republic, courts engaging in moral argument would secure the freedoms that are preconditions for the substantive republic.

Sandel's call for substantive moral argument in constitutional law is a form of what Ronald Dworkin calls "the moral reading of the Constitution."[3] That is, Sandel like Dworkin would interpret the Constitution as embodying principles of political morality, and would argue that courts should make recourse to those principles in interpreting it. (Of course, their moral readings would differ, because their principles would differ.) Sandel does not develop a division of institutional roles, or a conception of different types of arguments appropriate for courts and legislatures. He seems to contemplate that courts, as well as legislatures, will engage in moral argument in interpreting the Constitution.[4] Notably, Sandel does not make the traditional republican argument for judicial deference to the democratic process,[5] nor does he advance a republican argument for judicial reinforcement of the democratic process.[6] On these views, the domain of any substantive republic is outside the courts.

Just what is the substance of the substantive republic? What are the republican goods or virtues or ends that the Constitution should be interpreted to foster or further? Alas, Sandel fails to deliver the goods for a substantive republic. Indeed, he does not offer a substantive account of goods or virtues or ends so much as a call for a republican form of argument or justification for constitutional freedoms, and a commitment to a process of deliberation. He distances himself from the substance of classical republicanism, with its exclusiveness, coerciveness, and inegalitarianism, and instead emphasizes the need for a pluralistic republicanism in a diverse and mobile society. Moving beyond the encumbered self (with which he contrasted the liberal "unencumbered self" in his earlier work)[7] he advocates a republicanism that can accommodate "multiply-situated selves" with conflicting loyalties and obligations. And he contends that contemporary republicanism need not have a unitary and uncontestable conception of the common good but can be pluralistic.[8]

But how is this pluralistic republicanism possible? In what sense is such a capacious conception republican? What does it provide that liberalism lacks? What does it require that liberalism cannot provide? To the extent Sandel hints at substance, his republican virtues suitable for multiply-situated selves sound suspiciously liberal or at least compatible with liberalism, leading us to question whether there is a significant distance between his pluralistic republicanism and the most attractive form of liberalism.[9] To the extent Sandel's republicanism rejects central values of liberalism like autonomy, we question its feasibility and attractiveness.

We will assess Sandel's search for a substantive republic through analyzing his approach to the problem of moral disagreement and political conflict in a pluralistic polity, in particular, by considering his critique of the privacy cases from *Griswold* v. *Connecticut* to *Planned Parenthood* v. *Casey*. This cluster of Supreme Court decisions concerns the proper scope of substantive liberty protected by the Due Process Clause with respect to intimate association and reproductive freedom.

Sandel's Analysis of the Privacy Cases

Sandel uses the line of privacy cases from *Griswold* to *Casey* to chronicle the ascent of the procedural republic and its flawed model of liberal toleration or autonomy.[10] For him, the tale involves the Court's unfortunate move from the "old" privacy to the "new" privacy, and from a justification rooted in substantive moral goods to a justification based on autonomy. The Court began promisingly enough in *Griswold,* identifying a right of privacy of married couples as limiting the government's authority to ban their use of contraceptives.[11] On Sandel's account, *Griswold* emphatically did not rest on the flawed tenets of liberal toleration: the justification of rights premised on a "voluntarist" conception of the self and on the value of autonomy, independent of the moral goods it secures. Sandel praises the *Griswold* Court for resting the justification for a right of privacy on a substantive moral judgment about the value of marriage (which it called "intimate to the degree of being sacred," "a harmony in living . . . a bilateral loyalty," and "an association for [a] noble . . . purpose").[12]

But from this substantive republican justification for a right of privacy, the Court took a dramatic and fateful turn toward the liberal procedural republic in later cases, construing *Griswold* as enshrining the decisional autonomy of the individual—and the value of choice itself—as the core justification.[13] No longer limited to guarding the precincts of the "sacred" marital bed-chamber, privacy became in *Eisenstadt* v. *Baird* the "right of the *individual,* married or single, to be free from unwarranted governmental intrusion into matters so fundamentally affecting a person as the decision whether to bear or beget a child."[14] That individual right of privacy served as the basis for striking down, in *Eisenstadt,* a law restricting the distribution of contraceptives to unmarried persons and, in *Roe* v. *Wade,* a law forbidding women to terminate their pregnancies.[15] Then, in *Carey* v. *Population Services International,* another contraception case, the Court expressly cast the right of privacy as a right of "individual autonomy in matters of childbearing"[16] that extends to individuals independent of their roles or attachments (say, in marriage). So transformed, Sandel observes, privacy protects certain kinds of individual decisions rather than certain kinds of morally valuable social practices.

Sandel interprets *Casey,* which reaffirmed the central holding of *Roe,* as offering the "fullest expression" of this "new" notion of privacy as autonomy, pointing to *Casey*'s language about the relationship between the abortion decision and a woman's personal "dignity and autonomy."[17] He uses the language of *Casey* concerning the scope of *"Griswold* liberty" to show an explicit link between this notion of privacy and the voluntarist conception of the person: "At the heart of liberty is the right to define one's own concept of existence, of meaning, of the universe, and of the mystery of human life. Beliefs about these matters could not define the attributes of personhood were they formed under compulsion of the State."[18]

How should a republican court have decided these cases interpreting the scope of "*Griswold* liberty"? Sandel offers us clues in his critique of *Bowers* v. *Hardwick*.[19] For Sandel, *Bowers* starkly illustrates the limited ability of liberal toleration arguments adequately to ground rights. Justice White, writing for the majority, rejected a challenge rooted in the right of privacy to the application of Georgia's sodomy statute to private, consensual homosexual conduct. He summarily found no analogy or "resemblance" between homosexual sodomy and the choices and conduct protected under *Griswold* and its progeny. Instead, he analogized homosexual conduct to adultery, incest, and other sexual crimes committed in the home that are properly subject to governmental regulation. Moreover, with no critical evaluation of such belief, White concluded that the presumed belief by the electorate of Georgia in the immorality of homosexual conduct provided a rational basis for the statute. Sandel points to *Bowers* as an evident anomaly among the Court's new privacy cases in its rejection of the liberal ideal of the neutral state and its acceptance of the state's proper authority to express through criminal law a moral judgment about sexual conduct.

But Sandel does not embrace Justice White's opinion in *Bowers* as exemplifying republican moral discourse. To the contrary, he suggests that the challenge to Georgia's statute should have directly engaged the question of morality by drawing analogies between the human goods of homosexual intimacy and those of heterosexual unions previously protected by the Court. Such a justification for a right of homosexual intimate association would eschew the liberal ideal of state neutrality concerning citizens' conceptions of the good, because it would rest upon the good of the practices that the right protects. Rather than pursue this moral high ground, Sandel contends, the dissenting opinions in *Bowers* by Justices Blackmun and Stevens relied wholly on bare autonomy arguments, drawing an analogy to *Griswold* not as to the goods of marriage, but only as to the importance of choice to the voluntarist self. Worse, he contends, those defending or upholding privacy rights for gays and lesbians more frequently bracket the issue of the morality of homosexual intimate association and draw an analogy to *Stanley* v. *Georgia*, which upheld the right to possess obscene materials in one's home.[20] Here, for Sandel, is the epitome of the shortcomings of liberal toleration arguments: like obscenity, homosexuality is defended wholly independent of its moral worth and is demeaned as a "base thing that should nonetheless be tolerated so long as it takes place in private."[21]

Sandel contends that such bare autonomy arguments, because they eschew substantive moral discourse, may fail even to secure toleration. As a practical matter, "it is by no means clear that social cooperation can be secured on the strength of autonomy rights alone, absent some measure of agreement on the moral permissibility of the practices at issue."[22] Even if such arguments for rights succeed in court, they are unlikely to win more than a "thin and fragile toleration."[23] Because they leave unchallenged the negative views about gays and lesbians, they forego the opportunity to move citizens beyond empty toleration of private, disfavored conduct to respect and appreciation of the lives that homosexuals live.

On Sandel's republican alternative, grounding rights in the substantive moral good of social practices makes possible genuine respect and appreciation among citizens. Republicanism, he argues, interprets rights in light of their relation to its conception of the good society as a self-governing republic.[24] This link to republican self-government suggests that the full republican argument for a right would go along these lines: the social practice protected by a right allows the realization of something that citizens (through engaging in moral discourse) can recognize to be substantive moral goods, which in turn foster the citizens' engagement in republican self-government. Exactly what this means depends, of course, on the scope that Sandel gives to the term "self-government." His rejection of liberal notions of autonomy makes clear that we should construe the term to refer to deliberative democracy to the exclusion of deliberative autonomy.[25]

A Critique of Sandel's Analysis of the Privacy Cases

Is Sandel's critique of the "voluntarist conception" said to be dominating the privacy cases persuasive? Is his alternative republican justification altogether missing from such cases? And is it more attractive or persuasive than a liberal justification? We offer three responses.

First, Sandel's critique of the new privacy accurately identifies the emergence of a strong autonomy justification, but overstates the supposed dichotomy between the liberal appeal to choice and the republican appeal to moral goods. Undeniably, Sandel points to the central role that the appeal to a principle of autonomy plays in liberal constitutional argument, a principle that Blackmun and Stevens correctly concluded should have led the Court to strike the statute before it in *Bowers*. Yet Sandel's critique of the *Bowers* dissents in particular, and of liberal toleration arguments in general, draws too sharp a contrast between protection of rights for the sake of choice in itself and protection of them because of the moral good of what is chosen.

A more complete, less selective, reading of the dissents in *Bowers* reveals the argument that the protection of choice is important precisely because of the good of such things as marriage, family, and intimate association in persons' lives. As Justice Blackmun puts it: "[o]nly the most willful blindness could obscure the fact that sexual intimacy is 'a sensitive, key relationship of human existence, central for family life, community welfare, and the development of human personality.' "[26] This is an admittedly and inescapably liberal argument in the following sense: it is precisely because these matters are so important or significant in persons' lives, and for their pursuit of moral goods, that we protect, in Justice Stevens's words, an "individual's right to make certain unusually important decisions that will affect his own, or his family's, destiny."[27] Arguably, there is an analogical argument here in the contention that homosexual intimate association, like heterosexual sexual intimacy, is central to persons' lives, sense of place in society, identity, and happiness.

Of course, Sandel would find this fuller account of liberal toleration unsatisfying, for it is undeniably "voluntarist" in emphasizing the relationship between decisional autonomy and personal identity. Here, Sandel's analysis highlights that there is an undeniable and unbridgeable gap between liberal and republican justifications for rights of the sort he advocates. This gap has one basic source: Sandel's rejection of the moral principle of autonomy and its value (as liberals understand it) and his apparent exclusion of such autonomy from his conception of self-government. Notwithstanding Sandel, liberal justifications for rights such as privacy can and do make recourse to substantive moral goods, but they do so in order to augment rather than to supplant the appeal to autonomy. Furthermore, if, as Sandel argues, rights are to be justified with regard to their facilitation of self-government, a liberal argument must insist on a conception of self-government that includes not only deliberative democracy but also deliberative autonomy. This liberal commitment to a more complete conception of self-government reflects a moral judgment about the centrality of self-determination in securing the status of free and equal citizenship for everyone, and here liberals can only plead guilty to Sandel's charge.

Rather than flee the liberal commitment to autonomy, we would turn the tables on Sandel and ask: Is there no room in a republican justification of rights for a principle of protecting individual choice and autonomy? Sandel's republican model artificially separates moral goods from the process of choosing them. For example, marriage is an association and a social practice, but (absent a regime of arranged marriages) we do not just find ourselves in a marriage; we make a choice. While there are often constraints on choices and social norms and roles may shape choices, it is generally the case that procreation, parenthood, and other practices protected under the rubric of privacy or autonomy entail some element of choice. If republicanism's concern is simply that citizens engage in morally worthy social practices, then a regime that places no value on choice could simply assign citizens to engage in those practices. If Sandel objects that forcing persons into particular relationships and practices compromises the moral worth of those practices, he must implicitly assume that there is some value attached to the element of choice, autonomy, or personal self-government.[28] And if so, the gap narrows between Sandel and Justice Blackmun, who contends that "much of the richness of a relationship will come from the freedom an individual has to choose the form and nature of these intensely personal bonds."[29]

We question whether Sandel's distinction between liberalism's supposedly unencumbered selves choosing their ends, and pluralistic republicanism's "multiply-situated selves" claimed by "multiple loyalties," is as fundamental as he claims. Consider one of the specific examples he offers of the substance of his republicanism: "The civic virtue distinctive to our time is the capacity to negotiate our way among the sometimes overlapping, sometimes conflicting obligations that claim us, and to live with the tension to which multiple loyalties give rise."[30] Surely this capacity for self-direction bears a family resemblance to such liberal notions as revisability, or the capacity to form and to revise one's conception of the good life, including the capacity to enter into and to exit attachments and communities.[31] If so, Sandel practically embraces autonomy by another name. If we are correct, perhaps Sandel's republicanism can move closer to liberalism than his book suggests.

And perhaps liberalism can move closer to Sandel's republicanism than he allows. The justification for the right to abortion is illustrative. Sandel offers *Casey* as the fullest expression of the notion of privacy as autonomy, yet he ignores the role that substantive moral discourse plays in that case. In articulating a pregnant woman's liberty interest, the joint opinion speaks of the "unique" condition of pregnancy, stressing not only the moral good that women may bestow on children through childbirth and motherhood, but also the moral harm of denying women choice, due to the deeply personal nature of the pain and suffering of pregnancy, childbirth, and motherhood.[32] *Casey* sounds themes of self-government both in the liberal sense of autonomy, when it speaks of the role that procreation plays in a woman's self-definition and self-determination, and in a more republican sense, when it notes the vital role that the "ability to control their reproductive lives" has played in facilitating the "ability of women to participate equally in the economic and social life of the Nation."[33] Sandel's analysis of *Casey* also completely leaves out any discussion of sex equality as a component of women's full citizenship, a principle that some republicans have emphasized in justifying the right to abortion.[34]

Most interestingly, Sandel does not comment on perhaps the most republican aspect of the joint opinion in *Casey*: the latitude that it gives to the state to shape women's decision-making process in favor of childbirth over abortion to encourage "wise" or responsible decisions, in part because of the "consequences" of the abortion decision for the women, the community, and prenatal life.[35] Contrary to Sandel's characterization of the abortion cases as minimalist in their bracketing of the moral issues about abortion, *Casey* acknowledges that abortion is a matter as to which men and women of good conscience will always disagree and yet does not require that the state be neutral because of this moral conflict. Rather, that case permits the state, due to its "profound" interest in protecting potential life, to take sides by seeking to persuade women in favor of childbirth, so long as its measures aim to enhance informed decision-making rather than to impose an undue burden on decision-making.

Furthermore, it is telling against Sandel's account of the liberal procedural republic that he fails to acknowledge Dworkin's praise of the *Casey* joint opinion for recognizing a proper role for government in encouraging responsibility, in the sense of reflective decision-making, when intrinsic values, such as respect for the sanctity of life, are at issue.[36] Dworkin contends that the constitutional right to procreative autonomy rests on a right to make essentially religious decisions for ourselves; yet such a right entails a moral responsibility of reflective exercise, which government may encourage. Dworkin's analysis may remain too liberal for Sandel because it holds to a strong principle of ethical individualism, a right to decide for ourselves, even to make an immoral, or wrong, decision. (And Dworkin's apparent endorsement of *Casey*'s conflation of one-sided persuasion with facilitation of reflective decision-making raises concerns on liberal and feminist grounds.[37]) Yet his argument is notable as an attempt within liberalism to reconcile a principle of ethical individualism with a proper governmental role of shaping citizens and encouraging them to exercise their rights responsibly. Dworkin's attempt to give some credence to arguments about the ethical environment and a community's interest in its members' decisions suggests some common ground with a republican formative project. Moreover, Dworkin's argument for toleration on the issue of abortion seems far from minimalist, for it attempts to move citizens beyond pale civility and grudging toleration by recasting the abortion debate as a conscientious disagreement as to the interpretation of how best to respect the intrinsic value of the sanctity of life in particular circumstances.

Second, even assuming that Sandel's republican alternative offers a better justification for rights than liberal models, Sandel may overestimate the power of analogy about moral goods to move citizens from grudging toleration to respect and appreciation. To be sure, some critics of liberal toleration may find Sandel's critique and his plea to move from toleration to respect and appreciation inspiring and sound. For example, proponents of gay and lesbian rights might wager that engaging in and winning a substantive moral debate could lead to full citizenship and acceptance more readily than making toleration arguments.[38] But Sandel tells us little about how exactly the appeal to moral goods should be made and how judges, legislators, and citizens should evaluate such goods. Using his critique of *Bowers* as illustrative, we presume that his approach would encourage advocates of same-sex marriage to draw analogies between the goods realized in heterosexual marriage and those attained in same-sex relationships. *Griswold* spoke of the goods of bilateral loyalty and a harmony in living; contemporary accounts of marriage identify many goods, such as companionship, security, emotional commitment, and children. We assume that similar analogical arguments could be made concerning the moral goods of gay and lesbian families in order to secure rights to procreation and parenting.

Sandel may underestimate the intensity of moral disagreement about how persuasive these analogical arguments are, especially in the absence of any clear criteria for what counts as a moral argument. Suppose proponents of same-sex marriage offer numerous testimonials concerning the goods of gay and lesbian intimate association, along with psychological and sociological studies confirming such goods and further supporting gay and lesbian parenthood. And suppose opponents argue against the moral worth of such unions and contend that they are harmful to the participants and threaten the institution of marriage on these bases: biblical verses and religious teachings and convictions; philosophical arguments that the goods of marriage are realizable only by heterosexuals (e.g. Catholic natural law arguments); arguments about gay male promiscuity and the fear of AIDS; and arguments about alleged gender role confusion in children raised in same-sex marriages.

Sandel does not offer us guidance as to any requirements that his model would place upon citizens concerning what would count as a moral argument or as to any criteria to be used by judges or legislators in evaluating moral arguments. For example, he is critical of Rawls's requirement of public reason: that political and legal decisions be justifiable on grounds that citizens generally can reasonably be expected to accept.[39] Without knowing more about how the moral reasoning process is to unfold—whether judges or legislators may reasonably reject arguments rooted in homophobia, ignorance, and fear, and how they ultimately are to resolve matters of genuine moral conflict—we find Sandel's alternative to be perilous. As the unfolding battle over same-sex marriage suggests, moral argument in service of gay and lesbian rights may prevail in some judicial and legislative arenas, but its success depends critically on the framing of the moral debate.

For example, *Baehr* v. *Miike*,[40] the recent Hawaii case holding that the state failed to demonstrate a compelling interest for its ban on gay marriage, appears to be a successful example of engaging in moral argument. Hawaii asserted that the optimal development of children depended upon being raised by their two biological parents (or at least a married male and female), but the court found, based on expert testimony, that gays and lesbians can do as well as heterosexuals in parenting. This favorable outcome for gay and lesbian rights hinged on demonstrating sameness between homosexual and heterosexual parents, and the framing of the issue in terms of parental competence bounded moral discourse to consideration of the proper function of families and of what makes for good parenting. This issue was assessed, not through a judgment about the competing moral convictions of citizens concerning the comparative competency of heterosexual, gay, and lesbian parents, but through expert testimony, which led to the court's conclusion that children do best when they have a loving, nurturant parent, and that even the state's own experts conceded that gay and lesbian parents can be such parents.[41]

What was conspicuously absent in the Hawaii case was reliance upon heated rhetoric about the morality or immorality of homosexuality. In contrast, in the debate surrounding the Defense of Marriage Act, which Congress passed by an overwhelming vote, legislators deployed passionate rhetoric about saving marriage, the family, and the public from the immorality of homosexual intimate association and a parade of horribles that would follow in the wake of recognizing same-sex marriage. The challenge posed by opponents of the Act to explain how a loving, committed relationship between two persons of the same sex threatened anyone's heterosexual marriage was given no serious answer.[42]

Assessing the promise and peril of Sandel's republican justification for rights also requires a clearer elaboration than Sandel advances of its capaciousness and attention to whether his analogical method would move in a conservative or a more critical, transformative direction. A reasonable interpretation of his appeal to analogy is that it is inherently conservative because it entails that analogies in support of gay and lesbian intimate association be made to the human goods shared with relationships traditionally protected by the courts, namely, heterosexual marriage. Persons who cannot show the sameness of the goods of their relationship to those of such a traditionally protected relationship fail to secure protection.

Requiring such a demonstration of sameness may prevent Sandel's analogical method from taking a more critical and potentially transformative direction, whereby arguments for same-sex marriage would stress the different and distinctive goods of such unions. For example, consider the feminist argument that lesbian marriage offers a valuable alternative model to traditional heterosexual marriage: it is premised on love and commitment between equals, and it is free of a history as an unjust, hierarchical relationship within which inequality inheres in the differentiated gender roles themselves, and within which women had little to no protection against assaults on their bodily integrity.[43] This type of moral argument, far from sanctifying existing social practices, offers a fulcrum from which to criticize them.

If Sandel's republicanism were capacious enough to embrace such arguments, it would not confine itself to the search for sameness but would allow room for protection of a diversity of morally valuable social practices, and thus would be open to moral evolution and changing understandings of the worth of social practices.[44] If so, this would confirm our interpretation of Sandel's republicanism as wedded less to any particular substance (e.g. the good of traditional marriage) than to a form of argument or process of justification, which might prove open to different conceptions of moral worth. And if this type of argument is possible within Sandel's republicanism, how can he reject an argument for same-sex marriage rooted in a liberal commitment to diversity and the idea that there may be more than one morally valuable way of life (as Blackmun suggested in dissent in *Bowers*)? Or how can he reject the liberal idea that society benefits from different "experiments of living" because they may be worth emulating (to invoke Mill)?[45]

Third and finally, Sandel may be right that it is difficult to secure public support for constitutional freedoms on the strength of the appeal to autonomy alone. Yet, to jettison autonomy arguments entirely, rather than to supplement them with arguments based on substantive moral goods, may prove an even more difficult strategy for securing such freedoms. For example, the idea that even if one believes that it is morally wrong for a pregnant woman to have an abortion, it is wrong for government to prevent her from making that decision, has a powerful hold on the public. This suggests that, given the fact of reasonable moral pluralism, liberalism may have things about right: we should attempt to secure agreement on a principle of autonomy rather than to aim for moral agreement on the good. Or, as Rawls puts it, we should aim for an overlapping consensus on a political conception of justice, not for agreement on a comprehensive conception of the good.[46]

In some cases of persistent moral conflict, liberal toleration is a necessary starting point and may even be the most that can be achieved. But toleration need not be grudging and fragile if its proponents persuasively make a moral argument for it and its possible tempering of the formative project: autonomy is a human good, as are diversity, equal citizenship, and toleration itself, and a commitment to protecting those goods should often (but not always) constrain government from coercively acting to make citizens lead good lives by compelling "moral" and prohibiting "immoral" choices.[47] To the extent toleration, by its very definition, is "empty" in that it does not require respect and appreciation,[48] liberalism itself may be said to attempt to go beyond a model of "empty" toleration to a model of toleration as respect (and even appreciation) through the appeal to such a moral argument.[49] In any event, securing agreement on a principle of autonomy does not rule out more ambitious moral argument and attempts to persuade citizens concerning the moral goods realized through different choices and ways of life. Nor does it preclude an appeal in democratic arenas for expanded protections of rights premised on moral goods.

Conclusion

In conclusion, it is at once the appeal and the shortcoming of Sandel's project that he has not yet delivered enough. His republicanism seems more evocative than elaborated. (Indeed, this is often the case with works growing out of the republican tradition.[50]) He has done a more compelling job of showing us what we have lost than of showing us how we might reconstruct it for our time. Ultimately, Sandel fails to deliver the goods for a substantive republic. The few republican goods or virtues that he specifies fit comfortably within liberalism, and the liberal substance that he leaves out (especially autonomy) renders his republicanism problematic and perilous. What he provides is a call for a republican form of argument or justification for constitutional freedoms, and a commitment to a process of deliberation, that he claims will ameliorate discontent with democracy. In the end, this is Sandel's procedural republic.

That Sandel does not provide more may suggest just how formidable a task it is to articulate a republicanism that is appropriate for a pluralistic polity.

It remains an open question whether we should wish to revitalize the republican tradition and to search for a substantive republic. But even if we should, most of the work of developing a moral reading of the Constitution of the substantive republic remains to be done.

20

Gay Marriage and Liberal Constitutionalism: Two Mistakes

ROBIN WEST

Introduction

MICHAEL SANDEL has devoted himself to the work of challenging a part of our sadly privatized collective self-identity, and urging us to transform it. Whether that individuated, insulated, atomized, and disconnected individual that Sandel and other communitarians lament is the cause of our deomocracy's discontent or is necessary to liberalism I am not sure. But I do feel sure that such an individual is at the heart of one stunted ideal of human flourishing that is prevalent in both American culture and American constitutional law and legal thought generally. Sandel sees this truth clearly, sees the tragedy of it, expresses it eloquently, and for that contribution I am grateful. I wish to outline a more moderate version of the Sandelian thesis, as least as I understand it, and as it affects US American constitutional discourse, which I think is important and untouched by several critics whose work I assess below.

I

Let me begin by sketching and defending very briefly my moderate version of Sandel's thesis. Whatever this book gets wrong, it gets one thing exactly right, and that is the tendency of liberal constitutional argumentation to "bracket" moral argument, and I want to spend just two minutes expanding on that point. The problem is simple and stark. Liberalism rests, at heart, on a view of our nature that asserts that we are all, universally, rational. Over time, there have emerged two equally momentous implications: first, we are *all* rational—not just men, whites, or property owners, but all of us—and second, we are all rational—we are all capable of deciding for ourselves the content of the good life. Put a little differently, and more substantively, we all share in a human attribute—namely, the ability to decide for ourselves what we want in life—

the consequence of which is that we must all be accorded, and equally, basic rights of dignity and respect. Now, whatever the merits of its other implications, this basic liberal understanding of our nature has powerfully suggested, to liberal constitutional lawyers and theorists, a particular understanding of both the equality and the liberty protected by the Fourteenth Amendment of the United States Constitution. Equality, on this view, means respecting our human universality, it means treating likes alike, and legislation which does not, and does not for no good reason, is in trouble. Liberty, on this view, means respecting our right to fashion our own lives, to make and live with our own mistakes, in short, to respect our right to be left alone. Now of course the story is complicated, but I think it is just impossible to read the history of post-*Brown* and post-*Griswold* constitutional jurisprudence without acknowledging the tremendous influence this liberal conception of our basic rights has carried.

I want to make two critical, Sandelian points regarding this vision. This liberal conception, which stresses our universality on the one hand, and our individual competency on the other, leads the liberal constitutionalist toward two kinds of mistakes: it leads him to not see or to not appreciate the magnitude of our differences, and it leads him to not see or to not appreciate the interrelations and interdependencies of our lives. Neither of these mistakes is logically mandated: respect for our universally shared nature does not of course entail ignorance of or disregard for our differences, and attending to our individual and individuating impulses does not entail disregard of our interconnections. But nevertheless, the risk of both sorts of error is magnified when a liberal sensibility dominates. Both mistakes, I think, stunt contemporary liberal legal and constitutional discourse, and both peculiarly disable liberal constitutionalists from putting forward meaningful responses to conservative, and particularly cultural conservative arguments—arguments which have their own flaws but decidedly do not have those. There are, I think, many examples of this phenomenon, as has been the burden of a good deal of feminist and critical race theory over the last twenty years or so to show. Let me illustrate some of the costs of these mistakes, using the example of gay marriage.

The liberal constitutional argument for gay marriage is straightforward, and unsurprisingly stresses universalism—gay marriage is just like straight marriage—and individualism— it follows from our right to be left alone. Let me start with the universalist premise, and its implication for equal protection. Same-sex and opposite-sex marriages are in all legally relevant ways identical: they would serve comparable needs for intimacy and stability and they would entail comparable rights, duties, and liabilities in the various areas of law that impact family life. The only difference between them lies in the sex of the spouse, but this difference is simply immaterial—in all important, or essential respects that matter, the union is of the same sort. Gay men and lesbians, in Andrew Sullivan's liberal formulation of the point, are "virtually normal" in all ways relevant to law.[1] The now famous Hawaii Supreme Court opinion[2]—striking as unconstitutional a ban on gay marriage—is a virtual parody of it. To not allow same-sex marriage, the Court argued using straightforward liberal logic, is unlawful discrimination: why, because to marry someone of the same sex is just the same old thing as to marry someone of the opposite sex save for the irrelevant, minor, and anyway illegal factor of the sex of the spouse to be. So, it's just old-fashioned sex discrimination to permit an individual woman to marry a man but not a woman, or, of course, vice versa.

The liberty argument, although not yet elaborated in case law, is not hard to imagine. The right of the individual to marry within his sex is covered by the same right of privacy that protects the individual's right to marry outside his race, to take birth control, or procure an abortion.[3] It goes to the heart of our right to make fundamental decisions regarding our individual lives. It is quintessentially self-regarding behavior; a clear-cut example of conduct which is simply no one's business but my own. Expanding the freedom to marry implicates essentially no negative externalities and would constitute a dramatic expansion of individual liberty. It is accordingly, a paradigmatic freedom that ought to be—and hence is—protected by the Fourteenth Amendment.

There are of course many problems as well as some strengths with this liberal logic, but all I want to stress here are its opportunity costs. This argument for gay marriage based on its seamless sameness with straight marriage and the "equality" and equal treatment that sameness demands, deprives us of the opportunity to not only argue for gay marriage "on the moral merits," so to speak, but to make such an argument which stresses, rather than pointedly denies, the morally salutary differences between what gay marriage might be and what straight marriage in the here and now is. There are two such differences that come to mind. The first difference is that same-sex marriage, unlike traditional marriage, has never been predicated on the presumed desirability of subordinating the female sex. There is no history, in the history of same-sex marriage, of a "marital rape exemption," according to which one of the partners is entitled to sex on demand, regardless of the consent or desire of the other. There is no expectation, on the part of those contemplating same-sex marriage, as there still is with vast numbers of individuals contemplating traditional marriage, that one partner is privileged to demand sex, and the other obligated to provide it. There is no cultural construct, in other words, of marital roles, obligations, and identities constituted by an axis of subordination in turn constituted by legally privileged sexual violence. This is a difference that matters, and matters a lot.

It is a difference that matters, in short, because it is a difference that carries with it the promised potential to transform the very institution of marriage itself into a more truly liberal and even egalitarian community. Should same-sex marriage ever become a reality in this culture, it whould "normalize" the ideal of a for-life union between sexual equals. It would allow us an opportunity to glimpse the possibility of marital life freed of the illiberal and inegalitarian and unfree heritage of the institution's deeply patriarchal past. For liberalism to deny that opportunity in the name of formal equality is more than just perverse, although it is surely that. It is also self-defeating. In this instance, denial of difference is a denial, not an affirmation, of liberalism's deepest egalitarian and libertarian, as well as communitarian impulses.

The second difference between traditional and same sex marriage is the difference emphasized by conservatives, and particularly by the natural lawyer, Professor John Finnis: same-sex marriage, unlike traditional marriage, would legitimate and sanctify quintessentially nonreproductive, instead of reproductive, sex acts.[4] For Finnis, of course, this difference is fatal: such nonreproductive sex acts, for a variety of reasons or at least assertions, are paradigmatically immoral. Liberal political theorists and constitutional lawyers, and perhaps most persuasively Stephen Macedo, have responded true to form: by denying the difference.[5] The differences, Macedo argues, between the nonreproductive sex acts of a same sex couple and the reproductive-*type* sex acts of a sterile, post-menopausal, or infertile heterosexual couple using birth control, are just too miniscule to notice—surely, he stresses repeatedly, they are insignificant. Macedo's point is obviously well taken. But here again, we should at least hesitate before insisting so strenuously on sameness in the face of this apparent difference. There may well *be* a relevant difference between a marriage that sanctifies paradigmatically *non*-reproductive sexual acts, and one that sanctifies paradigmatically reproductive-type sex acts, and it may even be a difference that matters morally, but cuts the opposite way of that suggested by Finnis. What is it, after all, about the reproductivity of the reproductive-type sex act that makes it morally salutary, in the conservative imagination? One answer, I think, is that the reproductive-type sex act models a form of physically caring for the other within a committed marriage which either carries the potential for, or at least symbolizes, in the conservative imagination, biological reproduction—which is in turn an event which, when it occurs, demands considerable altruism, at least on the part of the mother. And altruism, after all, is quite a good thing, and a predisposition toward it is one which we should surely seek to foster. But on the other hand, that is only half of the reproductive story. Reproduction is also an event which, as sociobiologists never tire of reminding us, on a genetic and evolutionary scale, is through and through selfish. The care we bestow on family members genetically linked to us carries the same paradoxical quality. We might want to consider the possibility that the nonreproductive sex act, tamed, disciplined, and sanctified by a legal, religious, and socially recognized same-sex marriage, between two individuals committed to the care of each other and no less committed than their heterosexual counterparts to the possibility of raising children, presents a physical model of caring for the other that, precisely because it does not embed the giving of physical care in genetic replication, is less constrained by egoism. It is often observed, and quite rightly, that our capacity for care ebbs and flows depending on the strength or weakness of the genetic link between the subject and object of care-giving. The creation of a social institution defined by love-making not aimed toward genetic replication, but nevertheless aimed toward care, might at least expand our imaginative understanding of the limits and promise of the affective, physical, and sexual source of this communal, connective ethic.

I will be much more brief regarding liberty. There is just no good reason, and much to be lost, by denying the communitarian and communal nature of marriage, and hence of gay marriage. It is also unnecessary; there is nothing in the liberal regard for individual autonomy that commits one to the false claim that marriage is an individualistic institution, designed to enhance the autonomy of consenting adults by permitting them to contract with each other for sex, affection, and mutual support. Marriage just is, through and through, anti-individualistic. That is precisely its moral strength, and to no small measure, the source of its immense appeal.

Advocates of gay marriage in particular, outside of a dubious loyalty to liberalism, have no particular reason to deny this. Gay unions, first, have the potential to be significantly better, as communities, than their heterosexual counterparts: they may be just as violent, oppressive, suffocating, boring, tedious, or dreary, but they simply are not as vulnerable to the disabling and destructive possibilities of rape, legal and otherwise. Second, they share with heterosexual unions the redemptive potential to transform the individual into a person whose self-regarding preferences and desires are defined communally, and that is morally desirable, not undesirable, transformation of self-regard and identity. And third, the impact of these marriages on the larger culture would surely be for the good. Aside from the obvious benefits to gay and lesbian citizens themselves, the availability and legality of gay marriage would strengthen heterosexual marriages as well, leaving them more voluntary, less compulsory, more egalitarian, and for all of these reasons considerably more liberal.

II

Many of Sandel's critics say nothing that defeats the moderate version, the Sandelian thesis I have just defended. Mary Shanley offers both a narrow and a broad critique. Narrowly, Shanley contests Sandel's contention, which he shares with a good number of feminist scholars of the family, that family law rests on a voluntarist and contractual conception of marriage, a disembodied rather than embedded conception of the self, a disregard for the communal transformation of self that at least a good marriage ought to entail and that a bad marriage perverts, and that it does all of this to the detriment of women.[6] Professor Shanley paints a more nuanced and complicated picture. Pointing to the Indian Child Welfare Act as an example of at least a part of adoption law that seemingly rests on a radically communitarian conception of the self, she argues that family law, like liberalism at its best, embraces simultaneously a conception of the self that understands the person as simultaneously a situated individual, and as a citizen to be treated similarly to fellow citizens.[7] She is, I think, right about the ICWA, but I think wrong to treat it as exemplary of a meaningful counterweight in family law and theory to the individualism Sandel decries. The ICWA looks so strikingly different—and to many of us so wrong—precisely because it is so at odds with the liberal assumptions of identity and individualism that are for better or worse, and in my view it's some of both, carrying the day in family law. Family law is indeed moving rapidly, pell-mell and with the force of inexorable necessity, toward an individualistic, contractual and voluntarist conception of marriage and the family, which does, as Sandel argues, undermine the position of tranditional homemakers as well as undercut the essence of marriage itself—as I will argue in a moment. Against that migration, the ICWA is anomalous.

Now more generally, on Shanley's broad-based critique of Sandel's critique of family law. Sandel's most basic point—that the individualistic thrust of modern family law undermines the communitarian essence and hence the moral point of marriage—is fair enough, I think, and I also think Professor Shanley agrees with it.[8] The problem with Sandel's critique, as Shanley makes clear, is that it does not go far enough. As many, many feminist critics of liberalism have stressed—but as Sandel does not—the voluntarist, contractual conception of marriage at the heart of liberal individualist views of family law bars from the liberal imagination not only any understanding of the communitarian and moral point of the institution, but also bars the liberal from an understanding of its very real potential for devastating, life-long, damage—the murder of the spirit of its weaker and weakest members.[9] When the larger community, state and constitution respect and leave untouched and unexamined, either in the name of liberalism, privacy, individualism, or patriarchy, the individual, voluntary, private decisions of family members to be a family, that respect may leave insulated and unimpeded and unchallenged neither a community of embedded altruistic souls, as envisioned by Sandel, nor a union of cooperating egoistic individuals acting on their glorious preferences and living out their sovereign choices, as envisioned by contemporary liberals, but rather, what I have elsewhere called a separate sovereignty: a private and pitifully Hobbesian space in which there is no law, liberal or otherise, and in which as a consequence the strong dominate and the weak acquiesce.[10] In such a Hobbesian space the seeming altruism or cooperation of the weak comes not from an enriched and admirable sense of the worthiness of living a deeply connected life, but rather from an impoverished and embattled and belittled and trivialized sense of self-worth. It is, after all, easier and certainly more conducive to survival in a privatized Hobbesian world to give than to be violated, whether what is given by the weak to the strong is labor, or authority over decision-making, or the right to enjoy more leisure time and less responsibility for the second shift, or more sex. When all of this relentless and monotonous giving is driven, essentially, by ofttimes deeply rooted fear rather than genuine altruism, it is a gift which occasions tremendous psychic costs—costs to the integrity, the autonomy, the competencies, and the self-regard of the weaker party, and often over the course of an entire adult life-time.

It would be a very good thing, I think, and as Mary Shanley argues, if communitarians and other critics of liberalism who are nostalgic for the fault standard in the law governing divorce, would come to grips with this stark fact—the alternative to life in a liberally construed family, oftentimes, in private life, is not a life lived in accord with a high regard for the virtues of community but a life of fear. At the same time, however, it would be a very good thing, for those of us who, with Professor Shanley, decry the Hobbesian family not to lapse into an unexamined romance with the promise of liberalism. Here, I fear, Shanley's analysis replicates a recurrent but misguided tendency in the feminist critique of communitarianism. Feminists like Professor Shanley and myself, who are suspicious of communitarian sentimentality regarding the family, and who fear its potential whitewash of intra-family violence and violation, need to vigilantly remind ourselves that liberalism—even generously understood—with its privatization of family life, and its aspirational goal of contractual freedom and individual voluntarism, the bottom-line consequence of which is no more and no less than that from the legal point of view, you are stuck with what you chose, and that if you chose it, you've really no cause for complaint—has been, historically part of the problem, and may never be a part of the solution. The sovereign state's monopolization of violence has indeed been the liberal's response to the problem of individual violence in the public sphere, but a wall of privacy and a delegation of authority to the patriarch has been its response to the problem of individual violence in the private. Liberal privatization of family violation, in short, is not the cure for communitarian, sentimental denial of the same phenomenon. To sum up: Sandel is right that liberalism misses the moral point of family life. Professor Shanley is right that Sandel should be faulted for not seeing that communitarianism—his proffered alternative—misses the profound damage that a particular community can wreck on the lives of its members. But we should all be clear that the next step in this dialectic had better transcend both. Liberalism misses the damage done by intra-familial injustice as well. In fact it has done much to obscure it.

William Kymlicka's criticism of Sandel, in my view, begins with a stark challenge to Sandel's thesis, but in the end provides eloquent support for it, perhaps semi-intentionally. Toward the end of his chapter in this volume, Kymlicka suggests, entirely correctly, that broad public embrace of social Darwinism, contempt for failure, and adulation of individual success, is what drives US citizens toward inegalitarian social policies and ultimately to our discontent, not liberalism in any form, and certainly not liberal egalitarianism.[11] How, he asks, can *liberalism* of all things be faulted for the discontents of such a profoundly illiberal society? But his own critique suggests an answer to this not so obvious rhetorical question. Liberalism can, I think, to some degree be faulted for the discontents of illiberalism, for reasons Kymlicka's chapter suggests, and reasons which Sandel, I think would embrace. What drives politics in this society as in any other is to some degree the mythic stories we as a people tell ourselves about what is and is not admirable, noteworthy, and something to celebrate—what is and is not a life worth living, or at least worth striving toward.[12] The mythic story that has taken such root in this culture is the story of the successful individual who without benefit of family connections, benefactors, title, or inheritance, and using only his own pluck, initiative, cleverness, attraction to risk, and his God-given talents, pulls himself up and onward to wealth, fame, power, and preeminence. President Clinton, Bill Gates, Madonna, and Cal Ripkin, all fill this Horatio Alger bill. This myth, as Kymlicka suggests, has done this culture, constitutional and otherwise, tremendous harm—it is in many ways at the root of our cultural unwillingness to embrace the liberal egalitarian mandate to rectify inequalities attributable to circumstance rather than choice, and it is in many ways responsible for our consequent attraction to the panoply of illberal policies—from welfare reform to flattened taxes to opposition to affirmative action—that flow from that unwillingness.

Now the question Kymlicka nicely poses is simply whether *liberalism* can be charged with any aspect of our apparent inability to transcend the paralyzing grip of this mythology. I think it can, and for reasons that are related to the thesis of Sandel's book. The logic of liberalism—even in its left wing variant—drives us away from a direct and meaningful attack on the moral merits, so to speak, on this myth *as myth*. We need to do many things in this society to achieve a more progressive culture, but one thing we need to do is make the case that the vision of the good on which this myth rests is not a worthy one, and part of what we need to do to make that case is to replace it with visions of the good life that are simply better. It is better to live a more communitarian and egalitarian life than to spend one's life questing for the miniscule shot at the pot of gold and promise of fame accorded only the very few. Progressives—both liberals and communitarians—do not make those arguments very well—and the logic of liberalism, I think, is part of the reason we do not. Instead we argue on the solid ground of facts and principle, rather than the wispy, elusive cloud of myth and vision: we point out, for example, and quite rightly, that Clinton—often called our first "meritocratic president" because he was the first Ivy League president to gain entry on the basis of grades and Scholastic Aptitude Test (SAT) scores rather than through the gentlemanly route of winks and nods and alumni presidents—benefited from a public education skewed toward whites, and that Madonna, self-made though she may be, is enjoying as well as projecting an erotic ideal itself informed, partly, by racism; that the adoration of Ripkin, whatever his genuine accomplishments, is in part a function of a town in love with the prospect of a great white hope from a local working-class family. All of these debunking claims are true and important—there is no such thing as a "self-made man," no one's accomplishments can be attributable to character and choice unpolluted or diluted from the circumstances, environs, or simply the surroundings that embed us, the myth is indeed a myth, it is not fact, it is not true of anyone's life. But as true and as important as they are, these debunking disclaimers are not going to be sufficient to dislodge from the popular *Zeitgeist* this myth of the self-made, fully deserved, phenomenal success that is so central to our culture's resistance to redistribution and affirmative action both. To dislodge that myth we have to not only expose it as myth, but we also have to challenge it in kind; we have to replace it with better ones. I think Sandel's book generously read and to its credit challenges us to do precisely that.

While Professor Kymlicka faults Sandel for picking unfounded and counterproductive fights with liberal egalitarianism, Professor Frohnen faults him for collapsing his communitarian vision with liberal tolerance: Sandel, like all liberals, wants to direct our public institutions toward the end of human flourishing, albeit with an acknowledgement that the humans that should flourish are embedded in communities and systems of belief rather than individuated. Nevertheless, according to Sandel, the end of politics is human flourishing. That commitment alone, Frohnen complains, marks him as a liberal.[13] Like all liberals, he resists other ways to conceive of the end of politics: perhaps toward the greater glory of God, or the perfection of the species. I do not know, but I suspect that this is just too broad an understanding of liberalism. If liberalism is nothing but the identification of human flourishing as the end of politics then everyone in the canon of political thought from Aristotle to Marx and beyond is a liberal. But I realize I may be wrong about that. At any rate, I do not quite see why the labels matter so much. In this culture, here and now, the distinction between a vision of the end of politics that aims for human flourishing but conceives of the human as a sovereign consumer who produces and then consumes his or her own conception of that flourishing, so that all the state ought to do is butt out of the process, and a conception of the end of politics that aims for human flourishing but conceives of the human as embedded in a conception of the good and over which he accordingly has little control, but which ought nevertheless be valued, is a distinction that matters, and maybe even a lot. Whether the latter is or is not properly called "liberal" to my mind matters considerably less than whether or not it is a conception of politics that we ought to embrace.

Conclusion

Let me quickly conclude by noting that the liberal denial of difference and connection, in the area of gay marriage, and in the name of equality and liberty respectively, leaves in its wake one additional opportunity cost, of a peculiarly theoretical but perhaps not only theoretical, nature. We desperately need, in this culture and at this time, a reinvigorated and open dialogue regarding the point of marriage, of married life and of marital sex. If feminism continues to influence culture in the next century as it has in the one just past, then the point of that institution will no longer be, as it was for so much of the last millennium, to order social relations and life through subordinating the female sex. If liberalism holds its ground, nor will its point be the conception and rearing of children—so long as there are individuals who badly want to marry but have no desire or ability to parent. But nor can the point of marriage be what large numbers of liberals and libertarians are now arguing—a contract, no different in essence from any other, designed as to efficiently coordinate complementary preferences, maximizing wealth and efficiency for all. Marriage cannot be nothing but contract, for the straightforward reason that if it becomes that, it will wither away.

This leaves a void. What is the point of marriage? One possible answer, I think, is raised by the possibility and promise of gay marriage. It is also an old argument, dating at least from Mill's essays, but also echoed in the existential writings of Kierkegaard and in our own time the social utilitarianism of Peter Singer. The point of marriage, in theory as well as in our private lives, may be to provide a structure within which we learn to define and continually redefine ourselves as caring rather than egoistic beings—as connected to rather than alienated from the concerns and well-being of others. If so, then that is a central point of marriage which would indeed be shared by gay and straight marriage alike—as well as by marriages which do or do not, whether by choice or fate, produce children. It is a shared trait, however, and a common essence, which only comes into focus and can only come into focus when the transformative *difference* that gay marriage might make in the institution itself is highlighted, not obscured, and it is an essence which can only be captured when its communitarian rather than individualistic value is emphasized, rather than marginalized. Liberal constitutionalism, at least, obscures both and for essentially Sandelian reasons: the rational autonomous self at its heart seems to demand it. This is, simply, unfortunate: surely in this case, it is by highlighting difference that we might discard the institution's ignoble but ultimately inessential heterosexual and misogynist past, and by highlighting its communal essence we might better examine its transformative effects on the individuals who enter it. By blurring or denying difference, the liberal advocate, perversely, obscures the very universality among us that he relentlessly seeks to foster, and by blurring or denying connection, he frustrates an understanding of the impact of family living on the individual lives he seeks to honor. Sandel's work, read generously, challenges liberalism to correct this not only misguided, but also profoundly self-defeating impulse.

VI

Self-Government and Democratic Discontent

21

Fusion Republicanism

NANCY L. ROSENBLUM

Fusion Republicanism

IN 1997, in a legal battle over the First Amendment Establishment Clause, Alabama Circuit Court Judge Roy Moore refused to obey a higher court order to remove the Ten Commandments he had posted in his county courthouse and to stop the morning prayers he invited jurors to offer up. This was not a case of "ceremonial deism." Judge Moore was not one of those advocates of greater public recognition of faith who see themselves as trying to be as broad and inclusive as possible. He did not mean the prayers to stand in for all religions—he had favorite ministers. Nonetheless, the US House of Representatives voted overwhelmingly in favor of a resolution supporting the judge, proclaiming that the Ten Commandments "promote respect for our system of laws and the good of society." Congress was apparently undismayed that addressing a Southern Baptist prayer luncheon Alabama Governor Fob Jones announced, "The only way those Ten Commandments and that prayer will be stripped from that court is with the force of arms. Make no mistake about that statement."[1]

Hostility to decisions taken by courts, government agencies, and legislatures has become a familiar scenario, which includes threats of direct action by citizens or those representing them in the name of Americans' better, moral instincts and with a view to civic renewal. It is played out over "takings" of property, abortion, school curricula, and the right to keep and bear arms. This is the harsh face of democratic discontent.

"Fusion republicanism" is my name for the fluid mix of democratic ideology, potential militancy, and invocation of civic virtue prevalent in American political life. It is not a consistent ideology much less a systematic political philosophy. Rather, as "fusion" suggests, it is a conglomeration of disparate elements of political thought and practice that coalesce around certain unifying republican themes. Fusion republicanism covers a broad spectrum of positions, from respectable democratic theory to civic fundamentalism promulgated by extremists. It is manifest in many quarters of political life: it is institutionalized in "our localism," for example; it is latent in the conduct of juries with their potential for nullification—a characteristically republican form of opposition to proceduralism; and it is overt in self-styled citizen militias permanently poised for armed resistance. The elements of fusion republicanism are mutually reinforcing, even if their proponents are not always allies.

My objective is to set out the framework of contemporary American fusion republicanism and show that the public philosophy Michael Sandel prescribes in *Democracy's Discontent* has its home there. Commentary on Sandel's work has focused on the liberal side of the (overly sharp) dichotomy he draws between the two philosophies.[2] It centers on his interpretation of liberal thinkers (criticized as misleadingly selective or mistaken), his characterization of liberal politics and adjudication (criticized as an exaggerated portrait of neutrality and proceduralism), and on (largely futile) efforts to pinpoint just where Sandel *intends* his public philosophy to diverge from liberal policies and institutions in practice. What, for example, would Sandel take back from judicial interpretations of the Fourteenth Amendment, which enforce strong federal prohibitions against the states and against private individuals so that the people "do not have the power to govern their local lives apart from the nation as a whole"?[3] Intent aside, commentators explore the implications of Sandel's public philosophy for giving over decisions to democratic majorities, indeed to a sovereign "we the people" superior to the Constitution.

I want to shift attention to the family of concerns on the republican side of the divide. It is as important to locate Sandel's public philosophy in the company of fusion republicanism as to discriminate it from the liberalism he rejects; republicanism is, after all his avowed ideological framework. Like any much-used political concept, it gives rise to John Adams's lament that republicanism "may signify any thing, every thing, or nothing." Still, as Gordon Wood explains, from its first applications in America, it signified more than popular elections, more even than a form of government. Republicanism was celebrated for "its spirit, its morality, its freedom, its sense of friendship and duty, and its vision of society."[4] That is the bright side of republicanism, which also exhibits grimmer faces. If liberalism has excesses and errant strands, so does republicanism. The elements of fusion republicanism, including its pathologies, recur throughout American history and are exhibited plainly in contemporary public life. Republicanism as well as liberalism is "a tale fraught with moral complexity, replete with strange ideological bedfellows."[5] I intend to follow Sandel in bringing to the foreground the "often unreflective background" of our current political discourse. To the extent that Sandel would affirm or disavow contemporary expressions of republicanism, it should shed light on where he is positioned on the spectrum and may, secondarily, illuminate his relation to liberalism. In any case, it is necessary to fill out his map of the terrain.

Democracy's Discontent is a sober consideration of certain facets of republicanism in American political thought. Most importantly, Sandel describes the shift from an approach to political economy guided by considerations of the conditions of self-government to one directed mainly by the imperatives of growth and distributive justice. In doing so he adds an important dimension to the standard repertoire of the civic uses of property. Sandel takes us beyond the Jeffersonian insistence on real property as an aspect of personal identity and bulwark against influence and corruption, and beyond the notion that productive labor reflects republican virtue and marks the earner as a citizen in contrast to a slave on the one hand and the idle aristocrat on the other. Moreover, he sets out to provide a political, not just intellectual, history of this theme: identifying the strains of American public philosophy that relate to collective economic self-control, the politicians that promulgate them, and the associations (like the Knights of Labor) that have been its chief carriers.

This is a perceptive but selective account of the historical strands of republicanism in American political thought. It draws attention to vital subjects for democratic deliberation, but it also disregards much of the terrain of fusion republicanism, historical and contemporary. There is nothing wrong with selectivity, particularly if the principles of selection are pronounced. But the limited contours of Sandel's account are bound to affect our assessment of his diagnosis of the American political condition overall. His thesis—propounded with severe certainty—that the eclipse of republican public philosophy by a dominant procedural liberalism is the source of democracy's discontent may need modification if there are other contributing sources to discontent, among them arrant elements of republicanism.

Sandel's selectivity is also bound to effect our assessment of his ideas about what is necessary to counter democracy's discontent. The standard republican corrective is popular empowerment, tempered by the "formative project" of cultivating in citizens "the qualities of character necessary to the common good of self-government." Again, Sandel's specific contribution to this broad theme is a criticism of the economic arrangements that impede virtuous engagement. This orientation needs defending against liberal objections, of course. (In particular against the thesis, dating from early in the nineteenth century, that virtue flows not only from participation in politics but also from participation in society; that the pursuit of happiness and defense of interests generate forms of social cohesion; and that the impersonal world of commerce, occupations, etc., is a moral advance over a society held together by a stifling array of personal loyalties, obligations, deference, and dependencies.) More important for this chapter, Sandel's prescriptions need defending against alternative *republican* accounts of the obstacles to meaningful political agency, and against alternative republican accounts of how to reclaim self-government.

From the point of view of intellectual self-consciousness and philosophical acuity, Sandel situates himself on the high ground of American republicanism. The pedigree of his public philosophy can be traced to James Madison, not the radical Tom Paine. Its instruments are benign civic association and regular legislation, not direct action. Citizens are voters, deliberators, office-holders, not jurors engaged in nullification or armed militiamen invoking the Second Amendment. It is not my intention to paint *Democracy's Discontent* with the brush of republicanism's sometimes fantastic, subversive, even criminal elements, or to identify it with those who exploit republican rhetoric for partisan ends. Normally we can tell the difference between sober public philosophy and extravagant, often conspiracist, "civic fundamentalism." Still, careful dissection is in order. We can reasonably expect Sandel to be as alert to current expressions of republicanism and their consequences as he is to liberal ones, and to forecast *these* dangers, too. Given the promise of a public philosophy, we can reasonably expect sensitivity to distinctions within the family of positions exhibited in daily political life, and indications of which contemporary manifestations of fusion republicanism he would endorse, accommodate, or condemn. Perhaps the most important question raised by Sandel's stance as an advocate of a public philosophy is what responsibility he has to acknowledge the spectrum of related ideas, to recognize convergence between the republican high ground he stakes out and its dangerous, improbable expressions, and to draw sharp moral and political distinctions.

Fusion Republicanism and Democratic Discontent

I begin by considering the unifying elements of the fluid field of fusion republicanism. Three recognizable themes provide points of convergence among advocates, and give fusion republicanism its emotional force.

The first is a *perception of powerlessness*. It is a distinctively democratic perception because it is based on the sense of being deprived of legitimate public recognition and political influence. "Americans do not believe they have much say in how they are governed and do not trust government to do the right thing," Sandel writes. Accompanying this sense of disempowerment is the belief that others—some favored minority or privileged elite (procedural liberals, say)—have a disproportionate voice, even actual control.[6] According to recent testimony before the National Commission on Civic Renewal, "8 out of 10 Americans believe that our country is run by a close network of special interests, public officials, and the media."[7]

In the arena of religious "culture wars" with which I began, for example, both believers and militant secularists fire accusations and threats, and what is more, both sides claim not victory but victimization. Everyone sees his or her group as politically disadvantaged, democratically disarmed. Logically so, since when it comes to religion "minority status" is universal. We hear that atheists are winning all the battles: "They" (the conspiratorial "they") "are catering to these people."[8] It is not surprising that for their part, unbelievers feel at a political disadvantage too. Avowed atheists rarely run for public office, after all. There is a strong social gag rule against overt disbelief and expressed hostility toward religion.[9]

The sense of disempowerment disposes republicans to blur the line between unresponsive authority and abuse of authority; indeed, the line between hostility to specific acts of government and hostility to government is blurred as well. No wonder claims of disempowerment often have a conspiracist tenor. Fusion republicanism is not a matter of agreement about which policies or powerful groups are oppressive. But catch-all generalizations create a vague continuum from Ronald Reagan's promise to curb "bureaucratic cadres" and end "fifty years of failed federal programs" to characterizations of the USA as a police state where agencies like the FBI are immune from democratic control.[10]

In chronicles of democratic decline, the date of the Great Betrayal varies, too: 1913, the year the federal income tax (characterized as a form of "involuntary servitude") was declared constitutional, or the New Deal; the judicial decisions of the 1960s and 1970s ("forced" busing; abortion rights; changes in the legal status of women); gun control, or free-trade policy. Each is represented as the entering wedge of a program to deny citizens self-government and the moral capacity to reclaim it. Sandel's historical benchmark shifts, but he seems to signal 1968 as the year that America's moment of world mastery expired and the full force of procedural liberalism was brought to bear; by this measure we are thirty years into our current discontent.

The second point of convergence among elements of fusion republicanism is a *perception of political demoralization*. Nothing is more common in American history than jeremiads about a falling-off of civic virtue. What changes over time is whether the preoccupation is official corruption and the need for popular vigilance or the embarrassing absence of virtue in the populace overall. What is new is our adeptness at marshalling empirical evidence of decline. We have analyses of falling voter turnout, surveys documenting political mistrust and "pervasive contempt" for major institutions (ranging from greedy business corporations to suburbanized churches), updated data on crime rates and litigation explosions, even measures of clinical depression. Political agency is eroded by "sadness, depression, dysphoria of all kinds," Robert Lane explains, calling the USA a "joyless polity."[11]

Demoralization is sometimes linked to large-scale organization generally, that is, to nothing less than industrialization, urbanization, and modernization. As Sandel puts it, "the role of the individual as the center of a network of relationships has largely disappeared . . . it is as if the triumph of autonomy in matters of religion, speech, and sexual morality were a kind of consolation for the loss of agency in an economic and political order increasingly governed by vast structures of power."[12] Whatever other forces undercut self-government, however, discontent coalesces around expansive federal government. Government undermines healthy activism and pluralism directly by official regulation, subsidy, and control, or by gobbling up social functions and displacing secondary institutions in its ever-expanding roles as speaker, educator, employer, and player in the market. Republican critics diverge over whether imperialist political leaders act on their own or as tools of the forces of globalism, "one-world government," corporatism, or liberal elites and secular humanists. They diverge over whether the intermediate associations of civil society or decentralized political institutions offer the best hope for compensatory schools of virtue. But there is agreement that the federal government is chiefly responsible for eroding the independent life of civic groups and subcommunities, for the falling-off of civic engagement and democratic discontent.[13]

The third feature of fusion republicanism follows: *a propensity for direct political action*. When government is perceived as the source of our discontents and the threat to liberty, and when major social institutions are mistrusted as well, people are thrown back on themselves. This is in part a question of what sort of engagement is a corrective for the sense of powerlessness and demoralization. In part, too, it is foundational. Republicanism's first principle is that "there necessarily exists, in every government, a power from which there is no appeal, and which, for that reason, may be termed supreme, absolute, and uncontrollable," and which can only rest legitimately with the people.[14] In contrast to liberal constitutionalism and interest-group pluralism, the guarantee of free government "is not balance but responsibility."[15] Self-government, Sandel writes, "requires a knowledge of public affairs and also a sense of belonging, a concern for the whole, a moral bond with the community whose fate is at stake."[16]

Curbing the power of federal courts and agencies and restoring the prerogatives of state legislatures is on every republican agenda. (As of 1995, fifteen states had reaffirmed the Tenth Amendment and passed resolutions asserting state sovereignty.[17]) Still, fusion republicanism cannot be identified with states' rights simply, or with the "new federalism." Hopes turn to counties and localities, and even local authority must be subject to the jealous surveillance and influence of self-organized citizens. As Sandel puts it:

> [F]ederalism is more than a theory of intergovernmental relations. It also stands for a political vision that offers an alternative to the sovereign state and the univocal political identities such states require. It suggests that self-government works best when sovereignty is dispersed and citizenship formed across multiple sites of civic engagement.[18]

So despite presumed apathy, disassociation, and declining civic values, the distinctive response of fusion republicanism is a demand for *enhanced* self-government. It is as if the less citizens actually have to do with mundane political activity, and the less satisfying it is for those who are minimally active, the greater the insistence on strenuous forms of participation: term limits, popular recall, referenda, plebescites over party identification. In 1996 there were 90 initiatives on ballots in 20 states on issues ranging from hunting rights to a ban on affirmative-action programs. Groups agitate for record numbers of constitutional amendments to override judicial and legislative decisions on substantive policy matters. Political negativity seems to require some electric participatory jolt. For some citizens, "extremism in the cause of liberty" is excusable. David Brion Davis observed that discovery of a national conspiracy could counteract the corrosive effects of lethargy "by allowing the people to re-enact the primal drama of patriotism."[19] Groups define themselves as counterweights to overbearing government and as potential sources of popular resistance. "Citizen militias" are the fierce contemporary embodiment of private paramilitary groups presenting themselves as public defenders.

Against this background of the unifying elements of fusion republicanism, I want to make the spectrum of positions concrete by selecting three points on the terrain: localism, jury nullification, and citizen militias. Each emphasizes self-government, calls upon civic virtue, and aims at the common good. Each attends to the social environment and to specific institutions capable of cultivating civic-mindedness and engagement. Like Sandel's public philosophy, each is cast as a response to democracy's discontent. Together, they provide some initial substantive benchmarks for situating his public philosophy.

"Our Localism"[20]

The scale of self-government is a standard democratic theme, and republicanism militates in favor of localism. It is driven by concern that political representatives not be at such a distance from constituents that they are unaccountable; concern for a community's ability to control its own character; and concern for cultivating civic engagement. The assumption is that political loyalties affix most securely to this level of government, where residents can be consulted on particulars and representation is "actual." "As the republican tradition taught," Sandel advises, "local attachments can serve self-government by engaging citizens in a common life beyond their private pursuits, by forming the habit of attending to public things."[21]

In republican thought, localism underscores political authority and the corporate character of the municipality. From home rule to zoning, American commitment to local political autonomy is affirmed by public opinion and is judicially enforced. (Romantic versions of localism, by contrast, cast *neighborhoods* not political units as natural and familial; David Popenoe argues that the "tribal" structure of community is vital to civic renewal.[22]) Put strongly, the ideology of localism has it that policy "ought to be controlled locally, with the interests of local residents as the exclusive desideratum of local decision-makers."[23] Municipalities are "frequently created and defended . . . to insulate one set of local people or interests from the regulatory authority and population of another local government."[24] Once created, they are permanently protected against unwanted reorganization aimed at taking in poorer contiguous areas for reasons of diversity or distributive justice. Home rule is a system without guidelines or enforceable obligations to or for nonresidents or the wider region. Case law on local suffrage is clear on this point. For example, courts are concerned that voting schemes include all residents but are unconcerned about the effects of local decisions on nonresidents, who have no voice. Which is why local self-government owes more to the residency standard than to the constitutional principle "one person, one vote."[25]

Exclusionary zoning is a core mechanism of local self-government. It is designed to give people a degree of control over "the look of the place" and who their neighbors will be, and to "maintain the status quo within the community" defined in terms of "life-style."[26] The phrase "character of a community" is less a code for expensive homes than for self-government, including democratically condoned exclusion. Preserving property values is one aim, but personal assets are not the only thing at stake. Courts recognize avoiding economic harm to the circumscribed company of residents as a broad, legitimate goal that includes maintaining the tax base and conserving public services. Still, we begin to see why one expert on municipal law says that localism "calls into question basic assumptions about the 'public' nature of local political activity."[27] Municipalities have something of the character of those much-criticized homeowners' associations, commonly described in terms of "hostile privatism" and "secession."[28]

"The republican tradition taught that to be free is to share in governing a political community that controls its own fate," Sandel reminds us.[29] What does this mean for localism? Sandel approves of some forms of locally legislated "soulcraft." He would support moves by city councils to curtail both offensive political speech and pornography aimed at serving "not only the good of communal respect but also the good of self-governing communities"—disregarding the fact that offensive political speech and pornography have a very different status in constitutional law and liberal regard.[30] The ability to exercise local autonomy depends on more than formal legal authority and cutting back on constitutional constraints, though. Liberal concerns about localism are plain; the reasons internal to republicanism for skepticism about localism are less apparent.

They emerge in regard to Sandel's key concern, political economy. Local autonomy depends on actual revenues and fiscal strains. The property tax is the dominant local source of local revenue, and there is little relation between a city's resources and its financial needs. Both are the result of forces largely beyond local control—history, migration patterns, federal and state welfare mandates, the mobility of labor and capital.[31] That is why Herbert Gans cautions that municipalities can tolerate only moderate heterogeneity if they are to avoid irreconcilable conflicts of interest among residents on matters ranging from public services to zoning for low-cost housing: "since local institutions, including government, have little power to affect—and to ameliorate—the basic causes of such conflict, they [are] unable to handle it constructively."[32]

This only reinforces the republican wish to increase local economic control. In a well-known article, Gerald Frug invokes the free-chartered cities of medieval Europe and early American towns for the way they combined the characteristics of economic, communal, and political associations. Despite these oddly antirepublican models, the civic-minded spirit inspiring Frug's enthusiasm for localism is clear enough. The objective behind local economic autonomy is to institute a *democratic* political economy, and Frug proposes not only local regulation of business but the transference of "private" corporate power to municipalities; cities could take on banking, for example.[33]

Sandel's historical sympathies lie with decentralizing rather than nationalizing versions of economic reform and with movements aimed at "protecting local communities and independent producers from the effects of massive concentrations of economic power."[34] That said, his claims for the present are cautious. He is less interested in policy prescriptions than in simply urging that public deliberation take account of the civic consequences of political economy. His illustration of exemplary local self-organization is the community development corporation, which mixes self-help with federal and business support.[35] This sort of effort, while commendable, is a modest and typically short-lived "pocket of political activism."[36] It does not speak to the structural obstacles to casting cities as an alternative form of decentralized power with the capacity to moderate economic instability, say, or transform workplaces into scenes of civic education.

On the larger question of political authority, it is unclear under what conditions Sandel would favor local or state measures—either legal constraints or moral and material incentives—to prevent businesses from down-sizing or relocating, for example. It is also unclear how he judges the ceaseless competition among cities and suburbs to lure enterprises there. Is this a selfish scramble to advance private interests (corruption)? Or the lively expression of healthy localism on the part of equally civic-minded communities concerned about the social conditions of citizenship?[37]

Republicanism faces the challenge of determining *which* level of political community in a complex, pluralistic polity should regulate specific activities, and for whose benefit. Localism replicates the debate about business: whether corporate responsibility is to shareholders, stakeholders, or the wider public. The question of allocating authority is more acute when the principal consideration is promoting civic engagement by making self-government effective. For virtual authority without actual control is more likely to frustrate expectations for self-government than repair democracy's discontent.

Anti-Legalism: Community vs. the Procedural Republic

Another point on the terrain of fusion republicanism and potential locus of community activism is the jury. Political theorists typically follow Tocqueville in lauding the jury's benign educational function:

it teaches men to practice equity; every man learns to judge his neighbor as he would himself be judged . . . *It may be regarded as a gratuitous public school*, ever open, in which every juror learns his rights, enters into daily communication with the most learned and enlightened members of the upper classes, and becomes practically acquainted with the laws.[38]

But jury duty has always been more than a tutorial. It is a direct exercise of democratic will. *A Maryland Farmer* pronounced the jury trial more important than political representation as protection against arbitrary power because "those usurpations, which silently undermine the spirit of liberty, under the sanction of law, are more dangerous than direct and open legislative attacks."[39] For Tocqueville too, "the jury system as it is understood in America appears to me to be as direct and extreme a consequence of the sovereignty of the people as universal suffrage."[40]

Trial by jury is not just an individual right and guarantee of a fair trial to the accused, then: it is a constitutionally explicit, structural aspect of republicanism. Moreover, along with civic groups and voluntary political associations, the jury is a forum for community organizing. With its irreversible power of nullification—to acquit in disregard of the evidence and the court's instructions on the law—nullification is a shield against overzealous prosecutors, corrupt judges, and oppressive legislation. The jury is the final judge of who is victim and victimizer, patriot, criminal, or subversive. We can understand why assessing civic virtue has always been central to the composition and conduct of juries

Historical examples of nullification cut in every direction: Boston juries' refusal to convict under the Fugitive Slave Law as well as all-white juries' routine refusal to convict whites charged with violating the civil rights of blacks, effectively undoing Reconstruction statutes and condoning lynching and murder in the 1950s. Jury nullification was successfully used to free Vietnam War protesters prosecuted in the 1960s, and unsuccessfully urged by Operation Rescue defendants more recently.

The Supreme Court denied the right of criminal juries to judge the law in 1895, and today judges in most states tell jurors that their duty is to determine the facts and to apply the law as it is explained to them, whether they think it legitimate or not.[41] In a 1997 decision, the Second Circuit Court affirmed that unwillingness to apply the law is a proper basis for a judge to exercise unilateral authority to remove a juror.[42] But these restraints are not always effective, and some constitutional scholars advocate instructions to juries from the bench on nullification.[43] In 1990 the Fully Informed Jury Association was founded to lobby for laws legitimating nullification. Its membership mirrors the messy mix of reasons for nullification, not all republican, including religious conscience and the particular aims of "NRA members, antilogging environmentalists, advocates for the legalization of marijuana, tax protesters, and bikers opposed to mandatory helmet laws."[44]

The relation between the dual goals of a representative jury and an impartial jury is especially strained when juries engage in nullification. Today, racially based jury nullification by African-Americans is documented in some jurisdictions and jurors have been dismissed during deliberations for refusing to convict "because of preconceived, fixed, cultural, economic, or social . . . reasons that are . . . impermissible."[45] But one legal scholar offers "a principled framework" for this form of nullification. The Black community is better off when some nonviolent lawbreakers remain in the community rather than go to prison, Paul Butler argues, and

> the decision as to what kind of conduct by African-Americans ought to be punished is better made by African-Americans themselves, based on the costs and benefits to their community, than by the traditional criminal justice process, which is controlled by white lawmakers and white law enforcers.[46]

Consistent with this community-based justification for nullification, Butler recommends that information about nullification should be publicly disseminated in church, through rap music, newspapers, and magazines. He argues that jurors who engage in nullification "might be morally obligated to participate in black self-help programs" and in enforcing commuity norms against antisocial conduct; the Nation of Islam guards that patrol public-housing projects are an example.

The dangers of nullification are clear. We know that it is inspired by intimidation as well as a sense of justice. When juries act as mini-legislatures, they give local bias free reign. Nullification invites violation of due process and undermines the legalistic virtues of predictability and uniformity. No judicial system could function if it made "every jury, impannelled in every court in the United States . . . the rightful and final judge of the existence, construction, and effect of every law."[47]

For some citizen groups, however, that is precisely the objective. They would not restrict nullification to rare instances when acquittal seems like an act of mercy or a specific law is deemed unjust. Rather, nullification is a program of popular resistance, as it seems to be for the radical republican right today in its "self-defense" against tax and bankruptcy laws, weapons laws, and charges of sedition. A similarly radical rationale is evident in the proposition that jurors should consider the evidence in light of a criminal justice system that is presumptively discriminatory against Blacks, where not only law enforcement but criminal law (and property law) are seen as unjust. "As an African-American . . . it is difficult for me to encourage my people to relinquish the greatest power they have against the tyranny of the majority."[48]

At the limit, jury duty with its potential for nullification is seen as a standard mechanism of self-government. Against the federal courts' charge that "such verdicts are lawless . . . and constitute an exercise of erroneously seized power," advocates bring to bear classic republican responses.[49] Nullification is a legitimate, communal exercise of sovereignty, the argument goes, levied against the coersive apparatus of government at the point where authorities are least accountable and their power is most keenly felt by individual citizens.

"Civic Fundamentalism" and Citizen Militias

No thinker signals the unsettling fundamentalist tendencies of republicanism better than Tom Paine. Consent of the governed was not something to be granted once and for all in some original social contract; every political obligation must have the people's ongoing assent. "The earth belongs to the living" presumes a willingness to undo everything. Nothing could be more radical: "Every age and generation must be as free to act for itself, *in all cases*, as the ages and generations which preceded it."[50] Today, democratic discontent creates conditions ripe for direct action.

When Sandel refers to the tendency to political fundamentalism he has something in mind other than citizens taking "we the people" literally. By fundamentalism he seems to mean a form of nationalism (or exaggerated attachment to the national government?), which he attributes to those who are committed to sovereign states, abhor pluralism, and want to "take back our culture and take back our country."[51] Nationalism is a real danger, particularly when it involves restrictive definitions of citizenship, but there is little demonstrable affinity between aggressive nationalism and contemporary liberalism. Strangely, Sandel does not acknowledge the distinctive "civic fundamentalism" latent in republicanism: insistence on the civic virtue of vigilant patriots, a reluctance to relax jealousy and suspicion of government, and a propensity for direct action to "take back" power from corrupt or alien usurpers. Its fiercest face today is citizen militias.

One militia called its publication *Common Sense*, aptly, since these groups follow Paine in rejecting every authority but the Bible, and do not rue instability or share Publius' fear of "disturbing the public tranquillity by interesting too strongly the public passions."[52] Above all, in rhetorical imitation of Paine's famous familial metaphor, they insist that "the Federal government itself is the child of the armed citizen. We the people are the parent of the child we call government."[53]

By 1996 there were several hundred citizen militias in the USA, with membership ranging from fewer than a dozen to over a thousand.[54] Assuming the mantle of the independent militia that opposed the British army, their conspiracist thinking echoes the logic of that rebellion, where, as John Adams warned, the danger to America "was in fact only the small, immediately visible part of the greater whole whose ultimate manifestation would be the destruction of the English constitution with the rights and privileges embedded in it."[55] The original Minutemen of the towns were bound together by family loyalties as well as republican ideology, and the provincial armies were quasi-feudal bands of patrons and clients.[56] In any case, appropriating the title Minutemen became a historical pattern:

> It is hardly accidental that, in 1799, Fisher Ames called for a new generation of Minute Men to rise against the Jacobins, or that the same image was invoked by the anti-

Masons, anti-abolitionists, and anti-Catholics. In the 1880's a secret group of New York City Minute Men plotted aginst the Papists. And of course in our own time the heart-stirring name has been appropriated by militant right-wing extremists.[57]

Militia groups today represent themselves not as ordinary voluntary associations but as embodiments of popular sovereignty. The titles "posse" and "militia" evoke defense of liberty and order by an authorized group of citizens operating within the bounds of law (an implicit response to statutes that link these groups to domestic terrorism and disorder). Militias promise vivid displays of empowerment, with their symbolism of the gun. Like other paramilitary groups, some harbor ideologies of hate, separatism, and romantic militarism. The difference is that they represent themselves as republicans first of all. Self-styled Paul Reveres, their business is to alert others and demonstrate their preparedness to counter threats to democratic liberty, beginning with their own freedom of association.

Moreover, militias see themselves as the embodiment of civic virtue. "Patriots" are distinguished from nominal democratic citizens, and they echo Patrick Henry's grim caution: "Virtue will slumber. The wicked will be continually watching: Consequently you will be undone."[58] The temper of their pronouncements is moral outrage: *they*, at least, are vigilant and ready to sacrifice for the common good. They would agree with Garry Wills in assigning a purely military meaning to "keep and bear arms."[59] They are "well regulated." The Minutemen, one training pamphlet explained, are "the most experienced, most dedicated and best disciplined organization that is involved in this fight at the grass-roots level."[60]

Militias are not alone in arguing that the fight for democratic empowerment and civic renewal is joined over the Second Amendment, interpreted as a guarantee of republicanism not a personal right to gun-ownership for recreation or self-defense. "To see the Amendment as primarily concerned with an individual right to hunt, or protect one's home, is like viewing the heart of the speech and assembly clauses as the right of persons to meet to play bridge, or to have sex," one consitutional scholar observes.[61] From this republican perspective, the right to keep and bear arms is a structural defense of the federal balance; it secures officially authorized companies of "the people" under the jurisdiction of governors in order to offset a concentration of military power in the national government. The Second Amendment also secures self-selected, self-organized companies of citizens, insuring the possibility of popular resistance to undemocratic authority at any level.

From this standpoint, gun control is opposed not just as misguided anti-crime policy or a violation of a core constitutional right but as a step in a program of democratic disempowerment. This helps explain the familiar transformation of noncompliants and vigilantes into patriots and heroes. Who we view as virtuous, who as martyred, and why, depends on who we think presents the real clear and present danger. Which fear is greatest? Fear of ordinary crime? Of "domestic terrorism"? Or the civic fundamentalist fear of unaccountable agents of the state, unresponsive, arbitrary, and unjust? The conspiracist charge that proponents of gun control aim to literally disarm citizens is not relegated to some "fringe." It is echoed in mainstream electoral politics:

"What were those British soldiers coming for my friends?," Patrick Buchanan asked during his 1996 presidential primary campaign, "They were coming for the arsenal at Concord . . . they could impose their rule upon them, they could crush them . . . That right ain't about shooting ducks. That right is about a man's right to defend his wife, his family, his freedom and his country."[62]

As this demonstrates, the elements of fusion republicanism often converge. Despite differences in degrees of commitment to localism, say, or willingness to condone community-based anti-legalism, and despite political dispositions ranging from plausible democratic discontent to obscure and convoluted conspiracism, the discourse of republicanism can strike a uniform tone. This example undermines the comforting assumption that extremists alone create the climate of hostility and mistrust that makes a general tenor of anti-government hate talk and charges of disempowerment conceivable. Indeed, it suggests the reverse: that "civic fundamentalists" are the *beneficiaries* of a diffuse climate of republican discontent.

Public Philosophy and Democratic Responsibility

The usual response to any suggestion that the elements of fusion republicanism converge and are mutually reinforcing in practice is fierce denial. Understandably, even leaders who indulge in republican charges against their political opponents do not want to be held to account for excesses and abominations committed in the name of democratic discontent: "the attempt to locate in society's political discourse the cause of a lunatic's action is . . . contemptible"; the connection between political speech and hateful crime is "grotesque and offensive."[63]

The trouble is, in daily political life it is not always easy to draw a bright line separating points on the spectrum. When is militant republican rhetoric calculated to exploit popular feelings, or the exaggerated pose of partisans charging one another with disregard for the common good? When does it reflect the deep beliefs and herald the potentially violent action of civic fundamentalists? When is it the considered judgment of virtuous citizens? Is Alabama Governor Jones' threat to use state troops to resist a court order rhetorical defiance in the name of civic renewal, or extremism? Is the Governor safely ensconced on the civil side of democracy's discontent? In individual instances we try to sort out principled antifederalists, say, from true believers in some fantastic conspiracy. Despite the difficulty, as a practical matter we must insist strongly on drawing these distinctions.

From the standpoint of political theory, dissecting the elements of fusion republicanism and separating out proponents in a way that does not taint sober public philosophy or assign guilt by association is even more complicated. It is beyond the scope of this short chapter, but I want to conclude by briefly suggesting two areas where work needs to be done.

In part, the difficulty is a function of the genuinely perplexing relationships among political theory, "public philosophy," and popular ideology. What is the direction of intellectual influence? Bits and pieces of ideas from political theory, public philosophy, and ideology are exchanged. Bits and pieces are appropriated unsystematically in popular political discourse and as rationales for political action. Understanding these relationships involves a sociology of knowledge to explain how concepts move out into general circulation and are taken up. Karl Mannheim's writing on conservatism is a model, but this sort of study has not been applied to republicanism. How do ideas move out, become used and misused? What are the principal carrier groups? Contemporary citizen militias claim to be part of a long-standing civic tradition, but are they? Or are they sui generis, recent American originals? The ideology of localism, say, or the mechanisms of direct popular resistance have not been uncovered as well as the intellectual high ground Sandel recalls for us in his discussion of the political economy of citizenship. Tracing the lines of influence requires an exhaustive history of the strands of fusion republicanism.

The second difficulty concerns the political anatomy of the elements of fusion republicanism. The polemical objective behind labels of "extremism" applied to any ideological spectrum—left or right, liberal or republican—is to designate advocates as an insignificant "fringe" and to disavow any gradual continuum. We should not permit ourselves the comforting assumption that fringe groups are responsible for the climate of hostility that transforms democratic discontent into anti-government hatred. Again, "extremists" are the *beneficiaries* of a diffuse climate of hostility and of widespread agitation to correct the sense of disempowerment.

However, an accurate identification of a particular position as core and others as "extremist" is an empirical matter. It is particularly difficult when the center is shifting, as it appears to be in the USA.[64] Sandel sees a moving center to American political ideology overall, away from procedural liberalism toward some form of republicanism. As I have tried to show, the elements of fusion republicanism are fluid, and republicanism may have its own moving center.

Subtitled "America in search of a public philosophy," *Democracy's Discontent* suggests that Sandel's account of republicanism articulates widespread sentiment and addresses commonly felt needs. Do social science studies of public attitudes and beliefs sustain this assumption? Does Sandel track what Americans think? Are his examples of republican discontent and his model correctives representative? Sandel's public philosophy claims the intellectual high ground of republicanism, but it is an empirical question whether it is republicanism's current center. It may be that shifts along the spectrum of fusion republicanism—the real limits on local autonomy, say, or the experience of jury nullification, or the strengthening of civic fundamentalism—push Sandel's position closer to the edge of the republican spectrum, and closer to liberalism, even to the legalistic, procedural face of liberalism.

In any case, this sort of anatomy lesson is the responsibility of political theorists who advocate a public philosophy. Sandel should acknowledge the spectrum of fusion republicanism. He should be at least as attentive to its current expressions, including pathologies, as he is to liberalism's. He should indicate which expressions earn his enthusiastic support? Which are unfaithful to his understanding of republican principles? Which are aberrant? What institutions of self-government are vulnerable to abuse? What ideological alliances does he think are in the best interests of civic renewal? This responsibility is made more urgent to the extent that fusion republicanism is a real force in American political life.

22

Corporate Speech and Civic Virtue

MILTON C. REGAN, JR.

Introduction

MICHAEL SANDEL argues in *Democracy's Discontent* that Americans in recent years have become plagued with a sense of disempowerment—a feeling that they have diminishing control over the forces that shape their lives. An important reason for this anxiety, he maintains, is that Americans implicitly rely on a liberal public philosophy when they seek to interpret and order their common life. This philosophy characterizes freedom as the ability of the individual to choose her own values and ends. It depicts citizenship as membership in a political regime that attempts to honor her choices as much as possible, while imposing only those constraints necessary for others to pursue their goals. On this view, freedom and citizenship are antagonists: the demands of freedom set limits on what the state can ask of an individual; the duties of citizenship represent fetters on the enjoyment of individual freedom.[1]

This perspective is consistent with a pluralist model of politics, which sees political life as a process in which individuals seek to use collective means to satisfy the desires that they cannot fulfill on their own. As Cass Sunstein has put it, pluralism asserts that "[t]he goal of the system is to ensure that the various inputs are reflected accurately in legislation; the system therefore is one of aggregating citizen preferences."[2] A pluralist sees politics as akin to a marketplace in which individuals and groups compete for resources. Citizens press politicians to support their requests, in return for financial and political support. Political debate consists of appeals to others' interests in the hope of brokering an agreement in which as many people as possible get what they want. Economic arrangements are evaluated according to a similar criterion: how effective are they in satisfying individuals' material demands?

I would like to thank David Luban, Larry Mitchell, Roy Schotland, Mike Seidman, and Mark Tushnet for valuable comments on a draft of this chapter. I also would like to acknowledge the excellent research assistance of Shirley Woodward.

Sandel argues that the liberal vision of freedom and citizenship is powerless to respond to the anxiety that pervades modern American political life. Its emphasis on the freely choosing self in resolute pursuit of her interests is incapable of sustaining the civic commitment necessary for genuine self-governance. We need instead, he urges, a republican public philosophy, which sees freedom and citizenship as inextricably related. Republicanism asserts that "I am free insofar as I am a member of a political community that controls its own fate, and a participant in the decisions that govern its affairs."[3] On this view, citizens attain genuine freedom through the exercise of self-government. Political debate holds out the promise that individuals can develop civic virtue—that they will be moved to reformulate their ends so that concern for the common good outweighs attention to narrow individual interests. A republican sees politics not simply as a mechanism for satisfying preexisting preferences, but as a process in which preferences can be reshaped into public-regarding form. Similarly, she evaluates economic institutions not merely in terms of material efficiency, but according to the extent to which they enhance or inhibit the prospect of meaningful self-government.

Sandel's analysis offers an important corrective to current influential theories of politics. His insistence that we attend to the political implications of economic life is especially valuable. There is, however, a serious disjunction between the material conditions necessary for the development of civic virtue and the economic structure of modern American society. As Sandel himself acknowledges, the increasing influence of transnational business corporations contributes significantly to contemporary concern about diminishing self-governance.[4] The material dependence of citizens within such an economic system seriously complicates any effort to revive a republican ethos. On the one hand, sustaining this ethos as a regulative ideal is important in order to resist conflation of citizens' welfare with corporate interest. On the other hand, we must realistically acknowledge that individuals in modern society are crucially dependent on corporations for the basic elements of human functioning. Such dependence casts doubt on citizens' ability to attain critical distance from corporate demands when deliberating about political issues.

In this chapter, I want to examine the regulation of corporate political speech as an illustration of both the importance and the difficulty of attempting to reinvigorate the republican ideal in the modern age. Specifically, I will analyze the Supreme Court's decision in *Austin* v. *Michigan Chamber of Commerce*,[5] which upheld a prohibition on business corporation spending in support of or opposition to electoral candidates. Despite the pluralist rhetoric of the opinion, the decision in fact is most persuasively justified by a republican vision of the political process. My aim is not to explore all the nuances of doctrine that a comprehensive legal analysis would provide. Rather, it is to use *Austin* as a vehicle for exploring the tensions that law must confront in seeking to foster a republican model of political deliberation in a world of increasing individual dependence on corporate well-being.

The *Austin* Decision

At issue in *Austin* was the constitutionality of a Michigan law that forbids non-media corporations from using corporate treasury funds to make independent expenditures in connection with state elections for public office. These corporations are permitted instead to make such expenditures from segregated funds used solely for political purposes, commonly known as political action committees (PACs). The Supreme Court in *Austin* upheld the application of this law to the Michigan Chamber of Commerce, a nonprofit corporation funded by dues from members, three-quarters of whom are business corporations. The Court was particularly concerned about the ability of the Chamber to serve as an avenue for business corporations to circumvent restrictions on direct political speech. The decision thus is of particular interest because it effectively offers a discussion of why prohibiting such speech by corporations is consistent with the First Amendment.

The Michigan statute can be justified, said the Court, as a measure intended to protect the integrity of the political process. Firms that exploit the unique advantages that the state bestows on the corporate form are able to amass considerable wealth in the economic marketplace.[6] It would be unfair, however, to permit such firms to use this wealth to promote their ideas in the political marketplace. In that arena, advocates should compete solely on the basis of the strength of their ideas. Any disparity in resources available for political speech ideally should reflect only the fact that the most persuasive points of view attract the most financial support. Because the amount of corporate treasury funds is no indication of the popularity of the corporation's political views, companies should not be permitted to use this money to engage in political speech. By contrast, a PAC to which individuals have contributed will exhibit the necessary link between the amount of resources available and the power of the organization's political ideas.

Austin is notable for its articulation of a rationale for state regulation of campaign activity broader than the Court's traditional concern with the prospect of corruption, conceived narrowly as quid pro quo exchanges between political officials and supporters. Its concern about unfair advantage in the political "marketplace" suggests a pluralist conception of politics as fair competition among contending parties who seek to promote their own interests. The idea is that corporations have an unfair advantage over other political participants because their resources are acquired with the special help of the state. We must neutralize this advantage in order for political debate to be a true contest of ideas. In this sense, the prohibition at issue can be seen as a form of "First Amendment antitrust,"[7] intended to remedy political market failure.

As Justice Scalia's dissent argues, however, this rationale makes problematic any effort to single out business corporations for restrictive treatment. First, it is true that those who form corporations are able to amass wealth by using certain state-bestowed advantages, such as limited liability of investors and perpetual life of the organization. Nonetheless, other forms of association, as well as individuals, also are able to prosper by exploiting state-conferred benefits. These range from "tax breaks to contract awards to public employment to outright cash subsidies."[8] This point echoes the claims of Legal Realists of more than half a century ago, who pointed out that supposedly "natural" entitlements actually depend on state action for their acknowledgment and protection.[9] In this sense, the resources available to both corporations and individuals are a product of the existing legal regime.

Second, the resources available to wealthy individuals may no more reflect support for their political ideas than the money available to corporations. As Justice Scalia put it, "Why is it perfectly all right if advocacy by an individual billionaire is out of proportion with 'actual public support' for his positions?"[10] The desire to ensure a truly competitive political market necessarily must lead to limitations on the speech of wealthy individuals as well as corporations. For Scalia, this logical consequence reveals the indefensibility of the idea that the state should regulate the integrity of the political process. Solicitude for liberty and healthy mistrust of government mandates that the state not attempt to determine when any political participant has too much influence. Law should focus on corruption in the narrow sense of the term, not try to root out what Scalia calls the "New Corruption" by "calibrating political speech to the degree of public opinion that supports it."[11]

Scalia's opinion also represents a strand of pluralism, albeit one more laissez-faire in outlook than the majority's. It maintains that an uninhibited political process is the best guarantee of a citizenry that is both free and informed. If politics is to be a genuine marketplace of ideas, it is essential that corporations no less than any other actors be able to make their viewpoints known directly. Government should refrain from limiting competition except when necessary to prevent explicit trades of votes for favors.

A pluralist model of politics as fair competition thus seems unable persuasively to justify a prohibition on political speech imposed solely on business corporations. If *Austin* has coherence, I suggest, it is because of the implicit republican vision that animates the decision.

Corporations and Self-Interest

Civic republicanism urges that citizens deliberating about politics should attempt to expand their sympathies by looking beyond self-interest to the common good. Classic republicanism tended to posit a unitary common good, an assumption made more plausible because of the homogeneity of citizens achieved by various exclusionary measures. Contemporary neo-republicans reject both the notion of a single public interest and the restrictions that would limit the multiplicity of voices in political debate.[12] They argue that a republican ideal that speaks to modern concerns must place dialogue at its center.[13] Genuine dialogue requires a willingness to listen to the arguments of diverse others, and receptivity to the possibility of changes in one's values and preferences. In contrast to pluralism, individuals do not simply pursue the ends that they bring to debate, but engage in critical reflection on them in light of the views of others. Such a process may be more the exception than the rule for human beings who inevitably are animated by powerful drives of self-interest. It must at least be a possibility, however, if politics is to represent collective self-governance rather than mere brokerage of interests.

We can appreciate the republican underpinning of *Austin* by focusing on the importance of material independence in republican thought. Republicans regarded such independence as crucial to the cultivation of civic virtue.[14] A needy individual who is economically dependent on others will find it extremely difficult to adopt a perspective that reflects attention to the common good. First, she must devote most if not all of her energies to the task of self-preservation. The imperative to focus on material necessity offers little opportunity to look beyond self-interest; attention to some vague ideal of the public interest seems like a luxury that she can ill afford. Second, such a person will have her political judgment influenced by those on whom she is economically dependent. Most directly, she may be faced with the need to take certain political positions as a condition of continued support. More subtly, because her interest is so closely intertwined with that of her benefactor, she will naturally want to promote her benefactor's welfare in political matters.[15]

It was for these reasons that, as Sandel reminds us, republicanism evaluated economic arrangements not simply in terms of their contribution to material welfare, but according to the patterns of dependence and independence that they produced. The desire to maintain the independent political judgment necessary for civic virtue led many early republicans to advocate restricting the vote to property-holders, as well as to promote widespread property ownership. As Sandel observes, wage labor was regarded as incompatible with political self-government well into the nineteenth century, eventually gaining acceptance by republicans only because it might offer the opportunity for the worker eventually to establish himself in his own business.[16] Material dependence for a significant portion of the citizenry raised the specter of "corruption"—use of the political process to pursue private interests without regard to the common good.[17] For republicans, democracy requires citizens capable of civic virtue, and civic virtue requires freedom from material dependence that demands constant attention to self-interest.

The decision in *Austin* can be seen as resting on the view that business corporations are constrained in ways that systematically preclude them from cultivating civic virtue. Both legal directives and market pressures require that the corporation persistently pursue material self-interest. The corporation must take this end as a given, rather than treat it as subject to revision in light of critical reflection. For this reason, corporations *qua* corporations can be denied the ability to speak directly in political debate.

Let us consider why the corporation should be characterized in this way. As a preliminary matter, it makes sense to think of a corporation as having distinct interests that are not reducible to the mere sum of the interests of the individuals that comprise it. The firm is embodied in sets of procedures, policies, and roles that channel the behavior of persons within it in certain directions. Persons occupying roles within the corporate structure thus behave in ways they might not otherwise outside of those roles. The corporation acts and speaks through these persons-within-roles, most prominently managers and directors.[18] This conception of the firm as possessing intentionality and a sense of direction is reflected in the law's treatment of the corporation as a "person" for various purposes.[19]

The first constraint that tends to confine the corporation to the pursuit of self-interest is law. Both critics and supporters agree that the fundamental legal principle of corporate law is that corporate decision-makers' primary obligation is to increase shareholder wealth through profit maximization. The American Law Institute's *Principles of Corporate Governance*, for instance, state that: "A business corporation should have as its objective the conduct of business activities with a view to enhancing corporate profit and shareholder gain."[20] A well-known case enforcing this principle is *Dodge* v. *Ford Motor Company*, in which shareholders contested Henry Ford's plan to forgo the payment of special dividends.[21] Ford sought to reinvest earnings in the company in order to "employ still more men; to spread the benefits of this industrial system to the greatest possible number, to help them build up their lives and their homes."[22] The court upheld the shareholder challenge, declaring that directors could not lawfully "shape and conduct the affairs of a corporation for the merely incidental benefit of shareholders and for the primary purpose of benefiting others."[23]

The underlying assumption that animates the imposition of such a constraint is that corporate decision-makers are agents for shareholders who are the absentee owners of the company. At least since Berle and Means' *The Modern Corporation and Private Property*,[24] the central task of corporate law has been regarded as ensuring that management is held accountable for fulfilling this duty. Limiting managers' discretion by requiring them to pursue the narrow objective of profit maximization is an important means toward this end. As a result, "any suggestions that the law, as currently formulated and applied, permits consideration of non-shareholder interests in any meaningful way can be put to rest."[25]

It is true that corporate managers have some latitude in determining how best to enhance shareholder wealth. Courts rely on the "business judgment rule" in refusing to second-guess managerial decisions that plausibly can be defended as designed to benefit the corporation.[26] Decision-makers thus have some opportunity to forgo immediate gain for the sake of the long-term interests of the firm. By doing so, they also may benefit the larger community. Thus, for instance, had Henry Ford characterized his humanitarian plans as measures to promote the long-term profitability of the company, a court might well have upheld his decision. Similarly, steps to provide job training or education to disadvantaged potential workers, or to cease emissions into a river that supplies electrical power for a plant, may further both corporate and social interests.

Such a coincidence of benefits does not, however, undermine the claim that the corporation generally is precluded from cultivating civic virtue. Regardless of whatever social gains may result from a given action, management must use the language of corporate profitability to justify it. Law thus provides for corporate managers a vocabulary of motives that is based on self-interest. This vocabulary is impoverished compared to the one to which individuals have recourse in describing and justifying their political deliberation. Individuals of course may promote policies that benefit the larger society out of an appreciation of their enlightened self-interest. In this respect, they are no different than corporations. Individuals also, however, may be moved by arguments that elicit sympathy for others, or that persuade them that a given outcome is just regardless of personal advantage. By contrast, corporate decision-makers may not rely on such grounds alone to justify their actions.

Individuals' vocabulary of motives in the political arena thus is richer than the one-dimensional language available to corporations. It both permits and encourages the transcendence of self-interest, thereby holding open the possibility that political deliberation will be animated by civic virtue. Such a difference has implications not simply for the language that corporations and individuals use to justify their behavior. The normative vocabulary available to an actor shapes her perception of both the courses of action available and her own motives for acting.[27] If civic virtue is not an acceptable justification for corporate action, we cannot expect those who act on the corporation's behalf to develop it.

Recent enactment of corporate "constituency statutes" in several states is unlikely to alter the force of the law's command that managers focus on corporate financial self-interest. Such statutes authorize, although they typically do not require, directors to consider the interests of groups such as customers, suppliers, employees, and the larger community when making decisions.[28] As even supporters of these laws admit, "their effect is likely to be minimal."[29] None modifies the basic duty of directors to maximize profits. Furthermore, none provides for any means of enforcement by nonshareholder interests. Shareholders remain the only corporate constituency with legal authority to vote for directors, bring derivative litigation in the name of the corporation, and change control of the corporation by selling shares. Given this legal regime, "the likelihood that boards will give meaningful attention to social concerns is limited indeed."[30]

Even if corporate decision-makers were inclined to evade their legal responsibility to pursue corporate self-interest, competitive market pressures would rein in such impulses. Indeed, various practical concerns make it difficult for managers and directors to look even to long-term corporate interest, much less to take a broader social perspective. Intensified global competition and technological change create constant pressures to rationalize operations and to identify the contribution of each decision to profitability. The very survival of the firm is increasingly dependent on taking such a perspective. Furthermore, managerial and investor self-interest exert a pull toward focus on the short term. Corporate decision-makers who forgo short-term profit, even for the sake of anticipated long-term gains, risk lower immediate earnings and/or share prices. These may make the company vulnerable to a takeover, and leave managers and directors out of a job. Furthermore, those who control increasingly important institutional investment funds are under a fiduciary duty to maximize profits for beneficiaries.[31] With contributions to pension funds diminishing in comparison to payouts, and investment gains of growing importance to cash flow, many institutional investors are likely to exhibit little patience with corporate strategies that sacrifice short-term returns for long-term benefits.[32] As the work of Robert Jackall documents, the result of various market pressures is likely to be an institutionalized short-term focus in corporate culture.[33]

The operation of both law and the market therefore systematically tend to deprive corporations of the capacity to cultivate civic virtue. Ironically, despite its often enormous wealth, the corporation is a paradigm of the materially dependent actor that has no choice but to look relentlessly to its self-interest. As Lawrence Mitchell has suggested in criticizing corporate law's narrow definition of decision-maker responsibility, the roles filled by corporate actors are not those of persons who possess full moral autonomy. "[C]orporate actors within their roles are disabled from defining their ends and can only work toward the end that is given to them by the role."[34] The result, as Marc Galanter has observed, is that "[c]orporations enjoy a relative impunity to moral condemnation for single-minded pursuit of advantage that would be condemned as unworthy if done by [natural persons]."[35]

This is not to say that individuals act most of the time, or even often, on the basis of the common good. They too face constraints that make it necessary to look to their material self-interest a good part of the time. Nonetheless, we are committed to the idea that human behavior is not purely determined by such constraints, and that persons have the capacity to act on the basis of considerations that they themselves have chosen. Unlike corporations faced with the necessity of prospering at a certain rate, individuals have some latitude in determining what standard of living is sufficient and how much weight to attach to it. This offers an opportunity for the cultivation of public-regarding sentiments that the corporation generally cannot afford. It is our insistence on this possibility, rather than its complete realization, that distinguishes individuals from corporations as actors within the political sphere.

Austin's Republicanism

This analysis suggests a republican vision beneath the pluralist rhetoric of the *Austin* decision. Any hope of realizing republican aspirations for the political process requires that citizens possess at least the capacity to reflect critically on their ends, and the potential to be moved by dialogue with others to transcend self-interest for the sake of the common good. If corporations are not capable of such an orientation, then they should not be admitted as participants in political debate. The way to achieve this exclusion is to prevent the corporation from using corporate treasury funds to engage in political speech. These funds are resources available to the corporation *qua* corporation, accumulated through its profit maximization activity. Sales revenues represent the proceeds from transactions between self-interested buyers and sellers. The firm's capital reflects the provision of money by investors and creditors in the pursuit of economic gain. Those who control such money act as persons within constrained corporate roles, and the political speech on which they spend it will be driven by corporate self-interest.[36]

The exclusion of these actors from the political arena represents an effort to preserve a distinct sphere of political deliberation and debate. Collective self-governance requires the participation of autonomous moral beings, rather than those whose behavior is overwhelmingly determined by material interest. By restricting involvement to the former, the prohibition seeks to prevent the equation of political motives with economic ones. While actors in the economic market may legitimately be moved only by material self-interest, persons who deliberate in their capacity as citizens need not inevitably be so restricted in their outlook. In this sense, *Austin*'s reference to a political marketplace is somewhat misguided. The exclusion of speech funded by resources from the corporate treasury serves not simply to ensure a competitive contest of interests in political matters, but to preserve the possibility of a space in which broader concern for the common good also can serve as motivation.

We may accept that business corporations differ from individuals in their capacity for civic virtue, and still question whether they are sufficiently different from other organizations to justify being singled out for exclusion. One might argue that other forms of organization may also exhibit a tendency toward the uncritical pursuit of certain ends, which should disqualify them as well from direct political participation. For instance, was the Court wrong in *Federal Election Commission* v. *Massachusetts Citizens for Life*[37] to rule that a single-issue nonprofit advocacy corporation can use treasury funds to disseminate its message? Similarly, if we reject *Austin*'s reliance on the corporate form per se as the basis for prohibition, should unincorporated unions be forbidden to engage directly in political speech? If the absence of a capacity to cultivate civic virtue is the criterion for regulation, can we justify a prohibition that falls only on business corporations?

A crucial issue in answering this question is the extent to which an organization plausibly can be characterized as an association of individuals, whose political speech is funded by voluntary contributions from persons who have a meaningful opportunity to decide whether to support that speech. If this is the case, the organization serves as a vehicle for the enhancement of individuals' political voices. Those voices may speak in favor of self-interest, but this reflects the choice of individuals who at least have had the opportunity to weigh self-interest against other considerations in deciding which political causes to support. From this perspective, the Supreme Court in *Massachusetts Citizens for Life* was correct to protect the speech rights of an organization that had "features more akin to voluntary political associations than business firms."[38]

Despite Justice Scalia's reference in his *Austin* dissent to "that form of voluntary association known as a corporation,"[39] business corporations cannot plausibly be regarded as vehicles for advancing the considered preferences of individuals. Rather, as Daniel Greenwood has observed, the modern corporation is operated for the sake of "fictional shareholders" who are assumed to care only about maximizing the financial value of their shares.[40] Given the increasingly broad ownership of shares, shareholders also may well be employees of the company in which they hold stock or members of a community in which the corporation is an important economic presence. They also are likely, as are most people, to vary in the priority that they place on wealth maximization. At least some of these individuals may prefer a lower rate of return for the sake of job security, the economic viability of their community, or the promotion of noneconomic values. Despite the fact that shareholders are individuals with complex goals and concerns, corporate law imposes no responsibility on management to ascertain the wishes of the actual persons who own shares in the firm. Furthermore, shareholders have virtually no rights to participate in governance of the daily affairs of the corporation. They have only the authority to elect the board of directors, in whom the law vests broad discretion, and to effect changes in control by selling their shares. As a result, corporations operate on behalf of shareholders who are legal fictions, highly stylized persons whose interests are restricted to wealth maximization.

In addition, continuing increases in the proportion of shares held by institutional investors enhances the role of shareholders who seek not to maximize returns from a particular company, but within a portfolio of investments in several companies. Such investors generally do not regard themselves as "members" of any particular corporation. Firms are relevant to them only with respect to the relative risk/reward ratios that they offer; a portfolio investor "has no commitment to any product or institution behind that ratio."[41] As a result, "[t]he corporation's shareholders change continuously and continually";[42] it is difficult for either a corporation or an individual shareholder to know on a given day whether the individual owns shares in that specific corporation. The consequence is that "it is the market, not just (Wednesday's) shareholders, that controls the company's future—nonshareholders as much as shareholders."[43]

A business corporation engaging in political speech thus cannot realistically be regarded as simply the agent for individuals who have made considered decisions to promote certain political ends. The fact that the corporation is comprised of "fictional shareholders" means that it "will act as the market drives it to act, for good or bad, regardless of the interests or desires of any of its human participants."[44] For this reason, it is more plausible to think of a corporation as a collection of capital than as a collection of individuals.[45]

Other forms of organization in contemporary society more closely resemble associations of individuals, whose speech amplifies the voices of their members. Entities devoted to the promotion of political causes, such as the Sierra Club or the National Rifle Association, represent collections of individuals who contribute to the organization's political speech because of a deliberate choice to advance certain political interests. Such organizations, whether incorporated or not, readily can be characterized as vehicles for the enhancement of individuals' political voices. As such, the resources they have available represent decisions by persons in their capacity as citizens, rather than as consumers or investors. While we hold out the possibility that citizens may be moved by appeals to the common good, respect for human autonomy requires that we also honor individuals' decisions to promote political causes based on narrower considerations. Even organizations that relentlessly focus on a single issue are deserving of participation in the political sphere. Their relative strength reflects the judgments of individuals who have the capacity for reflective deliberation, and have chosen to support the organization's agenda. The importance of this capacity is underscored by the Supreme Court's pronouncements in *Massachusetts Citizens for Life* and in *Austin* that only political advocacy groups who do not receive contributions from business corporations have a constitutional right to use the organization's treasury funds to engage in political speech.

While unions are prohibited from using treasury funds to engage in political speech with respect to federal electoral candidates,[46] a law such as the one upheld in *Austin* permits speech by unincorporated unions in state electoral campaigns. Given the unpersuasiveness of a distinction based on the corporate form per se, is it possible to defend a prohibition on business corporations but not on unions? My analytical framework suggests that we can more easily regard the union rather than the business corporation as an association of individuals who band together to advance their common concerns. Their concerns as workers clearly include material interests in the form of economic benefits. They also, however, include nonmaterial ones, such as greater dignity and autonomy in the organization of work, and more free time to spend with one's family or in community pursuits. As Sandel observes, for instance, labor unions' advocacy of the eight-hour day in the late nineteenth century rested on the argument that workers needed more time to fulfill their duties as citizens by reading and participating in civic affairs.[47] Union activity thus represents an effort at self-governance in the workplace, which requires consideration of and trade-offs among a variety of both material and nonmaterial goods. Indeed, it can be seen as an effort to counter the tendency of corporations to view workers in much narrower terms as one of several factors of production that must be combined in the most efficient manner.

In addition, union membership often involves participation in a number of education and social activities that generate a sense of solidarity among workers. Labor's organizational unit is the union local, which provides opportunities for active participation in governance matters with those whom one sees on a daily basis at work. Voting is on a one-person, one-vote basis; by contrast, voting power in corporations is on the basis of shares, and some classes of shareholders have no voting rights at all. In contrast to a corporation, it is common to say that one "belongs to" or is a "member" of a union, terminology that "conveys a sense of personal commitment or engagement."[48] Finally, unions historically have supported broad political causes on behalf of various disadvantaged groups that did not necessarily serve, and indeed may have been contrary to, members' material interests. Many labor unions were prominent supporters of the civil rights movement, for instance, even though employment discrimination arguably limited the labor supply and pushed up wages. By contrast, "the common bond among stockholders lies almost exclusively in their mutual hope of profits."[49]

It is true that individual workers sometimes may be required to join a union.[50] In other instances, they need not become union members, but must accept the union as their collective bargaining representative and pay a fee for this service in lieu of union dues.[51] In these cases, the union does not represent an association constituted solely by the choices of individuals. Nonetheless, unions are constitutionally prohibited from using a worker's fees or dues to promote political positions with which the worker disagrees.[52] As a result, the funds that the union has available for political speech represent considered decisions by workers to use the union to advance certain political causes. A law prohibiting political speech funded by corporate treasury funds therefore need not include a ban on similar activity by labor unions in order to be valid. Whether incorporated or not, unions are far more plausibly described as associations that advance the goals and interests of individual members than are business corporations.

Finally, what of nonprofit, as opposed to business, corporations?[53] Such organizations play a prominent role in social and economic life, and range from entities such as the Salvation Army to nursing-home chains, hospitals, and day-care centers. Both the Federal Election Campaign Act and the Michigan law upheld in *Austin* prohibit political speech by all corporations, for profit or nonprofit, subject to the exception carved out by *Massachusetts Citizens for Life* for political advocacy corporations. Furthermore, as a practical matter, most nonprofits enjoy favorable tax treatment that is conditioned on abstention from involvement in political activity.[54] If, however, use of the corporate form is not the dispositive factor in regulation, can we justify at least as a theoretical matter a prohibition only on the political speech of business corporations?

I attempt no comprehensive analysis here, but an answer might begin with Henry Hansmann's distinction between "donative" nonprofits that receive their income from grants or donations from individuals (e.g. the Salvation Army), and "commercial" non-profits that receive their income from prices charged for their services (e.g. hospitals).[55] These are ideal types; many non-profits, such as universities, are a combination of the two. Nonetheless, the closer an organization is to the donative model, the better the argument that the political views that it espouses generally must be consistent with those of its donors if it is to survive. Whatever funds it has available for political speech thus tend to reflect the considered choices of individuals to use the organization to promote their political ends. By contrast, the treasury funds that a commercial nonprofit has available need not reflect approval of any political position that the organization takes. A need for the services that the nonprofit provides may prompt a consumer to engage in a transaction despite disapproval of the firm's political views. In such a case, it seems less plausible to characterize the organization as a vehicle for amplifying individual speech. This suggests that it is reasonable to exclude both business corporations and commercial nonprofit firms from engaging directly in political speech.

This is not to say, however, that a prohibition must apply to commercial nonprofits in order to pass constitutional muster. Indeed, business corporations could be singled out even if the other organizations that I have discussed are less akin to associations of individuals than I have claimed. Because political speech by the business corporation is not an extension of individual speech, it does not implicate any values of self-expression or autonomy. As Meir Dan-Cohen has suggested, the corporation's political speech rights therefore should be regarded as derivative, rather than original.[56] That is, we protect such speech not for the sake of the speaker, but because of the speaker's contribution to an informed audience of listeners. This instrumental justification means that regulation of this speech should not be subject to strict scrutiny, but to more lenient intermediate or even rational basis review.[57] Regulation of speech by artificial entities thus rests not purely on categorical principle, but on practical judgments about the extent to which various types of organizational speech may enhance or diminish the process of political deliberation. The state may reasonably conclude that business corporations present the most serious threat to civic virtue because they are the clearest instance of an unavoidably self-interested political actor, and because they possess more influence than does any other form of modern organization. Other entities may represent a more complex combination of features, so that a prohibition on their speech would risk inhibiting individuals' ability to amplify their voices by acting through an organization. In addition, as I will discuss at more length below, the state may decide that corporate political action committees offer an adequate vehicle for investors who wish to use the corporation to promote their political interests.

Finally, it is worth noting that concern about the distinctive potential for business corporations to undermine democratic self-government has been a persistent theme in American political life. Restriction of corporate political activity has a long history. Congress barred corporations from making financial contributions to candidates for federal office in 1907, prohibited all corporate financial contributions in 1925, and proscribed corporate expenditures in connection with federal campaigns in 1947. The statute upheld in *Austin* is but a recent example of a long-standing concern about direct corporate involvement in politics.[58]

Both practical and symbolic fears underlie this concern. First, as Charles Lindblom has pointed out, business corporations in a capitalist society are not simply one of several interest groups.[59] Rather, they are effectively delegated responsibility for ensuring society's economic welfare. They have the authority to make decisions that affect investment, employment, productivity, and the availability of various goods and services—decisions that in some other economic systems are made to varying degrees by the state. Given this allocation of power, citizens in a capitalist society are dependent on corporations in ways that citizens in other societies are not. Such a relationship of power and dependence necessarily generates considerable anxiety that citizens may effectively lose the power of self-governance.

This anxiety is exacerbated by the fact that the law historically has sought to promote economic development by giving corporations a license to ignore many of the social consequences of their activities. The directive that managers and directors must enhance shareholder wealth, combined with the limited liability of shareholders for corporate obligations, effectively allows the corporation to externalize the costs of profit maximization on parties such as employees, suppliers, communities, and society at large.[60] Corporate treasury funds thus represent resources accumulated by a narrowly egoistic legal actor. To permit that actor to use those resources in an effort to shape public policy in its interests risks even greater insulation of the corporation from social accountability. While not without controversy, we may accept the necessity of constructing a purely self-interested actor for economic purposes, as long as it is confined to that realm. To permit its entry into the political sphere, however, raises the prospect that its stylized, truncated orientation may come to dominate society as a whole. The result would be what republicanism terms "corruption"—the inability of citizens to transcend self-interest for the sake of the common good. Contrary to Justice Scalia's claim, *Austin* thus represents concern not about "New Corruption," but about an older form that has been feared since the inception of the republic.

Anxiety about corporations therefore is anxiety about ourselves—that we may lose the capacity for civic virtue through material dependence or preoccupation with self-interest. The corporation offers a way to externalize these fears. It serves as the paradigm of the materially dependent and self-interested actor incapable of reflective political deliberation. Banishing it from the political arena is a way of affirming our commitment to the ideal of civic virtue and the possibility of a politics of the common good. The corporation is formed by human beings and can act only through them. Yet we can treat it as not one of "us"; "we" are fit to engage in collective self-governance, but the corporation is not. This act of exclusion offers a narrative about our relationship to the business corporation—that it is our own creation designed to serve human purposes, that we can subject it to our will, and that the economic market is but one limited dimension of society. In this sense, it represents the citizenry's declaration of independence from corporations. By expressing the ideal that politics is a distinct sphere of human deliberation, this act seeks to instill trust in citizens that they are capable of looking beyond self-interest to join with others in pursuing the public good.[61]

Corporate Political Action Committees

Even as we prohibit corporations from using treasury funds to engage in political speech, however, we permit them to speak through political action committees. The resources of these committees come from the contributions of executive and administrative personnel and from shareholders, the only persons whom corporations are permitted to solicit.[62] Since the welfare of these persons tends to be dependent on the corporation, it is likely that contributors will want to promote corporate interests in the political arena. The funds that the corporate PAC acquires thus generally will reflect the materially self-interested decisions of contributors. Furthermore, the corporate officials who control the PAC will naturally want to use it to promote political outcomes that will benefit the company. The corporate PAC therefore has the potential to undermine the effectiveness of a prohibition on direct corporate political speech. Given our concern about corporations as resolutely self-interested actors, why do we readmit them into the political arena through the door of PACs?

The answer is realism. First, despite our ideals, we know that individuals in the modern age are in fact dependent on corporations in crucial ways for their welfare. We cannot afford to be ignorant of the impact of public policies on the health of corporations. Firms are especially well-positioned to provide information on such impacts, and PACs provide an effective vehicle for them to do so.

Second, it would be both unrealistic and unwise to attempt to eliminate self-interest from the political process. We must acknowledge that individuals quite often act on the basis of self-interest in politics, and that many times it is appropriate that they do so. Because employees and shareholders will generally be dependent upon the corporation to varying degrees, they will accurately perceive that furthering the company's political views will be in their material self-interest. Like any political association, a corporate PAC is an efficient vehicle for amplifying the voices of these individuals.

The PAC differs from corporate treasury funds, however, in that contributions to it reflect the exercise of choice by persons acting in their roles as citizens. Individuals have the capacity to make political decisions based on concern for the common good, even if they do not often exercise it. This existential margin of difference distinguishes the individual who *chooses* to promote her self-interest from the corporation who has no choice but to do so. By permitting the corporation to engage in political speech only with contributions designated for that purpose, the law requires individuals to engage in an act of deliberation specifically as citizens. An individual confronted with solicitation by a corporate PAC at least has the opportunity to reflect upon her ends and to decide whether promoting the corporation's political objectives would be consistent with them. She must deliberate about what weight to give her role as employee or shareholder in light of other personal and social interests. In this way, the law seeks to preserve political deliberation as a distinct process of individual and collective self-governance.

Regulations such as the one upheld in *Austin* therefore reflect a combination of republican idealism and pluralist realism. They represent an attempt to preserve the possibility of civic virtue in a world that has moved dramatically away from the material conditions that nurture it. Our dependence on corporations is something that we seek to limit, but also is something that we cannot afford to ignore.

Conclusion: Republicanism and Corporate Social Responsibility

There is a certain irony in the argument that I have presented: the prohibition of corporate political speech seeks to preserve civic virtue by assuming its inevitable absence in business corporations. Depiction of the corporation as an unavoidably self-interested actor is at odds with those who urge the corporation on its own initiative to take a broader political perspective and to assume greater social responsibility. Some advocates would expand corporate decision-makers' discretion by legally declaring that profit maximization in pursuit of shareholder wealth is but one of several lawful objectives of the corporation.[63] Others, such as supporters of corporate constituency legislation, would authorize directors to take into account the interests of groups other than investors when making decisions on matters such as plant closings and takeover offers. In general, advocates of corporate social responsibility encourage corporate involvement in public affairs in ways that may be only remotely, if at all, connected to the corporation's profitability. Only such latitude, they contend, will give managers and directors the opportunity to move beyond the narrow constraints of the corporate role to develop full moral autonomy and a sense of accountability for the impact of corporate actions on society—in short, to cultivate civic virtue.[64]

The prohibition of corporate political speech arguably moves in the opposite direction. It assumes that we cannot look to the corporation for civic virtue. We must instead accept the inevitable influence of role constraints on corporate actors, and seek to contain, rather than expand, corporate influence on matters of public significance. In this way, the prohibition contributes to a legal construction of the corporation that is at odds with those who would ask corporate agents voluntarily to take account of broader social concerns. Critics of my analysis may argue that, to the extent that this area of the law shapes the motives and self-understandings of corporate decision-makers, a prohibition sends the message that narrow self-interest is an inevitable orientation for which these actors cannot be blamed.

These different approaches to corporate social responsibility highlight the unavoidable dilemma that we must confront in attempting to respond to corporate influence in contemporary social life. On the one hand, there are risks in proceeding on the assumption that corporations are incorrigibly guided by self-interest. First, this approach accepts the permanent existence of a large group of individuals who are denied the exercise of full moral autonomy in their occupational life because they work within the corporation. This prospect is troubling in light of the fact that corporate managers and directors exert enormous influence over the deployment of resources in modern society. Second, it assumes that corporations usually will not take the socially responsible course of action unless it is consistent with their profitability. It thus seems resigned to the view that firms generally will not act responsibly on their own initiative, but must be subject to regulation that imposes costs or provides benefits that induce a socially desirable decision. Put differently, it assumes that law will have no independent normative force for corporations, but will be viewed instrumentally as but one factor in their cost–benefit equations. At best, we might hope that concern for long-term interest might sometimes prompt socially desirable decisions.

Finally, this model of the corporation may impose considerable social costs of its own. Law cannot anticipate every instance in which corporate actions may have broad social impacts. The cultivation of managerial judgment often may be the only assurance that corporations will take account of the externalities they impose. De-emphasizing voluntary compliance means that the state may need constantly to engage in the costly task of imposing obligations, monitoring behavior, and punishing violations. Corporate social responsibility, in other words, may require high transaction costs.

On the other hand, there are risks in assuming that corporations have any enduring capacity to proceed on the basis of civic virtue. First, the looser the legal constraints on officers and directors, the greater the danger that corporate elites will pursue their own agenda without accountability to anyone. The fear that shareholders will be exploited by corporate agents may have prompted excessive insistence that managerial discretion be limited to an unduly cramped compass. Nonetheless, the underlying general concern about accountability cannot be completely dismissed.

Furthermore, legal rules defining corporate decision-makers' responsibilities may be far less significant than the competitive pressures of global capitalism, investor demands, and the market for corporate control—all of which relentlessly direct attention to the material self-interest of the firm. If we permit corporate spending on political speech in the hope that enlightened corporate actors will engage in critical reflection on their interests, we run the risk that companies will use such speech to enhance their influence in modern life. This could occur not simply by the victory or defeat of particular candidates or ballot initiatives, or the enactment or repeal of specific legislation. It also could occur more subtly by shaping citizens' attitudes and self-understandings so that they are more consistent with corporate self-interest. Put differently, corporations may reshape individual citizens in their own image. They may increase their influence so significantly that individuals' dependence on them may erode any capacity for civic virtue among natural persons. Citizens may be no more able to afford deviation from material self-interest than corporations. If so, we will have lost the republican dimension of political life. We will all be pluralists who conform to the notion that politics involves nothing more than the pursuit of self-interest.

The debate over corporate political speech thus clarifies that calls for a rebirth of the republican ethos must attend closely to the conditions under which social norms are created and internalized. Neither intellectual insight nor sheer will is enough to ensure the viability of civic virtue. The world has changed dramatically since the eighteenth century, no more so than with the rise of massive entities designed deliberately to be egoistic actors insensitive to such virtue. These entities have shaped the norms of the larger social world that they inhabit, not least by forging patterns of power and dependence that Jefferson or Madision scarcely could have imagined. Efforts to reshape the normative contours of that world must come to grips with this development. As my analysis suggests, however, it is not self-evident how to reconcile the fact of corporate influence with the aspiration to self-government. Both expecting civic virtue from corporations and denying its possibility create risks that may exacerbate, rather than resolve, the tension. I have presented a tentative case for the latter approach, at least with respect to political speech. The most important point, however, may be that this issue illuminates the perplexing dilemmas that confront any attempt to sustain a civic republicanism that we can carry with us into the twenty-first century.

23

Federalism as a Cure for Democracy's Discontent?

MARK TUSHNET

IN a brief but important passage Professor Sandel invites us to "consider the unrealized possibilities implicit in American federalism."[1] His account of why those possibilities matter is sketchy, but it appears to be that American federalism offers opportunities for revitalizing democracy by enhancing the ability of citizens to participate in the kinds of formative projects that Professor Sandel believes essential to democracy in the modern world.[2]

On this account federalism is not of interest on two standard grounds frequently offered. States and local governments may *be* laboratories for social and political experimentation, as Justice Brandeis contended,[3] but a centralized constitutional system can foster experimentation when it is desirable. For example, recent changes in the system of providing public assistance to the poor occurred in two stages. First the centralized national authorities granted "waivers" of national regulations to allow state governments to experiment with new forms of providing assistance. Then Congress enacted a national reform, based in part on the experience gained from those experiments.[4] The example illustrates another point: experiments sometimes end, and the defense of federalism as a mechanism for experimentation must therefore allow for the possibility of a uniform and centralized imposition of the correct policy that localized experimentation helped identify. The Brandeisian defense of federalism, that is, may *require* some degree of commitment to centralization as a matter of principle.

The Brandeisian defense might have greater force if we could establish that policy-makers at the national level have smaller incentives to adopt programs that allowed for local experimentation than do policy-makers at the local level. As Susan Rose-Ackerman has argued, however, policy experimentation is a public good in the sense that no single policy-maker has strong incentives to be the first to experiment: better to sit back, let someone else run the risk of trying and failing at an experimental policy, and adopt only those policies that work out elsewhere.[5] Of course, as Rose-Ackerman points out, a local policy-maker may occasionally find it useful to engage in innovation, particularly if the policy-maker seeks higher office. But the incentives to innovate are not as strong as the Brandeisian defense of federalism suggests. And, it seems to me, national policy-makers have *some* incentive to authorize local experiments.[6] They can enhance their reputations, and to some extent their likelihood of reelection, by ensuring that their constituents benefit from national policy. But changing circumstances are likely to make it necessary to develop new policies to ensure that constituents continue to benefit. New policies, however, can be good or bad. By authorizing experiments, national policy-makers reduce the risk that a new policy, implemented in someone else's state, will turn out badly for them.[7] No doubt this incentive is offset by the interest in keeping control of policy, and by the psychological benefits that accrue from exercising centralized power. In the end, then, I think it hard to say that experimentation is more likely in a centralized or a federal system.

The second common defense of federalism that needs to be set aside is now well known under the name *subsidiarity*. This is a principle of efficient administration: Policy should be made and implemented at the level where it can be most effectively done, and frequently that is at the local level, at least with respect to many important policy areas. Again, however, a fully centralized government would have an interest in adhering to the principle of subsidiarity. National policy-makers' interest in reelection gives them an interest in ensuring that their constituents receive public services in the most efficient manner.

What makes federalism truly interesting in Sandel's framework are two other values of federalism, which I label, in standard ways, participation and value pluralism. Federalism promotes participation because, it is said, people find it easier to engage in political action in smaller jurisdictions: the smaller the jurisdiction, the more likely it is that a person's political action will actually affect policy, and the clearer it will be to the voter that his or her participation actually made a difference. An important definitional issue arises at this point. For federalism to serve the purpose of encouraging participation by guaranteeing greater influence on policy-making, federalism must mean the ability of the small jurisdictions to make ultimate policy choices that cannot be overridden by the larger jurisdiction. And the necessary finality of lower-level decisions in a truly federal system, I will argue, raises some real difficulties once we acknowledge the existence of value pluralism.

The important point about this formulation is that it does not assert that participation is valuable in itself.[8] Rather, participation is valuable because of its connection to policy-making. That connection, however, need not be as direct as I have asserted. Participation might be valuable because of a more indirect connection to policy-making: federalism encourages participation because people can actually influence some local-level policies, and having experienced political influence at that level, people become more vigorous citizens generally, participating more on higher levels as well.

Consider two local-level jurisdictions, A and B, which are federal units in a larger nation.[9] If people in jurisdiction A have the same values as those in jurisdiction B, which would lead to enacting policy X, federalism might be unnecessary as a means of ensuring that policy X be adopted. The nation might enact for all the laws that would be enacted separately in A and B, at least if the distribution of views among those who participate in national policy-making is the same as that among those who participate in local policy-making. But this might not be true. Active citizens might have views different from those of inactive citizens, and the set of people who participate in national decision-making might consist only of active citizens, excluding those who have been discouraged from participating in national policy-making because of their apparent lack of influence. Under these circumstances, a centralized government might adopt policy Y, preferred by the active citizens, rather than policy X preferred by the majority in both local jurisdictions A and B. In contrast, in a federal system jurisdiction A might choose policy X, and jurisdiction B might independently choose the same policy, because people residing in those jurisdictions, knowing that they will have the final word on the policy, might participate more actively in the process of selecting it.

This is a purely formal argument about the value of federalism, and it clearly has nothing whatever to say about the content of the alternative policies that might be chosen in federal and centralized systems. But that seems clearly at odds with Professor Sandel's concern that democracy today fails to identify formative projects that link citizen participation to the character-shaping dimensions of the economic order. It would seem, therefore, that the "unrealized possibilities" of American federalism must lie elsewhere for Professor Sandel.

Consider next the question of value pluralism, where people in jurisdictions A and B initially prefer different policies. Perhaps participation, which is encouraged by federalism, has a character-shaping effect that in turn affects the policies people prefer. So, for example, a person might go into the political arena thinking that it would be a good thing to suppress the expression of views that he or she believes erroneous. Confronting others in the political arena who disagree with him or her about which views are erroneous, or think it wrong to attempt to suppress erroneous views, the participant might come to see those people as engaging in the common venture of developing good policy, and might develop a more tolerant personality. He or she might come to think, "I deal with these people regularly on a range of issues, and they seem to me basically decent people; if such people think that suppression is a bad policy, perhaps I should reconsider my own position." Federalism then provides a vehicle for transforming value pluralism into value uniformity, at which point, clearly, one needs a defense of the uniform values that emerge over time in a federal system.

Value pluralism plays a key role in John Rawls's construction of political liberalism, and here too federalism may offer some institutional possibilities.

I think it helpful to distinguish in the first instance between value pluralism with respect to fundamental interests and with respect to nonfundamental ones. Fundamental interests, as I understand them, are values that a person believes must be implemented if the society in which he or she lives is to be regarded as minimally just. These are not merely personal values, the way of life that the person sets for himself or herself. Instead, they are values that must be generally implemented for all if the society is to be, in the person's view, minimally just. Nonfundamental interests, in contrast, are express values a person holds, but that the person acknowledges can be reasonably rejected by others.

Federalism of course provides an institutional mechanism for implementing value pluralism with respect to nonfundamental values, but as such offers little of philosophical interest: if people in jurisdiction A care about preserving the historic structures in their towns, and people in jurisdiction B prefer to destroy historic structures to pursue economic development, both groups can live comfortably with the other's decisions. Value pluralism with respect to fundamental interests, in contrast, cannot be a matter of mutual indifference.

According to Rawls's construction, disagreements with respect to fundamental interests lead to instability, which many people find quite costly. If they come to prefer stability to some aspects of their fundamental views, they may modify their fundamental views in ways that promote stability. They come to converge on a set of values that Rawls calls political liberalism. I have argued elsewhere in some detail that federalism may provide an institutional framework within which this convergence might comfortably occur.[10] In brief, I believe that federalism holds out the possibility of mutually profitable economic and cultural exchanges that gradually erode differences over fundamental interests, and that, given enough time, people may come to see that the benefits of those exchanges outweigh the incremental changes in fundamental interests that accompany each exchange, until the incremental changes accumulate into a larger transformation in fundamental views.

On this view, the "unrealized possibilities" of federalism lie in the fact that federalism can be something of a way station from a society in which people have widely divergent values into one in which they have convergent ones.[11] As Benjamin Barber puts it, federalism understood in this way gives people "sufficient time to live together to discover the need for more integrative remedies—and to acquire the trust and tolerance on which such remedies depend."[12] But, as Barber emphasizes, all this is in the service of "a gradualist, voluntary, trust-building strategy of supranationality."[13] The unrealized possibilities of federalism, that is, are *not* that it offers a framework for sustained value pluralism, but precisely that it offers a framework for the development of a universalist ethic. As I have argued elsewhere, something along those lines seems essential if we are to construct a politics with a formative project sufficient to the task of controlling the supranational economic entities that, in

Professor Sandel's view, play so large a role in generating democracy's discontent.[14]

The Supreme Court's recent decision invalidating the federal Religious Freedom Restoration Act provides an occasion for examining whether the perspective I offer gives us some purchase on a relatively narrow practical problem in designing federalist institutions. Congress enacted the Religious Freedom Restoration Act (RFRA) in 1993 against a complex legal background. The First Amendment says that "Congress shall make no law . . . restricting the free exercise [of religion]," and since the 1940s the Supreme Court has held that this ban applies against state and local laws as well because it was "incorporated" into the first section of the Fourteenth Amendment, which denies states the power to deprive people of liberty without due process of law. The protection afforded religious practices was relatively weak until the 1960s. The Court distinguished between religious beliefs, which were fully protected against regulation, and religious practices, which could be regulated to advance ordinary public purposes.[15] The Court appeared to change course in 1963. Finding it unconstitutional for a state to deny unemployment compensation to a woman who was unable to find an employer who would accommodate her religiously motivated need to avoid work on Saturday, the Court said that generally applicable state laws adversely affecting religious practices were unconstitutional unless they were justified by a compelling state interest.[16] The Court applied this standard to strike down several other denials of unemployment compensation, and in an important case also applied it to invalidate a requirement that children of members of the Old Order Amish denomination attend school until age sixteen, contrary to their parents' religiously motivated wish to terminate their education after they completed the eighth grade.[17]

These cases introduce some of the complexities of federalism understood as a way of protecting value pluralism. In each case there are two competing sources of value pluralism. The religious denominations are value locations for their members, but so are the state and local governments that seek to regulate the activities of members of religious denominations who are simultaneously citizens of the states. As the Court saw the problem, the centralized national government, acting through the national judiciary, would advance value pluralism better by protecting the value communities in the religious denominations than by protecting state and local regulatory authority.

At the same time, however, the Court acknowledged the importance of state regulatory power. In a series of cases decided in parallel with the unemployment cases, the Court upheld the government's authority to regulate.[18] The Court appeared to be concerned that a strict standard would unduly interfere with what it regarded as clearly justified exercises of government power. Finally, in 1990 the Court attempted to rationalize its cases. Rejecting the "compelling interest" standard, the Court decided that the free exercise clause was not violated when a state applied a neutral law of general applicability—

that is, one that in terms made no express reference to religious practices and that was not intended to suppress only religious practices—with the effect of making it more difficult for adherents of particular religious beliefs to practice their religion.[19] State and local governments as sources of value pluralism were, in the Court's eyes, to take precedence over religious denominations as sources of value pluralism.

The Court's decision created an uproar in religious communities, which formed an unprecedented coalition to seek legislation rejecting the Court's position. They sought once again to invoke the power of a centralized national government to protect subnational sources of value pluralism. Overcoming some resistance from state and local governments, which were particularly concerned about the problems they believed they would face in operating prisons, the coalition persuaded Congress to enact the Religious Freedom Restoration Act by huge margins. RFRA's preamble stated that its aim was "to restore the compelling interest test" the Court had adopted in 1963, because, in Congress's view, neutral laws could unfairly burden religious exercises.[20] The statute prohibited all governments—local, state, and national—from "substantially burdening" a person's exercise of religion unless the government showed that the burden advanced a "compelling governmental interest" and was "the least restrictive means" of doing so.

The Supreme Court considered a constitutional challenge to RFRA in *City of Boerne* v. *Flores*.[21] In 1923 St. Peter Catholic Church was built in Boerne, by the 1990s a suburb of San Antonio, Texas. As the city expanded, so did St. Peter's congregation. The church began to plan an expansion of the building. The city responded by enacting a historic preservation ordinance that required the church to obtain permission to expand; the city viewed the historic preservation district in which the church was located as a potential source of tourism and economic development. When the city denied the church's application for a permit, the church sued, claiming that applying the historic preservation ordinance to it violated its rights under RFRA. Without considering whether the denial did in fact violate RFRA, the trial court held that RFRA was unconstitutional. The church appealed, and the appeals court reversed. The city then took the case to the Supreme Court, which had before it only the question of RFRA's constitutionality.

Invoking principles of federalism, the Supreme Court found RFRA unconstitutional. The central national government in the United States is a government that has only the powers enumerated in the Constitution. Congress believed that it had the power to enact RFRA under §5 of the Fourteenth Amendment. That section gives Congress the power to "enforce, by appropriate legislation, the provisions of this article," including the due process clause through which the free exercise clause had been applied to the states. Congress believed that it was "enforcing" the free exercise requirement by enacting the "compelling interest" test. The Supreme Court disagreed. The 1990 law, the Court said, *defined* the precise scope of the free exercise clause. Congress could "enforce" the free exercise clause only by laws that dealt with free exercise violations *as the Court had defined them*. It could remedy free exercise violations, and it might act prophylactically if it showed that there was a widespread practice of suppressing religious practices under the guise of invoking neutral laws of apparently general application. But, the Court said, Congress had before it no record of violations that would justify treating RFRA as a statute designed to remedy constitutional violations that the Court itself would recognize as such.

The Court's doctrinal analysis is of less interest to me than the structure the Court's decision gives to the protection of value pluralism. The Court rejected the possibility of using centralized national power to protect religious communities as locations of value pluralism, once in the 1990 case when it abjured the use of its own centralized authority, and again in 1997 when it barred Congress from doing so. Notably, however, these decisions were made in the name of value pluralism itself: the Court allowed the institutions of state and local governments to enforce their own visions of the social good against competing visions emerging from religious communities.

Having noted that the Court spoke in favor of federalism as a protector of value pluralism, I must note my discomfort with the assertion that invalidating RFRA actually advanced value pluralism by vindicating the "unrealized possibilities" of American federalism. One reason is my general view that state and local governments in the United States are not truly sources of value pluralism. Consider the example of apparent regional differences in values in the United States. Do people in Montana, for example, think that their way of doing things is fine for them and the way people in California do things is equally fine for the people there? I have suggested that they do not.[22] They see people with a set of values—a certain kind of elitism that they roughly associate with "the coasts"—that they think no one should hold. It is just an unfortunate fact of life, to them, that they have not been able—yet—to guarantee that people in California hold the same values as those in Montana.[23] Local value pluralists, I am suggesting, are actually failed or incipient universalists, in just the way that Barber's defense of federalism is a defense of an incipient universalism.

Colorado's Amendment 2, invalidated in *Romer* v. *Evans*, is an example.[24] Because people in Denver and Boulder adopted gay rights ordinances applicable within those cities, people in Colorado Springs organized a statewide movement to slap Denver and Boulder down, even though Colorado Springs did not have, and was not likely to adopt, a gay rights ordinance. The people in Colorado Springs were not interested in value pluralism as such. They had a vision of universally applicable values and were in a position to enforce that vision—at least until the Supreme Court said no. Similarly, I doubt that anyone who opposes gay marriages in his or her own state thinks that it is all right for Hawaii to recognize gay marriages; it is simply that they cannot do anything about Hawaii.[25]

Commitment to value pluralism as such is surely hard to sustain even for those who might otherwise wish to do so. As Sandel himself suggests, the pressures exerted by a globalized economy in the direction of homogenizing local cultures seem to me quite large, which makes commitment to value pluralism as such seem increasingly utopian. Boerne's historic preservation district seems to me rather like an effort to capture some economic benefits by preserving something that may attract tourists precisely because it is "quaint," outdated, and no longer really available to us as a true cultural alternative.

But one might reject my skepticism about whether state and local governments in today's United States really are sources of value pluralism and still be uneasy with the Court's decision invalidating RFRA. I have argued that we should be concerned with value pluralism with respect to fundamental issues. Boerne's interest in historic preservation does not seem to me to qualify as fundamental in the relevant sense. Of course some people take a great deal of interest in historic preservation, while others do not. And yet that sort of pluralism seems to me largely unimportant in the defense of value pluralism. Value pluralism matters because it may be the most important source of social conflict, but differences over the importance of historic preservation seem rather like the song—"You say ee-ther, I say eye-ther"—and, as in the song, this sort of disagreement is not what leads people to call the whole thing off.[26]

Value pluralism with respect to these matters of relative indifference is not what Professor Sandel is interested in. Instead, he is interested in value pluralism with respect to things that matter. But at this point some of the problems with federalism in the abstract arise: few people are value pluralists with respect to the values they think most important, and many interesting and apparently divergent values make complex claims to universal truth in ways that complicate our ability to use federalism as a vehicle for vindicating value pluralism.

First, on the limited commitment to value pluralism as such: despite his interest in federalism, Sandel does not offer a sustained discussion of value pluralism with respect to some currently divisive issues, notably the issue of gay rights. The reason, I believe, is that Professor Sandel, like Barber and me, sees federalism as a valuable institution not because it promotes or protects value pluralism as such but because it offers the possibility of a transformation of values from those we do not approve into universalist values of which we do approve. Localized opposition to gay rights cannot be defended as a form of value pluralism, according to this view, because it rests on a set of undesirable values, which can, however, be eliminated over time through the gradual operation of universalizing processes associated with centralized economic and cultural forces set within a federal system.

Next, on the complexity problem: the RFRA case provides a minor example. The city of Boerne was attempting to advance its vision of the social good against a claim asserted by a parish of the Roman Catholic Church, which as a whole asserts an aspiration to universal jurisdiction. Under these circumstances, would allowing St. Peter's to expand actually promote its denomination's universalist aspirations rather than its (temporary, in its view) status as one of many competing religious denominations in the United States? Professor Sandel's discussion of the 1960s civil rights movement provides a more important example, which I have discussed in detail elsewhere.[27] The civil rights movement drew on local resources, but invoked universalist claims of Christianity and the Constitution understood in light of the Declaration of Independence.

Suppose I am right in thinking that contemporary American federalism is less about true value pluralism with respect to important matters than it is a means of dealing with everyone's perhaps temporary inability to implement his or her version of universalism. The complexity problem suggests the direction we ought to move in. And it is through the complexity problem that the *American* comes into my discussion of the unrealized possibilities of American federalism.

The idea I offer traces back to Abraham Lincoln's constitutionalism. It takes as its guide the universalism of the Declaration of Independence and the Constitution's Preamble. The Declaration and the Preamble, in this view, set the nation on a course to realize something I summarize somewhat inaccurately as a set of universal human rights justified to other people by reason.[28] This is a project, not a fixed accomplishment, and no one should think that we will determine the content of that set of rights by any way other than an historically extended discussion, which will take place among Americans because that discussion *is* the project of the United States.[29]

To put the point another way, to be an American is to orient your political action toward realizing the principles of the Declaration and Preamble. You have committed yourself, along with everyone else who is an American, to that project. Professor Beiner has described attempts by certain political theorists to liberalize nationalism by demonstrating how nationalism can be accommodated to liberal principles.[30] One might say, in contrast, that the US approach is the project of nationalizing liberalism. The American project is a universalist one: liberalism's universalist claims give American nationalism its particular content. Seen in this way, American federalism's unrealized possibilities lie not in providing the opportunity for the flourishing of an unrestricted plurality of values, but in providing the opportunity for alternative efforts to specify or realize the Declaration's principles and in providing the opportunity for a discussion among communities with different visions of how those principles should be specified. But the universalist dimension of the project licenses rejection of illiberal values in the long run, while the federalism dimension offers the hope that such a rejection will in fact occur. And, to complete the thought about federalism, to the extent that value pluralism takes the form of urging on us alternative specifications of the Declaration's universal principles, we would begin to realize some of *American* federalism's possibilities. When value pluralism takes forms not plausibly connected to the Declaration's principles, we as Americans can reject it.[31]

Sandel's concern here appears to be that the appeal to the Declaration's principles might degenerate into an abstract and arid rationalism. I suppose that *is* a risk, but, as Sandel himself says, in politics there are no guarantees. I would say, however, that the Declaration's principles are on their face rather thin, leaving much room for specification in the ongoing project of American constitutionalism. We can engage in the project of attempting to realize the Declaration's principles while sustaining value pluralism—for the moment, as the project works itself out over history—over a rather large range of important matters.

Finally, this account makes American universalism distinctive, to the extent that it connects that universalism to a project with roots not in the abstract philosophical theorizing that Professor Sandel argues cannot motivate appropriate citizen behavior, but in the Declaration of Independence, the Constitution, and more generally in the working out of the project of American constitutionalism through the course of United States history. We are not "formless, protean, storyless selves"; we are instead Americans seeking to continue a project with which we have chosen to affiliate ourselves.

VII

A Reply to His Critics

24

Reply to Critics

MICHAEL J. SANDEL

THE chapters in this volume pose a daunting array of criticisms and challenges, more than I can address in the detail they deserve. I am grateful to my friends and critics (often one and the same) for their searching responses to my work, even where they have taken me to task. I shall try in this chapter to identify some of the main lines of criticism and to reply as best I can, sometimes by clarifying arguments presented in *Democracy's Discontent* (hereafter *DD*), sometimes by revising or extending them.

Public Philosophy: Theory and Practice

Several critics raise questions about the idea of a public philosophy and about the way *DD* relates theory and practice. The book advances a philosophical argument and an historical one. The philosophical claim is that procedural liberalism—the political theory that says government should be neutral toward competing visions of the good life—is inadequate. The historical claim is that, in the past half-century, procedural liberalism has increasingly set the terms of American political discourse; it has crowded out republican understandings of citizenship and freedom and come to prevail as the reigning public philosophy.

But what, some critics ask, is the relation between the two? If liberal political theory is flawed, why not show this directly, through philosophical argument? And if American political discourse is impoverished, unable to address the erosion of community or the loss of self-government, why blame this condition on liberal philosophers like Rawls and Dworkin? Does this not attribute too great a role to ideas? If, as the historical narrative suggests, republican understandings of citizenship were in decline long before the philosophers of

I would like to express my appreciation to Anita L. Allen and Milton C. Regan, Jr. for conceiving of this project, for organizing the symposium at the Georgetown University Law Center where many of these chapters were presented and discussed, and for guiding this volume to completion.

liberalism arrived on the scene, there is all the more reason to doubt that procedural liberalism is responsible for our political condition.

Ronald Beiner poses the issue clearly by distinguishing two ways of relating the theory and practice of contemporary liberalism. The first makes an interpretive claim—that procedural liberalism sets the terms of political discourse and describes the self-understandings implicit in our political and constitutional practices. The second makes a causal claim—that statements of procedural liberalism by its philosophical proponents led citizens and public officials to embrace liberal policies and principles over republican ones. Beiner is right to suggest that I mean to make the interpretive, not the causal claim. Procedural liberalism constitutes the reigning public philosophy in the sense that it makes sense of our political and constitutional practices, taken as a whole; it describes the conceptions of citizenship and freedom that inform our public life.

What caused the shift from a republican to a liberal public philosophy is a further question. *DD*, concerned more with the interpretive question than the causal one, addresses it only obliquely. Broadly stated, the rise of the procedural republic might be explained as follows: the advent of a national, and now global economy complicated the republican project of subjecting economic power to democratic authority. Meanwhile, the emerging consumer society held out an alternative, privatized vision of freedom less demanding than the republican vision of freedom as self-rule. The great waves of immigration and the growing diversity of the nation rendered the formative project more difficult, and so heightened the appeal of a public philosophy that professed neutrality toward the ends its citizens espoused.

Although these and other changes prompted the emergence of the procedural republic, it was not altogether new. Both the liberal and republican strands of public philosophy had figured throughout the American political experience, but in shifting measure and relative importance. As Americans grappled over time with new social and economic circumstances, they elaborated a self-image present in American political culture from the start—the ideal of persons as free and independent selves, unencumbered by claims of custom or tradition or inherited status, bound only by ties we choose for ourselves. By the time procedural liberalism found its full philosophical expression in the 1970s, it was already deeply embedded in American public life. This is not to diminish Rawls's philosophical achievement. To the contrary, epic political philosophy often works this way. "When philosophy paints its grey in grey," Hegel wrote, "then has a shape of life grown old."[1] One need not accept Hegel's teleology of history to appreciate his insight that theory and practice are mutually constitutive. The political theory of procedural liberalism both shapes and reflects our political practice.

Beiner agrees that the interpretive conception of public philosophy avoids inflated claims about the causal efficacy of ideas, but worries that it carries "deflating consequences" for the enterprise of political theory. To reject a wholly idealist account of political change, he writes, is to concede that "writing a book like *Democracy's Discontent* surely won't by itself transform apathetic, disconnected, politically alienated quasi-citizens of contemporary America into Sparta-like paragons of republican virtue, nor will it turn hyper-individualistic consumers into whole-hearted citizens preoccupied with the common good." He is certainly right. Any sober political theory must distinguish between optimism and hope. If the diagnosis presented in *DD* is correct, there are reasons to doubt that the civic aspirations of the republican tradition will be realized in our time. But there are equally compelling reasons to reject the alternative—a public life that gives up on the project of freedom as self-government, that abandons the aim of calling economic power to democratic account, that fails to form in citizens the qualities of character that equip them for self-rule.

Richard Rorty raises a related set of issues about theory and practice. In an earlier article, "The Priority of Democracy to Philosophy," he argued against the idea that political arrangements depend for their justification on moral or philosophical principles.[2] Insofar as liberal practices take hold, he wrote, "the need for such legitimation may gradually cease to be felt. Such a society will become accustomed to the thought that social policy needs no more authority than successful accommodation among individuals." Rorty sought to enlist Rawls and Dewey on behalf of his claim that "liberal democracy can get along without philosophical presuppositions." He emphasized (and perhaps exaggerated) what he called the "historicist" aspect of Rawls's recent work, citing Rawls's statement that "what justifies a conception of justice is . . . its congruence with our deeper understanding of ourselves and our aspirations, and our realization that, given our history and the traditions embedded in our public life, it is the most reasonable doctrine for us." He attributed to Dewey the view that "communal and public disenchantment" is a price worth paying for "individual and private spiritual liberation." Finally, he urged critics of liberalism to shift their focus from philosophical debates about the self to a historically specific assessment of liberal political practice.[3]

Given his call for historically situated political argument, Rorty's chapter in this volume is puzzling. Consistent with his earlier views, he writes in defense of a pragmatic, or "minimalist" version of procedural liberalism and claims that the case for it is "historical, not philosophical." But he does not engage the historically specific, internal critique of procedural liberalism that constitutes most of the book. To those who defend the priority of the right over the good on the grounds that it fits with "our history and the traditions embedded in our public life," *DD* replies that the story is more complicated. The notion that government should be neutral toward competing conceptions of the good life so that people can be free to choose their values for themselves does figure prominently in contemporary political and constitutional discourse. But it is not characteristic of the American political tradition as such. To the contrary, the procedural republic is a recent arrival, a development of the last half-century. Republican understandings of citizenship and freedom have informed much of the American political experience, sometimes overlapping and sometimes contending with liberal understandings. To invoke the tradition of American liberty is to invoke a contest not a consensus. Moreover, the practice of procedural liberalism can be seen to display some of the defects characteristic of the theory. The rise of the procedural republic has coincided with growing anxieties about the loss of self-government and the erosion of community, anxieties that the reigning political agenda has failed to address.

This account may of course be wrong. But it is, on Rorty's own terms, the right kind of account. It is, as Michael Walzer notes, an example of "immanent social criticism, . . . a reflection upon experience rather than a pure reflection." This is an enterprise of which Rorty should approve. Instead of taking issue with the narrative, however, Rorty focuses on the philosophical prelude and complains of its abstraction. He states that the case for the procedural republic is "merely historical, not philosophical." The historical argument he offers consists of the bare assertion that republics that avoid taking sides on substantial moral questions "have the best track record among the regimes we have tried so far." But this begs the question (at once historical and philosophical) of how the strengths and deficiencies of the American republic are related to its civic and procedural aspects.

Turning to our contemporary political condition, Rorty disputes my suggestion that "the liberal self-image and the actual organization of modern social and economic life are sharply at odds." He rejects the notion that the ideal of the freely choosing, independent self looms large in American political culture, and does not think that Americans are troubled by a sense of disempowerment. I cannot rehearse here the evidence that supports the claims that Rorty contests. But it is surprising to find that Rorty rejects those features of my diagnosis that most closely parallel the critique of American democracy offered by his philosophical hero, John Dewey.

Far from valorizing "individual and private spiritual liberation," Dewey thought the central problem of American democracy was "the eclipse of the public," the loss of a public realm within which men and women could deliberate about their common destiny. In *The Public and Its Problems* (1927), Dewey argued that the threat to self-government arose, in the first instance, from the power and scale of modern industrial society. "The machine age in developing the Great Society has invaded and partially disintegrated the small communities of former times without generating a Great Community." According to Dewey, Americans were ill-equipped to contend with the social and economic forces they faced precisely because of "the enormous ineptitude of the individualistic philosophy to meet the needs and direct the factors of the new age." He remarked on the paradox that the theory of the freely choosing individual self "was framed at just the time when the individual was counting for less in the direction of social affairs, at a time when mechanical forces and vast impersonal organizations were determining the frame of things."[4]

Dewey offered a keen insight into the way the image of the free and independent self deepened its hold at the very time that circumstances were rendering it illusory. Modern economic forces liberated the individual from traditional communal ties, and so encouraged voluntarist self-understandings, but at the same time disempowered individuals and local political units. The struggle for emancipation from traditional communities was mistakenly "identified with the liberty of the individual as such; in the intensity of the struggle, associations and institutions were condemned wholesale as foes of freedom save as they were products of personal agreement and voluntary choice." Mass suffrage reinforced the voluntarist self-image by making it appear as if citizens held the power "to shape social relations on the basis of individual volition." But the "spectacle of 'free men' going to the polls to determine the political forms under which they should live" was an illusion. For the same technological and industrial forces that dissolved the hold of traditional communities formed a structure of power that governed people's lives in ways beyond the reach of individual choice or acts of consent.[5]

The role I attribute to the voluntarist self-image in my diagnosis of our present predicament is no more metaphysically ambitious than Dewey's. Now as then, there is a gap between the scale of social and economic life and terms in which we conceive our identities. The global economy is to our day what industrial capitalism and national markets were to Dewey's—a system of power that exceeds the reach of democratic authority and calls into question the prospect of self-government. Now as then, the image of the freely choosing self ill-equips us to contend with our condition. It is not a way to self-government but a source of consolation for the eclipse of the public, for the loss of civic freedom.

Republicanism

DD argues for a recovery of republican ideals, but a number of critics raise questions about the version of republicanism I seek to defend. Some object that the account presented in *DD* does not specify what civic virtues are most important or what political arrangements are most likely to produce them. The historical narrative shows that the language of civic virtue has figured prominently throughout much of American history, invoked by advocates of various political persuasions. But this leaves unclear, say the critics, which virtues I endorse or wish to emphasize. And without a more determinate account of civic virtue, it is difficult to assess the republicanism I defend. Two important issues lie behind this call for greater determinacy. One concerns the philosophical justification of republican theory; the other concerns its political implications.

Philosophical Justifications: Strong versus Weak Republicanism

Thomas Pangle, Philip Pettit, Clifford Orwin, and William Galston all point to the broad range of civic virtues that, according to my account, American republicans have embraced. Galston observes that "the general rhetoric of civic formation has proven compatible with almost any mode of economic organization," and that "the content of civic virtue was left largely undefined throughout our history (as it is in Sandel's account)." Orwin is struck by "the ubiquity and persistence" of republican arguments, and finds my notion of republicanism so broad "that it becomes the big tent of the American political tradition." Pettit, though sympathetic to republicanism, finds my argument "worryingly indeterminate about the precise nature of America's lost republican ideals, about what those ideals would require of us as citizens, and about where they would lead government policy." Whenever the book addresses the specific meaning of civic virtue, he states, "it fades out before achieving a sharp level of resolution" and "remains studiously uncommitted on what the content of that virtue is supposed to be." Similarly, Pangle wants "a clear and distinct account of precisely what character traits and what ways of life" a republican revival should aim at.

Pangle extracts from my account a litany of specific civic virtues that American republicans have emphasized: marital fidelity, economic independence, honesty, frugality, industry, simplicity of manners, self-control, discipline, moderation, temperance, self-denial, the capacity for shame, obedience, respect for authority, orderliness, religious piety, reverence for tradition, manliness, courage, ambition, the love of fame, patriotism, and a passion for the public good. Pangle's list, though true to the sources I cite, has a distinctly conservative bent. And even this list is partial, according to Pangle, because it leaves "hidden away in embarrassment" the aristocratic element in republicanism—the notion that virtuous and disinterested statesmen should govern.

Pangle chides me for failing to embrace what he sees as the conservative implications of republican virtue, for sweeping aristocracy and manliness under the rug. He is right that I "stand back in some hesitation" from my sources. The reason for this hesitation is not, however, that I am trying to evade the political implications that Pangle finds in republicanism. It is rather that I am trying to show how republican ideals informed political argument through much of our history. And if republican ideals set the terms of political discourse, it would be a mistake to assume that they support a single, determinate set of policies. Jefferson and Hamilton, Jacksonians and Whigs, artisan republicans and capitalist entrepreneurs, Lincoln and Southern defenders of slavery, Brandeis and Croly, all invoked different conceptions of civic virtue and the formative project. Some emphasized conservative virtues such as obedience, discipline, and reverence for tradition; others stressed the democratic virtues of active, critically-minded citizens who possessed sufficient economic independence and equality of condition to exercise political judgment and engage in public affairs.

That republicanism is sufficiently capacious to inform different political and economic outlooks is no argument against it. Procedural liberalism, which has its libertarian and egalitarian versions, is similar in this respect: given the notion that government should be neutral among ends in order to respect individual choice, it is a further question what political arrangements best respect neutrality and choice. Libertarians claim that an unfettered market economy leaves people free to choose their ends, whereas liberal egalitarians argue that people are not truly free without at least the minimal level of social and economic security assured by the welfare state.

Pangle and Pettit both press for an answer, in the case of republicanism, to the further question. Granted the importance of the formative project, what civic virtues should republican politics seek to cultivate? This question raises, in turn, a fundamental issue of political philosophy: What is the point of republican politics? Is political participation *instrumental* to liberty, a means to the end of enabling citizens to choose their own conception of the good life? Or is it *intrinsic* to liberty, an essential ingredient of human flourishing?

In *DD*, I distinguish these two versions of the republican political theory, but do not opt clearly for one over the other. The reason is that the American political tradition contains both, and my primary purpose was to contrast the republican strands of the tradition with the liberalism of the procedural republic. Pangle and Pettit both press me to specify more fully the version of republicanism I favor. Each presses in the opposite direction. Pangle finds the instrumental, or modest version of republicanism incoherent, and defends "the non-instrumental, intrinsic" account of civic virtue offered by Aristotle. Pettit rejects the Aristotelian idea that political participation is essential to human flourishing and argues for a republicanism whose purpose is to secure negative liberty.

Of the two versions of republicanism—the modest (or instrumental) version and the strong (or intrinsic) one—the second seems to me the most persuasive. The idea that political participation and civic virtue are important only for the sake of maintaining a regime that enables us to pursue our private ends is unlikely to be stable. Unless citizens have reason to believe that sharing in self-government is intrinsically important, their willingness to sacrifice individual interests for the common good may be eroded by instrumental calculations about the costs and benefits of political participation.

The strong version of republicanism, going back to Aristotle, finds the intrinsic value of political participation in a certain vision of human flourishing. Sharing in the governance of a political community that controls its own fate calls forth distinctive human capacities—for judgment, deliberation, persuasion, and action—that would otherwise lie dormant. One need not believe that civic virtue constitutes the whole of virtue in order to view it as an intrinsic good, an essential aspect of human flourishing. While other practices, such as art, philosophy, religion, and family life, engage other noble faculties and intrinsic goods, the goods at stake in the practice of self-government are of a different kind. For republican politics does not just involve reflecting and deliberating, but doing so under conditions of responsibility for the fate of the community as a whole. This is why civic virtue cannot be fully developed among those who do not live in a political community that controls its own destiny in some meaningful sense. However earnestly they may participate in the life of their society, their deliberations do not issue in significant action. Deliberation under conditions of collective impotence does not cultivate the sense of responsibility and moral burden associated with genuine self-rule. In the past, such conditions were the misfortune of small powers, disenfranchised minorities, and other disempowered groups. To the extent that the global economy now deprives even the most powerful nation-states of effective control over their destinies, however, there is reason to wonder whether the republican project can be realized in our time.

If sharing in self-rule cultivates qualities of character essential to human flourishing, it is easy to see why, despite the obstacles to self-government in the modern world, republican ideals persist. It also becomes clear what those obstacles consist in. The problem is not, as Jeremy Waldron suggests, one of population or scale, or the fact that people have a hard time perceiving the effect of their individual votes on the outcome of elections. It is rather that, whatever the outcome of elections, political communities large and small lack the agency or effective power to direct the social and economic forces that govern their lives.

Pettit defends a more modest republicanism ("a distinct neo-Roman republicanism, Ciceronian rather than Aristotelian in inspiration") that conceives freedom as "nondomination," or the absence of dependency on the will of another. Republican freedom, in Pettit's sense, is the condition enjoyed by citizens who live in a constitutional regime that avoids domination by limiting and dispersing power. Political participation and civic virtue are important, on his view, not intrinsically (because essential to human flourishing), but only insofar as they support institutions like the rule of law that prevent the arbitrary exercise of power.

Pettit proposes an intriguing "reworking" of my argument that substitutes his modest republicanism for my more strenuous version. The contrast is nicely illustrated by two different ways of understanding republican objections to the "dependency" that attended wage labor. I argue that republicans from Jefferson to Brandeis opposed the dependency of workers under industrial capitalism on the grounds that it deprived workers of the independence of mind and judgment necessary to meaningful participation in self-government. Pettit argues that these republicans were complaining about dependency as such (i.e. domination by employers), not about its effects on citizenship or self-government. It is difficult to resolve this interpretive dispute without turning to the sources themselves. But Pettit's alternative account of "dependency" offers an elegant illustration of the interplay between political theory and historical interpretation.

Pettit presents his republican revisionism as a friendly amendment to my thesis. Giving up on the idea that freedom consists in sharing in self-rule has the advantage, he argues, of "repairing" and "banishing" the indeterminacies of my republicanism. Shifting the focus from democratic participation to non-domination avoids the danger of "welcoming into the public forum all the discontented, moralistic voices that are currently marginalized." It provides a republican politics that does not "let loose the dogs of moral enthusiasm."

But the indeterminacies Pettit would banish are essential to the contestable, democratic character of republican politics. Avoiding domination is a worthy political end, but it is not the only end. And just as people of differing moral and ideological persuasions disagree about the meaning of civic virtue and the qualities of character self-government requires, so people disagree about what counts as domination: does the primary threat of domination come from big government or from big business and the power of special interests? No definitive answer to this long-debated question is likely to come, as Pettit hopefully suggests, from a "sensible research program." To the contrary, how to identify and cope with the sources of domination in the modern world is an intensely political question that too often goes unaddressed in our politics. One way of placing it on the political agenda might be, indeed, to "welcome into the public forum all the discontented, moralistic voices that are currently marginalized." Mobilizing citizens to contend with economic inequality and the power of special interests requires moral and civic energies now lacking in American politics. Under the circumstances, it is a defect of procedural liberalism that it keeps "the dogs of moral enthusiasm" on too short a leash. Pettit's tame republicanism offers little to remedy this condition.

Political Implications

A number of critics take issue with what they take to be the political implications of *DD*. Others object that the political implications are unclear. William Connolly, writing from the left, describes me as a "cultural conservative with a generous soul" who is insufficiently critical of conservatives such as William Bennett, Newt Gingrich, and George Will. Bruce Frohnen, writing from the right, complains that I am not a genuine critic of liberalism, but a proponent of "a more robust and activist form of liberalism." Mark Tushnet finds the reception of the book ideologically perplexing, even suspicious: "Any work praised, as *Democracy's Discontent* has been, by Social Democrat Eric Foner, Christian Democrat Mary Ann Glendon, and Tory George Will must be extremely wise, quite confused, or so abstract that each reader can find in it what she or he wants." He offers a class analysis: the book "responds to the discontent of today's professional-managerial class faced with reduced autonomy as corporate capitalism increasingly limits the domain in which professionals can exercise professional judgment and discretion." Meanwhile, Will Kymlicka, a defender of what he calls "left-wing procedural liberalism," places the republican critique of liberalism in "the long and unfortunate tradition of left sectarianism." Civic republicans committed to greater equality should spend less time criticizing procedural liberals, he suggests, and more time fighting for the political positions they share.

It is true that *DD* cannot easily be placed on the liberal-conservative spectrum of contemporary American politics. One of its purposes is to demonstrate the inadequacies of that spectrum and of the political discourse it organizes. The book tries to show that, despite their differences, contemporary American liberals and conservatives share assumptions drawn from the political theory of procedural liberalism and that these assumptions need rethinking. Admittedly, some confusion arises from the two different senses of liberalism: one describes the position of those in contemporary American politics who favor a more generous welfare state and a greater measure of social and economic equality; the other describes a tradition of political thought, going back to Locke and Kant, that emphasizes toleration and respect for individual rights. My quarrel is with a particular version of liberalism in the second sense, namely the procedural liberalism that constitutes the reigning public philosophy of American politics.

Kymlicka raises an important question about the two levels of argument. If civic republicans agree with liberals on the need for greater equality, why pick a fight? Why allow differences at the level of political theory to obscure agreements at the level of political advocacy? "People on the left who agree on 95 percent of the actual issues confronting our society spend all of our time arguing with each other about the 5 percent of issues we disagree about," Kymlicka laments, "rather than fighting alongside each other for the 95 percent of issues we have in common."

For purposes of political advocacy, Kymlicka is right. It is perfectly sensible for people who favor the same policies for different reasons to cooperate politically. But it is also important—politically as well as philosophically—to articulate the underlying differences of political theory. American liberalism has suffered in recent decades for its failure to address fears about the fraying of community, the erosion of moral authority, and the rising sense of disempowerment. After the civil rights movement, liberals ceded to cultural conservatives a monopoly on some of the most potent terms of political discourse—family, community, patriotism, morality, and religion. More than a mistake of political rhetoric, this failure reflected an impoverished political imagination, which reflected, in turn, the strictures of procedural liberalism. The insistence that government be neutral toward competing visions of the good life left liberals ill-equipped to engage moral and religious argument in political debate. The idea that freedom consists in our capacity to choose our own, individual ends left liberals inattentive to anxieties about the loss of collective agency and the erosion of community.

Liberals' attempts to expand the welfare state are hampered by the fact that their public philosophy does little to cultivate the social solidarity and sense of mutual obligation such policies require. Kymlicka attributes the failures of liberal egalitarian politics in the United States to endemic features of its political culture—the embrace of Social Darwinism, the contempt for failure, the adulation of individual success. But these cultural ideals are not prepolitical sociological facts that public philosophies cannot address. Robin West describes them well as "the mythic stories we as a people tell ourselves about what is and is not admirable, noteworthy, and something to celebrate—what is and is not a life worth living, or at least worth striving toward." If we hope to achieve a more progressive culture, she writes, we need to "make the case that the vision of the good on which this myth rests is not a worthy one, and part of what we need to do to make that case is to replace it with visions of the good life that are simply better." Liberalism is ill-suited to take on this task, because to challenge the myth is to take a stand on what ways of life are admirable and worthy of emulation. "The logic of liberalism—even in its left-wing variant—drives us away from a direct and meaningful attack on the moral merits, so to speak, of this myth *as myth.*"

If Kymlicka is right about the cultural obstacles to liberal egalitarian politics, he underscores the importance of a public philosophy that affirms what procedural liberalism avoids—a substantive engagement with moral and cultural questions. Kymlicka concedes that liberal neutrality encourages only "thin" national identities that do not affirm any particular conception of the good life. He does not consider that such identities may be too frail to support the ethic of mutual responsibility that liberal egalitarian policies presuppose. As Charles Taylor writes, the "modern democratic state demands a people with a strong collective identity." Procedural liberalism cannot supply, and may undermine, the strong moral bonds that a more generous welfare state requires.

A number of critics (including Kymlicka, Galston, Fleming and McClain) argue that I exaggerate the contrast between liberalism and republicanism in this respect. Liberalism does not reject the formative project altogether, they maintain; it recognizes the need to cultivate in citizens the virtues of toleration, respect, and a willingness to abide by principles of justice. The two theories differ, however, in the scope of the formative project, and this difference matters politically. The republican tradition seeks to shape a public culture of a certain kind, even where doing so privileges certain conceptions of the good life over others. Kymlicka asks for an example of a formative project (presumably judgmental in some respect) that I would endorse but that procedural liberals would not. Here is one: it would be defensible, from the standpoint of republican freedom, to discourage practices that glorify consumerism on the grounds that such practices promote privatized, materialistic habits, enervate civic virtue, and induce a selfish disregard for the public good. The republican tradition has long considered an excessive preoccupation with consumption a moral and civic vice, inimical to self-government. From the standpoint of procedural liberalism, by contrast, what matters is fair access to the fruits of consumption. The debate between procedural liberals and civic republicans is not a sectarian squabble but a contest between two visions of citizenship and the public realm.

In recent decades, talk of civic virtue has come mainly from the right. One of the aims of *DD* is to show how republican themes have also inspired attempts to bring economic power to democratic account. William Connolly and Nancy Rosenblum are aware of this aim, but worry that republicanism today is likely to wear an intolerant face. They want me to distance myself more decisively from the company I keep.

Connolly suggests that I am "abstractly drawn" to William Bennett's invocation of national unity, civic virtue, and mediating institutions, and so "skate too lightly" over his use of republican virtues as "weapons of cultural war in the domains of race, ethnicity, religion, gender, and sexuality." Rosenblum invites me to separate myself from yet darker expressions of republicanism in our time, such as the militia movement and other forms of "civic fundamentalism." Prevalent among contemporary responses to democratic discontent is what Rosenblum calls "fusion republicanism," a "fluid mix of democratic ideology, potential militancy, and invocation of civic virtue." Its unifying themes include perceptions of powerlessness and moral decline and a propensity for direct political action.

Rosenblum invites me to specify my relation to "fusion republicanism" by giving my views on three concrete issues: localism, jury nullification, and citizen militias. For reasons she anticipates, I am sympathetic to localism, but not without ambivalence. Republican freedom requires a sense of belonging, a moral bond with a particular political community. Neighborhoods, townships, and cities have traditionally served as sites of civic engagement. But self-government also requires political communities that have some effective control over their destinies. Given the hyper-mobility of capital, information, and industrial production, it is unclear whether localities today can meet that test. The scramble among cities and suburbs to lure businesses often leads to a kind of extortion, in which localities agree to relax health, safety, and environmental regulations and to forgo tax revenues in exchange for enterprises that may one day leave without notice. Some have proposed that metropolitan or regional forms of governance can lessen these difficulties and still provide a sense of place, a possibility worth exploring. Another way that localist impulses can undermine republican ideals can be seen in the tendency of the affluent to retreat to private enclaves and gated communities. Unless rich and poor alike have a stake in the quality of public schools, transportation, parks, libraries, downtown areas, and community centers, such class-mixing institutions will wither and die, and with them, the possibility of deliberating about the common good. Rosenblum is right to suggest that, liberal objections aside, there are reasons internal to republicanism to view at least some expressions of localism with ambivalence.

Jury nullification is the doctrine that jurors have the right not to enforce a law they consider unjust. It reflects a republican view of the jury as a democratic institution in which citizens deliberate, not only about the facts of the case but also about the justice of the law as applied to the case. As Jeffrey Abramson explains in his excellent book on the jury, the doctrine was prevalent in the early decades of the republic but fell into disuse by the twentieth century as juries were restricted (at least officially) to questions of fact.[6] Once invoked by Northern juries unwilling to enforce the Fugitive Slave Law, it was also employed by juries in the segregationist South that refused to convict whites of crimes against African-Americans.

From the standpoint of republican ideals, a case can be made for reviving the doctrine of jury nullification. Admittedly, it poses the danger that biased jurors will acquit defendants they should convict. But all democratic institutions make mistakes and commit injustices. (Consider elected legislatures.) Whether democracy is a risk worth taking in any particular arena depends on balancing the likelihood and gravity of unjust outcomes against the benefits of participation, deliberation, and civic education. In the days of segregation, when the bias of white Southern jurors was pervasive and predictable, the case for jury nullification was weak. Under present circumstances, however, the republican advantages of the practice might well outweigh the risks.

Rosenblum's third case, the militia movement, is easier than the first two. While she is right to suggest that the citizen militias of our day invoke the tradition of armed republican virtue, they now represent a pathological expression of that tradition. The right to bear arms guaranteed by the Second Amendment once served republican ideals by preventing the national government from monopolizing the instruments of violence and coercion. In the nuclear age, however, it is ludicrous to think that allowing citizens to possess handguns, hunting rifles, and automatic weapons is a sensible way of checking federal power. We should repeal the Second Amendment and find other ways to guard against arbitrary state power. In the meantime, however, we should lessen the appeal of civic fundamentalism by acknowledging the legitimate frustration about powerlessness and devising a politics that addresses it.

Feminism and the Family

In *DD*, I argue that family law has come increasingly to reflect assumptions drawn from procedural liberalism, including the voluntarist conception of the self, and that this tendency is harmful to women and undermines the goods that families at their best can realize. Mary Shanley criticizes this account on two grounds. First, she claims that I overstate the extent to which the law treats families in voluntaristic, contractarian terms. Second, she argues that, by criticizing liberal approaches to the family, I sentimentalize the traditional family and overlook its oppressive character.

In support of the first point, Shanley cites the Indian Child Welfare Act of 1978, which regulates the adoption of Native American children in ways that respect the cultural identity of tribal communities. The law does not treat Native American children as "unencumbered selves," but instructs courts to give preference in adoptions first to members of the child's extended family, then to members of the child's tribe, and finally to other Indian families. This is an intriguing counterexample, but I am inclined to agree with Robin West that it is an exception to the tendency of mainstream family law, which is moving rapidly "toward an individualistic, contractual, and voluntarist conception of marriage and the family" in ways that threaten to "undercut the essence of marriage itself."

Shanley's second objection raises a deeper challenge. Even if it is true that contemporary family law reflects a flawed vision of persons as unencumbered selves, my critique of the liberal vision leaves the impression that I am uncritical of the oppressive features of traditional marriage law. While I deplore the subordination of woman and have no desire to resurrect traditional gender-based roles, Shanley's chapter helps me see how this misimpression could arise from two aspects of my work.

One source of misunderstanding arises from my discussion of justice and the family in *Liberalism and the Limits of Justice*.[7] Some critics of that book took me to suggest that justice does not apply to families, which should be governed instead by nobler virtues like generosity and benevolence. They charged that I idealized the family, overlooked the conflicting interests of husbands and wives, implicitly affirmed patriarchy, and ignored domestic violence. This misunderstanding arises from what I thought at the time was a fairly technical point about Rawls's notion of the "circumstances of justice," and the role it plays in his theory. In a fateful passage that has perhaps been quoted more than any other in the book (mainly by critics), I cited Hume's claim that in families, the need for justice recedes as mutual benevolence increases. My point in citing Hume was not to endorse his vision of the family, or to suggest that families are beyond justice. It was simply to show that Hume's account of the circumstances of justice, which Rawls himself invokes, does not support Rawls's claim that justice is the first virtue of social institutions. My point was that for Rawls, the primacy of justice cannot be based on Hume's empiricism, but must depend on more contestable Kantian assumptions about the nature of the moral subject.[8]

As Shanley rightly observes in a footnote to her chapter, the fact that I have not responded to this objection has allowed the misunderstanding to persist. Bruce Frohnen's chapter in this volume contains yet another instance of this misreading, now applied beyond the context of the family: "On Sandel's reading justice is a remedial virtue, needed only when the shared goals and aspirations of a group crumble and are replaced by conflict over the distribution of necessary goods." The fact that this misunderstanding is so persistent and widespread suggests that my original formulation invited it. I am grateful to Shanley for drawing attention to this question.

The second reason Shanley thinks my account invites the charge of nostalgia for traditional gender roles is that I offer little in the way of proposals for reform. I criticize the liberal conception of marriage and describe the harsh economic consequences for women of no-fault divorce. But as Shanley points out, I do not "suggest reforms that would create greater equality between men and women," or propose ways of restructuring the economy to enable men and women to balance remunerative work and the care of children. Shanley is right that "protecting women who chose to stay home in the absence of broader reforms places the costs of sustaining family relationships disproportionately on women."

My primary purpose in discussing family law was to show how vividly (and how recently) it has come to embody the assumptions of procedural liberalism. My aim was less prescriptive than interpretive—to examine the defects of liberal theory through the lens of an important social institution. But here, as in other areas of social and political practice, the critique of procedural liberalism requires for its plausibility at least a gesture in the direction of alternative possibilities. The call for greater equality among men and women in public and private life is one that liberals and republicans can readily share. But the problem of the family will not be solved simply by ensuring men and women an equal opportunity to choose their roles. The greater challenge is to imagine ways of reorganizing the relation between family and work so that the distinctive goods of each are accorded the social recognition and prestige they deserve. Since this task requires explicit social choices about the place of family and work in a good life, it is unlikely to be advanced within the terms of procedural liberalism. It requires a form of public discourse that does not shrink from morally contentious questions about the nature of the good life.

Pluralism

The essays by Charles Taylor, William Connolly, and Michael Walzer display different sensibilities but share a common theme: All sympathize with my critique of procedural liberalism but none thinks that the republican tradition offers a wholly satisfactory alternative. Each emphasizes, though in different terms, the need for a public philosophy that gives greater expression to pluralism.

Taylor offers a pluralist vision that goes beyond liberal toleration. Rather than abstract from all moral, religious, and cultural differences, Taylor argues, we should appreciate such differences as possible complements to our own identities. Following Herder and Humboldt, he suggests that our humanity is not something we realize as individuals but a common project. We should therefore respond to the pluralism of the modern world by engaging outlooks different from our own, not by abstracting from them, as procedural liberalism insists. We should be open to the possibility that our own identities may be deepened and enriched by a critical yet sympathetic engagement with other cultures and traditions.

Connolly proposes a different way of living with difference. He welcomes my suggestion that the civic virtue distinctive to our time is the capacity to live with the ambiguity of complex identities and multiply-encumbered selves. But Connolly claims that this revision "waves goodbye to the classical dogma of civic republicanism," and gestures toward a more promising "civic pluralism." The civic pluralism he favors emphasizes the "contingency and contestability" of identities. It does not rely on Kantian respect for persons or Taylor's "Herder–Humboldt complementarity view." For Connolly, the moral source of cultural pluralism lies in a heightened awareness of the fragility of our seemingly fixed and secure identities. The more alive we are to the contingency and contestability of our own identities, he maintains, the more generous we are likely to be toward others.

Taylor's pluralism, demanding though it is, seems to me the more compelling of the two. First, as a matter of moral psychology, decentering or disrupting people's sense of who they are does not necessarily inspire greater openness toward the practices and convictions of others. To the contrary, generosity of spirit is more likely to flow from confidently situated selves than from persons constantly confronted with the contingency and contestability of their identities. Second, the dogmatism and fundamentalism that Connolly fears may themselves be symptomatic reactions to dislocating forces of contemporary life—the insecurity of work in a world with fewer life-long careers; the erosion of the family; the fragmented, sensationalized, commercial-driven blur of images that constitute our media-saturated culture; the disempowerment associated with the global economy; the emptiness of a public life that fails to engage substantive moral questions. The best response to the intolerance that fuels the culture wars is not to deconstruct the identities of the combatants but to challenge the economic forces and cultural tendencies that enervate citizenship and erode the dispositions that equip us for self-rule.

Walzer offers yet a third account of pluralism—a "meat and potatoes multiculturalism" in which different racial, ethnic, and religious groups compete for resources to provide for the welfare of their communities. Their political activity provides an important source of civic engagement and commitment. But as Walzer points out, the immediate object of their efforts is not the common good of the nation as a whole. Their primary motivation is to advance the interests of their particular communities.

Walzer suggests that this "mediated, group-focused version of distributive justice," more liberal than republican, is the form of pluralism best suited to an immigrant society like the United States. He considers it more realistic than stronger accounts of citizenship and social solidarity, for two reasons. First, communities whose members are most fully encumbered, such as the Amish, orthodox Jews, and the Native American Church, are unlikely to leave much room for civic energy and commitment. They are, so to speak, "greedy" communities that absorb so much of the identity of their members that little is left for the republic. Second, citizens who are not religious sectarians, the vast majority, "carry their obligations more lightly." In the United States, the experience of immigration not only made for a heterogeneous society; it also loosened the hold of ethnic and religious encumbrances. Walzer argues that the heterogeneity of American society and the weakening of communal identities, taken together, make social solidarity and republican citizenship difficult to achieve.

Walzer may be right that we must settle for the civic engagement that results as a by-product of interest-group pluralism. But to do so is to give up on an aspiration we should be reluctant to concede. The idea that freedom consists in shaping the forces that govern our collective life is difficult to sustain in the modern world. Not only the diversity of our society, but the scale of the economy and the depredations of the culture complicate the republican project. Under conditions such as these, however, the republican tradition reminds us that politics is not only about the size and distribution of the national product. It is also about bringing economic power to democratic account, and equipping men and women with the habits and dispositions that suit them to self-rule.

NOTES

Introduction

1. Michael J. Sandel, *Democracy's Discontent: America in Search of a Public Philosophy* (Cambridge, Mass.: Harvard University Press, 1996).
2. Sandel tends to suggest that liberal public philosophy shapes liberal jurisprudence. But it is not implausible to think that the causal arrow could go the other way. Consider, for instance, the following claim in Brian Barry, "How Not to Defend Liberal Institutions," in Barry, *Liberty and Justice: Essays in Political Theory 2* (Oxford: Clarendon Press, 1991), 30: "the best way of looking at the principle of neutrality [that defines liberal political philosophy *à la* Rawls, Dworkin, and Ackerman] is to see it as a generalization of the line of postwar Supreme Court cases that interpreted with increasing stringency the constitutional requirement that Congress shall make no law establishing a religion."
3. For a fuller elaboration, see Ronald Beiner, *What's the Matter with Liberalism?* (Berkeley: University of California Press, 1992), ch. 2; and id., *Philosophy in a Time of Lost Spirit: Essays on Contemporary Theory* (Toronto: University of Toronto Press, 1997), ch. 1.
4. For an excellent discussion of the clash between different kinds of community, different kinds of "encumbrance," see Michael Walzer's Chapter in this volume. Similar dilemmas also run through Nancy Rosenblum's Chapter in this volume.
5. One should not be misled by this into thinking that neutralist or proceduralist accounts of liberalism exhaust contemporary liberal thought. Therefore one can sympathize with critics who complain that Sandel, in *Democracy's Discontent*, fails to address the more virtue-oriented or perfectionist versions of liberalism that arose subsequent to the initial liberal-communitarian debate: see, for instance, Daniel A. Bell, "Liberal Neutrality and Its Role in American Political Life," *The Responsive Community*, 7/2 (Spring 1997), 62. But the attempt to show that the liberal tradition has the intellectual resources to generate more ambitious kinds of social theory than the proceduralist versions of liberalism that were dominant in the 1970s and early 1980s somewhat misses the point of Sandel's new book. In *Democracy's Discontent*, the central issue is not the limits or potentialities of political philosophies as such, but rather, their symptomatic character in relation to *public* philosophies. Hence what concerns Sandel in Rawls's thought is not its (perhaps inadequate) character as a political philosophy but rather the way it reflects (*accurately*) the reigning public philosophy.
6. Michael J. Sandel, "Political Liberalism," *Harvard Law Review*, 107/7 (May 1994), 1767. In his presentation at the McDonough Symposium, William Galston suggested that the supposed contest between appeals to "the right" and appeals to "the good" is in fact a contest between two competing conceptions of the good. According to Galston's wonderful formulation, "the right" is really the liberal conception of the good "that dare not speak its name."

7. Cf. Sandel, "Political Liberalism," 1767 n. 12.
8. I can report from personal experience how difficult it can be to shake off this annoying label. Despite the fact that one of the sections of my book on liberalism carries the subtitle "Why I am Not a Communitarian," Brenda Almond, in a review essay on that book, is not deterred from classifying me as a communitarian ("The Retreat from Liberty," *Critical Review*, 8/2 (Spring 1994), 236); Jeffrey Friedman, in an article in the same issue ("The Politics of Communitarianism," 328), softens this somewhat by calling me a "quasicommunitarian." Cf. Alasdair MacIntyre, "The Spectre of Communitarianism," *Radical Philosophy*, 70 (Mar./Apr. 1995), 34: "I have myself strenuously disowned this label, but to little effect."
9. As Nancy Rosenblum wrote in an unpublished draft, "The public philosophy Sandel prescribes . . . is sympathetic to decentralization and to the inadequacies of national community, but exhibits reservations in its commitment to local autonomy".
10. Alasdair MacIntyre, "I'm Not a Communitarian, But . . .," *The Responsive Community*, 1/3 (Summer 1991), 91.
11. Alasdair MacIntyre, "A Partial Response to My Critics," in John Horton and Susan Mendus (eds.), *After MacIntyre* (Notre Dame, Ind.: University of Notre Dame Press, 1994), 302–3. Cf. MacIntyre, "Nietzsche or Aristotle?" in Giovanna Borradori (ed.), *The American Philosopher* (Chicago: University of Chicago Press, 1994), 151: "large-scale politics has become barren. Attempts to reform the political systems of modernity from within are always transformed into collaborations with them. Attempts to overthrow them always degenerate into terrorism or quasi-terrorism. What is not thus barren is the politics involved in constructing and sustaining small-scale local communities, at the level of the family, the neighborhood, the workplace, the parish, the school, or clinic, communities within which the needs of the hungry and the homeless can be met." See also, MacIntyre, "Poetry as Political Philosophy: Notes on Burke and Yeats," in Vereen Bell and Laurence Lerner (eds.), *On Modern Poetry: Essays Presented to Donald Davie* (Nashville: Vanderbilt University Press, 1988), 152–4, 156–7.
12. This is the crux of the Sandel–Kymlicka debate. With the debate cast in these terms, Sandel's view seems to me the more persuasive one.
13. This volume, p. 88.
14. Cf. Galston's Chapter in this volume, p. 81: "Sandel cannot escape a tension between the authority of the state to shape character and the kinds of 'encumbrances' on which he dwells. To the extent that we take seriously particularist duties (for example, to family members) or group identification (for example, with faith communities), we may be inclined to resist rather than embrace public direction of civic character formation"; also, p. 84: "the extent to which the power of the national state should be deployed against local communities and civil associations in the name of shared citizenship raises moral and prudential considerations that do not always favor enhanced localism."
15. See *Democracy's Discontent*, 314, 320–1, 347–8. A key notion in this context is Sandel's idea of a "dispersal of sovereignty" (pp. 345, 347).
16. This volume, p. 179.
17. Cf. Orwin, this volume, p. 89: "It is because we are claimed to be constituted by our communities that loyalty to communities overrides any broader patriotism. . . . . The teaching that our identities are communal from the ground up has thus proved every bit as corrosive of the bond of common citizenship as the individualism blamed by Sandel."

18. Here one can point out a remarkable reversal in the Sandel–Rawls confrontation. The following is Sandel's rebuttal in *Democracy's Discontent* of Rawls's strategy, in *Political Liberalism*, of neutralizing the communitarian challenge by "communitarianizing" his own liberalism (that is, by construing it as an interpretation of the American tradition): "the liberal conception of the person . . . has only recently come to inform our constitutional practice. Whatever its appeal, it does not underlie the American political tradition as a whole, much less 'the public culture of a democratic society' as such. Any role it may play in the justification of liberalism *must therefore depend on moral argument, not cultural interpretation or appeals to tradition alone*" (*Democracy's Discontent*, 103; my italics). In other words, Sandel rebukes Rawls for being too communitarian!
19. Amitai Etzioni, *The New Golden Rule* (New York: Basic Books, 1996), 269 n. 20.
20. For an instructive account of what is morally attractive about this liberal conception, see Richard Rorty's Chapter in this volume.
21. This volume, p. 175.
22. *Democracy's Discontent*, 193.
23. Ibid. 231, 242, 250.
24. It is not the case that all critics of liberalism are committed to coming up with remedies for the disabilities of a liberal social order. MacIntyre, for instance, writes: "I am not a communitarian. I do not believe in ideals or forms of community as a nostrum for contemporary social ills. I give my political loyalty to no program" (Borradori, *The American Philosopher*, 151). I strongly agree with MacIntyre here: as I have tried to argue in various places, the business of social criticism should not oblige one to legislate an alternative for the social order one is criticizing (see, for instance, *What's the Matter with Liberalism?*, ch. 7).
25. *Democracy's Discontent* 348–9. Cf. Richard Rorty's Chapter in this volume, p. 123.
26. See *Democracy's Discontent*, 336–7.
27. Mark Hulliung, "The Use and Abuse of History," *The Responsive Community*, 7/2 (Spring 1997), 68. Cf. R. Bruce Douglass, "A House Built on Sandel," *Commonweal*, 22 (Nov. 1996), 27. Jeremy Waldon, in his Chapter in this volume, mounts a vigorous case against Sandel on a charge of aggravated nostalgia.
28. Ronald Dworkin, *A Matter of Principle* (Cambridge, Mass.: Harvard University Press, 1985), 191.
29. Ibid. 203. Kymlicka offers a very clear restatement of this view in his Chapter in this volume: "The state should be neutral amongst conceptions of the good, in the sense that it should not justify its legislation by appeal to some ranking of the intrinsic worth of particular conceptions of the good" (this volume, p. 133); also: "The state should leave judgments about the good life to individuals, and should seek instead to ensure a free and fair context for individuals to make these judgments" (pp. 138–9).
30. *Democracy's Discontent*, 322.
31. Michael J. Sandel, "Easy Virtue," *The New Republic*, 2 (Sept. 1996), 23.
32. While Sandel would not necessarily want to align himself with Clinton's politics, I think the proven appeal of Clinton's political rhetoric, with its unmistakable communitarian resonance, offers some evidence that Sandel's project may be a quite promising one for those concerned with rebuilding an egalitarian or social-democratic politics in the United States and elsewhere. Cf. Charles Taylor's Chapter in this volume, p. 223; Michael Walzer's Chapter in this volume, p. 181; Robin West's Chapter in this volume, pp. 267–8; Joan Chalmers Williams's Chapter in this

volume; each of these, in various ways, presents Sandel's book as an attempt to remedy the deficiencies of procedural liberalism as a basis for egalitarian politics.

33. Although Christopher Lasch presents a rather different "meta-narrative" of American history, I interpret the essential thrust of Lasch's enterprise in a very similar way: for elaboration of Lasch's social theory, and its affinities to Sandel's project, see my essay, "Left-Wing Conservatism: The Legacy of Christopher Lasch," in Beiner, *Philosophy in a Time of Lost Spirit*, 139–50.
34. Again, one certainly should not make the mistake of assuming that procedural liberalism of the Rawls-Dworkin variety is the only available version of liberal theory (*Democracy's Discontent* perhaps tends to encourage this false assumption). Neither should one think that contemporary liberalism has been left untouched by the communitarian critique. On the contrary: communitarianism has been very good for liberalism. It has elicited a much more robust engagement with issues of civic virtue and character formation in the work of, for instance, Galston, Stephen Macedo, Stephen Salkever, and Peter Berkowitz; and it has helped to provoke Kymlicka's interesting work exploring how liberal theory ought to deal with problems of group membership for minority cultures.
35. See Mary Lyndon Shanley's critique of Sandel in her Chapter in this volume (see, especially, n. 27, where Shanley complains about Sandel's failure to address feminist criticisms of his first book), as well as Robin's West's partial critique and partial defense of Sandel in her Chapter in this volume, pp. 260–6, pp. 268–9. In her oral presentation at the conference from which this volume arose, Shanley mentioned Christopher Lasch's *Haven in a Heartless World*, and recalled the critical response when that book was published: "haven *for whom*?" Along with many other feminist critics, Shanley clearly sees Lasch and Sandel as sharing a presumed communitarian nostalgia for the patriarchal family. Equally clearly, Sandel sees this as a "bum rap."
36. See, for instance, Eric Foner, "Liberalism's Discontents," *The Nation*, 6 May 1996, 36–7.
37. Let me just say, in support of Sandel, that it is not clear to me why, in order to avail himself of a civic republican vocabulary, he is obliged to take responsibility for all the sins of the republican tradition going back to Aristotle (which is what some of his liberal and feminist critics imply).
38. *Democracy's Discontent*, pp. ix–x.
39. See *Democracy's Discontent*, 354 n. 28. It's worth noting that Rawls seems more or less to share Sandel's idea of public philosophy. In a recent text, Rawls writes: "Debates about general philosophical questions cannot be the daily stuff of politics, but that does not make these questions without significance, since what we [i.e. we philosophers—R.B.] think their answers are will shape the underlying attitudes of the public culture and the conduct of politics" (*Political Liberalism*, paperback edn. (New York: Columbia University Press, 1996), p. lxi.). It would seem to follow fairly directly from this statement that philosophers are the ones who "shape" public culture, and nonphilosophical ordinary citizens enact in their political conduct the attitudes thus shaped.
40. Cf. Galston's Chapter in this volume, pp. 81–2. The issue of Sandel's idealism was also highlighted in exchanges between Galston and Sandel at the McDonough Symposium. (Galston: "I am not a materialist, but reading Sandel's book is almost enough to turn me into one.") See also Rorty's chapter in this volume, pp. 122–4.
41. *Democracy's Discontent*, 322; my italics.
42. Cf. Susan Okin's review of *Democracy's Discontent* in *American Political Science Review*

91/2 (June 1997), 441, explaining why one can hardly blame "the teenaged John Rawls or the infant Dworkin" for the arrival of the procedural republic *in 1943* (she cites *Democracy's Discontent*, 54).

43. As Michael Walzer forcefully argued in a dialogue with Sandel at the conference that inspired this volume, precisely if Sandel's diagnosis of the pervasive atomization and consumerization of contemporary American life is *correct*, Americans today are grossly ill-fitted for the duties and responsibilities of citizens. Hence Walzer's own preferred response: building up a kind of surrogate citizenship founded on existing ethnic and class allegiances that define the reality of American pluralism. Cf. Walzer, *What It Means to Be an American* (New York: Marsilio, 1996), 37–8, 47, emphasizing the tension between republican and cultural-pluralist notions of citizenship; but see also 10–12, 17, on how the two kinds of politics can work together.
44. Nancy Rosenblum's Chapter in this volume, p. 277; Rosenblum borrows these phrases from Robert Lane.

Chapter 1

1. Michael J. Sandel, *Democracy's Discontent: America in Search of a Public Philosophy* (Cambridge, Mass.: Harvard University Press, 1996), p. ix. Unless otherwise indicated, the following citations refer to this publication.
2. 6, 24, 26, 117, 321.
3. 14, 16, 66, 93, 96, 104, 322, 369 n. 54.
4. 18, 322.
5. 116–17.
6. 24, 323.
7. 19, 322–3.
8. 16, 117–19.
9. 324.
10. 103.
11. 26.
12. 191.
13. 250.
14. 235, 237, 246.
15. 240.
16. 268, 270.
17. 103.
18. 96, 104, 105.
19. 97, quoting the Court in *Eisenstadt* v. *Baird* 405. U.S. 438 (1972).
20. 113.
21. 109.
22. 113, 114.
23. 126, 218, 327.
24. 126, 145, 146.
25. 145, 146, 171, 312, 327.
26. 144.
27. 145.
28. 136, 144–7, 159, 161, 169, 182, 234, 243.
29. 126, 145, 146.

30. 126.
31. Ibid.
32. 312.
33. 165, 310.
34. 162.
35. 164, 327.
36. 310.
37. 171.
38. 145.
39. 191.
40. 164, 165.
41. 327.
42. 162, 164–5.
43. 145.
44. 142.
45. 141, 145, 159, 218, 234.
46. 141.
47. 312.
48. 126.
49. 132.
50. 138.
51. 162.
52. 131, 166.
53. 151, 187, 191, 219.
54. See, e.g. 250.
55. See also Aristotle, *Politics*, bk. 3, chs. 12–13; Plato, *Laws*, 756e–758a; Isocrates, *Areopagiticus*, 21–2; for a fuller discussion, see T. L. Pangle, *The Ennobling of Democracy: The Challenge of the Postmodern Age* (Baltimore: Johns Hopkins University Press, 1992), ch. 7.
56. Preamble to the proposed Bill for the More General Diffusion of Knowledge (1779), in Julian Boyd, et al. (eds.), *The Papers of Thomas Jefferson*, 22 vols. to date (Princeton: Princeton University Press, 1950), ii. 526–7. See similarly Jefferson's statements of the aim of elementary and of higher academy education in "The Rockfish Gap Report" (Saul Padover (ed.), *The Complete Jefferson* (New York: Duell, Sloan, and Pearce, 1943), 1097–8). See also Jefferson's letter to Joseph Cabell, 14 Jan. 1818, in Paul L. Ford (ed.), *The Works of Thomas Jefferson*, 12 vols. (New York: G. P. Putnam's Sons, 1905), xii. 85–6; and see Noah Webster, "On the Education of Youth in America," in Frederick Rudolph (ed.), *Essays on Education in the Early Republic* (Cambridge: Harvard University Press, 1965), 55–7. For a fuller discussion, see Lorraine Smith Pangle and Thomas L. Pangle, *The Learning of Liberty: The Educational Ideas of the American Founders* (Lawrence, Kan.: University Press of Kansas, 1993).
57. *Notes on the State of Virginia*, Query 14 (New York: W. W. Norton, 1972), 146; Jefferson to John Adams, 28 Oct. 1813, in Lester J. Cappon (ed.), *The Adams–Jefferson Letters*, 2 vols. (Chapel Hill: University of North Carolina Press, 1959), ii. 388.
58. Indeed, one may wonder whether Sandel does not in fact exaggerate somewhat the revolutionary leaders', as well as the Founders', attachment to classical or Aristotelian republicanism. The full reasons for my skepticism about the "classical republican" reading of the Founders which Sandel adopts, pretty much uncritically

or second-hand, from the Pocockian school of intellectual history (Gordon Wood, Lance Banning, and Drew McKoy—see esp. 371 nn. 9, 12–15, 18, 22, and above all 33) are laid out in my *Spirit of Modern Republicanism: The Moral Vision of the American Founders and the Philosophy of Locke* (Chicago: University of Chicago Press, 1988).

59. This quotation comes, as Sandel notes, from an unpublished note written in April 1787. But the note in fact does *not* refer to "the aim" or even to the system aimed at, but instead to what Madison calls "an auxiliary desideratum" only supplementing what Madison in the previous paragraph has discussed as the "great desideratum," namely, government "neutrality" in supervising the competition among selfish factions and "interests." This government neutrality and selfish interest-group competition is of premier importance because it will secure protection of "*rights*." So, once replaced in its proper context, Madison's remark on virtue is not nearly as distant in spirit from interest-group pluralism as Sandel claims; and this mistaken use of Madison's words is a vivid illustration of the misunderstanding of the Founding into which I believe Sandel has been led by his overly-trusting reliance on the secondary sources, and his failure to confront the difficult question of what the character and status of civic virtue really is in the thought of the Founders.
60. 128–31; see also 166.
61. See esp. 318–20.
62. 103.
63. 26, 132, 138.
64. 138.
65. 126.
66. 350.
67. 26; italics in the original.
68. 132, 138; see Aristotle's refutation of this claim, in *Nicomachean Ethics*, bk. 1, ch. 5.
69. John Trenchard and Thomas Gordon, *Cato's Letters*, 3rd edn., 4 vols. (New York: Russell & Russell, 1733), ii. 52–3 and 236. (Letters 40 and 61).
70. 132.
71. Washington to Warner Lewis, 14 Aug. 1755, and Washington to Henry Lee, 22 Sept. 1788, in John C. Fitzpatrick (ed.), *The Writings of George Washington from the Original Manuscript Sources* (Washington: Government Printing Office, 1931–44), i. 162 and xxx. 97–8. For a fuller discussion and analysis of Washington's complex meditations on the relation of virtue and fame or honor, see Lorraine Smith Pangle and Thomas L. Pangle, *The Learning of Liberty*, ch. 12
72. 9.
73. See esp. *Nicomachean Ethics*, bk. 3, ch. 8.
74. Ibid., bk. 10, chs. 7–8; *Politics*, bk. 7, ch. 3; *Metaphysics*, bk. 1, chs. 1–2.
75. 116.

Chapter 2

1. Michael J. Sandel, *Democracy's Discontent: America in Search of a Public Philosophy* (Cambridge, Mass.: Harvard University Press, 1996), 322.
2. Ibid. 323. See also 294.
3. Ibid. 275.
4. Ibid. 278.
5. Ibid.

6. Benjamin Constant, *Constant: Political Writings*, ed. B. Fontana (New York: Cambridge University Press, 1988), 314, 316.

Chapter 3

1. Michael Sandel, *Democracy's Discontent: America in Search of a Public Philosophy* (Cambridge, Mass.: Harvard University Press, 1996).
2. Ibid. 5.
3. Philip Pettit, *Republicanism: A Theory of Freedom and Government* (New York: Oxford University Press, 1997).
4. Quentin Skinner,"The Paradoxes of Political Liberty," in *The Tanner Lectures on Human Values* (Cambridge: Cambridge University Press, 1985).
5. Sandel, 33.
6. Ibid. 35.
7. Ibid. 37.
8. Ibid. 39.
9. Ibid. 41.
10. Ibid. 43, 46.
11. Ibid. 70.
12. Ibid. 73, 90.
13. Ibid. 94–100.
14. Ibid. 144.
15. Ibid. 153.
16. Ibid. 172–4.
17. Ibid. 183–4.
18. Ibid. 187.
19. Ibid. 225.
20. Ibid. 267.
21. Ibid. 5, 166.
22. Ibid. 320.
23. See Cass R. Sunstein, *After the Rights Revolution: Reconceiving the Regulatory State* (Cambridge, Mass.: Harvard University Press, 1990); *The Partial Constitution* (Cambridge, Mass.: Harvard University Press, 1993); *Democracy and the Problem of Free Speech* (New York: The Free Press, 1993); "The Enduring Legacy of Republicanism," in S. E. Elkin and K. E. Soltan (eds.), *A New Constitutionalism: Designing Political Institutions for a Good Society* (Chicago: University of Chicago Press, 1993).
24. Sandel, 131.
25. Ibid. 4.
26. Ibid. 6.
27. Ibid. 4.
28. Ibid. 26.
29. Ibid. 9.
30. Ibid. 274.
31. Ibid. 26.
32. Ibid. 25.
33. Ibid.
34. Ibid. 5.

35. Ibid. 318–19.
36. Ibid. 320–1.
37. Ibid. 330.
38. Ibid. 309.
39. Ibid. 107.
40. Ibid. 290.
41. Ibid. 23.
42. Ibid. 202, 274.
43. Ibid. 355.
44. Benjamin Constant, *Constant: Political Writings*, ed. B. Fontana (New York: Cambridge University Press, 1988).
45. Quentin Skinner, "Machiavelli on the Maintenance of Liberty," *Politics*, 18 (1983), 315.
46. Machiavelli, *The Chief Works and Others*, trans. Allan Gilbert, 3 vols. (Durham, NC: Duke University Press, 1965), 2043.
47. Sandel, 36.
48. Ibid. 130.
49. See Philip Pettit, *Republicanism: A Theory of Freedom and Government* (Oxford: Oxford University Press, 1997); M. N. S. Sellers, *American Republicanism: Roman Ideology in the United States Constitution* (New York: New York University Press, 1994); Quentin Skinner, *Liberty before Liberalism* (Cambridge: Cambridge University Press, 1997).
50. See Sellers on these themes.
51. See Pettit, *Republicanism: A Theory of Freedom and Government*, and Skinner, *Liberty before Liberalism.*
52. Algernon Sidney, *Discourses Concering Government*, ed. T. G. West (Indianapolis: Liberty Classics, 1990), 441.
53. Richard Price, *Political Writings*, ed. D. O. Thomas (Cambridge: Cambridge University Press, 1991), 77–8.
54. John Locke, *Two Treatises of Government*, ed. P. Laslett (New York: Mentor, 1965), 325.
55. Ibid. 348.
56. Price, 81.
57. Charles de Secondat Montesquieu, *The Spirit of the Laws*, ed. T. A. M. Cohler, B. C. Miller, and H. S. Stone (Cambridge: Cambridge University Press, 1989), 187.
58. Pettit, 106–9.
59. Pettit, ch. 8.
60. Machiavelli, 241.
61. Jean-Fabien Spitz, *La Liberté Politique* (Paris: Presses Universitaires de France, 1995).
62. Adam Ferguson, *An Essay on the History of Civil Society* (Edinburgh: Millar and Caddel, 1767; repr., New York: Garland, 1971), 167.
63. Pettit, ch. 3.
64. Christine Korsgaard, "Commentary on Cohen and Sen," in M. C. Nussbaum and A. Sen (eds.), *The Quality of Life* (New York: Oxford, 1993).
65. Sandel, 106–7.
66. Ibid. 107.
67. Ibid. 21.
68. Ibid. 187.
69. Ibid. 153.

70. Pettit, 147–50.
71. Ibid. 76–7.
72. Sunstein, *Democracy and the Problem of Free Speech.*
73. Joshua Cohen, "Deliberation and Democratic Legitimacy," in A. Hamlin and P. Pettit (eds.), *The Good Polity* (New York: Blackwell, 1989), 17–34.

Chapter 4

1. Michael J. Sandel, *Democracy's Discontent: America in Search of a Public Philosophy* (Cambridge, Mass.: Harvard University Press, 1996), 323.
2. Ibid. 203.
3. Ibid. 124.
4. Ibid. 234.
5. Ibid. 231.
6. Ibid. 321.
7. Ibid. 129.
8. Ibid. 209.
9. Ibid. 275 ff.
10. John Rawls, *A Theory of Justice* (Cambridge, Mass.: Harvard University Press, 1971), 515.
11. Sandel, 7.
12. Ibid. 113.
13. Ibid. 348.

Chapter 5

1. Steven Kautz, *Liberalism and the Community* (Ithaca, NY: Cornell University Press, 1995).

Chapter 6

1. See Eric Foner, "Liberalism's Discontents", *The Nation*, 6 May 1996, 34.
2. See Mary Ann Glendon, "Civil Service," *New Republic*, 1 Apr. 1996, 39.
3. For an argument reconstructing communitarian thought more generally as a political philosophy and criticizing it from a conservative perspective, see Bruce Frohnen, *The New Communitarians and the Crisis of Modern Liberalism* (Lawrence: University Press of Kansas, 1996). The reconstruction is quite interesting, as are those parts of the critique that do not degenerate into standard Republican rhetoric against the Clinton administration. (The book's jacket identifies the author as a speech writer for Republican Senator Spencer Abraham of Michigan.)
4. For a recent work by a sociologist describing and accounting for shifts in the power of professionals in similar terms, see Elliott A. Krause, *Death of the Guilds: Professions, States, and the Advance of Capitalism, 1930 to the Present* (New Haven: Yale University Press, 1996). See ibid. 22 ("[G]uild power . . . is declining as state power and capitalist power encroach upon it."); ibid. 280 ("[F]ormerly self-run professional groups have slowly been losing the ability to control their own associations, *to control the workplace,* to control the market for their services, and to control their relation to the state." Emphasis added).

5. The chapter in which Sandel discusses the Progressive era opens with a more extended evocation of today's discontents than the other chapters in Part II, and contains phrases like "[t]hen as now." (Sandel, p. 205.)
6. See generally Robert Wiebe, *The Search for Order, 1877–1920* (New York: Hill and Wang, 1967); Daniel Rodgers, "The Search for Progressivism," *Reviews of American History*, 10 (1982), 113.
7. Some analysts suggest that contemporary communitarianism reproduces the Progressive emphasis on expertise. See, e.g. Charles Derber, "Coming Glued: Communitarianism to the Rescue," *Tikkun* (July–Aug. 1993), 27; Kenneth Anderson, Review Essay, "A New Class of Lawyers: The Therapeutic as Rights Talk," *Columbia Law Review*, 96 (1996), 1062, 1089 ("[T]he unhappiness of lawyers looks rather less like professionals experiencing the loss of fulfillment . . . and rather more like the unhappiness of experts who, having established to their own satisfaction the certainty of ends not open for argument by non-experts, wonder why they are not also loved."). These criticisms, except for the more modest claim that there are substantive arguments for political positions, properly apply to communitarians who are less committed democrats than Sandel. Sandel does not claim much for experts on these matters because he does not specify what the winning substantive arguments might be, although his discussion of gay rights does hint at the answers he would give.
8. Sandel's disparagement of popular culture, however, in his concluding reference to "the vacant, vicarious fare of confessional talk shows," (Sandel, 351) is dismaying, albeit typical of intellectuals speaking for and to the professional-managerial class. For a discussion of the popular culture issue, see J. M. Balkin, "Populism and Progressivism as Constitutional Categories," *Yale Law Journal*, 104 (1995), 1935 (book review).
9. See Sandel, 334–5.
10. See Thomas K. McCraw, *Prophets of Regulation: Charles Francis Adams, Louis D. Brandeis, James M. Landis, Alfred E. Kahn* (Cambridge, Mass.: Harvard University Press, 1984), 101–9, 135–41. McCraw summarizes his analysis of Brandeis's position: "Brandeis' fixation on bigness as the essence of the problem doomed to superficiality both his diagnosis and his prescription. . . . It meant that he must argue against vertical integration and other innovations that enhanced productive efficiency and consumer welfare. . . . It meant that he must promote retail price fixing as a means of protecting individual wholesalers and retailers, even though consumers again suffered. It meant, finally, that he must become in significant measure not the 'people's lawyer' but the spokesman of retail druggists, small shoe manufacturers, and other members of the petite bourgeoisie." (p. 141.)
11. See, e.g. Sinclair Lewis, *Babbitt* (New York: Harcourt Brace, 1922).
12. Andrew Friedman, "Citizens Fight Wal-Mart Sprawl," *Neighborhood Works* (Oct.–Nov. 1994), 10, cited in Sandel, 335.
13. Sandel, 275.
14. Ibid. 221.
15. Ibid. 294–5.
16. Ibid. 294.
17. In the late 1970s and early 1980s, sociologists influenced by Marxist theory engaged in an extended discussion of the characteristics of the professional-managerial class. See, e.g. Pat Walker (ed.), *Between Labor and Capital* (Boston: South End Press, 1979);

Erik Olin Wright, *Classes* (London: Verso, 1985). For a recent application, see Deborah C. Malamud, "Class-Based Affirmative Action: Lessons and Caveats," *Texas Law Review*, 74 (1996), 1847.

18. See Foner, 34 (referring to Sandel's "tendency to romanticize the past as a golden age of community responsibility").
19. Sandel, 109.
20. Ibid. 111. Sandel relies in part on research reported by Lenore Weitzman, finding that "[f]or men, divorce brings a 42 percent increase in standard of living, while divorced women and their children suffer a 73 percent decline. Ibid., citing Lenore J. Weitzman, *The Divorce Revolution* (New York: Free Press, 1985), 186, 265, 338–9, 362. Professor Weitzman now agrees that these figures are inaccurate; her data actually showed a 10 percent increase for divorced men, and a 27 percent decline for divorced women. See Richard R. Peterson, "A Re-evaluation of the Economic Consequences of Divorce," *American Sociological Review*, 61 (1996), 528; Lenore J. Weitzman, "The Economic Consequences of Divorce Are Still Unequal: Comment on Peterson," *American Sociological Review*, 61 (1996), 537, 538.
21. Sandel, 289.
22. Ibid. 330
23. Ibid. 332.
24. See ibid. 330–2, citing Robert B. Reich, *The Work of Nations: Preparing Ourselves for 21st Century Capitalism* (New York: A. A. Knopf, 1991), 268–77.
25. See ibid. 331, quoting Reich, 268.
26. See ibid., citing Reich, 269–70.
27. Ibid. 127.
28. Nor does he describe the class basis of the procedural republic, although *corporate capitalism* seems to be the natural candidate.
29. See Sandel, 142–50.
30. See ibid. 155–60.
31. Ibid. 181.
32. See ibid. 189–92.
33. Cf. Kenneth Anderson, "A Class of Lawyers: New Therapeutic as Rights Talk," *Columbia Law Review*, 96 (1996), 1037.
34. Sandel, 202.
35. Ibid. For an argument that capital mobility has a smaller causal impact on disintegration of communities and neighborhoods than expansion of government, see David Conway, "Capitalism and Community," *Social Philosophy and Policy*, 13 (1996) 137, 152–3, 159. I find the argument unpersuasive on its own terms, but in any event, it does not establish that making government smaller would overcome whatever effects capital mobility *does* have.
36. Sandel, 203.
37. See ibid. 333–7.
38. Ibid. 338–9.
39. Ibid. 338.
40. See ibid. 339–41.
41. See ibid. 216–17.
42. See ibid. 227–31.
43. Ibid. 231.
44. For a discussion of the democratic deficit in the institutions of the European

Community, see Shirley Williams, "Sovereignty and Accountability in the European Community," in Robert O. Keohane and Stanley Hoffman (eds.), *The New European Community: Decision-making and Institutional Change* (Boulder, Colo.: Westview Press, 1991), 155, 153–9.

45. Sandel, 339.
46. Ibid.
47. Ibid. 341.
48. Ibid. 342.
49. Ibid.
50. Ibid. 344.
51. Ibid. 345.
52. Ibid.
53. Ibid.
54. The class's public philosophy has to get from here to there, which means that we should not be surprised to find false starts or residues of the inadequate prior public philosophy, as in division within the class over support for the North American Free Trade Agreement.
55. Sandel, 341. As my colleague Mitt Regan put it in his comments on a draft of this chapter, Sandel "advises us to 'Act Locally,' but doesn't tell us how to 'Think Globally.' "
56. Ibid. 342. For a discussion of political and legal strategies to address problems created by transnational employment of workers under conditions often regarded as below minimal standards, see Laura Ho, et al. "(Dis)Assembling Rights of Women Workers Along the Global Assembly Line: Human Rights and the Garment Industry," *Harvard Civil Rrights—Civil Liberties Law Review* (1996), 383, 394–413.
57. For an argument that the international human rights movement involves appeals to rights that are minimal in one sense but maximal in another, see Michael Walzer, *Thick and Thin: Moral Argument at Home and Abroad* (Notre Dame: University of Notre Dame Press, 1994), 6–11.
58. Consider in this connection the widespread, and not entirely admirable, "Not In My Back Yard" (NIMBY) phenomenon associated with environmental politics.
59. Sandel, 342.
60. It used to be that "member of the international proletariat" was thought to be such an identity, but it is no longer (or at least not widely) thought to be so.
61. Sandel, 350.
62. See John B. Judis, "Public Freedoms, Personal Liberties," *Washington Post Book World*, 5 May 1996, 6, expressing disappointment with Sandel's "saccharine conclusion" and arguing that "[a]s economic power has become increasingly concentrated in transnational corporations, only collective efforts that can match the power of these behemoths will restore the basis of popular liberty."
63. Sandel, 346.

Chapter 7

1. Michael J. Sandel, *Democracy's Discontent: America in Search of a Public Philosophy* (Cambridge, Mass.: Harvard University Press, 1996).
2. Ibid. 318.
3. Louis Hartz, *The Liberal Tradition in America: An Interpretation of American Political Thought Since the Revolution* (New York: Harcourt Brace, 1955). For important

concise summaries of the debate within history, see James T. Kloppenberg, "Republicanism in American History and Historiography," *Tocqueville Review* 13/1 (1992), 119–36; Daniel T. Rogers, "Republicanism: The Career of a Concept," *Journal of American History*, 79/1 (1992), 11–38; Gordan S. Wood, "The Virtues and the Interests," *New Republic*, 11 Feb. 1991, 32–5.

4. Sandel, 117.
5. Keith Bradsher, "Gap in Wealth in U.S. Called Widest in the West," *New York Times*, 17 Apr. 1995, A1 (includes data cited; quote from Edward N. Wolff).
6. Paul Starobin, "Unequal Shares," *National Journal*, 11 Sept. 1993: 2176–9. Helpful books are Kevin Phillips, *The Politics of Rich and Poor: Wealth and the American Electorate in the Reagan Aftermath* (New York: Random House, 1990) and Edward N. Wolff, *Top Heavy: A Study of Increasing Inequality of Wealth in America* (New York: Twentieth Century Fund Press, 1995).
7. Mrs. Cecil Frances Alexander, " All Things Bright and Beautiful," *Hymns for Little Children* (n.p.: 1848).
8. Curtis J. Berger and Joan C. Williams, *Property: Land Ownership and Use*, 4th edn. (New York: Aspen Law & Business, 1997), 11.
9. Sandel, 305.
10. Cornell West, *The American Evasion of Philosophy: A Genealogy of Pragmatism* (Madison: University of Wisconsin Press, 1989), 6.
11. Thomas Jefferson, *Notes on the State of Virginia*, ed. William Penden (Chapel Hill: University of North Carolina Press, 1955).
12. Dorothy Ross, *The Origins of American Social Science* (New York: Cambridge University Press, 1991), 97–101, 145–6, 187.
13. Stanley N. Katz, "Thomas Jefferson and the Right to Property in Revolutionary America," *Journal of Law & Economics*, 19 (1976), 480.
14. Ibid. 480–1.
15. For three assessments in recent legal literature, see Richard D. Parker, *Here, the People Rule: A Constitutional Populist Manifesto* (Cambridge, Mass.: Harvard University Press, 1994); William E. Forbath, "Why Is This Rights Talk Different from All Other Rights Talk? Demoting the Court and Reimagining the Constitution: The Partial Constitution by Cass Sunstein," *Stanford Law Review*, 46 (1994), 1171–1804; Jack Balkin, "Populism and Progressivism as Constitutional Categories: Democracy and the Problem of Free Speech by Cass Sunstein," *Yale Law Journal*, 104 (1995), 1935–90.
16. Joe Dominguez and Vicki Robin, *Your Money or Your Life: Transforming Your Relationship with Money and Achieving Financial Independence* (New York: Penguin Books, 1992), 97.
17. Charles Reich, "The New Property," *Yale Law Journal*, 73 (1964): 733.
18. All quotations are from Constance Perin, *Everything in its Place: Social Order and Land Use in America* (Princeton: Princeton University Press, 1977).
19. Fannie Mae, *Fannie Mae National Housing Survey*, 8 (1992).
20. Berger and Williams, 60–3.
21. Nancy F. Cott, *The Bonds of Womanhood: "Women's Sphere" in New England 1780–1835* (New Haven: Yale University Press, 1977), 3; Clarissa W. Atkinson, *The Oldest Vocation: Christian Motherhood in the Middle Ages* (Ithaca, NY: Cornell University Press, 1991).
22. Ruth H. Bloch, "The Gendered Meaning of Virtue in Revolutionary America," *Signs: Journal of Women in Culture and Society*, 13/11 (1987), 37–58; ead., "American

Feminine Ideals in Transition: The Rise of the Moral Mother, 1785–1815," *Feminist Studies*, 4 (1978), 101–25.

23. For a good concise survey of this history, see Faye D. Ginsburg, *Contested Lives: The Abortion Debate in an American Community* (Berkeley: University of California Press, 1989), 227–47. See also Nancy S. Dye and Noralee Frankel (eds.), *Gender, Class, Race and Reform in the Progressive Era* (University of Kentucky Press: Lexington, 1991), esp. Nancy S. Dye, "Introduction"; Marlene Wortman, "Domesticizing the 19th-Century City," *Prospects: Annual of American Culture Studies* 3 (1977), 531–72; Dolores Hayden, "The Grand Domestic Revolution: A History of Feminist Designs for American Homes, Neighborhoods, and Cities"; Eileen Boris, "The Power of Motherhood: Black and White Activist Women Redefine the 'Political,' " in Seth Koven and Sonya Michel (eds.), *Mothers of a New World: Maternalist Politics and the Origins of Welfare State* (New York: Routledge, 1993), 213–45.
24. Cott, 70, 67–8.
25. Ibid. 68, 71. This argument tracks Joan C. Williams, "Deconstructing Gender," *Michigan Law Review*, 87 (1989), 797–845. "A Marxism you can bring home . . ." was originally used by Carlo Romano to describe Gramsci, see Joan Williams, "Domesticity as the Dangerous Supplement of Liberalism," *J. Women's History*, 2 (1991), 69.
26. Mary P. Ryan, *Cradle of the Middle Class: The Family in Oneida County, New York 1790–1865* (New York: Cambridge University Press, 1981).
27. Ginsburg, 188–93.
28. Deborah Fallows, *A Mother's Work* (Boston: Houghton Mifflin, 1985).
29. Joan C. Williams, *Reconstructing Gender* (forthcoming).
30. Anne E. Tergensen, "Survivors of Corporate Layoffs Bear Heavy Burden," *Record*, 5 July 1996, A01; Stephen S. Roach, "A Battle Over Fruit From Productivity," *Buffalo News*, 2 Apr. 1995, 7; Paul Weinberg, "Canada—Labor: Auto Workers Take On General Motors and Win," *International Press Service*, 25 Oct. 1996; Paul Casciato, "GM Striking Workers Dig In, City Braces," *Reuters*, 3 Oct. 1996.
31. Sue Myrick, "GOP Response to President Clinton's Weekly Radio Address," *Federal News Service*, 15 Mar. 1997; Linda Feldmann, "How Congress Wants to Balance Work and Family," *Christian Science Monitor*, 25 Feb. 1997, 1.
32. Albert R. Hunt, "Clinton's Edge With Women Goes Far Beyond Abortion Issue," *Wall Street Journal*, 20 Sept. 1996, R1; "Why Women Like Big Government: Explaining the Gender Gap," *Christianity Today*, 40/13, (11 Nov. 1996), 112; Robin Toner, "With GOP Congress the Issue, 'Gender Gap' is Growing Wider," *New York Times*, 12 Apr. 1996, A1.
33. Peter D. Hart Research Associates and Mellman Group, *The Economic Situation Facing Working Families 1996*; Peter D. Hart Research Associates and Mellman Group, *Summary of Opinion Research on Living Standards* (1996).
34. Poster published by Working Women's Department of the AFL-CIO.
35. "Thumbs Up," *Dallas Morning News*, 27 Nov. 1996, 20A; "Programs that Work: Women's Self-Empowerment Project," *Essence* (March 1997), 44.
36. A somewhat arbitrary selection of sources for this are: Edward McGlynn Gaffney, Jr., "Politics Without Brackets on Religious Convictions: Michael Perry and Bruce Ackerman on Neutrality," *Tulane Law Review*, 64 (1990), 1143–94; Richard Wightman Fox and James Kloppenberg (eds.), *A Companion to American Thought* (Oxford and Cambridge, Mass.: Blackwell, 1995), entries on "Liberal Protestantism."

37. Gaffney, 279.
38. Sean Wilenz, *Chants Democratic: New York City and the Rise of the American Working Class* (New York: Oxford University Press, 1984), 92, 94. In a more contemporary example, Habitat for Humanity melds the liberal dignity strain stated in religious language with a republican focus on homeownership to give people with a stake in the community.
39. Thomas Skidmore, *The Rights of Man to Property* (New York: A. Ming, Jr., 1829).
40. Wilenz, 185 (quote), 187.
41. John Locke, *Two Treatises of Government: A Critical Edition With An Introduction and Apparatus Criticus by Peter Laslett* (New York: Cambridge University Press, 1960), 309.
42. *The Holy Bible* (New York: American Bible Society, 1989), 1194.
43. Immanuel Kant, *The Moral Law: Kant's Groundwork of the Metaphysics of Morals*, trans. H. J. Paton (New York: Barnes & Noble, 1967), 84; John Rawls, *A Theory of Justice* (Cambridge, Mass.: Harvard University Press, 1971), 12–13.
44. Michael J. Perry, "Toward an Ecumenical Politics," *George Washington Law Review*, 60 (1992), 599–619, 614 n. 16 (quoting Basil Mitchell).
45. *State* v. *Shack*, 58 N.J. 297, 277 A.2d 369 (1971).
46. *Hilder* v. *St. Peter*, 478 A.2d 202 (Vt. 1984).
47. Berger and Williams, ch. 11.
48. Margaret Jane Radin, "Market Inalienability," *Harvard Law Review*, 100 (1987), 1879; Robert S. Prichard, "A Market for Babies?", *University of Toronto Law Journal*, 34 (1984), 341–57.
49. Henry F. May, "Religion and American Intellectual History, 1945–1985: Reflections on an Uneasy Relationship," in Michael J. Lacey (ed.), *Religion and Twentieth-Century American Intellectual Life* (New York: Cambridge University Press and Woodrow Wilson International Center, 1991), 12.
50. Sandel, 17.
51. Amy Waldman, "Why We Need A Religious Left," *Washington Monthly Co.* 27/12 (1995), 37.
52. Ibid. 43.
53. Ibid. 59–60.
54. Berger and Williams, 94.
55. Michael J. Perry, "Toward an Ecumenical Politics," *George Washington Law Review*, 60 (1992), 599–619, 603 (quoting John A. Coleman, *An American Strategic Theology* (New York: Paulist Press, 1982).
56. Id. (Although by his test I am not even religious!)
57. Juliet B. Schor, *The Overworked American: The Unexpected Decline of Leisure* (New York: Basic Books, 1991), 108.
58. Paul Wachtel, *The Poverty of Affluence: A Psychological Portrait of the American Way of Life* (New York: Free Press, 1983), 13.
59. Schor, 11, 13, 117.
60. Schor, 7.
61. Dominguez and Robin, 69.
62. Laura Geyer, Conversation, Mar. 1997.
63. For a classic example of populist anti-corporate rhetoric, see Richard Neely, *The Product Liability Mess: How Business Can Be Rescued From the Politics of State Courts* (New York: Free Press, 1988).

64. Allan Sloan, "The Hit Men," *Newsweek*, 26 Feb. 1996, 44.
65. For an example with explicit religious overtones, see Jim Wallis, *Who Speaks for God? An Alternative to the Religious Right—A New Politics of Compassion, Community, and Civility* (New York: Delacorte Press, 1996), 88–97; for an analysis of tort law as redistribution, see Neely, 9 ("massive wealth-redistribution system").
66. James T. Kloppenberg, "The Virtues of Liberalism: Christianity, Republicanism, and Ethics in Early American Political Discourse," *Journal of American History*, 74/1 (1987), 9–33; Eric Foner, "Liberalism's Discontents," *The Nation*, 6 May 1996, 36. The "in solution" metaphor is from Dorothy Ross.

Chapter 8

1. Michael J. Sandel, *Democracy's Discontent: America in Search of a Public Philosophy* (Cambridge, Mass.: Harvard University Press, 1996), 5.
2. Ibid. 10.
3. Ibid. 48.
4. Ibid. 44.
5. Ibid. 51–2.
6. Ibid. 39.
7. Ibid. 40.
8. Ibid.
9. Ibid. 40–1.
10. Ibid. 1.
11. Ibid. 2.
12. Ibid. 3.
13. Ibid. 2.
14. Ibid. 348.
15. Ibid. 4.
16. Ibid. 12.

Chapter 9

1. Michael J. Sandel, *Democracy's Discontent: America in Search of a Public Philosophy* (Cambridge, Mass.: Harvard University Press, 1996), 14.
2. Ibid.
3. Ibid. 100–8.
4. Richard Rorty, "Comments on Michael Sandel's Democracy's Discontent", American Political Science Association symposium (1 Sept. 1996), 2.
5. Ibid. 3.
6. Sandel, 40.
7. Ibid.
8. Rorty, 6.

Chapter 10

1. Although left-wing liberalism has arguably been the less influential of the two in American politics, Sandel views Rawls's theory as the most important statement of procedural liberalism. So my focus on left-liberalism is consistent, I think, with Sandel's own emphasis.

2. The claim that our conceptions of the good are rationally revisable does not entail, as Sandel sometimes suggests, that all of our ends are "chosen." On the contrary, many of our ends are inherited from our family or community. Liberals simply insist that however we originally acquired our ends, we are capable of rationally evaluating and potentially revising them. Nor does the revisability claim entail, as Sandel sometimes suggests, that our conception of the good is a matter of "preference" rather than "obligation." On the contrary, conceptions of the good typically specify desirable roles and relationships, each of which carries with it various obligations. A conception of the good, in other words, is not just a list of preferences, but also a specification of obligations. However, the rational revisability view insists that we are capable of rationally reflecting on the worth of the roles and relationships entailed by our conception of the good. We can judge whether the obligation-imposing roles we have entered into are still worthy of our allegiance. In short, the crux of the view is not that our conceptions of the good are chosen rather than inherited, nor that they are matters of preference rather than obligation. The crux of the view is that our conceptions of the good are rationally revisable, and that the state should make possible the development and exercise of this capacity for rational revisability.
3. John Rawls, "Social Unity and Primary Goods," in A. Sen and B. Williams (eds.), *Utilitarianism and Beyond* (Cambridge: Cambridge University Press, 1982), 172.
4. These three claims are interrelated, though not logically entailed by each other. For example, the commitment to a nonperfectionist state flows naturally from a commitment to rational revisability. It seems plausible to suppose that the best way to ensure that everyone has an equal and effective capacity to rationally reflect on their ends is if the state avoids giving official sanction to some (justice-respecting) ways of life over other (justice-respecting) ways of life. However, this is not strictly logically entailed, and there are some liberals who endorse rational revisability but reject the commitment to a nonperfectionist state (e.g. Raz).
5. Of course, liberal states have promoted national identities for other, less praiseworthy, goals—e.g. to encourage uncritical patriotism, and the willingness to die for one's country.
6. John Rawls, "The Priority of Right and Ideas of the Good," *Philosophy and Public Affairs,* 17/4 (1988), 272–3. Although Sandel quotes repeatedly from Rawls, it is interesting to note that he never mentions this passage, which is perhaps the most directly relevant to the argument of his book.
7. Rawls, "Priority," 252.
8. Sandel might reply that even if promoting certain virtues and identities is not strictly equivalent to promoting conceptions of the good, the reasons liberals have for objecting to the latter apply equally to the former. This would be true if the basis for the liberal objection to state perfectionism is simply that it is controversial, and hence likely to cause social conflict. But this cannot be the predominant objection, for as Sandel himself notes, avoiding perfectionism can be just as controversial as engaging in it. Moreover, enforcing norms of justice is also very controversial (particularly left-wing norms of justice). So liberal egalitarians can hardly be committed to minimizing controversy. Instead, the major reason why liberals object to state perfectionism is that it is seen as a threat to foundational liberal values of individual agency and social justice. State perfectionism is seen, rightly or wrongly, as likely to impede rational revisability and distort the fair distribution of resources. By

contrast, the state promotion of responsible citizenship and national identities can promote, not hinder, these foundational liberal values.

9. See the works on citizenship education by Spinner, Callan, Gutmann, Macedo, etc. For references and discussion, see my "Education for Citizenship," in Terence McLaughlin and Mark Halstead (eds.), *Education in Morality* (Routledge, forthcoming).
10. See the works of liberal nationalists and liberal multiculturalists, including David Miller, Joseph Raz, Yael Tamir, and my own work.
11. e.g., *Shaw* v. *Reno*, 509 U.S. 630 (1993).
12. The situation of "multination" states which contain large, territorially concentrated ethnolinguistic minorities—e.g. Canada, Spain, Belgium—may be seen to be an exception. But in fact they are the exception which proves the rule, since these minorities view themselves precisely as "nations" which happen to be incorporated (often involuntarily) into a larger state. They are challenging the primacy of the larger state, not because they are disputing the centrality of national identities in the modern world, but precisely because the larger state does not define their nation. See, on this, my *Multicultural Citizenship: A Liberal Theory of Minority Rights* (Oxford: Oxford University Press, 1995).
13. On this, see my "Prospects for Citizenship: Domestic and Global," in Thomas Courchene (ed.), *The Nation-State in a Global/Information Era* (Kingston, Ont.: John Deutsch Institute for the Study of Economic Policy, Queen's University, 1997), 315–25.

Chapter 11

1. Michael Sandel, *Democracy's Discontent: America in Search of a Public Philosophy* (Cambridge, Mass.: Harvard University Press, 1996), 116.
2. See John Rawls, *Political Liberalism* (New York: Columbia University Press, 1996).
3. Ibid. 154.
4. Sandel, *Democracy's Discontent*, 23.
5. Ibid. 21.
6. Ibid. 23.
7. Ibid. 102.
8. Ibid. 103.
9. Rawls, *Political Liberalism*, p. xlv.
10. Ibid. 18.
11. Ibid. xlvi.
12. *Roe* v. *Wade*, 410 U.S. 113, 162.
13. Ibid. 163.
14. Rawls, *Political Liberalism*, 243 n. 32.
15. See Judith Jarvis Thomson, "A Defense of Abortion," *Philosophy and Public Affairs*, 1/1 (Fall 1971); Donald Regan, "Rewriting *Roe* v. *Wade*," *Michigan Law Review*, 77 (1979), 1569; Cass R. Sunstein, "Neutrality in Constitutional Law," *Columbia Law Review*, 92/1, 29–44.
16. The National Abortion Federation "Fact Sheet" (Nov. 1989) states that most women base their decision to have an abortion principally on "the inability to afford and/or unreadiness to start or expand their families due to existing responsibilities."
17. Cf. Steven L. Ross, "Abortion and the Death of the Fetus," *Philosophy and Public Affairs* 11/3 (1982).

18. Ronald Dworkin, *Life's Dominion* (New York: A. A. Knopf, 1993), 155.
19. Sandel, *Democracy's Discontent*, 21.
20. For an extensive analysis of abortion and infanticide which supports this conclusion, see Michael Tooley, *Abortion and Infanticide* (Oxford: Clarendon Press, 1983).
21. Of course, one could appeal to other grounds for opposing infanticide, such as the consequentialist argument that the practice would result in diminished respect for other human lives. I simply reject that such arguments can fully capture the moral psychology which underlies the opposition to infanticide.
22. Rawls, *Political Liberalism*, p. lv.
23. Sandel, *Democracy's Discontent*, 103.
24. Ibid. 23.
25. Ibid. 116.
26. Ibid.
27. Ibid. 107
28. Ibid. 108

Chapter 12

1. Charles Taylor, "Cross-Purposes: The Liberal-Communitarian Debate," in Nancy L. Rosenblum (ed.), *Liberalism and the Moral Life* (Cambridge, Mass.: Harvard University Press, 1989), 165, 171–4. See also William Galston, *Liberal Purposes Goods, Virtue, and Diversity in the Liberal State* (New York: Cambridge University Press, 1991).
2. See for example "In this issue . . . ," the introduction to a symposium on communitarianism in *The Intercollegiate Review* (Spring 1997). For a discussion of communitarianism's educational roots see Stephen J. Tonsor, "A Place Apart: The Architecture of Ideas," in *The Intercollegiate Review* (1997), 6. See also Robert Nisbet, who argues in his *The Quest For Community* (New York: Oxford University Press, 1953) that

> [i]n earlier times, and even today in diminishing localities, there was an intimate relation between the local, kinship, and religious groups within which individuals consciously lived and the major economic, charitable, and protective functions which are indispensable to human existence. There was an intimate conjunction of larger institutional goals and the social groups small enough to infuse the individual's life with a sense of membership in society and the meaning of the basic moral values. (p. 53)

According to Nisbet the modern welfare state has made the fundamental institutions of life seem irrelevant. This state is committed to "social justice" and insists that we can achieve justice only by gathering everyone into large bureaucratically designed and integrated categories and organizations. It has destroyed the connections between private associations and public life, and with them the bases of community and virtue. And see Russell Kirk, the father of modern American conservatism, who observed in his *The Politics of Prudence* (Bryn Mawr, Penn: Intercollegiate Studies Institute, 1993):

> It has been said by liberal intellectuals that the conservative believes all social questions, at heart, to be questions of private morality. Properly understood, this statement is quite true. A society in which men and women are governed by belief in an enduring moral order, by a strong sense of right and wrong, by personal convictions about justice and honor, will be a good

> society—whatever political machinery it may utilize; while a society in which men and women are morally adrift, ignorant of norms, and intent chiefly upon gratification of appetites, will be a bad society—no matter how many people vote and no matter how liberal its formal constitution may be.

3. See especially Robert Booth Fowler, *The Dance with Community* (Lawrence, Kan.: University Press of Kansas, 1991), ch. 1.
4. See for example the leading communitarian Charles Taylor. In his *The Ethics of Authenticity* (Cambridge, Mass.: 1991), Taylor notes we are living in a "culture of authenticity." In such a culture, being in touch with your instinctive "moral sense" is no longer good because it makes you treat others as you ought to—according to some transcendent set of standards such as the Golden Rule. Instead, in a culture of authenticity, being in touch with your internal instincts, being "true to yourself" is good for its own sake. It makes you a "true and full human being."

   Communitarians are liberal because they reject any formulation of the goals of life that transcends development of our individual talents and capacities—that, for example, sees loyalty to one's family, class, or God as imperative even if it means leading an impoverished life in terms of both material rewards and personal development. They do not wholly dismiss visions of the good, such as religious salvation. But communitarians such as Taylor insist that such visions are good only instrumentally. They should be used when and to the extent that they help individuals flourish.

   See especially Taylor's discussion of the possible "backgrounds" against which we must "define our identities." These include religion, history, class solidarity, and natural law. We each need one or more of these "things that matter" in order to develop our selves. Taylor does not, however, want us to join together as a community and *choose* among or order these "things that matter." The authentic self must define what matters by conversing with other selves. In the end each of us must decide for himself what matters.

   > We lack any set of common beliefs to order our common life. We have no common set of principles that in and of themselves tell us what is right. Thus moral choice is and should be a matter of individual desires and dispositions. Taylor, 3.

5. Fowler, *Dance with Community*, ch. 1.
6. The connection between justice and distribution in the liberal-communitarian debate is discussed in Charles Taylor, "Cross-Purposes: The Liberal-Communitarian Debate," 161.
7. Michael Sandel, *Liberalism and the Limits of Justice,* (Cambridge: Cambridge University Press, 1982), 9. References omitted.
8. Ibid. 6.
9. Ibid. 9.
10. Ibid. 178.
11. Ibid.
12. Ibid. 179.
13. Ibid. 35.
14. Ibid. 30–1.
15. For a hostile reaction to Sandel's view of the family as natural, see Susan Okin, "Humanist Liberalism," in Rosenblum (ed.), *Liberalism and the Moral Life,* 31. Okin argues that the family itself rests on sex roles that are unjust. She in effect provides

evidence for Sandel's criticism of the contemporary liberal refusal to recognize any institution or relationship that transcends the demands of justice.

16. Sandel, *Liberalism*, 31.
17. Ibid.
18. Ibid. 36.
19. Ibid. 179.
20. Ibid.
21. Ibid.
22. John Stuart Mill, *Three Essays* (Oxford: Oxford University, 1975), 83.
23. John Locke, *Second Treatise of Government*, ed. C. B. McPherson (Indianapolis: Hackett, 1980), paras. 77–86. Subsequent references, by paragraph, given in the text.
24. Ruth Grant, "Locke's Political Anthropology and Lockean Individualism," *Journal of Politics* (Feb. 1988), 59.
25. Of course, Grant recognizes the central role of the family in her "anthropological" treatment of Locke's philosophy. See esp. pp. 45–6.
26. Alex Neill, "Locke on Habituation, Autonomy, and Education," *Journal of the History of Philosophy* (Apr. 1989), 233.
27. Incompetents, incapable of reason, are to be treated as perpetual children, with their natural rights and duties held in perpetual trust and exercised for their own good (para. 60).
28. Sandel, *Liberalism*, 180–1.
29. Michael Sandel, *Democracy's Discontent: America in Search of a Public Philosophy*, (Cambridge, Mass.: Harvard University Press, 1996), 320.
30. Ibid. 329.
31. Ibid. 322.
32. Ibid. 70.
33. Ibid. 68–71.
34. Ibid. 71.
35. See esp. ibid. 71 and 89. Curiously, Sandel makes much of American liberalism's "individualistic" view that honor is merely one asset among many, to be seen as a commodity rather than an intrinsic part of the self, capable of being harmed. He prefers the European model which, on his reading, treats honor as a much more important attribute than does American law. Yet his discussion of the Nazi march in Skokie shows that, for him, "respect for persons as situated selves" necessitates tender care for the self-esteem of the individual, lest it lose its capacity for self government. Ibid. 82–9.
36. See especially the discussion of early American political and religious arrangements in *Jaffree* v. *Board of School Commissioners*, 1104, 1114–15 (1983) and the sources cited therein.
37. Sandel, *Democracy*, 320–1.
38. On the fundamental distinction between social and political institutions in Tocqueville, and in his view of America, see Bruce Frohnen, in *Virtue and the Promise of Conservatism: The Legacy of Burke and Tocqueville* (Lawrence, Kan.: University Press of Kansas, 1993), ch. 1.
39. Sandel, *Democracy*, 318.
40. Ibid. 319.
41. Ibid.
42. Ibid. 336–7.
43. Ibid.

Chapter 13

1. Michael Sandel, *Democracy's Discontent: America in Search of a Philosophy* (Cambridge, Mass.: Harvard University Press, 1996), 66.
2. Ibid. 343.
3. John Higham, *Send These to Me: Jews and Other Immigrants in Urban America* (New York: Atheneum, 1975), 242.
4. See, for example, Sidney Verba and Norman H. Nie, *Participation in America: Political Democracy and Social Equality* (New York: Harper & Row, 1972).
5. See my essay, "Multiculturalism and the Politics of Interest," in David Biale, Michael Galchinsky, and Susannah Heschel (eds.), *Insiders/Outsiders: Multiculturalism and the Jews* (Berkeley: University of California Press, 1988).

Chapter 14

1. In preparing this chapter, I have relied on Amitai Etzioni, *The New Golden Rule: Community and Morality in a Democratic Society* (New York: Basic Books, 1996).
2. Michael Sandel, *Democracy's Discontent: America in Search of a Public Philosophy* (Cambridge, Mass.: Harvard University Press, 1996), 19–20.
3. For a particularly cogent discussion of the role of reason in deliberations of ends and not just of means, see Philip Selznick, *The Moral Commonwealth: Social Theory and the Promise of Community* (Berkeley and Los Angeles: the University of California Press, 1992), esp. 524–6.
4. Dennis Wrong in his *The Problem of Order* (New York: The Free Press, 1994) illustrates the tendency toward reason in stating:

   > Many sociologists confine themselves, implicitly at least, to the cognitive rather than the motivational or emotional aspects of interaction, often making tacit assumptions about the latter or simply taking them for granted. Berger and Luckmann explicitly call their vivid account of how actors construct an objective social world that then confronts and constrains them a contribution to the "society of knowledge." (p. 60)

   Although Wrong speaks directly of sociology, the affinity for the rational applies to many disciplines.
5. Ibid. 286.
6. James Kuklinski, et al., "The Cognitive and Affective Bases of Political Tolerance Judgments," *American Journal of Political Science*, 35/1 (1991), 22.
7. James Q. Wilson, "Interests and Deliberation in the American Republic, or Why James Madison Would Have Never Received the James Madison Award," *PS: Political Science and Politics* (Dec. 1990), 559.
8. James Hunter, *Culture Wars: The Struggle to Define America* (New York: Basic Books, 1991).
9. James Hunter, *Before the Shooting Begins: Searching for Democracy in America's Culture War* (New York: The Free Press, 1994), p. viii.
10. Ibid. 4–5.
11. Charles E. Lindblom, *The Intelligence of Democracy: Decision-Making Through Mutual Adjustment* (New York: The Free Press, 1965).
12. For further discussion, see Amitai Etzioni, *The Moral Dimension* (New York: The Free Press), 136–50; Charles Lindblom, *The Intelligence of Democracy* (New York: The Free

Press, 1965); Kenneth E. Boulding, "Review of a Strategy of Decision: Policy Evaluation and as a Social Process," *American Sociological Review*, 29 (1962), 930–1.

13. Bette Hileman, "Fluoridation of Water," *Chemical and Engineering News*, 66/31 (1988), 26, 27, 42.
14. Amy Gutmann and Dennis Thompson, *Democracy and Disagreement* (Cambridge, Mass.: Harvard University Press, 1996).
15. Jane J. Mansbridge, *Beyond Adversary Democracy* (Chicago: University of Chicago Press, 1983). See ch. 5, "The Town Meeting," 47–58.
16. Jürgen Habermas speaks to this in his book *Moral Consciousness and Communicative Action* (Cambridge: MIT, 1993). In discussing the"discursive redeemability" of dialogue, Habermas outlines characteristics of dialogue that can facilitate the course to shared core values. He states, "Obligations to act flow directly from the meaning of an expressive speech act in that the speaker specifies what it is that this behavior does not contradict and will not contradict in the future" (p. 59). The relationship between future action and community dialogue represent the "procedures" necessary to move to the realization of shared core values. Bruce Ackerman also contributes to the understanding of the meaning of discussion and conversation when he outlines the importance of mutual intelligibility", although he does indeed agree that facts and values cannot be completely separated, and like Habermas, sees different conversations. Also see Bruce Ackerman, "Political Liberalisms," *Journal of Philosophy*, 91/7 (1994), 364–86. id., "Why Dialogue?" *Journal of Philosophy*, 86/1 (1989), 5–22.
17. Robert E. Goodin, *No Smoking: The Ethical Issues* (Chicago: University of Chicago Press, 1989).
18. Michael Lerner and Cornel West, *Jews and Blacks: Let the Healing Begin* (New York: G. P. Putnam's Sons, 1995).
19. Anti-Defamation League, *The Religious Right: The Assault on Tolerance and Pluralism in America* (New York: Anti-Defamation League, 1994).
20. Sidney Blumenthal, "The Newt Testament," *New Yorker*, 70/4 (1994), 7.
21. Courtney Leatherman, "Whither Civility?," *Chronicle of Higher Education*, 42/26 (1996), 21.
22. Sarah Lyall, "Tories Learn Limits of Personal Attacks on Demons (e.g. Laborites)," *New York Times,* 29 Aug. 1996.
23. Closely related is drawing *a line between one's legal right to free speech,* which allows one to say most things however offensive, and the communitarian merit of not voicing whatever offensive thoughts come to mind. See Amitai Etzioni, *The Spirit of the Community: Rights, Responsibilities, and the Communitarian Agenda* (New York: Crown Publishers, 1993) and William Galston, "Rights Do Not Equal Rightness," *The Responsive Community*, 1/4 (1991), 71.
24. Mary Ann Glendon, *Rights Talk: The Impoverishment of Political Discourse* (New York: The Free Press, 1991).
25. Ibid. 9.
26. Daniel A. Bell, *Communitarianism and its Critics* (Oxford: Clarendon Press, 1993).
27. Etzioni, *The Spirit of the Community*, 175–7.
28. Etzioni, *The New Golden Rule.*
29. David Lamb, *Death, Brain Death, and Ethics* (London: Croom Helm, 1985).
30. Robin M. Williams, Jr., *American Society: A Sociological Interpretation* (New York: Alfred A. Knopf, 1952).

31. Rachel Carson, *The Silent Spring* (Boston: Houghton Mifflin, 1962).
32. Marc Mowery and Tim Redmond, *Not in Our Backyard: The People and Events that Shaped America's Environmental Movement* (New York: William Morrow and Company, 1993).

Chapter 15

1. Page references here and below to Michael J. Sandel, *Democracy's Discontent: America in Search of a Public Philosophy* (Cambridge, Mass.: Harvard University Press, 1996).
2. Reference to human commitments, freely chosen or otherwise, recalls Sandel's concept of the "unencumbered self." This notion is central to *Democracy's Discontent*, as it is to much of Sandel's writings. Because the topic has been so widely discussed, we are not going to take it up here.
3. The fear that civic republicanism might entail some form of coercion is fairly ubiquitous within contemporary liberal theory. Nevertheless, as we note later in this chapter, John Rawls (along with many other liberals) distinguishes between more or less coercive, and thus, more or less acceptable, forms of civic republicanism. The question that is left unanswered is what, if anything, civic republicanism necessarily *does* entail.
4. John Wise, "Vindication of the Government of the New England Churches", in Kenneth Dolbeare (ed.), *American Political Thought* (Chatham, NJ: Chatham House P[ublishers, 1984), 36.
5. Sydney E. Ahlstrom, *A Religious History of the American People* (New Haven: Yale University Press, 1972), 351.
6. See, Barry Alan Shain's corrective, *The Myth of American Individualism: The Protestant Origins of American Political Thought* (Princeton: Princeton University Press, 1994).
7. Sidney Verba, Kay Lehman Schlozman, and Henry Brady, *Voice and Equality: Civic Voluntarism in American Politics* (Cambridge, Mass.: Harvard University Press, 1995), 320.
8. Quoted in Joe Klein, "In God They Trust," *New Yorker*, 16 June 1997, 42.
9. Alexis de Tocqueville, *Democracy in America*, trans. by George Lawrence, ed. J. P. Mayer (Garden City, New York: Anchor Books, 1969), 692.
10. Ibid.
11. This paragraph draws on Elshtain's piece, "The Hard Questions: Sense and Sensibility," *New Republic*, 30 Sept. 1996, 29.
12. See his now celebrated essay, "Bowling Alone: America's Declining Social Capital," *Journal of Democracy*, 6 (1995), 71.
13. John Rawls, *Political Liberalism* (New York: Columbia University Press, 1993), 135.
14. Ibid. 205.
15. Tocqueville, 434.
16. Ibid. 189–95.
17. Mary Ann Glendon, "Forgotten Questions," in Mary Ann Glendon and David Blankenhorn (eds.), *Seedbeds of Virtue* (New York: Madison Books, 1995), 4.

Chapter 17

1. Michel Foucault, "Politics and Ethics: An Interview," in Paul Rabinow (ed.), *The Foucault Reader* (New York: Pantheon, 1984), 373–80.
2. Id., *Surveiller et Punir* (Paris: Gallimard, 1976).
3. See Hubert Dreyfus and Paul Rabinow, *Michel Foucault: Beyond Structuralism and Hermeneutics*, 2nd edn. (Chicago: University of Chicago Press, 1983), 237, 251.

Chapter 18

1. Michael J. Sandel, *Democracy's Discontent: America in Search of a Public Philosophy* (Cambridge, Mass.: Harvard University Press, 1996), 108; hereafter referred to in the text as Sandel 1996.
2. The statistics on divorce, working mothers, and out of wedlock births are taken from Elaine Tyler May, "Myths and Realities of the American Families," in Antoine Prost and Gerard Vincent (eds.), *A History of Private Life* (1991), v. 583–7.
3. Janet L. Dolgin, *Defining the Family: Law, Technology and Reproduction in an Uneasy Age* (New York: New York University Press, 1997) says that the law is faced with making choices between models of the family that incorporate assumptions of "holism, fixed relationships, and enduring connections" and models that assume "autonomy, negotiated bargains, and fungible choice" (p. 13). Milton C. Regan, Jr., has moved from advocating a return to status as an antidote to exaggerated individualism in family law, his proposal in *Family Law and the Pursuit of Intimacy* (New York: New York University Press, 1993), to a view that family law can encompass competing but coexisting models of family relationships in his most recent book, *Alone Together: Law and the Meanings of Marriage* (New York: Oxford University Press, 1998).
4. Michael J. Sandel, *Liberalism and the Limits of Justice* (Cambridge: Cambridge University Press, 1982), hereafter referred to in the text as Sandel 1982.
5. Sandel 1996, 116.
6. Sandel 1982, 7, 2.
7. Ibid. 10.
8. Ibid. 183.
9. Ibid. 14.
10. Ibid. 31, quoting David Hume, *An Enquiry Concerning the Principles of Morals,* 1777.
11. Ibid. 172.
12. Ibid. 169.
13. Michael J. Sandel, "Morality and the Liberal Ideal," *New Republic*, 7 May 1984, 17.
14. Sandel 1982, 172–3.
15. Sandel 1996, 108.
16. On the history of marriage and divorce law see Norma Basch, *In the Eyes of the Law: Women, Marriage and Property in Nineteenth-Century New York* (Ithaca, NY: Cornell University Press, 1982); Michael Grossberg, *Governing the Hearth: Law and Family in Nineteenth-Century America* (Chapel Hill: University of North Carolina Press, 1985); Regan, *Family Law and the Pursuit of Intimacy*; Mary Lyndon Shanley, *Feminism, Marriage and the Law in Victorian England* (Princeton: Princeton University Press, 1989).

17. On no-fault divorce see Lenore Weitzman, *The Divorce Revolution: Unexpected Social and Economic Consequences for Women and Children in America* (New York: Free Press, 1985); Herbert Jacob, *Silent Revolution: The Transformation of Divorce Law in the United States* (Chicago: University of Chicago Press, 1988); Mary Ann Glendon, *Abortion and Divorce in Western Law* (Cambridge, Mass.: Harvard University Press, 1987) and *The Transformation of Family Law* (Chicago: University of Chicago Press, 1989); Allen M. Parkman, *No-Fault Divorce: What Went Wrong?* (Boulder, Colo.: Westview Press, 1992).
18. Sandel 1996, 112.
19. Ibid. 111.
20. Milton C. Regan, Jr., "Family Law at Century's End," *Focus on Law Studies: Teaching about Law in the Liberal Arts* (publication of the American Bar Association) 12/1 (Fall 1996), 1 ff.
21. Weitzman, *The Divorce Revolution*; Martha Albertson Fineman, *The Neutered Mother, the Sexual Family and Other Twentieth-Century Tragedies* (New York: Routledge, 1994); June Carbone, "Economics, Feminism, and the Reinvention of Alimony: A Reply to Ira Ellman," *Vanderbilt Law Review*, 43 (1990), 1463.
22. This observation is not new; it was brilliantly noted in John Stuart Mill, *The Subjection of Women* (1869), in *Three Essays*, ed. Richard Wollheim (Oxford and New York: Oxford University Press, 1975).
23. Susan Moller Okin, *Justice, Gender, and the Family* (New York: Basic Books, 1989), 137–8.
24. Sandel 1982, 32.
25. Sandel 1996, 115.
26. Milton C. Regan, Jr., "Spouses and Strangers: Divorce Obligation and Property Rhetoric," *Georgetown Law Journal*, 82 (Sept. 1994), 2306.
27. Sandel's failure in *Democracy's Discontent* to address the issue of the oppressive nature of traditional marriage law along with the dangers of irresponsible individualism, is particularly troublesome since several commentors on Sandel's treatment of the family in *Liberalism and the Limits of Justice* drew attention to the relationship between the assumption of family unity and women's subordination; see among others Okin, *Justice. Gender, and the Family*, 29–31 and Will Kymlicka, *Liberalism. Community and Culture* (Oxford: Clarendon Press, 1989), 113–24. It is disconcerting to find *Democracy's Discontent* reiterating the view of the earlier book without mentioning these objections, even if only to refute them.
28. *Bowers*, 478 U.S. at 191.
29. Sandel 1996, 105, quoting 478 U.S. at 217.
30. Ibid. 108.
31. Ibid. 117.
32. *Bowers*, 478 U.S. at 204.
33. Blackmun writes that "The Court recognized in *Roberts*, 468 U.S., at 619, 104 S. Ct., at 3250, that the "ability independently to define one's identity that is central to any concept of liberty" cannot truly be exercised in a vacuum; we all depend on the "emotional enrichment of close ties with others." *Bowers*, 478 U.S., at 204.
34. *Bowers* 108 S. Ct. 2841 at 2852.
35. Sandel sees the dissent in *Bowers* as following in the highly individualistic language of *Eisenstadt* v. *Baird*, 405 U.S. 438 (1972) . Indeed, he seems to regard most cases dealing with family after 1972 as progeny of *Eisenstadt*. (Janet L. Dolgin, *Defining the*

Family, reads *Eisenstadt* in a similar vein.) Like Sandel, I find the language of *Eisenstadt* unfortunate and ill-advised. But unlike Sandel I do not think it has taken over discourse on family issues. In addition to my different reading of the *Bowers* dissent, I would point to Justice Brennan's dissent in *Bowen* v. *Gilliard*, 483 U.S. 587, a case dealing with whether a father's support payments to a child whose mother received AFDC benefits could be used to cut her benefits. Justice Brennan wrote insightfully about the importance of framing law to offer support to family relationships.

36. As Sandel tells it, assertions of individual rights and the maintenance of community are nearly always in tension. But in many instances assertions of individual rights have revealed the power relationships upon which the seeming unity of the community rested. This was true of the women's suffrage, labor, and African-American civil rights movements as it is in the assertion of women's rights with respect to marriage and divorce, and of gay and lesbian rights.
37. 25 U.S. C. §§1901–63 (Pub. L. No. 95–608, 92 Stat. 5069).
38. Anita Allen draws a connection between issues of cultural identity in adoption and Sandel's views. She writes: "Respecting a group's identity means tolerating and appreciating (as Professor Michael Sandel now stresses) key linguistic, religious and other cultural practices that comprise its identity." Anita L. Allen, "Does a Child Have a Right to a Certain Identity?," in Mikael M. Karlsson, Olafur Páll Jónsson, and Eyja Margrét Brynjarsdóttir (eds.), *Recht, Gerechtigkeit und der Staat* (Law, Justice and the State: Proceedings of the IVR 16th World Congress, Reykjavik, 1993) (Berlin: Duncker & Humbolt, 1993).
39. Michael Grossberg, *Governing the Hearth: Law and the Family in Nineteenth-Century America* (Chapel Hill and London: University of North Carolina Press, 1985), 268–73.
40. Ibid. 278–83.
41. *Indian Child Welfare Act: Hearings on S. 1214 Before the Senate Select Committee On Indian Affairs*, 95th Congress, 1st Session (1977); *Indian Child Welfare Program: Hearings Before the Subcomm. On Indian Affairs of the Senate Committee On Interior and Insular Affairs, 93rd Congress, 2nd Session (1974)* [Hereafter *1974 Hearings*].
42. Halting (or at least slowing) this placement of Indian children away from reservations and Indian homes was meant to serve the interests of both the children and the tribes. Witness after witness at the 1974 Congressional Hearings testified that Indian children placed away from Indian families often suffered two kinds of hardship. First, they frequently were placed in a series of foster homes or institutions, and did not find permanent homes. Second, those children raised without knowledge of and exposure to Indian culture seemed to fare less well psychologically than those who were raised with knowledge and appreciation of Indian culture. Dr. Joseph Westermeyer of the Department of Psychology at the University of Minnesota, who had worked extensively with the Chippewa, observed, for example, that while many of the problems encountered by the people he saw were not unusual in persons who had spent significant portions of their childhood in a series of foster homes, those problems were exacerbated in adolescence when the Anglo identity they had been asked to assume was denied them by white society. As Westermeyer put it, "[A]mong the patients that I encountered that had a high identity with Chippewa culture . . . [many] had good coping skills. . . . Those with a low cultural identity . . . tend to have poor coping [skills] and also significant social

problems." (1974 Hearings at 46–7) The tribes, for their part, lost many children who would have been future adult members of the tribe; many feared a kind of "cultural genocide" was taking place, with the removal of children depleting the tribe's population and undermining the vitality and continuity of Indian culture. See Alice Hearst, "The Indian Child Welfare Act," unpub. paper, Smith College, Northampton, Mass. (1996), 17–18.

43. Ibid. 16–18, and Joan Heifetz Hollinger, "Beyond the Best Interests of the Tribe: The Indian Child Welfare Act and the Adoption of Indian Children," *University of Detroit Law Review*, 66 (1989), 454.
44. 25 U.S.C. §1902.
45. 25 U.S.C. §1911(a) and (b). For a discussion of these provisions see Christine Metteer, "*Pigs in Heaven*: A Parable of Native American Adoption Under the Indian Child Welfare Act," *Arizona State Law Journal*, 28 (1996), 602, ref. omitted.
46. 25 U.S.C. §1915(a). In an attempt to clarify the meaning of "good cause" the Department of the Interior Bureau of indian Affairs issued nonbinding guidelines to assist state courts. The BIA Guidelines suggest that factors for the courts to consider include the child's or parents' placement preference, the child's extraordinary emotional or physical needs, and the unavailability of suitable homes fitting the placement preferences. Guidelines for State Courts, Indian Child Custody Proceedings, 44 Federal Register 67,584 (1979).
47. 25 U.S.C. §1915(c).
48. Although tribal membership is not identical to race (since some Native Americans are not members of a tribe either because their group is not on the federal register of tribes or because they have lost contact with their group, and because in rare instances non-Indians have been enrolled as tribal members), tribal membership nonetheless has a strong racial component.
49. Twila L. Perry, "The Trans-racial Adoption Controversy: An Analysis of Discourse and Subordination," *New York University Review of Law and Social Change*, 21 (1993–4), 38. Color-blind individualism, in Perry's view, has three defining characteristics: optimism about the ultimate eradication of racism in the USA; a belief that race should not be an important factor in evaluating individuals and that a color-blind society is a desirable goal; and a methodological commitment to focus on the individual as the primary unit for the analysis of rights and interests. Color and community consciousness, on the other hand, sees racism as a pervasive and difficult-to-eradicate aspect of American life; embraces multiculturalism and cultural preservation rather than assimilation or color-blindness; and focuses as much on groups with which the individual is identified as on the individual. Underlying the color and community consciousness perspectives, Perry says, "is a strong belief in the interrelationship between the subordination of a group as a whole and the oppression of the individuals within that group." (p. 43)
50. Some members of Congress recently attempted to make the ICWA conform to the color-blind individualism of the Multiethnic Placement Act by proposing amendments to the Adoption Promotion and Stability Act of 1996; those amendments were pulled, however, after protests by the tribes. See Parnell, "The Existing Indian Family Exception," 394. The Multiethnic Placement Act was repealed by the Small Business Job Protection Act of 1996, which forbids agencies receiving federal funds from using race as a factor in deciding adoptive or foster care placements, and again exempts cases governed by the ICWA.

51. Sandel 1996, 12.
52. Ibid. 113.
53. Ibid. 117.
54. Ibid. 116.
55. *Mississippi Band of Choctaws* v. *Holyfield*, 490 U.S. 30 (1989). The Supreme Court's analysis of the policy issues involved in the ICWA in *Mississippi Band of Choctaws* v. *Holyfield* shows a strong concern for tribal rights. "The protection of this tribal interest [in the future of Indian children] is at the core of the ICWA, which recognizes that the tribe has an interest in the child which is distinct from but on a parity with the interest of the parents. This relationship between Indian tribes and Indian children domiciled on the reservation finds no parallel in other ethnic cultures found in the United States" (*Holyfield*, 490 U.S. at 52, citing *In re Adoption of Halloway*, 732 P.2d 962, 969–70 (Utah 1986)).
56. State courts are divided over the "existing Indian family exception"; while some accept it, others regard the exception as judicially created law and refuse to recognize such an exception.

    Many, although not all, of the cases in which state courts have recognized the "existing Indian family exception" involve the placement of children born out-of-wedlock to non-Indian mothers and Indian fathers. In such cases some courts say that since the father is not living with the child, there is no viable "Indian family." Moreover, once the mother has relinquished the child for adoption, she is not a legally recognized parent. I suggest below that in some instances the "existing Indian family exception" may seem to have some merit because it provides a way to oppose a kind of biology-based notion of who is a father by insisting that there be a social as well as a genetic relationship between father and child before the ICWA apply. However, I think there are better ways of countering a genetic understanding of who is a child's "parent." Moreover, the "existing Indian family exception" limits the power of the tribe by giving authority not to gestational mothers (whose interests and wishes should be taken into account) but to the state.
57. 25 U.S.C. §1915(c).
58. Erik W. Aamot-Snapp, "Note: When Judicial Flexibility Becomes Abuse of Discretion: Eliminating the 'Good Cause' Exception in Indian Child Welfare Act Adoptive Placements," *Minnesota Law Review*, 79 (1995), 1190 and n. 129.
59. Joan Heifetz Hollinger notes that the ICWA placement preferences raise the question of "whether the goals of protecting the best interests of Indian children and promoting the security, stability and survival of Indian families and tribes are ever compatible with the adoption of Indian children by non-Indians, and if so, under what circumstances." The wishes of the biological parents would constitute, I believe, one such circumstance. See Joan Heifetz Hollinger, "Beyond the Best Interests of the Tribe," 451–501, at 452 and 497. See also Barbara Bennett Woodhouse, "Protecting Children's Rights of Identity across Frontiers of Culture, Political Community, and Time," in *Families Across Frontiers* (Martinus Nijhoff Press, forthcoming). For a different perspective (more focused on the tribes), see the discussion in Parnell, "The Existing Indian Family Exception," 431, n. 289.
60. Donna J. Goldsmith questions whether the ICWA should recognize the right of the gestational mother to influence the placement of her offspring: "The concept that a mother has the right to remove her child from its extended family and community, thereby depriving the child of its heritage . . . is foreign to American Indian

cultures." Donna J. Goldsmith, "Individual vs. Collective Rights: The Indian Child Welfare Act," *Harvard Women's Law Journal*, 13 (1990), 8. Evelyn Blanchard gave similar testimony before Congress in 1988:

> Indian people have two relationship systems. They have a biological relational system, and they have a clan or band relational system. It is the convergence, if you will, of these two systems in tribal society that creates the fabric of tribal life. And each of us as an Indian person has a very specific place in the fabric. Those responsibilities are our rights, individual rights. And even our mother has no right to deny us those rights.

To Amend the Indian Child Welfare Act: Hearings on S. 1976 Before the Senate Select Comm. On Indian Affairs, 100th Congress, 2nd Sessioin 48 (1988), 97–8 (Statement of Evelyn Blanchard).

Such testimony raises tremendously difficult issues for an Anglo feminist like me who wishes both to defend women's autonomy and to respect indigenous cultures and tribal self-determination. But I am unconvinced that outright denial of the relevance of the wishes of any gestational mother in the name of a group can be justified, and I do not think that obliteration of the voice of the mother is necessary to defend tribes and Native American families from unjustifiable incursions of state courts.

On the rights of gestational mothers see Barbara Katz Rothman, *Recreating Motherhood: Ideology and Technology in a Patriarchal Society* (New York: W. W. Norton & Co., 1989); Martha Albertson Fineman, *The Neutered Mother, the Sexual Family, and Other Twentieth-Century Tragedies* (New York: Routledge, 1994); Barbara Bennett Woodhouse, "Hatching the Egg: A Child-Centered Perspective on Parents' Rights," *Cardozo Law Review*, 14 (1993), and " 'Are You My Mother?': Conceptualizing Children's Identity Rights in Transracial Adoptions," *Duke Journal of Gender Law and Policy* 1/2 (Spring 1995), 107–29; and Mary Lyndon Shanley, "Unwed Fathers' Rights, Adoption and Sex Equality: Gender-Neutrality and the Perpetuation of Patriarchy," *Columbia Law Review*, 95/1 (Jan. 1995), 60–103.

61. Parnell, "The Existing Indian Family Exception," 419.
62. 25 U.S.C. §1903, emphasis added.
63. 25 U.S.SC. §1903 (9).
64. See Twila L. Perry, "The Trans-racial Adoption Controversy"; Alice Hearst, "The Indian Child Welfare Act," unpubl. paper, Smith College, Northampton, Mass. (1996); and Janet Farrell Smith, "Analyzing Ethical Conflict in the Transracial Adoption Debate: Three Conflicts Involving Community," *Hypatia*, 11/2 (1996), 1–33 on the question of how to balance the claims of group membership and individual autonomy.
65. Tribal membership need not be pitted against all other interests or claims in a zero-sum contest. A court may be able to construct an arrangement that will allow for recognition of the importance of the birthmother's wishes and the child's right to an Indian heritage—or, perhaps better put, to a complex heritage. Stan Watts reports a case in which a Navajo tribal court succeeded in doing just that. Stan Watts, 'Voluntary Adoptions Under the Indian Child Welfare Act of 1978: Balancing the Interests of Children, Families, and Tribes," *Southern California Law Review*, 63: 213–56, at 253–4. In her novel *Pigs in Heaven*, Barbara Kingsolver imagines a similar resolution of the competing claims of a child's Anglo caretaker and the tribe to which its parents belonged. Barbara Kingsolver, *Pigs in Heaven* (New York: HarperCollins, 1993).) Such complex arrangements may not, however, always be feasible or desirable. In such cases, the court must weigh the claims before it,

including the interest of the tribe as defined by the ICWA and the preference of the birth-parent(s).

66. Anita Allen makes the interesting argument that much of the concern about a child's right to a particular cultural identity (which is often used in arguments against trans-racial adoption) "is largely a surrogate for another idea . . . [i.e.] that adults have a right to respect for their identities." Allen, "Does a Child Have a Right to a Certain Identity?" For an interesting discussion of the ways in which "the tale told by law" may influence as well as reflect general cultural attitudes see Mary Ann Glendon, *Abortion and Divorce in Western Law* (Cambridge, Mass.: Harvard University Press, 1987), 112–14.
67. See Kymlicka, *Liberalism. Community and Culture,* 52.
68. See John Wallach, "Liberalism, Communitarians, and the Tasks of Political Theory," *Political Theory,* 15/4 (Nov. 1987), 518–611.
69. Will Kymlicka attempts to formulate a theory of group rights in *Liberalism, Community and Culture,* and in *Multicultural Citizenship: A Liberal Theory of Minority Rights* (Oxford: Clarendon Press, 1995).
70. Hannah Arendt also emphasized the importance of storytelling to civic life. See "Action" in *The Human Condition* (Chicago: University of Chicago Press, 1958). Where Arendt talked about the construction of a public narrative as a contest involving the interpretation of action, however, Sandel's narrative largely concerns battles of ideas.

Chapter 19

1. Michael J. Sandel, *Democracy's Discontent: America In Search of a Public Philosophy* (Cambridge, Mass.: Harvard University Press, 1996).
2. By "too thick," we mean that Sandel's theory presupposes or requires more or deeper agreement on goods or virtues or ends than seems feasible, given the fact of reasonable pluralism, without intolerable state oppression.
3. Ronald Dworkin, *Freedom's Law: The Moral Reading of the American Constitution* (Cambridge, Mass.: Harvard University Press, 1996), 1–38.
4. Sandel's claim that courts interpreting constitutional freedoms should engage in substantive moral argument about the good does not always entail removing moral issues from the political process of deliberative democracy. For example, his approach might lead to the conclusion that certain categories of speech are of low value for self-government and therefore should be subject to regulation through the political process. Sandel 1996, 71–90.
5. See, e.g. James Bradley Thayer, "The Origin and Scope of the American Doctrine of Constitutional Law," *Harvard Law Review,* 7 (1893), 129–56; Learned Hand, *The Bill of Rights* (Cambridge, Mass.: Harvard University Press, 1958). In this chapter, we distinguish between "traditional republicanism," illustrated by Thayer and Hand, which argues for judicial deference to the democratic process, and "classical republicanism," associated with Aristotle and Rousseau, which emphasizes government's formative project of inculcating civic virtue in the citizenry.
6. See, e.g. Cass R. Sunstein, *The Partial Constitution* (Cambridge, Mass.: Harvard University Press, 1993); id., *Legal Reasoning and Political Conflict* (Oxford: Oxford University Press, 1996).

7. Michael J. Sandel, *Liberalism and the Limits of Justice* (Cambridge: Cambridge University Press, 1982), 21.
8. Sandel 1996, 318–21.
9. At the April 1997 Georgetown University Law Center conference on *Democracy's Discontent*, Will Kymlicka argued that Sandel's civic republicanism and the liberal egalitarianism of Rawls and Dworkin were allies on "95% of the actual issues confronting our society," although their arguments for governmental policies characteristically—but not always—diverge in appealing to, respectively, civic virtues and the obligations of justice. See Will Kymlicka, "Liberal Egalitarianism and Civic Republicanism: Friends or Enemies?" (Ch. 10 this volume). Another participant, Bruce Frohnen, argued that Sandel's conception of the self is fundamentally liberal. See Bruce Frohnen, "Sandel's Liberal Politics" (Ch. 12 this volume).
10. Sandel 1996, 94–100.
11. 381 U.S. 479 (1965).
12. Ibid. 486.
13. Sandel 1996, 97–8.
14. 405 U.S. 438, 453 (1972) (emphasis in original).
15. 410 U.S. 113 (1973).
16. 431 U.S. 678, 687 (1977).
17. Sandel 1996, 99.
18. 505 U.S. 833, 851, 857 (1992) (joint opinion).
19. Sandel 1996, 103–8 (critiquing *Bowers* v. *Hardwick*, 478 U.S. 186 (1986)).
20. 394 U.S. 557 (1969). Sandel gives the example of *People* v. *Onofre*, 51 N.Y.2d 476 (1980), in which New York's highest court struck down that state's sodomy law on the ground that it violated the right of privacy. (Sandel 1996, 106)
21. Ibid. 107.
22. Ibid. 106.
23. Ibid. 107.
24. Ibid. 25.
25. For a constitutional theory with these two themes, see James E. Fleming, "Constructing the Substantive Constitution," *Texas Law Review*, 72 (1993), 211–304; id., "Securing Deliberative Autonomy," *Stanford Law Review*, 48 (1995), 1–71.
26. 478 U.S. at 205.
27. Ibid. 217.
28. One justification for toleration, both historically and today, is the conviction that coercion and compulsion corrupt belief.
29. *Bowers*, 478 U.S. at 205.
30. Sandel 1996, 350.
31. See Will Kymlicka, *Liberalism, Community, and Culture* (Oxford: Oxford University Press, 1989), 47–73; Nancy L. Rosenblum, "Pluralism and Self-Defense," in Nancy L. Rosenblum (ed.), *Liberalism and the Moral Life* (Cambridge, Mass.: Harvard University Press, 1989), 207–26.
32. 505 U.S. at 852.
33. Ibid. 851–2, 856.
34. See, e.g. Sunstein, *The Partial Constitution*, 283–4.
35. 505 U.S. at 852.
36. Ronald Dworkin, *Life's Dominion: An Argument About Abortion, Euthanasia, and Individual Freedom* (New York: Alfred A. Knopf, 1993), 151–9.

37. Elsewhere, one of us has criticized Dworkin's analysis on these grounds. See Linda C. McClain, "Rights and Irresponsibility," *Duke Law Journal*, 43 (1994), 989–1088.
38. See e.g. Chai R. Feldblum, "Sexual Orientation, Morality, and the Law: Devlin Revisited," *University of Pittsburgh Law Review*, 57 (1996), 237–335.
39. See John Rawls, *Political Liberalism* (New York: Columbia University Press, 1993), 212–54; id., "The Idea of Public Reason Revisited," *University of Chicago Law Review*, 64 (1997), 765–807. Sandel criticizes Rawls's idea of public reason in Michael J. Sandel, "Political Liberalism," *Harvard Law Review*, 107 (1994), 1765–94, 1789–94 (reviewing Rawls, *Political Liberalism*).
40. 1996 WL 694235 (Hawaii Cir. Ct. 1996).
41. Ibid. 15–20. Thus, the Hawaii case seems wholly compatible with an argument within political liberalism for same-sex marriage: Impose no requirement as to the specific form that a family must take, so long as it can perform the roles and responsibilities required of it within the basic structure of society.
42. See 142 Cong. Rec. H7278 (daily edn., 11 July 1996) (statement of Rep. Barney Frank).
43. See, e.g. Robin West, "Integrity and Universality: A Comment on Ronald Dworkin's *Freedom's Law*," *Fordham Law Review*, 65 (1997), 1313–34, 1329–34; Nan Hunter, "Marriage, Law, and Gender: A Feminist Inquiry," *Law & Sexuality*, 1 (1991), 9–30.
44. At the Georgetown conference, when Robin West offered the argument sketched in the text, Sandel expressed interest in such an argument about the substantive moral vision offered by same-sex marriage (Robin West, Ch. 20 this volume). Similarly, in response to Mary Shanley's paper, in which she criticized Sandel's analysis of family law for his inattention to liberal and feminist critiques of the family as oppressive and subordinating to women, Sandel commented that he rejected patriarchy and was not nostalgic, although he did not have a fully worked out model of what marriage should be. (Mary Lyndon Shanley, Ch. 18 this volume.)
45. John Stuart Mill, *On Liberty* (New York: W.W. Norton, 1975), 54.
46. Rawls, *Political Liberalism*, 133–72.
47. Michael Moore refers to the "goodness of pluralism, tolerance, and autonomy" in formulating a liberal response to Sandel. See Michael S. Moore, "Sandelian Antiliberalism," *California Law Review*, 77 (1989), 539–51.
48. A common definition of toleration includes an attitude of disapproval or even disgust toward, and thus an impulse to suppress, the tolerated belief or conduct. See Joseph Raz, *The Morality of Freedom* (Oxford: Oxford University Press, 1986), 401–2.
49. See Linda C. McClain, "Toleration, Autonomy, and Governmental Promotion of Good Lives: Beyond 'Empty' Toleration to Toleration as Respect," *Ohio State Law Journal*, 59 (1998), 19–132.
50. See, e.g. Richard D. Parker, "The Past of Constitutional Theory—And Its Future," *Ohio State Law Journal*, 42 (1981), 223–59.

Chapter 20

1. Andrew Sullivan, *Virtually Normal* (New York: A. A. Knopf, 1995).
2. *Baehr* v. *Lewin*, 74 Hawaii 530 (1993).
3. See Ronald Dworkin, "Sex, Death and the Courts," *New York Review of Books*, 8 Aug. 1966, 44, 50.

4. See generally, Robert P. George and Gerard V. Bradley, "Marriage and the Liberal Imagination," *Georgetown Law Journal*, 84 (1995), 301.
5. Stephen Macedo, "Homosexuality and the Conservative Mind," *Georgetown Law Journal*, 84 (1995), 261.
6. Michael Sandel, *Democracy's Discontent: America in Search of a Public Philosophy* (Cambridge, Mass.: Harvard University Press, 1996), 108–19. For a discussion of feminist responses and analyses of the contractual model of marriage, see Jana Singer, The Privatization of Family Law, *1992 Wisconsin Law Review* (1992), 1443.
7. Shanley, Ch. 18 this volume, p. 240.
8. Ibid. pp. 232–7.
9. See, for example, Reva Segal's striking study of ideological history of the state's refusal to address domestic violence, in Reva Segal, "The Rule of Love: Wife-beating as Prerogative and Privacy," *Yale Law Journal*, 105 (1996), 2117.
10. Robin West, *Progressive Constitutionalism* (Durham, NC: Duke University Press, 1994) (marital rape and equality chapters).
11. Kymlicka, Ch. 10 this volume, pp. 136–7.
12. Sandel makes a related point in *Democracy's Discontent*, 350–1.
13. Frohnen, Ch. 12 this volume.

Chapter 21

1. *New York Times*, 5 Mar. 1997, A 16.
2. For an exhaustive discussion of the overlap between republican and liberal elements at the time of the American Revolution see Gordon S. Wood, *The Radicalism of the American Revolution* (New York: Vintage, 1991).
3. George P. Fletcher, "Unsound Constitution," *The New Republic*, 23 June 1997, 16.
4. Wood, 95–6, 99.
5. Michael J. Sandel, *Democracy's Discontent: America in Search of a Public Philosophy* (Cambridge, Mass.: Harvard University Press, 1996), 171.
6. Ibid. 3.
7. *The Newsletter of the National Commission on Civic Renewal*, 1/1 (Spring 1997), 2.
8. Alan Wolfe, "From War of Religion to War Over Religion," unpub. paper.
9. Surveys conducted in the 1980s show that while nearly 70 percent of Americans agree that freedom to worship applies to all religious groups regardless of their views, only 26 percent thought that freedom of atheists to make fun of God and religion should be legally protected. Cited in Wendy Kaminer, "The Last Taboo," *The New Republic*, 14 Oct. 1996, 24–32, 26.
10. Cited in David H. Bennett, *The Party of Fear* (Chapel Hill: University of North Carolina Press, 1988), 344.
11. Robert Lane, "The Joyless Polity," in Stephen Elkin (ed.), *Citizen Competence* (State College, Pa.: Pennsylvania State University Press, forthcoming).
12. Sandel, 118.
13. For criticism of this position see Nancy L. Rosenblum, *Membership and Morals: The Personal Uses of Pluralism in America* (Princeton: Princeton University Press, forthcoming).
14. James Wilson, cited in Akhil Amar, "Popular Sovereignty and Constitutional Amendment," in Sanford Levinson (ed.), *Responding to Imperfection: The Theory and*

Practice of Constitutional Amendment, (Princeton: Princeton University Press, 1995), 98.

15. Herbert J. Storing, *What the Anti-Federalists Were For* (Chicago: University of Chicago Press, 1981), 56.
16. Sandel, 5.
17. *New York Times*, 6 July 1996, A 1.
18. Sandel, 347.
19. David Brion Davis (ed.), *The Fear of Conspiracy* (Ithaca, NY: Cornell University Press, 1971), p. xxii.
20. Richard Briffault, "Our Localism: Part I: The Structure of Local Government Law," *Columbia Law Review*, 90 (1990), 1: ibid. "Part II: Localism and Legal Theory," 346.
21. Sandel, 314.
22. David Popenoe, "The Roots of Declining Social Virtue: Family, Community, and the Need for a 'Natural Communities Policy'," in Mary Ann Glendon and David Blankenhorn (eds.), *Seedbeds of Virtue* (New York: Madison Books, 1995), 94, 97.
23. Richard Briffault, "Our Localism: Part II," 364.
24. Ibid. "Part I," 84.
25. These themes come together in the New Jersey Supreme Court decisions collected under the title *Mt. Laurel*, the principal challenge to the exercise of zoning authority solely for the welfare of a particular community. In 1975 a unanimous New Jersey court reasoned that since zoning is a delegation of state police power, any scheme having an impact beyond the borders of the local community must promote the general welfare of the "affected region" rather than impair it. In this case, the failure to make "realistically possible a variety and choice of housing" sufficed to violate state constitutional due process and equal protection. *Southern Burlington County N.A.A.C.P.* v. *Township of Mount Laurel* 336 A.2d 713 (N.J. 1975).
26. *Mount Laurel* 336 A.2d 713 (N.J. 1975).
27. Cited in Briffault, "Our Localism: Part I," 5.
28. Indeed, the notion of privatizing local neightborhoods has been advanced. For a full discussion see Rosenblum, "Corporate Culture at Home," *Membership and Morals*, ch. 4; and "Democratic Education at Home: Residential Community Associations and 'Our Localism'," *Political Economy of the Good Society* (Spring, 1997).
29. Sandel, 202, 205.
30. Sandel, 89.
31. That is, "the decisions of private taxpaying individuals and revenue- and employment-generating businesses to move to, remain in, expand in or depart from the geographical confines of the city," Paul E. Peterson, *The Price of Federalism* (Washington: Brookings Institution, 1995), 187.
32. Herbert J. Gans, "The Balanced Community: Homogeneity or Heterogeneity in Residential Areas," in Jon Pynoos, Robert Schafer, and Chester W. Hartman (eds.), *Housing in Urban America* (New York: Aldine Publishing, 1980), 141–52, at 141, 148.
33. Gerald E. Frug, "The City as a Legal Concept," *Harvard Law Review*, 93 (Apr. 1980), 1056 at 1069, 1068, 1083 ff., 1126, 1137. Cities should be given "the kind of power wielded by those entities that still exercise genuine decentralized power—private corporations," (at 1130, 1144).
34. Sandel, 227.
35. Sandel, 303–4.
36. Sandel, 333.

37. Suburbs compete with cities and with one another for businesses and affluent residents that add to the tax base with minimal fiscal impact. (The boroughs of New York City compete with one another to lure businesses or get them to expand there. "The Wrong Way to Lure Business," *New York Times*, editorial, 8 Sept. 1996, Sec. 4, p. 16.)
38. Tocqueville, cited in Akhil Amar, "The Bill of Rights as a Constitution," *Yale Law Journal*, 100 (1991), 1186.
39. Cited in Storing, 19, 64.
40. Cited in Amar, "The Bill of Rights," 1185, 1196.
41. 156 US 51 cited in Jeffrey Abramson, *We, the Jury: The Jury System and the Ideal of Democracy* (New York: Basic Books, 1994), 62–3, 85.
42. *U.S.* v. *Thomas et al.*, 95–1337; U.S. Court of Appeals for the Second Circuit, 1997.
43. Abramson takes this position. Amar is equivocal: "I do not mean to suggest that I am wholly persuaded." (Amar, 1195).
44. Abramson, 59.
45. *U.S.* v. *Thomas, et al.*, 116 F. 3d 606 (1997) at 25.
46. Paul Butler, "Racially Based Jury Nullification: Black Power in the Criminal Justice System", *Yale Law Journal*, 105 (1995), 679.
47. Benjamin Curtis *vis-à-vis* the Fugitive Slave Law, cited in Abramson, 81.
48. Butler at 717 n. 214, 723, 724 n. 236.
49. *U.S.* v. *Thomas, et al.*, 116 F. 3d 606 (1997) at 30.
50. *The Rights of Man*, in *Thomas Paine: Collected Writings* (New York: Library of America, 1995), 438, 594.
51. Sandel, 350.
52. "Publius" cited by Storing, 74.
53. Norman Olson, testimony before Senate Subcommittee on Militias, June 1995.
54. Morris Dees and James Corcoran, *The Gathering Storm* (New York: HarperCollins, 1996), 199.
55. Bernard Bailyn, "The Logic of Rebellion: Conspiracy Fears and the American Revolution," in Richard Curry and Thomas Brown (eds.), *Conspiracy: The Fear of Subversion in American History* (New York: Holt, Rinehart, Winston, 1972), 22.
56. Gordon Wood, 45, 74.
57. Davis, p. xxii.
58. Cited in Storing, 52.
59. Garry Wills, "To Keep and Bear Arms," *New York Review of Books*, 21 Sept. 1995, 62–73 at 64–6. This is in contrast to those who argue that the Second Amendment right applies to gun ownership per se, for private uses.
60. J. Harry Jones, Jr., *The Minutemen* (Garden City, NY: Doubleday, 1968), 57.
61. Amar, "The Bill of Rights," 1164.
62. "Gun Owners No Easy Audience for Candidates," *New York Times*, 15 Jan. 1996, A 12.
63. Columnist George Will, cited in Lewis H. Lapham, "Seen But Not Heard: The Message of the Oklahoma Bombing," *Harper's Magazine*, July 1995, 32; Newt Gingrich, Speaker of the House of Representatives, cited in Lapham, 34.
64. Alan Wolfe, "Sociology, Liberalism, and the Radical Right," *New Left Review*, 28 (1987), 3–27.

Chapter 22

1. Michael Sandel, *Democracy's Discontent: America in Search of a Public Philosophy* (Cambridge, Mass.: Harvard University Press, 1996), 25–6.
2. Cass Sunstein, "Beyond the Republican Revival," *Yale Law Journal*, 97 (1988), 1539, 1543.
3. Sandel, 26.
4. Ibid. 344.
5. 494 U.S. 652 (1990).
6. 494 U.S. at 657–660.
7. David Cole, "First Amendment Antitrust: The End of Laissez-Faire in Campaign Finance," *Yale Law and Policy Review*, 9 (1991), 236.
8. 494 U.S. at 680.
9. *See*, e.g. Morris Cohen, "Property and Sovereignty," *Cornell Law Quarterly*, 13 (1927) 8.
10. Ibid. 685.
11. Ibid. 692.
12. See, e.g. Sunstein, above n. 2.
13. See, e.g. Frank Michelman, "Law's Republic," *Yale Law Journal*, 97 (1988), 1493.
14. See Gregory S. Alexander, "Time and Property in the American Republic Legal Culture," *New York University Law Review*, 66 (1991), 273.
15. Rawls makes a similar argument in contending that citizens must be assured of a minimum amount of "primary goods" in order to act autonomously. John Rawls, *A Theory of Justice* (Cambridge, Mass.: Harvard University Press, 1971), 92–3.
16. Sandel, 179.
17. On republican concern about corruption, see David C. Williams, "Civic Republicanism and the Citizen Militia: The Terrifying Second Amendment," *Yale Law Journal*, 101 (1991), 551, 553–5.
18. See Meir Dan-Cohen, *Rights, Persons, and Organizations* (Berkeley: University of California, 1985) 41–51; id., "Freedoms of Collective Speech: A Theory of Protected Communications by Organizations, Communities, and the State," *California Law Review*, 79 (1991), 1229, 1235–41.
19. See, e.g. *Santa Clara* v. *Southern Pac. R.R.*, 118 U.S. 394 (1896)(equal protection); *Minneapolis & St. Louis Ry.* v. *Beckwith*, 129 U.S. 26 (1889)(due process). See also American Bar Association Model Rules of Professional Conduct, Rule 1.13 (lawyer for organization represents the entity rather than any of its agents).
20. American Law Institute, Principles of Corporate Governance, sect. 201(a)(1992).
21. *Dodge* v. *Ford Motor Co.*, 170 N.W 668 (Mich. 1919).
22. Ibid. 683.
23. Ibid. 684.
24. Adolph A. Berle and Gardner C. Means, *The Modern Corporation and Private Property* (New York: Macmillan, 1932).
25. Lawrence E. Mitchell, "A Critical Look at Corporate Governance," *Vanderbilt Law Review*, 45 (1992), 1263, 1284.
26. For a useful overview of the application of this doctrine, see Kenneth B. Davis, Jr., "Discretion of Corporate Management to Do Good at the Expense of Shareholder Gain—A Survey of, and Commentary on, the U.S. Corporate Law," *Canadian–U.S. Law Journal*, 13 (1988), 7.

27. See Kenneth Burke, *A Rhetoric of Motives* (New York: Prentice-Hall, 1950); C. Wright Mills, "Situated Action and the Vocabulary of Motives," *American Sociological Review*, 6 (1940), 904.
28. See, e.g. N.Y. Bus. Corp. Law 717(b)(McKinney Supp. 1991). Connecticut is the only state that requires consideration of nonshareholder interests. See Conn. Gen. Stat. Ann. 33–313(e)(West Supp. 1991).
29. Lawrence E. Mitchell, "Cooperation and Constraint in the Modern Corporation: An Inquiry into the Causes of Corporate Immorality," *Texas Law Review*, 73 (1995), 477, 533.
30. Ibid. 533.
31. Mitchell, "A Critical Look at Corporate Governance," 1290–3.
32. Ibid. 1291.
33. Robert Jackall, *Moral Mazes: The World of Corporate Managers* (New York: Oxford University Press, 1988), 96–100.
34. Mitchell, "Cooperation and Constraint," 525.
35. Marc Galanter, "Planet of the APs: Reflections on the Scale of Law and its Users," (draft, 25 Nov. 1996), 10.
36. C. Edwin Baker draws on the market-driven character of both political and nonpolitical corporate speech in making a somewhat different argument. He maintains that such speech should not be afforded constitutional protection because it does not reflect autonomous expression that furthers self-realization. C. Edwin Baker, *Human Liberty and Freedom of Speech* (New York: Oxford University Press, 1989), 195–224.
37. 479 U.S. 238 (1986).
38. Ibid. 263.
39. *Austin*, 494 U.S. at 680.
40. Daniel J. H. Greenwood, "Fictional Shareholders: For Whom Are Corporate Managers Trustees, Revisited," *Southern California Law Review*, 69 (1996), 1021.
41. Ibid. 1082.
42. Ibid.
43. Ibid. 1087. For an overview of the increasing influence of institutional investors, see Michael Useem, *Investor Capitalism: How Money Managers Are Changing the Face of Corporate America* (New York: Basic Books, 1996).
44. Ibid. 1089. For a more extensive argument in favor of a prohibition on corporate political speech based on the character of the corporation as comprised of "fictional shareholders," see Daniel J. H. Greenwood, "Fictional Shareholders and Real Speech: The Compulsion of Corporate Free Speech" (unpublished manuscript, 26 Feb. 1997).
45. Mark M. Hager, "Bodies Politic: The Progressive History of Organizational 'Real Entity' Theory," *University of Pittsburgh Law Review*, 50 (1989), 575, 650.
46. Federal Election Campaign Act, 2 U.S.C. 441b(a).
47. Sandel, 191.
48. Hager, 651.
49. Ibid.
50. Under a union shop agreement, employees must become union members, but can be required only to pay dues or fees to the union. *NLRB* v. *General Motors*, 373 U.S. 734, 742 (1963).
51. This is known as an agency shop agreement.
52. *Chicago Teachers' Union* v. *Hudson*, 475 U.S. 292 (1986); *Abood* v. *Detroit Board of Education*, 431 U.S. 209 (1977).

53. Most nonprofits of any significance are incorporated. Henry Hansmann, "The Evolving Law of Nonprofit Organizations: Do Current Trends Make Good Policy?" *Case Western Law Review*, 39 (1988–9), 807, 807.
54. IRC §501(c).
55. Henry Hansmann, "The Role of Nonprofit Enterprise," *Yale Law Journal*, 89 (1980), 835, 840.
56. Dan-Cohen, "Freedoms of Collective Speech," 1245.
57. Ibid. 1247.
58. For a discussion of the history of restrictions on corporate political activity, see *Pipefitters Local Union No. 562* v. *U.S.*, 407 U.S. 385, 401, 403 (1972).
59. Charles Lindblom, *Politics and Markets* (New York: Basic Books, 1977).
60. See, generally, David Millon, "Communitarianism in Corporate Law: Foundations and Reform Strategies," in Lawrence E. Mitchell (ed.), *Progressive Corporate Law* (Boulder, Colo.: Westview Press, 1995); Lawrence E. Mitchell, "A Theoretical and Practical Framework for Enforcing Corporate Constituency Statutes," *Texas Law Review*, 70 (1992), 579.
61. For a thoughtful discussion of the potential of corporate law to promote trust, see Mitchell (ed.), *Progressive Corporate Law*, 185.
62. 2 U.S.C. 441b(b)(4)(A).
63. See, e.g. Mitchell, *Cooperation and Constraint.*
64. For varying expressions of such an aspiration, see the essays in Mitchell (ed.), *Progressive Corporate Law*; Christopher D. Stone, *Where the Law Ends: The Social Control of Corporate Behavior* (New York: Harper Colophon Books, 1975).

Chapter 23

1. Michael J. Sandel, *Democracy's Discontent: America in Search of a Public Philosophy* (Cambridge, Mass.: Harvard University Press, 1996), 347.
2. For a more complete argument that this is the best interpretation of Professor Sandel's interest in American federalism, see Mark Tushnet, "A Public Philosophy for the Professional-Managerial Class," *Yale Law Journal*, 106 (1996), 1571, 1595–9 [excerpted above, in Ch. 6].
3. *New State Ice Co.* v. *Liebman*, 285 U.S. 262, 311 (1932) (Brandeis, J., dissenting). It may be worth noting that Brandeis offered this argument to support a statute that used entry regulation to stabilize competition in a market— for the sale of ice—that seems to be fully competitive in the ordinary course. On standard economic theory, this was an experiment whose outcome could have been predicted.
4. This is an overly generous description of the actual process, but it does illustrate how a centralized political system *could* foster experimentation.
5. Susan Rose-Ackerman, "Risk-Taking and Reelection: Does Federalism Promote Innovation?," *Journal of Legal Studies*, 9 (1980), 593.
6. Because I am considering the possibility of experimentation in a wholly centralized system, I put aside the point that, in the United States, national politicians have some incentive to authorize local experimentation because they are structurally responsive to the interests of local-level policy-makers. This is Herbert Wechsler's classic point, about which most constitutional scholars are today highly skeptical. Herbert Wechsler, "The Political Safeguards of Federalism," in *Principles, Politics, and Fundamental Law*, (Cambridge, Mass.: Harvard University Press, 1961), 49.

7. Perhaps the best strategy, then, would be to vote in favor of a general statute authorizing all sorts of innovation and then fight against implementing any particular one in the politician's home state, or stand back and let state-level politicians run the risk that the experiment will fail. The national politician can take credit for letting the experiment occur if it succeeds, and can blame the local-level politicians for their mistakes if the experiment fails.
8. Indeed, I find it difficult to see what defense there might be for the claim that participation is a value in itself, divorced from a direct or indirect connection to policy-making.
9. In what follows, I describe a territorially-based federalism. One can imagine other frameworks, in which the connection between value pluralism and territory is looser, as in some forms of consociational governance. Here two imperfect examples are the evolving Belgian constitutional system, part of which creates governing bodies based on a person's membership in a linguistic community no matter where that person resides, and the new New Zealand electoral system, which allows Maoris to choose whether to vote for candidates on either of two lists, one reserved for Maoris and the other open to all. For a description of the New Zealand system, see Jack H. Nagel, "Constitutional Reform and Social Difference in New Zealand," *Cardozo Journal of International and Comparative Law*, 4 (1996), 373.
10. Mark Tushnet, "Federalism and Liberalism," *Cardozo Journal of International and Comparative Law*, 4 (1996), 329.
11. It seems worth noting that this defense of federalism differs from the use of federalism to promote experimentation. In both settings diverse local actions are ultimately replaced by uniform national ones, in the case of experimentation when the experiment yields a definitive conclusion and in the case of value convergence when the values converge. But value convergence can only occur when people in the local jurisdictions choose to alter their values, knowing that their choice to maintain a divergent set of values cannot be coercively displaced by a centralized government. Federalism, in short, is essential for value convergence; it is not essential for experimentation.
12. Benjamin Barber, *Jihad* vs. *McWorld* (New York: Times Books, 1995). 290.
13. Ibid.
14. Tushnet, above n. 2.
15. See *Reynolds* v. *United States*, 98 U.S. 145 (1879) (upholding federal statute making bigamy a crime, against challenge by religiously motivated Mormons); *Cantwell* v. *Connecticut*, 310 U.S. 296 (1940) (distinguishing between belief and conduct, and protecting belief under the First Amendment's free-speech provision).
16. *Sherbert* v. *Verner*, 374 U.S. 398 (1963).
17. *Wisconsin* v. *Yoder*, 406 U.S. 205 (1972).
18. Most of these cases involved exercises of regulatory power by the national government, but the Court's analysis did not take the distinctive role of the national government into account, and at least one case did involve state regulatory efforts. See, e.g. *O'Lone* v. *Shabazz*, 482 U.S. 342 (1987) (upholding state prison regulation that had the effect of denying Muslim prisoner access to one form of religious service).
19. *Employment Division, Department of Human Resources* v. *Smith*, 494 U.S. 872 (1990).
20. 42 U.S.C. § 2000bb ff.
21. 117 S.Ct. 2157 (1997).

22. Mark Tushnet, "What Then is the American?" *Arizona Law Review*, 38 (1996), 873, 877 .
23. Professor Vicki Jackson has disagreed with me on this issue. In her view people in Montana like the fact that people in New York and California are driven in ways that make the coasts centers of economic activity, from which people in Montana benefit. I agree that this is possible, but my guess is that people in Montana think they could get the same economic benefits if people on the coasts held the values Montanans did.
24. 116 S.Ct. 1620 (1996).
25. As I read *Democracy's Discontent*, Professor Sandel does not say that limiting gay rights is just fine *for the people of Georgia*, and protecting gay rights is equally fine *for the people of New York*, which is what a value pluralist might say
26. To the extent that historic preservation is connected to economic revitalization, its interest does approach being fundamental, but one would have to know much more about the facts about Boerne's economic situation than I do to be comfortable with the claim that its historic preservation ordinance was a key to preserving the city, not as a historic district, but as a viable entity altogether.
27. Tushnet, above n. 2, at 1603–6.
28. The Declaration's key phrases suggest such a formulation: "All men are created equal" and "unalienable rights" evoke the idea of universal human rights, and "a decent respect for the opinions of mankind" evokes the idea of justification by reason.
29. The parochialism of this account is only provisional, for reasons I offer below.
30. On Professor Beiner's account, the project may be flawed to the extent that it accommodates nationalism to liberalism by stripping all particular nationalistic commitments of what makes them distinctive from other nationalist commitments.
31. Obviously, the phrase "not plausibly connected to the Declaration's principles" conceals a great deal.

Chapter 24

1. Georg Hegel, *Philosophy of Right* (1821), T. M. Knox, trans. (London: Oxford University Press, 1967), 13.
2. Richard Rorty, "The Priority of Democracy to Philosophy," in Merrill D. Peterson and Robert C. Vaughan (eds.), *The Virginia Statute for Religious Freedom* (Cambridge: Cambridge University Press, 1988), 257–82.
3. Ibid. 261, 264, 265, 273. Rawls's quotation from John Rawls, "Kantian Constructivism in Moral Theory," *Journal of Philosophy*, 77 (1980), 515, 519.
4. John Dewey, *The Public and Its Problems* (126), repr. in *The Later Works of John Dewey, 1925–1953*, ed. Jo Ann Boydston (Carbondale: Southern Illinois University Press, 1984), ii. 304, 314, 295.
5. Ibid. 296–8.
6. Jeffrey Abramson, *We, the Jury: The Jury System and the Ideal of Democracy* (New York: Basic Books, 1994), 57–95.
7. Michael J. Sandel, *Liberalism and the Limits of Justice*, 2nd edn. (Cambridge: Cambridge University Press, 1998).
8. Ibid. 28–35.

INDEX